JUCHE

A CHRISTIAN STUDY OF NORTH KOREA'S STATE RELIGION

Thomas J. Belke

Living Sacrifice Book Company
Bartlesville, OK

Published by
Living Sacrifice Book Company
P.O. Box 2273
Bartlesville, OK 74005-2273

Unless otherwise indicated, Scripture quotations are taken from *The Holy Bible, New International Version* (NIV), © 1973, 1978, 1984 by the International Bible Society. Published by Zondervan Bible Publishers, Grand Rapids, Michigan.

Scripture quotations designated KJV are from the King James Version.

Scripture quotations designated NKJ are from the *New King James* version, © 1979, 1980, 1982 by Thomas Nelson Inc., Publishers, Nashville, Tennessee.

Design and production by Genesis Publications.

Cover by David Marty Design.

Printed in the United States of America.

Library of Congress Cataloging-in-Publication Data
Belke, Thomas J. (Thomas Julian), 1958–
    Juche : a Christian study of North Korea's state religion / by Thomas J. Belke.
        p.   cm.
    Includes bibliographical references.
    ISBN 0-88264-329-0 (pbk.)
    1. Religion and politics—Korea (North) 2. Kim, Il-sung, 1912–
—Philosophy. 3. Self-reliance—Korea (North) 4. Korea (North)
—Church history.   I. Title.
BL65.P7B43   1999
261.7'095193—DC21   99-30315
                                                                    CIP

To the embattled saints in North Korea,
the faithful in Christ Jesus.

In memory of
the Reverend Robert J. Thomas,
martyred on the bank of the Taedong River,
near Pyongyang, 1866

Precious in the sight of the LORD
is the death of his saints.
Psalm 116:15

Who shall separate us from the love of Christ? Shall trouble or hardship or persecution or famine or nakedness or danger or sword? As it is written:

> "For your sake we face death
>   all day long;
> we are considered as sheep to
>   be slaughtered."

No, in all these things we are more than conquerors through him who loved us. For I am convinced that neither death nor life, neither angels nor demons, neither the present nor the future, nor any powers, neither height nor depth, nor anything else in all creation, will be able to separate us from the love of God that is in Christ Jesus our Lord.

Romans 8:35–39

Contents

Acknowledgments

I wish to express my deep gratitude to the following people who helped make this book possible:

Mr. Tom White, USA Director of Voice of the Martyrs, Inc., whose belief in this project, photos, source information, and ongoing support of the persecuted church made this book possible.

The principals of Living Sacrifice Books, for their courage in committing the financial resources that made my dream a reality;

The Communications Department at The Voice of the Martyrs, for coordinating the layout and production of this book;

Professors Howard L. Foltz, Joseph L. Umidi, and Peter E. Prosser, all from Regent University, under whose guidance this investigation was conducted, for their careful reading of the manuscript, timely guidance, and for their generous academic flexibility in granting me the privilege of running with this project;

Dr. Charles A. Wickman, Executive Director of the Center for American—North Korean Understanding, who offered valuable insights and research data;

Dr. Dale Kietzman, William Carey International University, for his significant contribution of research material;

Dean Vinson Synan of Regent University's School of Divinity, for his insightful comments, encouragement, and vision to raise up Christian leaders in ministry;

Mr. Robert Felsing, research librarian at the University of Oregon, for his splendid North Korean website;

Professor Hubert Morken, Regent University, for challenging me, helping me ask the tough questions, and encouraging me take the time to probe deeper in search of truth;

Ms. Catherine Sexton, SPOT Image Corporation, for use of unclassified satellite imagery;

Mr. Robert Sivigny, research librarian at Regent University, for his friendship and research advice;

Mr. Li Yang Su, Vice Editor-in-Chief of the Korean Central News Agency, for taking the time to answer some of my many questions about Juche;

Ms. Kim Raina, Republic of Korea Embassy, Washington, D.C., for the use of several excellent photos;

Ms. Rebecca A. Livingston, U.S. National Archives, Washington, D.C., for primary source information on the *General Sherman* incident;

Professor Murooka Tetsuo, National Institute for Defense Studies, Tokyo, Japan, for his historical and Juche-related insights;

Mr. Alex Stewart, analyst, North Asia Research Associates, London, UK, for information regarding offshore oil off the DPRK coast;

Mr. Tom Corcoran, Executive Director, Eurasia Group, New York, NY, for forwarding numerous news articles;

Dr. Stephen Linton, Director, Eugene Bell Foundation, for his insights and research tips;

Mr. Walter Summerville, Executive Director, Christian Friends of Korea, for sharing American missionary primary source material;

Rev. Byoungyoung (John) Lee, for his friendship, love, prayers, and encouragement;

Mr. Robert W. Schubring, explosives expert, for his friendship, analysis, and for FedExing the designer chocolates for my wife;

Cornerstone Ministries International, for carefully reading and critiqueing the manuscript;

Rev. David Yonggi Cho, Senior Pastor, Yoido Full Gospel Church, for taking the time to come to the other side of the world to preach at a small Sunday evening service at a little church in Virginia Beach and impart his vision for evangelizing North Korea;

Dr. Jay K. Yoo, for his encouragement, vision, sound advice, and brotherly love;

Rev. Earl D. Bergman, my father-in-law, for his prayers and frequent encouragement during my graduate studies;

Lorrie, my lovely wife, for her many prayers and for often calling to my attention television reports and newspaper articles on North Korea and her grace to me during my immoderate zeal for this project;

Those contributors, not recognized by name, who provided me with research tips, insights, and information through the course of this project;

and, most of all, to

My Lord and Savior, Jesus Christ, to whom all praise, glory, and honor is due.

Any mistakes are mine.

Foreword

North Korea, the Hermit Kingdom, has been closed to outsiders for over fifty years. In the past decade, famine, flooding, and economic hardship have forced the doors to open slightly. The view inside is appalling. It is clear that the long dictatorship of Kim Il Sung was founded upon demonic power and a crafty ideology called Juche—self-reliance.

Representing the sun goddess once worshipped by the entire Korean peninsula, Kim Il Sung set himself up as a powerful god in the 1950s. His dream was to exist forever, long after his death in 1994, through his son, Kim Jong Il. Having been raised in a Christian environment, Kim Il Sung copied and twisted the Christian Trinity, imposing an ungodly trinity on the people of North Korea. In his warped vision, Kim Il Sung was the almighty, eternal father; Kim Jong Il was the active word, the son; and Juche ideology was the very spirit of the revolution, the spirit ruling the nation, the life-giving breath of their god.

Kim Il Sung's plan and the Juche ideology were initially presented as a political ideology. Soon after his taking control of North Korea, though, it became a manifest part of a plan for Satan to assume rights and authority over the North Korean people. The country was dominated by force, ruled by fear, controlled by death. Hundreds of thousands have been killed during this regime. Satan cut these lives short, preventing them from ever having the opportunity to hear of the real Messiah, Jesus Christ.

The veil continues to cover the eyes, minds, hearts, and spirits of the North Korean people. Even the defection of Hwang Jang Yop, the engineer of Juche ideology, has not eroded the nation's belief in Jucheism. North Koreans, Hwang Jang Yop included, still believe that Juche (self-reliance) ideology will save the world. Hundreds die every day in total ignorance of God's love and mercy.

When I first met Tom Belke at Regent University, I was surprised at his interest in studying North Korea's Juche ideology. I thought it was rather odd. Now I realize that God revealed to him that the Juche philosophy was the real religion of North Korea. The Juche mentality is Satan's fetter, shackling people's minds. Juche must be broken, so that the people can be truly free. Tom has spent years researching this truth and shining God's light on the great darkness oppressing North Koreans.

Rebellion separates man from the true God. Self-dependence, Jucheism, is the epitome of rebellion. God created us in His image to be fully dependent on Him. Juche holds the direct opposite. Through Tom's efforts, we learn more about this philosophy and the strategies that the devil has used to gain control over the North Korean people.

The small Kim Il Sung pin covering every North Korean's heart is in fact a symbol of worship, spiritually hindering them from giving their hearts to Jesus. Their slogans and songs deifying Kim Il Sung, Kim Jong Il, and Juche are used to keep them in spiritual darkness. As North Koreans are forced to worship the images of Kim Il Sung daily, they remain ignorant offenders, breaking God's commandment and falling under His curse.

For too long, North Korea has been a playground of principalities and powers. Millions of souls have entered eternity without having heard the name of Jesus. This must stop. Every Christian missionary with a burden for North Korea should learn as much as possible about the devices Satan is using to keep the North Korean minds and hearts in bondage. Let us pray that, through the words in this book, the Holy Spirit would teach us new intercession and ministry strategies, so that we can work together, as the Body of Christ, to break Satan's crushing hold on the people of North Korea.

REV. BAHN-SUK LEE
M.Div., Fuller Theological Seminary
Ph.D. candidate studying the theology of
underground Christians in North Korea

Preface

This book aims to provide the reader with a window into North Korea's totalitarian culture and its state religion, Juche, which guides it. Contrary to contemporary notions, Juche, which literally means "self-reliance," is not merely a North Korean version of Marxist atheist philosophy, but rather a highly developed religion. As will become clear in the chapters that follow, references to Juche as "totally secular" or "atheist" convey a complete misunderstanding of North Korean society.

The truth is that North Korea is controlled by the Juche religious system, an idolatrous religion that both binds and blinds the people of North Korea while actively promoting an ongoing war upon the underground Christian church. There are those who maintain that Juche is not a religion. It is my hope that this book will dispel ignorance among readers about the situation in North Korea, and enable them to understand the Juche worldview.

This book is written to benefit the Korean people, not to harm them. Koreans are a wonderful people. Multitudes of Koreans—including North Koreans—will worship with all other believers before the throne of God in eternity. This book also does not condemn humanitarian aid. I heartily applaud the ongoing stream of Christian humanitarian aid which continues to show the love of Jesus Christ to the starving masses of North Korea apart from any political agenda. Nothing in the self-centered, self-reliant system of Juche can explain or comprehend this great outpouring of love from Juche's arch-enemy: the Church of Jesus Christ.

My purpose in writing this book is to irreversibly rend the veil of secrecy that masks the Juche religious system—and to expose Juche for what it truly is. Also, this book is intended to equip the Church to pray for victory over the spiritual forces of darkness so God may deliver the people of North Korea from bondage (Ephesians 6:12). God so loved the Korean people that He gave His one and only Son that whoever believes in Him will not perish but have eternal life. He says, "Ask of me, and I will make the nations your inheritance" (Psalm 2:8). North Koreans need the real Jesus

Christ of the Bible, not a counterfeit. We need to pray that they will find Him.

Make no mistake: as long as the Juche religion continues, judgment is fixed in North Korea's future. The coming spiritual storm ultimately will expose the Juche religious system for what it really is: a house built upon the sand. But grace is also in North Korea's future. The Bible's unchanging proclamation that "this gospel of the kingdom will be preached in the whole world as a testimony to all nations, and then the end will come" (Matthew 24:14) is the devil's undoing in North Korea. Jesus made no exceptions in His Word—there are no "gospel-free zones." Thus, it is my steadfast conviction, based on the unchanging, inerrant Word of God, that the gospel of Jesus Christ shall be openly preached in North Korea in the near future.

THOMAS J. BELKE

Quoted material from North Korean propaganda publications is indicated as follows:

PUBLICATION	NOTATION
Democratic People's Republic of Korea magazine	*DPRK*
Korean Central News Agency (main state daily organ)	*KCNA*
Rodong Sinmun (organ of the Korean Workers' Party)	*Rodong Sinmun*
People's Korea (*Choson Sinbo*) (DPRK Internet monthly)	*People's Korea*
Kuguk Jonson (organ of the pro-North National Democratic Front of South Korea, or NDFSK)	*Kuguk Jonson*
Minju Choson (organ of the government)	*Minju Choson*
Korea Today (KCNA/Korean News Agency-related organ)	*Korea Today*
Choson Inmingun (organ of the Korean People's Army)	*Choson Inmingun*
Kulloja (or *Kuroja*) (monthly magazine of the Korean Workers' Party)	*Kulloja*
Youth Vanguard (organ of the Kim Il Sung Socialist Youth League)	*Youth Vanguard*

CHAPTER 1

Introduction

What we don't know about North Korea is so vast that it makes the Kremlin of the 1950s look like an open book. The communist northern tier of a peninsula once known as the Hermit Kingdom has lived up to that name with a vengeance, enveloping its 22 million people in a bell jar of propaganda, thought control and mythology glorifying the Kims, often in public pageants that would dwarf a Cecil B. DeMille production.[1]

ARNOLD KANTER
U.S. UNDERSECRETARY OF STATE
UNDER PRESIDENT GEORGE BUSH

Welcome to Juche [Joo-chay], the world's "newest" major religion. If you have never heard of Juche before, you are not alone. Few people outside of North Korea have. Most general volumes on world religions mistakenly state that North Korea is a "Marxist-Leninist dictatorship" where religious practices are virtually non-existent. Any such notion falls widely short of reality. In fact, Juche's approximately 23 million adherents, who worship their former and current dictators, outnumber those of more well-known world religions such as Judaism, Sikhism, Jainism, Bahaism, and Zoroastorianism.

In the following chapters, we will embark on a journey into North Korea—the Hermit Kingdom—to view what is possibly the most rigidly controlling religious system on the planet. Through the use of unchallengeable totalitarian power, North Korea's ruling elite enforces Juche ideology into every aspect of the culture. No competing ideologies are permitted.

We will also explore the classic question, "How did Kim Il Sung, a Communist, create a religion?" In the mind of the average North

1

Korean, Juche is not viewed as a religion. The North Korean people's view of religion is different from the Western world's concept of "religionized faith." For example, in North Korea, every individual is owned by the nation. In one sense, this view is similar to Christianity in that Christians also are not their own, but belong to Jesus Christ. However, a difference arises in the cultural use of common terms. Consider the Korean concept of "father." One may properly address an old man on the street as "grandfather." Likewise, you might call a man who is kind to you "uncle." You would address your good friend's father as "father" to show respect. However, when the North Koreans, under Juche, look to Kim Il Sung as "Father" in the sense of provider, sustainer, and savior—and worship him in the place of Almighty God—then they are revealing the true nature of Juche as a religion.

In the chapters that follow, we will separate fact from fiction in this world of the Hermit Kingdom, where politics, philosophy, worship, and all aspects of culture are intertwined under the auspices of the "Dear Leader" Kim Jong Il, the son of the "eternal, immortal Great Leader" Kim Il Sung—Father of the revolution, "Eternal President," and author of the Juche idea.

The home of the Juche religion is officially known as the Democratic People's Republic of Korea (DPRK). North Korea, called "Choson" by its residents, occupies the northern half of East Asia's Korean peninsula between the Korea Bay (Yellow Sea) and Eastern Sea (Sea of Japan), bordering China and Russia. North Korea's total land area is slightly smaller than Mississippi. Aside from the coastal plains, North Korea's terrain is mostly hills and mountains separated by deep, narrow valleys. The forested interior is nearly inaccessible and sparsely populated.

North Korea's economic infrastructure is backward compared to other nations. While there are 5,000 kilometers of railroads, less than 7% of their roughly 28,000 kilometers of roads are paved. Telephones are available only to government officials. The radio and television infrastructure is also state-controlled. North Korea's capital is Pyongyang, which has a population of 2.3 million. Two-thirds of the country's labor force of nearly ten million people serve in urban nonagricultural occupations; the rest work on farms.

As we begin to explore the Juche religion, it is essential to remember that Juche represents a radical departure from Korea's earlier religious system. Before 1945, Korean religion was dominated by a mixture of Confucian thought, Buddhism, and shamanism (communication with demons and ancestral spirits). There was also a vibrant growing Christian community. However, under Juche, these competing religions were systematically eliminated, suppressed, or persecuted through a totalitarian system of fear and thought control. The majority of North Koreans today have never heard the name of Jesus. The knowledge of God has been obliterated for most by an Orwellian nightmare of repression, demands for total conformity, and isolation from the outside world.

During the two decades prior to the death of Kim Il Sung in May 1994, the Juche religious system took root in North Korea. Under Juche, the former dictator was deified and worshipped by the Koreans. He was presented as omniscient and omnipresent. Surprisingly, Kim Il Sung, the founder of Juche, had a Pentecostal Christian mother, Kang Ban Sok. His background might help to explain the strange mixture of Christian and Communist terminology used within the Juche religious system. Table 1-1 provides a sample of Juche religious beliefs and terminology reflected in recent North Korean propaganda.

In the Juche belief system, man is proclaimed God in a nation whose government has officially decided against Christianity for all of its citizens. Far from being a passing philosophy or minor cult, Juche religious ideology is the cornerstone of North Korea's totalitarian society. It holds sway over the entire population through a stifling system of party and government organizational controls. North Korea's leaders advocate Juche ideology as the only standard of morality in their ongoing revolution against all foreign and domestic enemies, real or imagined.

Juche ideology is the supreme symbol of North Korea and serves as mechanism to tame the people to become blind followers of the Leader. North Koreans are told that they live in "paradise on Earth" while, according to the United Nations, they are in the midst of the greatest famine since Ethiopia's in 1984.[2] Such practices are possible only because the Big Brother society of George Orwell's science fiction novel, *1984*, truly has become a reality. Today Big Brother has a name. His name is Kim Jong Il. Kim Jong Il is promoted as the new god-man who reveals the will of the deceased Kim Il Sung, and his regime is as repressive as his father's.

In the chapters that follow, we will explore the various aspects of Juche, including its central teachings, spiritual dimension, its spiritual archenemy, origins, and Juche holy sites. We will also consider the Juche worldview, the architect of Juche, propagation of the Juche culture, and Juche as a religion in transition. Our journey into the realm of Juche will conclude by considering a biblical view of the future of Juche.

TABLE 1-1. Juche Religious Beliefs Reflected in North Korean Propaganda

JUCHE BELIEF	RELATED PROPAGANDA
The identity of God	"…the firm belief that he [Kim Jong Il] is identical to President Kim Il Sung and is god of the Korean nation…" [KCNA].
Salvation and the Bible	"His [Kim Jong Il's] work is a great bible which indicates the way of saving the nation, the path of national reunification…"[3] [KCNA].
Prayer and immortality	"Then they [the visiting Japanese delegation led by Shizue Araya] held a meeting to pray for the immortality of the President in front of his statue on Mansu Hill" [KCNA].
Benevolent totalitarianism "as in heaven"	"President Kim Il Sung with the idea of "believing in the people as in heaven" devoted all his life to the welfare of the people…As mentioned above, the guidance of the President and Secretary Kim Jong Il for the welfare of the people continues" [KCNA].
Legendary exploits	"After Korea's liberation…the President made a 550,000-kilometer-long[4] journey, going to the places where the people live and gave on-the-spot guidance to some 18,000 units on more than 8,000 occasions. Secretary Kim Jong Il has made a journey for the welfare of the people as the President did. Secretary Kim Jong Il put forward the slogan 'We serve the people!'" [KCNA].

TABLE 1-1. *(continued)*

JUCHE BELIEF	RELATED PROPAGANDA
Kim Il Sung is the Father of Juche	"It comprehensively elaborates on the immortal feats of President Kim Il Sung who put forward the Juche-based idea and theory of Party building and ceaselessly strengthened and developed the WPK into a revolutionary Party with the solid monolithic ideological system, a militant Party with strong organization and discipline and a Party deeply rooted among the broad masses, and indicates the tasks and ways of the Party to defend its revolutionary character as the Party of President Kim Il Sung" [*Rodong Sinmun*].
Kim Jong Il will continue Kim Il Sung's Juche morality to the end	"All the ideas and theories indicated in the work carry the steadfast will of Secretary Kim Jong Il who is leading the revolutionary cause of Juche straight to victory with unfailing loyalty and filial piety and noble moral obligation to President Kim Il Sung...Since the General led the party and the revolution, the cause of the Juche-based Party building has developed on to a new higher stage... He also has thoroughly applied the idea of believing in the people as in heaven and further strengthened the relations between the Party and the people sealed in blood" [the latter phrase could refer to their blood having been spilled during the Korean War] [*Rodong Sinmun*].
Nature witnesses that Kim Jong Il is heaven-sent	"Mysterious natural phenomena were witnessed on September 28, when...Secretary Kim Jong Il in a car arrived at the entrance to the [army] unit, the fog cleared off and the sun shone bright in the blue sky. Two apricot trees on either side of the road to the unit had 28 and 26 blossoms respectively."[5] Seeing the mysterious natural phenomena, the unit servicemen said that Secretary Kim Jong Il is the famous general produced by heaven [*KCNA*].

CHAPTER 2

Central Juche Teachings

Living in the Korean way means thinking with our own heads, acting and solving everything with our own strength according to the interests of our country's revolution and people, as demanded by the Juche idea.[1]

KIM JONG IL

Woe to those who call evil good and good evil, who put darkness for light and light for darkness, who put bitter for sweet and sweet for bitter.

ISAIAH 5:20

The Juche religious system does not exist to promote the welfare of North Korea's citizens, nor to ascribe worship to the one true God. Instead, Juche's central teachings exist solely to promote and sustain the totalitarian regime of Kim Jong Il. These central teachings underpin five primary ideological goals shown in Table 2-1.

TABLE 2-1. Five Primary Goals of Juche Ideology

– The justification of Kim Jong Il as dictator-god
– Hereditary power succession
– Xenophobic isolationism
– National reunification (Kim Jong Il's rule over all Korea)
– Export of the Juche system on a worldwide basis

Article 3 of North Korea's Constitution designates Juche as the state religion when it declares, "[The North Korean government] shall make the Juche Ideology of the Workers' Party the guiding principle for all its actions." Similarly, the Charter of the Korean Workers' Party (WPK) reveals a commitment to Juche in its pre-amble: "The Workers' Party is guided only by Kim Il Sung's Juche Ideology and revolutionary thoughts."[2] Table 2-2 provides a look at some core teachings of the Juche religion.

TABLE 2-2. Core Teachings of the Juche Religion

JUCHE DOCTRINE	CORRESPONDING TEACHING [*KCNA, DPRK*]
Leader worship	Kim Il Sung and Kim Jong Il are divine, immortal, and worthy of all prayer, worship, honor, power, and glory.
Totalitarian subordination of the individual to the nation	The individual must guide all his or her actions according to the Juche ideal as revealed by the immortal Comrade Kim Jong Il. Juche is "the socialist cause of Korean style, is the cause of national independence which places the destinies of the country and nation ahead of other things and subordinates everything to it."
Man as the beginning and end of all things	"The revolutionary cause of Juche started by President Kim Il Sung and being carried forward to completion by Secretary Kim Jong Il is the revolutionary cause of genuine national independence started and advanced by the Korean people with their own faith and will."
Self-validation	"The revolutionary cause of Juche has become the cause of genuine national independence because it has been led by President Kim Il Sung and Secretary Kim Jong Il."
Korea ethnocentrism	"This is the sacred country. As a result of Juche, the powerful socialist country, strong in the Juche character and national character and independent in politics, self-supporting in the economy and self-reliant in national defense, has been built in this land." "Because of our Party, the position of our country has been raised beyond comparison and the dignity and honor of the nation shine all over the world." "The Korean people are blessed most in the world with the peerless great man Comrade Kim Jong Il whom they have held in high esteem as the leader of the WPK."

TABLE 2-2. *(continued)*

JUCHE DOCTRINE	CORRESPONDING TEACHING [*KCNA, DPRK*]
North Korea is "paradise on earth"	North Korea, despite her ongoing "struggle," is paradise on earth. Other nations, such as "the south," that do not have the benefit of Juche are poor, miserable places to live.
Juche is uniquely Korean	"All the lines and policies of the Korean revolution which have been shaped and pursued historically have never based on the established theories or experience of others."
Reunification	Reunification of the divided Korean peninsula along Juche guidelines is not only a political agenda, but a sacrosanct principle of Juche religion. "Juche is the cause of national reunification...the revolutionary cause of genuine national independence."
Extreme national self-reliance	"It is the Korean people's way of making revolution and their basic stand to push ahead with the revolution and construction with their own viewpoint, will and decision and to hold fast to independence in external relations."
Interdependence brings disaster	Any calamity can be attributed to the improper reliance upon other nations. "The WPK and the Korean people have held high the banner of self-reliance, mindful that dependence on outside forces leads to the collapse of the country and self-reliance guarantees the prosperity of the country and nation."
The cause of Juche will ultimately be victorious	"The revolutionary cause of Juche is the cause of self-reliance which emerges victorious ever by the efforts of the Korean people...Juche is the nation-loving struggle to establish the sovereignty of the nation throughout the country and guarantee the welfare of posterity for all ages."

These core teachings of Juche have been imposed upon millions of Koreans through a mass system of controls. Koreans dare not question why their leader-god, who supposedly has power to make the trees blossom and sun break through the fog, cannot likewise prevent the drought, floods, and tidal waves that ravage the nation. According to Juche, all such disasters are caused by some combination of Korea's enemies, the inevitable result of reliance on other nations, and just part of the "arduous ever-victorious struggle."

Political analysts who have little or no concept of Juche's spiritual roots underestimate its nature. No place on earth compares to North Korea with its highly developed system of institutionalized brainwashing and control that spans the entire culture. Spiritually sensitive men and women who visit North Korea by way of Beijing frequently breathe a sigh of relief when stepping off the plane in the People's Republic of China. They sigh because, by spiritual comparison, China—where the Church is heavily persecuted—seems like a free country!

In the pages that follow, the specific teachings of Juche will be further explained. These teachings stem from the "Juche idea," which has been developed into the "philosophy of Juche." This analysis will also include an in-depth look at the core teachings of reunification and the concept of the Juche religious pantheon.

The Juche Idea

My political philosophy is the Juche idea.[3]

KIM JONG IL

Though various sources agree that Juche is "man-centered" and related to "self reliance," what exactly is the "Juche idea that forms the cornerstone of the Juche religion? To answer this question, the *KCNA* presented excerpts from Kim Jong Il's book *On the Juche Idea of Our Party.*

> [The] Late President Kim Il Sung created [the] Juche idea after acquiring a deep insight into the requirements of a new era when the oppressed and humiliated masses of the people became masters of their destiny. Thus he developed their struggle for *Chajusong* [collective social life attribute given to man by society[4]] onto a higher plane and opened up the age of Juche, a new era in the development of human history...The revolutionary idea of the working class emerges as the reflection of the mature demand of history and the revolution in their development. In order to advance the revolution under the new historical conditions, the revolution in each country should be carried out responsibly by its own

people, the masters, in an independent manner, and in a creative way suitable its specific conditions. It is the essence of Juche idea. The Juche idea is a new philosophical thought which centers on man. It raised the fundamental question of philosophy by regarding man as the main factor, and elucidated the philosophical principle that man is the master of everything and decides everything. The philosophical principle of the Juche idea is the principle of man-centered philosophy which explains man's position and role in the world. That man is master of everything means that he is the master of [the] world and plays the decisive role in transforming the world and in shaping his destiny. *Establishing Juche in ideology is the primary requirement of the masses' struggle for Chajusong.* The revolution and construction are man's conscious activities. Establishing Juche in thinking, therefore, is the only way to establish Juche in politics, the economy, defense, and all other domains. The Juche idea was created by late President Kim Il Sung and is developed and enriched by General Secretary Kim Jong Il [*KCNA*].

The editor of the *Korean Central News Agency*, when asked for a concise "non-psycho-babble" definition of Juche, provided an exact quote from Kim Jong Il's book *On the Juche Idea of Our Party:*

> The Juche idea is a new philosophical thought which centers on man. The Juche idea is based on the philosophical principle that *man is the master of everything and decides everything.* The Juche idea raised the fundamental question of philosophy by regarding man as the main factor, and elucidated the philosophical principle that man is the master of everything and decides everything. That man is the master of everything means that he is the master of the world and his own destiny; that man decides means that he plays the decisive role in transforming the world and in shaping his destiny. The philosophical principle of the Juche idea is the principle of man-centered philosophy which explains man's position and role in the world.[5]

Lee Wha Rang, analyst for the *Korea Web Weekly*, explains that this "new philosophical thought" borrows from a wide variety of philosophies while somehow retaining its uniqueness:

> The basic idea of Jucheism is to think on your own and not copycat foreign ideas.

Lee Wha Rang further states that, according to the Juche idea,

> Human beings and society are governed by manmade laws which are not found in the material world or [in] other biological beings. The social changes are advanced by man and its laws are imposed by man. The main engine of the social movement is man himself.[6]

Probably the most concise definition of the Juche idea is expressed by practitioners of the Juche martial arts on their website:

> Juche is a philosophical idea that man is the master of everything and decides everything. In other words, it is the idea that man is the master of the world and his destiny. It is said that this idea was rooted in Paektu Mountain, which symbolizes the spirit of the Korean people.[7]

Yet to the chagrin of the Juche faithful, this anthropocentric Juche idea is almost identical to the classical humanist ideology. Christian author Francis Schaeffer wrote:

> The term humanism used in this wider, more prevalent way means Man beginning from himself, with no knowledge except what he himself can discover and no standards outside himself. In this view, Man is the measure of all things, as the Enlightenment expressed it.[8]

Original or not, the Juche idea has given rise to a system of Juche philosophy that lies at the heart of North Korea's state religion.

The Philosophy of Juche

This [Juche] philosophical cloak has helped the communist system to turn out to be an evil one satisfying the interests of only the ruling elite but suppressing the freedom of ordinary citizens.[9]

KIM GAHB CHOL
PROFESSOR EMERITUS
KONKUK UNIVERSITY, SEOUL

The philosophy of Juche is a system of humanistic thought that emerged from the North Korea of the early 1970s. It builds on the Juche idea of self-reliance to emphasize the importance of developing the nation's potential using its own resources and reserves of human creativity. Juche has such a radical emphasis within North Korea that the term was used fifteen times in the following 1998 propaganda article:

A national meeting of example-setters in *Juche* was held at the 6,000-seat theater of the April 25 house of culture on January 29 and 30. It was attended by Vice President Ri Jong Ok, other senior officials of the party and state, officials of example units of *Juche* and innovators. It summed up achievements and experience gained in the course of the "arduous march" and discussed tasks and ways to push ahead with the forced march for the final victory by giving fuller scope to the revolutionary spirit of *Juche*.

In a congratulatory message to the participants in the meeting, the Central Committee of the Workers' Party of Korea said that the history of the Korean revolution is a proud history of *Juche* and all the victories made by the WPK and the Korean people in the revolutionary struggle and construction work are a brilliant fruition of *Juche*. It recalled that, in recent years, the Korean people, upholding the slogan *"Juche is our only choice,"* have firmly defended and exalted Korean socialism in teeth of the vicious moves of the imperialists to isolate and stifle them and unprecedented hardships caused by severe natural disasters, thus working historic miracles. It pointed out that it is the pride of the WPK and the Korean people to have a large army of example-setters in *Juche* who have supported the party in practice by creditably performing their revolutionary duties under any circumstances in the revolutionary spirit of soldiers and *Juche*.

It further said: Today, the WPK requires the whole party, the whole army and all the people to make a decisive turn in the revolution and construction by pressing ahead with the forced march for the final victory in a high-pitched spirit of *Juche*. To uphold General Kim Jong Il with loyalty and filial piety is an ideological and spiritual quality of the example-setters in *Juche*. Herein lies a basic source of the revolutionary spirit of *Juche*. The congratulatory message called upon all the example-setters in *Juche* to become ardent loyalists who play a vanguard role in the struggle to put the plan and intention of the party into practice.

Kim Ki Nam, Secretary of the WPK Central Committee, delivered a report "let us accelerate the forced march for the final victory under the uplifted revolutionary banner of *Juche*."

The reporter recalled that General Kim Jong Il set forth a revolutionary policy of meeting the anti-socialist offensive of the imperialists with the strategy of *Juche* and has led the whole party, the whole army and all the people along the road of victory, setting great examples in the van[guard] of the "arduous march."...Speakers introduced achievements and experience gained in the revolutionary spirit of *Juche* [*KCNA*].

The Juche philosophy transforms this self-reliant nationalism into extreme cultural, economic, and political isolationism. This xenophobic hyper-nationalism is accomplished by labeling the imitation of or reliance upon foreign countries as inherently evil.

The philosophy of Juche captures the essence of Marxist-Leninist concepts of the Party and the masses. However, Juche deviates sharply from Marxism-Leninism philosophy through its additional ingredient of the cult of the "Su-ryong" (leader). Since it serves to deify the leader, the concept of the Su-ryong gives Juche philosophy a distinct religious quality. Not surprisingly, in the 1970s, Kim Jong Il suggested that Juche be renamed Kim Il Sung Chuui (Kim Il Sung-ism). It has also been called Kim Jong Il Chuui (Kim Jong Il-ism). Ironically, Communism's godless ideology has come full circle in Juche's deification of Kim Il Sung and Kim Jong Il. Nevertheless, Juche's leaders are quite adamant that faith in their gods does not comprise a religion. Thus they retain Communist and atheistic terminology while theorizing a new emperor-worship religion. Beyond these general principles, Juche retains an amorphous quality seemingly to accommodate its many inherent contradictions. Juche's adherents are more apt to describe it in terms of what it not rather than what it is. Consider the typical philosophical statements by Juche believers shown in Table 2-3.

As the table shows, Marxism did not present North Korea's leaders with an adequate political model for achieving socialism—only an set of opaque prescriptions. Or, from another perspective, Marxism's lack of a specific political model opened the way for North Korea's Juche architects to develop a tailor-made version of totalitarianism for their own indigenous political culture. However, Juche's theorists rebel against any notion that Juche evolved out of Marxism since this would not be "self-reliance."

The remarks shown in the table include the assertion that "Jucheism is not humanism" and then go on to redefine humanism. (Such redefinitions are common in Juche.) Before we bypass such a remark, it is worthwhile to consider that *humanism* is defined as "the placing of Man at the center of all things and making him the measure of all things." Thus, the Juche idea is, by definition—and at its core—pure, unvarnished humanism. A philosophical and historical understanding of humanism is therefore beneficial in understanding Juche thought. Likewise, the Juche religion provides an example of what will occur when

TABLE 2-3. Typical Philosophical Statements by Juche Believers[10]

TOPIC	JUCHE PHILOSOPHICAL VIEW
Juche vs. humanism	*Jucheism is not humanism.* Jucheism states that man is the master of everything and man decides all things. Jucheism deals with the relationship between man and the world. It is true that humanism, too, regards man as being the central element, but it does not recognize man's social nature and emphasizes man's instinct and individualism; humanism says man is an island to himself.
Juche, man, and society	*Jucheism regards man not as an isolated island but an integral part of the society.* Jucheism recognizes man being independent, creative, and conscious of his responsibilities to the society. He is the master in his own society and world. He can change the world. Jucheism clarifies the essential qualities of man and the forces of social changes. Jucheism recognizes that the world is composed of materials, changing and developing; the world is dominated and transformed by man.
Juche vs. Marxism	*Jucheism is not Marxist dialectical materialism.* Marxism says that the world is made of materials and dialectics; that the world undergoes constant changes and evolution. Marxism tries to explain the underlying forces that drive the changes in terms of class struggle (conflicts and confrontation: dialectics) and production mechanics (materialism). Jucheism cannot be understood in terms of Marxism-Leninism. It is a man-centered philosophy which begins by clarifying what a human being is. Things change because people make them change. It is the man-world interaction that drives the changes.

TABLE 2-3. *(continued)*

TOPIC	JUCHE PHILOSOPHICAL VIEW
Juche and social change	*Marxism applies physical laws to social changes.* The changes cannot be regarded as arising purely from material causes. The social movement is not a pure natural process, either. Jucheism asserts that the social changes are primarily caused by man. The social movement is pushed forward by actions of man. In some ways, human beings and the society are governed by the universal laws of the material world. For instance, human beings are governed by the action of gravity and man dies just as all other biological beings must die sooner or later.
Juche and manmade law	On the other hand, *human beings and the society are governed by manmade laws* which are not found in the material world or other biological beings. The social changes are advanced by man and its laws are made and imposed by man. The main engine of the social movement is man himself. The clearer the role of man in social changes, the more purposeful and conscious man becomes. Even in a capitalist society, the purposeful and conscious actions of human beings dominate. The more human beings develop ideologically, the more their purposeful and conscious factors will impact the society.

the full philosophical agenda of humanism is implemented across an entire society.

Definitions are very important when entering any discussion where the terms *humanism, human beings, human-centered,* and *humanitarian* are involved. People should not confuse Christian *humanitarianism* with *humanism. Humanitarianism* is helping people through kindness—treating people humanly. Christians should be the most humanitarian of all people. Similarly, the biblical God-centered philosophy elevates the *human being* by recognizing that man is created in God's image. By contrast, the *humanist* man-centered philosophy dismisses the spiritual dimension of man and tends to dehumanize *human beings* by viewing them as no different than evolved apes. Thus, humanism has much to do with imposing a godless societal agenda and very little to do with humanitarianism.

In North Korea, Kim Il Sung and Kim Jong Il have systematically implemented the humanist Juche religion throughout their society. It is important to understand that Juche man-centered humanism has absolutely nothing to do with treating people as *human beings*. Inalienable human rights are God-based, and the denial of God also denies any absolute basis for *human beings* being fundamentally different than a dog or a mosquito. Thus, classifications of *human beings* become arbitrary. Moreover, the rejection of a God-based philosophy permits the reclassification of *human beings* as "non-humans," making the extermination of the opponents (real or imagined) of Juche that much easier.

Failure to distinguish between these definitions can result in confused observations. For example, Professor Shin Il Chul, author of *A Study of North Korea's Juche Philosophy*, remarked:

> North Korea insists that Juche philosophy is a "human-centered view on the world." This remark can be cited as an expression that the philosophy takes into consideration an idea that "socialist humanism" must enable the people to live like "human beings." *But the reality is that Juche philosophy rejects humanism*, labeling it bourgeois culture; instead, it tries to justify the personality cult of one man. Juche philosophy has replaced the "materials" appearing in materialism with "human beings," but it tries to define the concept of human beings within the framework of collectivism, thus resulting in denying individual human rights. Therefore, Juche ideology was degraded into a mere political ideology lacking Juche (self-determination).[11]

In actuality, Juche philosophy matches the doctrine of humanism articulated in the Humanist Manifestos I and II almost in entirety. Thus, any claims by Juche proponents that they have rejected humanism are based on lack of information, intentional deception, or the overriding desire for Juche to retain both its "uniqueness" and its "made in Korea" label.

One of the alleged differences between Juche philosophy and classical Marxist Communism is in Jucheism's virtual omission of the term "dialectic." The Marxist concept of the dialectic proposes the view that the constant cultural changes and societal evolution are driven by the ongoing contradictions in terms of class struggles and materialism (production mechanics). These struggles and contradictions are the prime movers that shape developments in the world. The dialectic is considered to be the soul of Marxism and a law which lies at the very heart of Communism. Yet, Juche ideology omits the term "dialectic."

Proponents of Juche ideology assert that Jucheism is not Marxist dialectical materialism. For example, consider the following propaganda excerpt:

> [The Juche] theory on the independent and creative stands clarified by General Kim Jong Il is the most scientific one…General Kim Jong Il clarified the essence of the independent and creative stands and their fundamental requirement, thus scientifically making clear the basic features of these stands different from the preceding dialectical materialist stand…It is hard to regard this stand as the same with the materialistic stand that everything should be viewed by focusing on material conditions since the world consists of material. The creative stand is one that the masses of the people ought to play the role as transformers of the world and shapers of their own destiny…This stand is different from the dialectical stand of the preceding philosophy considering that the world consistently changes and develops, so everything should be viewed as a process of change and development. The might of the Juche idea as an instrument of practice can be increased only when the people have a correct understanding of the independent and creative stands and adhere to them in the revolution and construction…[12]

Yet, this "no dialectic" assertion really is more one of form and not substance. Any admission, according to the dialectic theory, that contradictions exist within North Korean society may be viewed as possibly undermining the hereditary dictatorship. The Pyongyang regime may fear that admission of a dialectic would result in some sort of reform in its political system.

Notwithstanding the "invented here" view of Juche by North Koreans, some experts believe that the Chinese system of Communism has had the strongest foreign influence on Juche's architects. Like Mao Zedong in the Chinese model, Kim Il Sung has been portrayed as the quintessential leader of the masses. Propaganda has frequently touted Kim's visits to factories and the countryside. Kim, like Mao, sent Party cadres down to the local levels to help implement policies, solicit local opinion, and require small-group political study. Kim Il Sung also implemented the so-called criticism and self-criticism of Mao's Cultural Revolution through the use of periodic campaigns to mobilize both the masses and soldiers for production or education in true "people's army" fashion.

Yet, despite many such similarities and an apparent common ideological ancestry, the Juche philosophy is significantly different from the Communist philosophies of the People's Republic of China and the former Union of Soviet Socialist Republics. For example, the Korean Workers' Party symbol is a hammer and sickle with a superimposed writing brush, symbolizing the "three-class alliance" of workers, peasants, and intellectuals. Unlike Communism in China and Cambodia, North Korea's Juche regime has never ostracized, persecuted, and purged intellectuals as a potential "new class" of exploiters of the masses. In contrast, Juche has pursued an inclusive policy toward them. Perhaps this deviation from classical Communism came about because of the shortage of experts and technocrats after so many people fled from the North to the South in the late 1940s.

There is also the unmistakable flavor of a reactionary element within the philosophy of Juche. North Korean political essays consistently proclaim that Juche has succeeded where China, the Soviet Union, and Eastern Europe's Warsaw Pact nations failed. Juche and the victory it represents are synonymous and attributed to Kim Il Sung. He is the "creator," "father," and "Great Leader" whose unfathomable genius originated Juche to "provide a complete answer to any question that arises in the struggle for national liberation and class emancipation, in the building of socialism and communism." Kim Il Sung, and Kim Jong Il after him, are believed to be the personification of revealed truth and wisdom.

In the Juche ideological view, the Chinese and Soviets did not go far enough to implement Communism. An example of this is given in the following excerpt from Lee Wha Rang's article, "What is Jucheism?":

> You Korean comrades are *not* Communists at all;
> you are nationalists. All you are after is our ruble.
>
> VLADIMIR LENIN TO GEN. YI TONG WHI,
CHAIRMAN OF THE KOREAN
COMMUNIST PARTY (C. 1920)

Of course, Lenin was right about the Oriental Communists. Mao Zedong was expelled from Commintern, Deng Xiaping was more capitalist than Bill Clinton, Ho Chi Minh was a "Sunday" Communist, and Kim Il Sung went so far as to rename the Communist Party of Korea to "Workers' Party of Korea."

They all professed Marxism-Leninism adapted to "local and today's" conditions. If you rewrite the Bible to adapt to today's problems, would it still be the Bible? Would you still be a Christian? If you take an old Ford Model T and replace its engine, gears, body, paint, etc., the result would look, feel and run different than the original. Mr. Ford would have trouble recognizing it—for it is no longer a Ford T! Mr. Marx and Comrade Lenin would be shocked to see the "revised" Communism of China, for example.

Kim Il Sung ordered his scholars to come out with a new political philosophy germane to Korea. Unfortunately for Kim, his scholars in the 1950s were mostly Marxist-Leninist dogmatists[13] trained in the old schools of Communism in Russia. These fellows could recite the Communist Bibles (selected works of Lenin, Stalin, etc.) backward and forward, but they did not quite understand what they meant for Korea.

They did not understand the basic tenets of Communism and they did not practice Communism either. They formed a new exploitation class—the Party cadres—with subsidized food, housing and other Capitalist amenities, while the working poor got poorer and poorer. The poor folks began to long for the good old days of the Japanese colonialists.

In China, Mao Zedong organized Red Guards to smash the bourgeois life style of the new elite. Mao figured that only the new generation could save China from the old ways of corruption and exploitation of the people by the ruling elite.

Was Mao's Cultural Revolution good for China? It was bad for China's economy. It disrupted education for a whole generation of China. On the other hand, the ruling elite became more egalitarian and Mao's slogan, "Serve the People," took on more substance among the officials. For the first time in China's modern era, the common people were given the power of confronting and toppling arrogant or corrupt government and Party officials.

The basic idea of Jucheism is to think on your own and not copycat foreign ideas. Kim told the Party ideologues to be more creative and original. In China, Mao initiated his

"Let One Hundred Flowers Bloom" campaign which he had to terminate because it created more factionalism by dogmatists and opportunists than any creative ideas by true believers.[14]

In light of such beliefs, Juche proponents consider any inferences that Juche is a philosophical outgrowth of communism as equivalent to religious heresy.

The philosophy of Juche can be viewed as a socialist hybrid of Marxism-Leninism, indigenous Korean leader worship, and nationalist reactionarism—all with the distinct moral overtones of religious validation. This concept of divine "manifest destiny" was apparent in Kim Il Sung's 1992 New Year's message, in which he proclaimed the invincibility of this Juche ideology:

> I take great pride in and highly appreciate the fact that our people have overcome the ordeals of history and displayed to the full the heroic mettle of the revolutionary people and the *indomitable spirit of Juche* Korea, firmly united behind the party...No difficulty is insurmountable nor is any fortress impregnable for us when our party leads the people with the *ever-victorious Juche-oriented strategy and tactics* and when all the people turn out as one under the party's leadership.[15]

As these remarks indicate, the Juche socialist doctrine provides the philosophical underpinnings for the Su-ryong and the Party's monolithic totalitarian social structure to rule over the masses.

From a philosophical standpoint, Jucheism flows from a group adaptation of existentialist philosophy articulated by the French philosopher Jean Paul Sartre. Sartre's first premise of existentialism is that, "It is a random universe to which we bring meaning." Sartre, who was also once a member of the French Communist Party, proclaimed that all aspects of life, including original and learned aspects, are self-created. For example, if we agree that "Kim Il Sung is God," then Kim Il Sung is God. One simply has to create the title, delegate the power, defer the responsibility, and choose the man. "Kim Il Sung is God" is all self-created (or man-created). Under Juche, it is "people-created" when Party consensus is reached. Jucheism extends the existentialist concept of the individual man to emphasize the group perspective. However, it retains the trademark existential notion that "*we* (man and mankind) create our own world." Yet, while man is at the center of both Juche and existentialism, Juche deviates from Sartre's consciousness-centered philosophy by substituting a man-centered one. This key substitution leaves Juche's architects with total freedom to define "the man" in any way they want. That man who is at the center is the Su-ryong.

The Su-ryong

See to it that no one takes you captive through hollow and deceptive philosophy, which depends on human tradition and the basic principles of this world rather than on Christ.

COLOSSIANS 2:8

In the 1980s, Kim Il Sung's Juche theorists, under Hwang Jang Yop, developed the "Theory of the Su-ryong."[16] With notable similarities to Nazi Führer ideology, this theory explained that "the Su-ryong is an impeccable brain of the living body [the masses]." Thus, "the masses can be endowed with their life in exchange for their loyalty to him, and the Party is the nerve of that living body." The "Theory of the Su-ryong" lies at the heart of Juche religious ideology. This theory argues that the rightful and truly self-reliant (Juche) leader of the masses must have a blood relationship with the preceding Su-ryong. Based on this theory, the Su-ryong can command the people's worship, trust, wealth, and honor with the moral force of law. Moreover, the Su-ryong theory enables North Korea's leaders to claim divine status, powers, and abilities.

It was Hwang Jang Yop, the behind-the-scenes leader who solidified Kim Il Sung's power base in the late 1950s, who actually devised the Juche theory in the late 1960s. He later developed the "Theory of Immortal Socio-Political Body," also called the "incarnational theory," to justify the Kim-to-Kim hereditary succession plan. Yop explained that the absolute power of the Su-ryong is essential to the implementation of Juche ideology:

The most important thing for human beings is a socio-political life. A healthy body guarantees the intellectual and physical activities of human beings, but a man, if he is backward ideologically and if he lacks a revolutionary lifestyle, despite his healthy flesh, will not be able to enjoy a worthy life as a member of society for whom Jajusong [self-determination] is the lifeline. *The individual physical life span is mortal, but the political life span is immortal* because the social group, represented by the working masses, will live forever together with the Party, the Su-ryong, and the history of the fatherland and the people. The physical life given by the parents will last only for one generation, but the political life given by the Party will enable a man to enjoy a worthy life while he is alive, and will let others remember him forever generation after generation, and therefore this political life is immortal. *Political life is given only by the socio-political body the center of which is the Su-ryong...*

The Su-ryong nurtures and protects the political talent of every member of the socio-political body, and every member comes to be endowed with precious political life by endeavoring to equip himself with the revolutionary ideology of the Su-ryong and by sharing his fortune with the Su-ryong. *Therefore, the Su-ryong of the people is the father of the political life.* Juche ideology teaches that the true lifestyle of human beings is a self-determined and creative lifestyle which is designed to rally themselves around the Su-ryong, and under his leadership, to make their political life shine brilliantly.[17]

In effect, this "Theory of Immortal Socio-Political Body" presents the Juche theology of eternity. Hwang Jang Yop's Juche theology contends that a human being has both a bodily life and a socio-political life. A person's eternal socio-political life shares the same fate as the associated "socio-political organism." Since the most self-reliant "socio-political organism" is defined to be the Su-ryong, people are taught to both pray for the immortality of the Su-ryong and devote their entire existence to serve him to the death.

As the Su-ryong, Kim Jong Il wields uncontested dictatorial power over North Korea regardless of the various political titles he assumed following the death of Kim Il Sung in 1994. For example, Kim Jong Il presides over the government as head of state; over the military as both Commander-in-Chief and head of the National Defense Commission; and over the Party as General Secretary, the only living member of the Presidium and head of the Central Military Committee. North Korea's political structure over which the Su-ryong presides is shown in Figure 2-1.

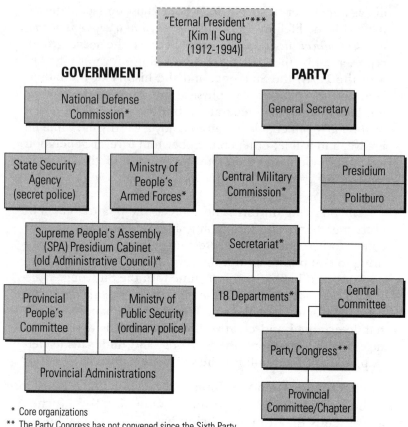

FIGURE 2-1. North Korea's Political Structure[18]

In 1991, American scientist Jeremy Stone asked Hwang Jang Yop about the power of the Su-ryong in determining what is and is not Juche. Stone asked, "Can the President overrule experts on what constitutes Juche?" Yop replied:

> The president listens to the opinions of officials below him a lot. Sometimes the experts make a mistake. And then he corrects them. *He is the final arbiter of what is Juche.* This is why the people in the theoretical research regard the President as their teacher.[19]

According to the philosophical principle of Juche ideology, only those loyal to the Su-ryong (the Party faithful) are recog-

As the sole members of the Juche Su-ryong (leader), the late Kim Il Sung and his reigning son Kim Jong Il are ascribed superhuman god-like powers of intelligence.

nized as truly Juche self-reliant beings. Thus, under Juche theology, the masses are taught that both their individual and collective eternal existence depends on their unquestioning loyalty to the Su-ryong. The "Socio-Historical Principle of Juche" further explains that it is essential for the masses to be guided by the Su-ryong and the Party for them to become masters of history. Thus, this theory both provided self-validation to North Korea's totalitarian government and enabled Kim Il Sung's regime to justify the eventual father-to-son succession of Kim Jong Il in the 1990s.

More importantly, however, the Juche religion's "incarnation theory," whereby Kim Jong Il must carry out his father's will, compels his deification. As Kim Jong Il continues to justify his hereditary succession, North Korean authorities are calling the late Kim Il Sung the Eternal Su-ryong. Meanwhile, Kim Jong Il is trying to assume Kim Il Sung's title of Great Su-ryong (Great Leader). This trend is a concerted attempt to manipulate the masses into thinking that Kim Jong Il is himself Kim Il Sung, the incarnation of the Eternal Su-ryong, while maintaining that Kim Jong Il is not personally responsible for the economic crisis and famine. The problems inherent with Kim Jong Il promoting himself as being "one with his father" make it totally unrealistic to expect that any political reform or meaningful foreign policy reform will ever come from the top in North Korea.

The Party

> *The Party is the core of the independent socio-political organism, as a pivotal contingent of the popular masses, firmly united organizationally and ideologically, with the leader [Su-ryong] as center.*[20]
>
> KIM JONG IL

The Charter of the [North] Korean Workers Party (KWP or "The Party") stipulates that "the ultimate goal [of the KWP] is to establish a Juche ideology-oriented society and construct a communist society [throughout all of Korea]." Since its official founding on October 10, 1945, the Party has served as the power center for Kim Il Sung's totalitarian state.

> He [Kim Il Sung] laid down the establishment of the monolithic ideological system of the Party as the basic line of Party building and led the struggle to implement it. Thus, he achieved the firm unity of the Korean communist movement and guaranteed a high standard of iron-willed, ideological unity and *the cohesion of the whole Party based on the Party's monolithic idea, the Juche idea [DPRK]*.

According to the *Rodong Sinmun*, the Party implements the Su-ryong's (Kim Jong Il's) true and collectivist Juche "revolutionary concept of life," which "glorifies the life of a human being." The article further defines the Party's role in implementing the Juche concept of life:

> The Party should bring up and take care of [all] people in a responsible manner *from their birth to their death*, put them forward in society and exalt their eternal political life *even after their death* [*Rodong Sinmun*].

The KWP, whose members are elected without opposition, have always sustained Kim Il Sung, and now Kim Jong Il, as North Korea's sole totalitarian rulers and champions of national re-unification according to the "communization of the south" ideal.

By its Charter, the KWP is superior to the Constitution. Thus, the Party, not the Constitution, guides and controls all policy. Article 11 of the Constitution also recognized the Party's supremacy: "The Democratic People's Republic of Korea shall conduct all the activities under the leadership of the Workers' Party." At present, the five major tasks Party cells must tackle include:

1. To support the unified leadership of the Party Central Committee with loyalty

2. To organize and guide Party life effectively to train all the Party members into the revolutionaries of Juche type

3. To do work with the masses efficiently to strengthen the blood-sealed ties between the Party and the masses

4. To expedite the three revolutions—ideological, technical, and cultural—to promote socialist construction

5. To defend the security of the country and the socialist gains [*DPRK*]

The KWP's Charter expressly declares that the Party's present task is to achieve totalitarian rule throughout the Korean peninsula:

[The Korean Workers' Party exists] to ensure the complete victory of socialism in the Democratic People's Republic of Korea and the accomplishment of the revolutionary goals of *national liberation and a people's democracy in the entire area of the country.*[21]

When the Charter was revised in October 1980, Juche terminology was added:

...the Workers' Party of Korea shall be guided in its activities *solely by Kim Il Sung's Juche Ideology* and revolutionary ideology.[22]

This modification codified the KWP's role to serve as the prime agent of the Su-ryong's monolithic dictatorial rule through Kim Il Sung and Kim Jong Il.

The Party is organized around the Party Central Committee. Subordinate organs include the Political Bureau, Secretariat of the Party Central Committee, Central Military Commission, and 22 specialized bureaus. The Political Bureau wields the core of the Party's power. It is the organ of absolute authority through which all Party decisions are made. The Political Bureau consists of the Presidium, regular members, and alternate members. With the death of Kim Il Sung, Kim Jong Il is now the sole member of the Presidium. As such, he exercises absolute authoritarian power and reigns over both the Party and the masses of North Korea.

Party members are expected to act in total conformity to their leaders. This pyramidal structure serves to squelch non-conformity by requiring leadership approval for all key policy decisions.

> This is the standard formulation which I came to understand in the following way: The entire Government bureaucracy operates without instructions on major issues because only Kim Il Sung [now Kim Jong Il] makes the final decision. Accordingly, the bureaucracy generates vague phrases such as "the way will be opened" or "there will be a way forward" to encourage Western concessions without committing themselves to do anything in particular. Moreover, the North Korean bureaucrats are as adept as Jesuitical scholars in coming up with new reasons for their policies and, where logic is unable to bridge gaps, they are also adept at blind leaps into implausible arguments.[23]

George Orwell's description of Big Brother's expectations of a Party member apply equally to those under the Juche system. Orwell wrote:

> A Party member is expected to have no private emotions and no respites from enthusiasm. He is supposed to live in a continuous frenzy of hatred of foreign enemies and internal traitors, triumph over victories, and self-abasement before the power and wisdom of the Party.[24]

Orwell's description of a Party member is almost identical to that of North Korea's dictator. By comparison, Kim Jong Il wrote:

> Our party is the mother party. Therefore, a party activist must always have the traits of a mother and have warm contact with the people. He should listen to the masses and work energetically and tirelessly for their interests. This is the style and basic character of our party's activist [KCNA].

Kim Jong Il uses similar Orwellian terminology to characterize one's duty to the Party in his book, *Let Us Exalt the Brilliance of Comrade Kim Il Sung's Idea on the Youth Movement and the Achievements Made Under His Leadership* (1996):

> Our young people…regard it as the highest honor and revolutionary duty to return the love and trust of the Party and the leader by remaining faithful and filial, as befits all true sons and daughters. They are the young vanguard of our Party who uphold the Party's leadership loyally by rallying firmly around the Party with one mind and purpose and who carry out the aims and wishes of the Party without fail, even going through fire and water if necessary. They trust and follow only our Party in any adversity, defend it with their lives ahead of all others and breathe and move in accordance with its ideas and intentions.[25]

As the Presidium of the Party, Kim Jong Il's goals, whatever they may be, are by extension the Party's goals. It is through this organ of the Party that the Su-ryong continues to exercise totalitarian control over North Korea's masses.

> By attaching *prime importance* to imbuing the Party ranks with *the Juche idea*, our Party has continued to strengthen the ideological and iron-willed, moral and loyal unity and cohesion of the whole Party, through the *intensification of education on the Juche idea in various forms, to meet the needs of changing conditions* [*KCNA*].

Besides sustaining Kim Jong Il in leadership, the KWP exists to complete the important revolutionary task of national reunification and to continue the arduous struggle to achieve material prosperity for the motherland.

> Today, the Party cells are performing their noble mission and duties with credit in further developing the Party into a revolutionary party of Juche and carrying on and promoting the Juche revolutionary cause [*KCNA*].

Elections, or "election struggles," are always the same under the Juche system. There is always only one candidate, always 100% participation in voting, and always 100% approval for the Party-designated candidate. North Korean officials take great pride in their Constitution regarding their system of universal, equal, and direct suffrage through "secret" ballot. They boast that they have the "most democratic election system in the world." But how does a North Korean "election struggle" really work?

Polling procedures commence with individuals standing in line according to the number written on their ballot paper. When it is a person's turn to vote, he or she politely bows before Kim Il Sung's and Kim Jong Il's photographs as two Party members watch. Then the voter places the ballot in the ballot box. Placing the ballot in the ballot box without making a mark means a vote in favor of the Party-designated candidate. If one wants to cast a dissenting vote, one has to take an the additional step of putting a mark on the ballot. To do so is to risk one's life, especially since all the ballots are numbered. Those believed to be disloyal are sandwiched between and zealously watched by two Party members throughout the entire voting process. Absentees in an election are treated as if they are disloyal to Kim Jong Il unless they have someone vote by proxy for them.

The centerpiece of the Party's "revolutionary cause" is national reunification. In the speeches and propaganda following Kim Jong Il's unanimous October 1997 election to Party General Secretary, there was an often nauseating overuse of Juche national reunification slogans. These speeches are more to showcase the Party's religious fervor for Kim to complete the nation's destiny than to preserve any vestiges of political process. Here is one of many such Party propaganda pieces:

> [The] politics of General Secretary Kim Jong Il are an *invincible politics* which are original in method and content and which is matchless in might. The author of the article says: The politics of the Workers' Party of Korea is an ever-victorious politics which has never undergone failure. Herein lie the basic characteristics and *inexhaustible might* of Kim Jong Il's politics. The history of his revolutionary activities is a history of a great statesman *who has never made the slightest error or deviation in his lines and his fighting career* recorded with rich political practices…There is no such statesman in the world as General Secretary Kim Jong Il who has strong courage and faith. *His politics is aimed at truth and justice.* It is an important lesson left by the fighting history of the Workers' Party of Korea that *if it informs the people of the truth* and opens its heart to them, they will rise up as a mountain. The Party and the people approach each other with sincerity and share the fate with each other. Herein lies the greatness of Kim Jong Il's politics.

His politics are magnanimous politics. The politics of the Workers' Party of Korea is magnanimous in its ideology. *Let us build a new society with trust and love.* This is a motto of General Secretary Kim Jong Il [*Rodong Sinmun*].

Considering the importance of the Party in theory, the current Korean Workers' Party seems to be seriously trouble-ridden. For example, analysts report:

> Since Kim Il Sung's death, there have been no reports on any session of the Party Central Committee or the Politburo while military influence has been steadily on the rise. Strangely, the Party did not hold a session even to elect Kim its general secretary. He was given the title as the top Party leader simply in a joint statement of the Party Central Committee and the Party Central Military Committee. This joint statement was issued following a series of rallies of Party cadres held throughout North Korea.[26]

Nevertheless, at least in theory, the Korean Worker's Party serves as the main vehicle for not only sustaining the Juche religious system and its associated utopian totalitarian society, but for mobilizing the masses to carry out Juche's sacred and righteous cause of reunification.

The Masses

The popular masses are the teachers of all things.[27]
KIM JONG IL

Under Juche, the masses serve to carry out the will of the Suryong through the organ of the Party. The collective and individual consciousness of the masses are controlled through the totalitarian state. Juche's ideological basis for the masses' unquestioning obedience is derived from the "Revolutionary View of the Leader." A 1987 *Rodong Sinmun* article explains:

> "The Revolutionary View of the Leader" stipulates that though the masses are the masters of history and the motivators of revolution, they cannot take up spontaneously any revolutionary course unless they are organized into revolutionary forces and led by the Leader. They can act as the masters only when the Great Leader gives them the necessary instructions and clears the path before them.[28]

Thus, obedience is a paramount necessity. Non-conformity is not tolerated. These views track closely with the classical Communist view of the masses:

> In the Communist view, the individual means little. He has no soul, no spirit, no eternal worth. He is nothing but a highly complex ape. He has no rights, only such privileges as the state chooses to give or take away...and even those [best interests] of the community may be subordinated to the "best interests" of the human race...[by] the leaders of the Communist party, for they are working to bring the classless society, the workers' paradise on earth. Lenin declared, "We repudiate all morality, that is taken outside of human, class concepts...We say that our morality is entirely subordinated to the interests of the class struggle...At the root of Communist morality, there lies the continuation and completion of Communism."[29]

Other than the aspect of the deification of the Su-ryong, the Juche concept of the masses does not differ noticeably from the Marxist-Leninist notion of the masses. Yet, one would not readily guess the slavish reality and hopeless plight of the masses based upon Kim Jong Il's statements, such as:

> The popular masses are the most excellent, the greatest and the most beautiful beings in the world. Because of this, I enthusiastically adore the popular masses. Our best teacher is the popular masses. There is no teacher in this world wiser and more intelligent than the popular masses. There are big things and small things in our work, but there should be no big or small things in the heart of service to the people. Even if the work is small, we must do it with the utmost enthusiasm and sincerity, if it is for the people. We must be true servants of the people [*KCNA*].

In true Juche fashion that is oblivious to reality, Juche believers suppose that their masses are somehow viewed as more significant than the masses under traditional Communist philosophy:

> *Man is not a mere means of production. Jucheism regards man as an individual being,* whereas Marxism regards man as a production means. Jucheism regards a human being as a social being with independence, creativity and consciousness. Man is what he is today because he has formed the social collective and lived in it with social cooperative relationship with

other members.

Man's social being has evolved over the eons. It is not correct to cast man's essential features as the product of the material development, from non-living matters to living matters, from the living matters at low level, animals in general, to the living matters at high level, human beings. Man's main features cannot be explained purely in terms of biochemical processes.

Jucheism states that man is a social being who forms a social collective, lives in it and develops with social cooperative relations with other members of the society. *Jucheism is a guiding principle which should be applied in solving our daily problems.*[30]

To be fair to Karl Marx, the above contrast between man as a means of production and a "social creative being" is a misrepresentation. Marx, to his credit, was very precise in the use of terms, using man as "production factor" only for the sake of analysis. His "dictatorship of the proletariat" terminology assumes the masses to be a social and creative entity capable of working together.[31]

Although we will not analyze the role of the masses at length, we should consider the impact of the Juche philosophy on the masses. According to Juche theory, a society governed by Juche is "the most superior society" because it is developed on the basis of a collectivist view of life. The socio-political integrity of the masses as a whole is emphasized, while the comparative value of

Juche's loyal masses gather in Pyongyang's Kim Il Sung Square (1994).

any individual is rather small. In theory, when the Juche socialist democracy is enforced, it should be "incomparably superior to bourgeois democracy."[32]

Yet, that is not the reality of life for the masses in North Korea. The imposition of the Juche caste system and self-preservationist view of the Su-ryong have resulted in the suffering of the masses being of little consequence as long as the "arduous struggle" continues "toward inevitable victory." Bettering the existence of the masses means little according to Jucheism, if such action would also weaken the power of the Su-ryong. This callous Juche view of the masses as pawns on a philosophical chessboard exists even in the face of widespread deprivation, hunger, and starvation. With hard-line Communism collapsing all over the world, Kim Jong Il's ruling philosophy of Juche continues its hard-line policies toward the masses, apparently in dread for its survival.

Reunification

True patriotism is in the struggle for fatherland reunification.[33]

KIM JONG IL

According to Kim Jong Il, "National reunification is the supreme desire of the nation...the great unity of the whole nation, set forth by the great leader, Comrade Kim Il Sung."[34] As we continue our discussion of the central teachings of the Juche religion, it will become apparent what the doctrine of "national reunification" really means.

On April 18, 1998, as North Korea neared its 50th anniversary as a nation, Kim Jong Il presented his "five-point principle for national unity." Kim's "new" principle calls for: (1) national independence; (2) the unity of the people under the banner of patriotism; (3) the improvement of relations between the South and the North; (4) struggles against foreign powers and anti-reunification forces; and (5) the strengthening of solidarity among all Koreans in the North, South, and abroad. Though on the surface this "new" principle seems progressive, an examination of Juche teachings reveals Kim Jong Il's true intent.

National reunification along Juche guidelines is both a core belief of the Juche religion and the heartfelt desire of many

Korean people. For example, the following poem was written by a young South Korean woman and the chorus was sung by both North and South Koreans at the 1990 National Reunification Rally at Panmunjon.

Yet, reunification under Juche is primarily a religious tenet of faith rather than a political concept. For the

> **"Our Wish is Reunification"**
>
> Our wish is reunification.
> Even in dreams, our wish is reunification.
> By sacrificing our lives for it,
> Let reunification happen!
>
> Reunification saves our people.
> Reunification saves our nation.
> Reunification, come quickly!
> Let reunification happen!
>
> *[DPRK]*

Juche believer, the same lyrics to "Our Wish is Reunification" speak of an entirely different vision for Korea than the South's. In the North, "national reunification" means that the army and masses reasonably can be expected to sacrifice their all, in "the spirit of human bombs," to achieve the communization of the South. For example, a typical propaganda article stated:

> We must turn the military stronghold into an iron-wall ...Our People's Army is the pillar of the socialism of our own style...our People's Army will deal a fatal blow to them [the U.S. and the South] with its strong power accumulated in tens of years and achieve the reunification of the fatherland by the guns of justice.[35]

The Korean people are a single homogenous ethnic group who have lived on the Korean Peninsula for 5,000 years. However, the first "unification" of the peninsula did not occur until 668, when Shilla in the south conquered Koguryo in the north to form the kingdom of Koryo. Recalling Korea's history, Kim Il Sung proposed the founding of the Democratic Confederal Republic of Koryo (DCRK) at the Sixth Congress of the KWP in October 1980. From the North Korean viewpoint, a new "Koryo republic" should have come about following World War II after their arduous revolutionary struggle to throw off the yoke of Japanese oppression. However, Korea was divided into two due to "the United States troops' unjust occupation of 'south' Korea." For the last fifty years, the people of the North have been told that their brothers and sisters are "enslaved in the south by the ruthless Americans." There in the south, as the story goes, the Americans have made over 45 million fellow Koreans undergo

*Juche reunification poster from the
1990 National Reunification Rally.*

untold hardships over the last half century. Thus, both the United States and the "illegitimate puppet regime of the south" are seen as the denizens of division. Meanwhile, Kim Il Sung and now Kim Jong Il are proclaimed to be the true champions of the sacred cause of national reunification.

Juche ideology teaches that continued national division threatens the very existence of the nation of Korea. However, given the sharp contrast between life in the two Koreas, many South Koreans are losing their vision for national reunification. In the process of pursuing reunification, Kim Il Sung advanced the "10-Point Program of Great Unity of the Whole Nation for Reunification of the Country" at the Ninth Supreme People's Assembly of the DPRK on April 6, 1993. The text of the 10-Point Program is shown in Table 2-4.

Despite the highly idealistic wording of the 10-Point Program, at least two fundamental flaws doom it to remain a utopian dream. First, Point 5 speaks lightly and naively of the fundamental spiritual, political, economic, ideological, and cultural differences between the "communization" and "prevail over communism" systems. There is absolutely no way in which totalitarianism can coexist with freedom. Second, despite the fine-sounding ideology of the 10-Point Program and "Koryo Republic," Kim Jong Il and the Party are bound by the Juche religion to implement Kim Il Sung's vision to communize all of Korea under totalitarian rule. The nice sounding words are intended to present the kinder, gentler, more peaceful facade that students are enamored with and that the general populace desires to hear. Yet only a Korea reunified under Juche, which extends the brutal totalitarian rule of the Su-ryong over all of Korea, has ever been envisioned by the North's leadership. For example, the following propaganda shows the North's view of implementing the 10-Point Program under Kim Jong Il:

TABLE 2-4. "10-Point Program of Great Unity of the Whole Nation for Reunification of the Country"

Preamble: To put a period to the nearly half-a-century-long history of division and confrontation and reunify the country…All those who are concerned for the destiny of the nation, whether they be in the north, or in the south, or overseas, and whether they be communists, or nationalists, haves, or have-nots, atheists, or theists, must unite as one nation, above all…

NO.	POINT
1	A unified state, independent, peaceful, and neutral should be founded through the great unity of the whole nation.
2	Unity should be based on patriotism and the spirit of national independence…[T]he nation should unite with one will…They should reject flunkeyism and national nihilism that erode the nation's consciousness of independence.
3	Unity should be achieved on the principle of promoting co-existence, co-prosperity, and common interests, and subordinating everything to the cause of national reunification.
4	All manner of political disputes that foment division and confrontation between the fellow countrymen should be stopped and unity be achieved.
5	They should dispel fears of invasion from the south and from the north, prevail-over-communism and communization altogether, and believe in and unite with each other.
6	They should set store by democracy and join hands on the road to national reunification, not rejecting each other for the difference in "isms" and principles.
7	They should protect material and spiritual wealth of individual persons and organizations and encourage them to be used favorably for the promotion of great national unity.
8	The whole nation should understand, trust, and unite with one another through contacts, travels, and dialogues.
9	The whole nation in the north and the south and overseas should strengthen solidarity with one another on the way to national reunification.
10	Those who have contributed to the great unity of the nation and to the cause of national reunification should be highly estimated.

...in regard to implementation of the resolution of the 30th U.N. General Assembly Session on Korea. Now that structure of the Cold War has been destroyed and great changes have taken place in correlations among countries, the U.S. troops' military occupation of South Korea cannot be justified by anything, he said, and stressed: For successful "four way talks" in Geneva, the U.S. should, before anything else, discard the anachronistic way of thinking and take practical steps for ensuring a lasting peace in the Korean Peninsula with its independent viewpoint and judgment... *divided Korea will be reunified under the banner of the Democratic Confederal Republic of Koryo under the wise guidance of General Kim Jong Il* [*KCNA*].

Similarly, one should not lightly dismiss the title "lodestar of national reunification" that Kim Jong Il has taken upon himself. For example, Pyongyang delivered 1998 New Year postcards throughout South Korea. The front of these postcards proclaimed, "Let us pray for the immortality of President Kim Il Sung, the eternal father of the nation, and wish the leader Kim Jong Il, the lodestar of reunification, a long life in good health on the morning of the New Year Juche 87 of a great hope." On the back of the postcards was written, "We cannot live without reunification of the country. Let us invigorate the movement for reunification under the guidance of the leader Kim Jong Il, the lodestar of national reunification" [*KCNA*].

The 10-Point Program is framed within "the three principles (or charters) of national reunification" put forth by President Kim Il Sung in meetings with delegates from South Korea on May 3, 1972. These three principles are independence, peaceful reunification, and great (or grand) national unity. At first glance, arguing against any one of the three would seem about as absurd as arguing against motherhood. However, these three principles are usually accompanied by propaganda that insists upon adoption of the 10-Point Program, founding the Democratic Confederal Republic of Koryo, immediately withdrawing U.S. troops from South Korea, pulling down the concrete wall dividing Korea, and abolishing South Korea's "fascist" National Security Law. Ironically, all of these conditions basically existed on May 1, 1948, when the United Nations commissioned a general plebiscite for the Korean people. However, it was Kim Il Sung and the Communists who opted against a reunified Koryo Korea in favor of choosing a Communist totalitarian society and attempting to impose this totalitarian system on all the Korean people by force of arms in June 1950. Since that time, the goal to communize the South has both intensified and taken on the force of religion under Juche.

The pullout of U.S. troops from Korea is, in particular, a sore spot in Juche ideology. The presence of U.S. troops on Korean soil is an ongoing thorn in the side of those in the North who desire to communize the South before the start of the 21st century. Current North Korean propaganda seems to indicate that there is growing Juche religious pressure for the North to initiate a new "war for national reunification." In addition, Pyongyang has been spending an enormous amount of money on anti-South operations despite its worsening economic and famine conditions. If Kim Jong Il does not initiate such a war soon, then, according to Juche ideology, Kim Jong Il would be guilty of the unthinkable—violating the will of Kim Il Sung. According to Juche ideology, the Korean people should enter the new millennium of "The Juche Era" with a reunified and communized Koryo Korea.

> U.S. troops present in South Korea, first of all, should be pulled out for peace and security on the Korean Peninsula ...It would *be a disgraceful and cursed thing* if the U.S. enters *the 21st century* with its troops remaining in South Korea and the Korean armistice agreement kept intact [*Rodong Sinmun*].

Many people in South Korea are either reluctant or unwilling to paint a bleak picture regarding peaceful reunification. Due to distaste, they willingly overlook the irreconcilable nature between a totalitarian police state under Juche's enforced idolatry and the capitalistic representative democracy of the South which is heavily influenced by Christianity. Somehow they feel that being "too negative" about the brethren in the North will be the main obstacle to reunification—not the fundamental spiritual, political, and economic differences between their respective ideologies.

North Korea's use of the term "flunkeyism" in Point 2 of the 10-Point Program is worth additional scrutiny. Point 2 states that all Koreans "should reject flunkeyism and national nihilism that erode the nation's consciousness of independence." What is this "flunkeyism" that all Koreans are to reject? To the North, it is any voice that is "counterrevolutionary." Kim Jong Il, in his book *On the Juche Idea of Our Party*, describes flunkeyism as "the evil practice of...trying to carry out the revolution...by depending on foreign forces."[36] The phrase "great-power chauvinism and flunkeyism" may be compared to the biblical phrase "tax collectors and sinners," where great-power chauvinism (like Roman tax collecting) is a particularly grievous form of flunkeyism. Thus, given an understanding of the term "flunkeyism," the basic Juche view of Point 2 really means "Unity under Juche." In the following January 1998 *Rodong Sinmun* article (which quotes from Kim Jong Il's essay, "On Preserving the Juche Character and National Character of the Revolution and Construction"), "flunkeyism" is used to mean "counterrevolutionary" (counter-Juche):

> In invariably keeping the Juche character the WPK has also strictly *rejected all hues of counterrevolutionary trend* of thought including great-power chauvinism and *flunkeyism* and led the uncompromising struggle against it. Great-power chauvinism and *flunkeyism* were the main obstacle to and the first target of our party's struggle for maintaining the Juche character. Our party and people have waged ceaseless and acute struggle against *flunkeyism* while rejecting great-power chauvinism *that goes against the Juche character* [*KCNA*].

American scientist Jeremy J. Stone got a firsthand view of the reunification fervor in Pyongyang during his 1991 visit. The city was festooned with banners such as "Warm Welcome to Participants in International Solidarity Marches for Korea's Unification." Students marched through the streets while loudly shouting slogans. Later, when Stone asked a sweet-faced, 18-year-old girl on the subway if she had any questions about the United States, she said, "Get your troops out of south Korea!"[37]

From a Juche perspective, reunification is as sacred as—or even more than—the view of the Union during the American Civil War (1861–1865). Northern soldiers and civilians viewed the Civil War as a war to end slavery. They viewed "states rights," the claim of the southern states to self-determination, as a fundamental threat to the continued existence of the Union. The phrase "His truth is marching on" in the popular "Battle Hymn of the Republic" serves as a time capsule reminding us of the religious motivation behind the sacrificed lives of over 400,000 Northern soldiers out of a population comparable to North

Korea's 23 million to achieve "national reunification" for the United States. Do you think that Abraham Lincoln was, for one minute, about to seek a compromise solution with the "illegitimate regime of the south"? Take that 1861 picture, superimpose a pagan cult religion (the main issue), take it halfway around the world to Korea and advance the clock of history about 136 years. Now you can begin to appreciate why national reunification is a religious tenet under Juche. Though any comparison does Lincoln an injustice, Kim Jong Il, like Lincoln, is not about to forsake what he believes is Korea's ancient Koryo birthright and divine destiny: the restoration of a unified Korea.

The 1998 "Joint New Year Editorial" even recast the veiled plight of North Korea's starving masses in terms of pursuit of a holy Juche crusade for national reunification. *Rodong Sinmun* proclaimed, "The struggle waged by the Workers' Party and people of Korea last year was one deciding whether the people remain an independent people or be reduced to slaves." The term "arduous march" was used five times in conjunction with the "*sacred* struggle for the acceleration of the independent and peaceful reunification" and "bringing earlier the victory of the cause of global independence and socialism." Similarly, a 1998 *Korean Central News Agency* editorial portrayed reunification as a "big tent" concept that encompasses both capitalists and Communists, those for God and those against God:

> The entire fellow countrymen should unite as one under the banner of great national unity to form a strong driving force for the *reunification* of the country...There is neither reason nor condition for proletarians and men of property, atheists and believers, communists and nationalists not to get united, *if they subordinate everything to the sacred cause common to the nation, that is reunification* and independence of the country and prosperity and development of the reunified country [*KCNA*].

The sacred nature of national reunification seems to be lost not only on Western political analysts, but remarkably even on some South Koreans as well. Instead of basing their policies, expectations, and diplomatic strategies on the framework of reunification from the North's Juche religious worldview, they err in superimposing secular metrics. Their analysis focuses on the outlook in terms of economic strength, North Korea's ongoing famine, speculative notions of an internal coup, and "saving face." In this writer's opinion, such analysis reveals a widespread underestimation of the force of the Juche religion. Once Juche is seen as the religion it is, application of the German reunification paradigm to Korea seems like a square peg in a round hole. Consider the following two examples of the misapplication of the German reunification paradigm:

> North Korea has been organized so tightly into a pyramid of power with Kim Il Sung at its apex that the possibility of a cataclysmic *social implosion cannot be ruled out.* Not that many years ago, Pyongyang still confidently spread the word that Kim's homeland was a paradise on earth and that South Korea was a brutally poor, miserable place under Uncle Sam's boot heel. "The game is finished," observed one South Korean official. "Not only is the South's *economy* 14 times stronger than the North's," he pointed out, but "the ideological game is also over. The only rational way for the North is to cooperate, *save face* and *gradually integrate.*"
>
> "We have to acknowledge collapse and a *German-style unification* by absorption as a real possibility," says Sohn Hak Kyu, a spokesman for South Korea's ruling Liberal Democratic Party. "On the one hand, this would be a great historic event. On the other, *it will cost a lot.*" One recent study in Seoul estimated that it would take $1.2 trillion and perhaps 20 years to raise the North's economy to parity with the South's —an effort that would cripple Seoul's prosperity. Even short of that, a tidal wave of refugees crossing the DMZ is a possible nightmare to come.[38]

> To be sure, South Korea and its president have much on their plate...South Korea's next president, in office till 2003, will be *fated to play Chancellor Kohl and preside over Korea's reunification.* Is he ready for this, and are his people? I doubt it.[39]

A writer for the DPRK's *Kulloja,* the monthly news magazine of the Korean Workers' Party, speculated that a reunified Korea would become the fourth most important economic center in the world (probably after the United States, European Commonwealth, and Japan). Nevertheless, such analysis generally ignores the overriding importance of the Juche religion upon any reunification scenario.

The following estimate of North Korea is slightly better, although it describes Juche reunification as only a dream. "Dream,"

*Participants at the rally for reunification in the '90s
march along the streets of Pyongyang.*

however is a gross understatement. Reunification is an abiding passion, a quest for eternal glory, something to die in valor for—indeed, the very pulse of Pyongyang's religion.

North Korea, the conventional wisdom goes, has a death wish. Ruled by an unstable Stalinist "monarch," the Democratic People's Republic of Korea is so determined to realize its *dream* of reuniting the peninsula under communist rule that it could invade the South at a moment's notice, irrespective of the inevitability that it would lose. The metaphor of North Korea as a powder keg, governed by an irrational and unpredictable leader, is misleading at best. While it often operates out of "basements of fear," *North Korea is a fundamentally rational state* that has in many ways reaped the fruit of its foreign policies, however *quixotic* they may once have seemed to observers. Between its birth as a nation in 1945 from the ashes of World War II through 1994, North Korea's statehood was invested in one man: Kim Il Sung.[40]

If reunification is viewed solely as a lame unrealistic "dream," then an analyst might reject an otherwise good analysis, such as above, and throw out a wild statement like "North Korea is a fundamentally rational state..." Instead, viewing reunification as a core religious tenet of the Juche faith helps, in part, to explain many of North Korea's seemingly irrational foreign policies.

Even the "soft landing theory" that is coming into vogue in Washington does not reflect appropriate respect for the Juche religious aspect of national reunification. The "soft landing" theory maintains that the West should neither save nor let down North Korea with a "bang." Instead, minimal aid will be used to string North Korea along until its economy strangles on its own accord. Meanwhile, inside North Korea, ongoing privation is proclaimed to be part of the "arduous struggle" of national reunification.

However, as irrational as Juche may seem to other worldviews, Kim Jong Il remains consistent to the Juche worldview—particularly with regard to national reunification. For example, consider the following article, which demonstrates Pyongyang's continuing resolve regarding national reunification:

> The south Korean magazine *Mal* carried in its August issue the letter that Secretary Kim Jong Il sent to Mun Myong Ja, a U.S.-resident Korean woman journalist, on July 13... Summing up the letter, she said, *"It reiterated no change in the north's system."* General Kim Jong Il stressed the three principles of national reunification, the proposal for founding the Democratic Confederal Republic of Koryo, and the 10-point programme of the great unity of the whole nation for the reunification of the country are guidelines which should be adhered to and implemented to the last by the Korean nation in the struggle for national reunification, Mun wrote. She said: clarifying the DPRK's position toward relations with the United States and Japan, the General stressed the settlement of the matter depends on their attitude toward the DPRK [*KCNA*].

The North's impeccable—and arguably religious—consistency with regard to national reunification is also carefully framed and validated to their populace in a historical-cultural context. The following article recounts how Kim Il Sung associated his Democratic Confederal Republic of Koryo theme with a Juche educational institution by renaming it after the ancient Koryo dynasty.

> The *heritage of national culture* is brilliantly inherited and developed in Korea. This year Koryo Songgyungwan [University] greets its 1,005th birthday. In May Juche 81 [1992] President Kim Il Sung visited Songgyungwan in Kaesong...*He went on to...rename the university "Koryo Songgyungwan"* inheriting "Songgyungwan" built by the *Koryo dynasty* [918–1392], and personally wrote the name of the university...The contents and purpose of education remained unchanged...Koryo Songgyungwan has been a pride of time-honored education and culture of the Korean nation [*KCNA*].

As if the continual parade of propaganda was not enough to convince them of their own resolve for national unity, on August 4, 1997, Kim Jong Il issued a new political essay entitled "Let Us Carry Out the Great Leader Comrade Kim Il Sung's Instructions for National Reunification." Since then, North Korean leaders have continuously referred to this new essay in almost every major speech. Consider the following excerpts from recent North Korean speeches. The first speech before the United Nations General Assembly in New York, on October 7, 1997, begins by summarizing the core Juche reunification beliefs:

> Like all the other UN member nations, the Democratic People's Republic of Korea is a sovereign state that has the rights to choose a political system and to keep it from being violated, and the Korean-style socialism is not a system that can be stifled by anyone...The question of *Korea's reunification is the question of retaking the sovereignty of a nation which is being violated by outside forces* and, at the same time, an issue of international peace and security to remove the legacy of the Cold War. The government of the DPRK, he noted, regards the three principles of independence, *peaceful reunification and great national unity, the Ten-Point Programme of the Great Unity of the Whole Nation and the proposal for founding a Democratic Confederal Republic of Koryo* as the three charters of national reunification [*KCNA*].

As the speech continued, South Korea, the United States, and Japan were identified as the chief opponents of Korean reunification.

On the very same day, on the other side of the globe, Kim Hyong Sop delivered a similar speech in Pyongyang. This speech, which was largely incorporated into a *Rodong Sinmun* article on October 9, invokes the passion, history, and destiny of North Korea's people toward the sacred issue of reunification:

> All the Koreans in the north, south and overseas will make redoubled efforts to found the *Democratic Confederal Republic of Koryo* (DCRK) and achieve the independent and *peaceful* reunification of the country,...through the establishment of a unified national government on condition that the north and the south recognize and *tolerate each other's ideas and social systems*, a government in which the two sides are represented on an equal footing and under which they exercise regional autonomy respectively with equal rights and duties...
>
> *The Great Leader Comrade Kim Jong Il, who puts his heart and soul into realizing the President's idea of reunification* and leadership, has wisely led the Korean people to fight for national reunification through the establishment of the DCRK...In order to realize the proposal for founding the DCRK and re-unify the country, *we must hold fast to the principle of national independence, resolutely smash the domestic and foreign bellicose elements' new war preparations and preserve a lasting peace on the Korean Peninsula.* If the tension is to be

> **"Korea is One"**
>
> Korean people, unite and open the door to reunification.
> We are one people under the revolutionary sun.
> Illumined by the leader's five-point programme
> We go to independence and reunification.
> Korea is one.
>
> [DPRK]

> eased and the danger of war to be removed in Korea, the United States must renounce its hostile policy...Japan must repent of its past...hostile policy toward the DPRK and refrain from encouraging the south Korean rulers to division and war [*Rodong Sinmun*].

At first glance, the "toleration terminology" used in this speech actually sounds a bit progressive and reasonable. However, the call for the formation of the Koryo republic based on toleration of "each other's ideas and social systems" contradicts Juche's fundamental religious call to establish Kim Jong Il's rule over all of Korea's 70 million people. For example, the above remarks contradict the joint resolution by the Workers' Party of Korea Central Committee and Central Military Commission published on the very next day (October 8) to communize the South under Juche and Kim Jong Il. The Party resolution inaugurates the Juche era as ushering in the time when Kim Jong Il will rule over all of Korea. No words such as "tolerate each other's ideas and social systems" are found in the October 8th document. Until one recalls that all of these documents are cleared by the same totalitarian regime, it almost seems like "a tale of two Koryos"!

The inseparable link between the push for Korean national reunification and the Juche religious system is cause for reflection. For example, consider the implications of routine propaganda statements such as the following:

> We, the followers of the Juche idea, are determined to take the immortal Juche idea created by the great leader as our unwavering will and faith, and to vigorously fight for the completion of the independence cause under the leadership of the dear leader Comrade Kim Jong Il [*DPRK*].

This article emphasizes the fundamental tenet of Juche that peaceful coexistence between capitalism and Juche socialist communism must not and cannot be tolerated. According to this logic, the North's justification for carrying the revolution to the South takes on religious overtones.

When one realizes the religious crusade–like meaning of national reunification under Juche, then the futility of the four-way talks among the People's Republic of China, the United States, and the two Koreas becomes apparent. For North Korea to formally grant diplomatic recognition to South Korea as a separate nation would be the same as giving up the half-century-old theory of "The Revolution of the South." Any such notion would be impossible for Kim Jong Il since it would be against the core teachings of the Juche religion.

Can one think, even for a moment, that a "peace at any price" negotiation style will dissuade those that wield god-like power over the masses? Can such a regime change overnight at the negotiating table and enact "rational" reforms? British Prime Minister Neville Chamberlain thought so when he signed the Munich Pact on September 30, 1938, with Nazi Germany's dictator, Adolf Hitler. At the price of Czechoslovakia and the World War that followed, Chamberlain maintained the temporary illusion of "peace in our time." After Chamberlain signed the historic agreement, Winston Churchill told the House of Commons, "The people should know that we have sustained a defeat without a war…the first foretaste of a bitter cup."[41] Do Pyongyang's gathered millions at routine reunification rallies of the 1990s, which dwarf Hitler's legendary Nazi rallies of the 1930s, send us a different message?

Critically, even if North Korea's leaders wanted to change, could they? Or are they trapped by their own Party lines, propaganda, and years of frenzy? If one peels back the veil even farther to the spiritual dimension, dare we view Juche-style totalitarian enslavement of all Korea as an inherent effect of a demonic influence that rules over North Korea? If such demonic control is a spiritual reality, then can we expect a totalitarian terrorist leader who is under such demonic bondage to be "free" to make the right choice? After all, one can make a choice only if one is truly free. North Korea, including its leader, is not free. Both the nation and its leader are slaves to this influence and the "arduous struggle" for the sacred cause of national reunification.

The Juche Pantheon: "The Three Generals of Mt. Paektu"

Let us boast of and uphold the three generals from Mt. Paektu, the most famous mountain in the world: ever-victorious brilliant commander Kim Il Sung, peerlessly brilliant commander Kim Jong Il and heroine of Paektu General Kim Jong Suk.

NORTH KOREAN POSTCARD

The Juche pantheon is an implementation of the age-old satanic lie in the garden of Eden, "…and you will be like God." Through the Juche religious system, Kim Il Sung was proclaimed as the immortal God and eternal Father. Upon Kim Il Sung's death in 1994, twenty years of elaborate propaganda set the stage for his son Kim Jong Il to be proclaimed a god, too. The resulting

Juche pantheon now provides for the worship of the deceased Kim Il Sung and the living Kim Jong Il. Pyongyang's propaganda demonstrates that, under the Juche religious system, Kim Jong Il is fully vested as a deity co-equal with his father:

> We regard the leader Kim Jong Il, who is *identical to President Kim Il Sung in idea, leadership and virtue,* as our mental support... *"We believe in the leader Kim Jong Il, who is the savior of nation and lodestar of national reunification"* [*Kuguk Jonson*].

Kim Il Sung is also worshipped in the sense that his spirit will live forever through the collective consciousness of the Party and masses.

The most recent development in Juche theology is the elevation in late 1997 of Kim Jong Il's mother, Kim Jong Suk, to the status of a Juche goddess. Possibly because of the historical strength of Christianity in the North, Christian influence on Juche theology is reflected in the Trinity-like image of the Juche godhead and the surrogate gospel of Juche. However, unlike the co-equal three-Persons-in-One God of Christianity, Juche propaganda presents three separate gods with Kim Jong Suk in a non-Su-ryong supporting role to Kim Il Sung (the father) and Kim Jong Il (the son). The following 1998 sample of North Korean propaganda provides an example of how these three personages are now glorified as "The Three Generals of Mt. Paektu":

> Cards carrying pictures of the three great persons of Mt. Paektu were recently distributed to houses in...South Korea ...Printed on the front side of each card are letters *"Let us boast of and uphold the three generals from Mt. Paektu, the most famous mountain in the world"* against the background of Mt. Paektu at sunrise. Carried on its back are pictures of the three generals in army uniform, with letters *"ever-victorious brilliant commander Kim Il Sung," "peerlessly brilliant commander Kim Jong Il,"* and *"heroine of Paektu General Kim Jong Suk."* Seeing the pictures, people expressed deep reverence for the great men and woman of the nation, the information said [*KCNA*].

The following paragraphs take a closer look at this man-centered pantheon including a more detailed discussion of the Juche pseudo-Trinity godhead of Kim Il Sung, Kim Jong Il, and Kim Jong Suk.

Man at the Center

The Juche idea is a new philosophical thought which centers on man...Man is the master of everything and decides everything.

LI YANG SU
VICE EDITOR-IN-CHIEF
KOREAN CENTRAL NEWS AGENCY

Juche establishes its gods based on the man-centered or anthropocentric philosophy of Juche. For example, the Chairman of the Supreme People's Assembly, Yang Hyong Sop, delivered a report on December 27, 1997, in which he stated:

> ...the socialist constitution of Korea worked out by President Kim Il Sung is a new-type *anthropocentric* one, which is the embodiment of the immortal Juche idea. With the Juche-based socialist constitution instituted and being enforced, he noted, the Government of the DPRK has had a mighty instrument of the People's democratic dictatorship for guaranteeing the political leadership of the Workers' Party of Korea and the political domination of the working class and people of other social strata over the whole of society [*KCNA*].

The term "man-centered" is used synonymously with "anthropocentric" by North Koreans in characterizing Juche. For example, a December 6, 1997, propaganda release by the *Korean Central News Agency* declared:

> In order to achieve greater victory in today's struggle to glorify a new era of the *Juche revolution*, it is necessary to carry through the call of the Workers' Party of Korea, *"Let us live our own way!"* in all domains of the revolution and construction. *Rodong Sinmun* says this in an editorial today. The daily goes on: For the WPK and the Korean people to live their own way at present means to cherish deep in their mind General Kim Jong Il's idea of and faith in independence and carry out the revolution and construction the way he does. The Korean way contains *man-centered philosophy* and patriotic soul. The Korean people have no better slogan than this.

From a philosophical perspective, this "man at the center" premise is a non-premise. Great philosophers from Aristotle to the present have assumed the primacy of man without using such a concept to initiate a new religion. Analysts can make little sense of many Juche philosophical statements:

> "The clearer the role of man in social changes, the more purposeful and conscious man becomes." *I have no idea what this means.* The psychological study of consciousness has never found any relationship between "role of man" and "level of consciousness." Neither has it found a relationship between "purposeful" (motivation studies) and "role of man."[42]

From a philosophical viewpoint, given that there are not "elephant-centered" or "monkey-centered" philosophies, Juche's "man-centered" basis appears to be pure psycho-babble.

The "man-centered" Juche psycho-babble, however, makes more sense from a biblical worldview. The discerning Christian will recognize it as having many common characteristics with Satanism, secular humanism, and historical pagan emperor worship. All three of these deny the existence of the one true God, deny the atoning death on the cross of Jesus Christ, the Son of God, and elevate man to the status of a false god in God's place. The relative merit of such religions or philosophies is of no consequence. From a biblical perspective, all such "man-centered" philosophies or religions openly aim at the same root spiritual deception: "The fool says in his heart, 'There is no God'" (Psalm 14:1).

So, regardless of its philosophical coherency, "man-at-the-center" lies at the heart of the establishment of the Juche pantheon system. The following excerpt from an interview with Li Yang Su, Vice Editor-in-Chief of the *Korean Central News Agency*, provides a sample of this Juche man-centered view:

> The Juche idea is a *new* philosophical thought which centers on man. The Juche idea is based on the philosophical principle that *man is the master of everything and decides everything.* The Juche idea raised the fundamental question of philosophy by regarding man as the main factor, and elucidated the philosophical principle that man is the master of everything and decides everything. That man is the master of everything means that he is the master of the world and his own destiny; that man decides means that he plays the decisive role in transforming the world and in shaping his destiny. The philosophical principle of the Juche idea is the principle of man-centered philosophy which explains man's

position and role in the world.[43]

This man-centered worldview allows for "mysterious natural phenomena" to occur in response to Party resolutions deifying Kim Jong Il as "indeed the greatest of great men produced by heaven," while denying the supernatural view of man's role in the world. This enables both the masses and Pyongyang's Korean Christian Federation "Christian religionists" to unify,

> ...determined to turn out as one in a sacred struggle for reunifying the country in hearty response to the noble patriotic intention of the General [Kim Jong Il] with firm belief that he is identical to President Kim Il Sung and is god of the Korean nation.[44]

Kim Il Sung: "The Great Leader"

Through court trials, we have executed all Protestant and Catholic church cadre members and all other vicious religious elements have been sent to concentration camps.[45]

KIM IL SUNG
EXCERPT FROM A 1962 SPEECH

The "Great Leader" Kim Il Sung (1912–1994), the Juche god-king of the North Korean people, remains an enigmatic figure to most of the world even beyond his death. During his almost half century of rule over North Korea from 1945 to 1994, Kim Il Sung became the mystical god of his people, a monster to those on whom he waged war, and a riddle to almost everyone else. Just before his death in 1994, prominent Americans, including evangelist Billy Graham and former President Jimmy Carter, courted Kim as a fellow peacemaker. They hoped Kim, with his fledgling atom bomb program, would work with them to avoid a nuclear showdown.

Former President Carter discussed his attitude toward world leaders in his 1996 book, *Living Faith.* Carter stated, "Americans tend to see conflicts in terms of friendly/enemy, angel/devil," and such views were a "major impediment" to global peace. He said that American and other global leaders "must be willing to deal with" leaders such as Kim Il Sung "to avert war and suffering." Carter said that in his meeting with Kim Il Sung, Kim "extolled the virtues of Christian missionaries who saved him" from his Japanese captors and had a "desire for good relations with the U.S." But he also added that there was "no way to confirm his sincerity." Yet, former President Carter did not show any appreciation for the ongoing war against the Church by Kim Il Sung or the massive level of human suffering occurring within the Juche totalitarian system. Kim Il Sung seemed to have used Carter's personal altruism and desire for "peace" against them much as Hitler did against Neville Chamberlain at Munich a generation earlier. Having heard President Carter's viewpoint, let us ask, "Is it fair for Americans or Christians at large to characterize Kim Il Sung as an 'enemy' or 'devil'?" Just who really was this Kim Il Sung that the American leaders were negotiating with?[46]

In a way, developing a composite portrait of Kim Il Sung is like painting a picture of the devil himself. To the deceived, he is the angel of light, the surrogate god and the self-exalted one. To the elect, he is the deceiving, despotic, God-hating tyrant who enslaves people and makes war upon the saints. A true picture of the man might best be achieved by superimposing two hologram images. At first glance, you see the "Great Leader," "Father," and "God," a true, just, and compassionate benefactor of the Korean people. However, when the light hits the image from a slightly different angle, the picture changes to an evil-motivated, fear-bound murdering despot whose all-consuming passions are to destroy the Church and elevate himself to immortality. The discussion that follows considers the "pleasant" side of the hologram, before, like the picture of Dorian Gray, Kim Il Sung's true portrait emerges.

A look at the mass outpouring of emotion at Kim's funeral in July 1994 is helpful to understand what Kim Il Sung meant to the North Korean people. Millions of onlookers assembled in Pyongyang and lined the streets for the funeral procession of the 82-year-old autocrat. Their passionate tears and genuine grief demonstrated that a nation had lost both its god and the only leader it had ever known. Pyongyang's radio broadcasters nearly sobbed as they announced news of Kim Il Sung's death from the rain-swept capital: "He was the greatest of the great men." Foreign diplomats inside the country reported that thousands of school children were bursting into tears. They stood amazed as countless masses of stunned, flower-laden mourners filed through Pyongyang's streets. Govind Narain Srivastave, Secretary-General

North Korea's mass outpouring of emotion at the death of their god in 1994.

of the Asian Regional Institute of the Juche Idea, captured the sentiment as he lamented, "We, the followers of the Juche idea, have never thought of Korea without the great leader Comrade Kim Il Sung, even in a dream" [*DPRK*].

Then something amazing happened. After ten days of this nationwide mourning characterized by "a sea of tears," mourning suddenly ceased on July 20th. Overnight the Korean Workers' Party had passed word throughout North Korea to direct the masses to stop mourning. This decision was made so that a massive memorial rally could be convened in Pyongyang's Kim Il Sung Square. The abrupt halt in mourning gave eyewitnesses another astounding indication of the absolute totalitarian control that Kim Il Sung's Juche system had over North Korea's people. Even their emotions were subject to state control.

What image in the hearts and minds of people could invoke such an outpouring of genuine heartfelt emotion? A brief look at some North Korean propaganda helps to answer the question. In the decades before his death, propaganda had systematically built Kim Il Sung into an all-wise and all-knowing god. For example, consider the following quotes written by Kim Il Sung in his book, *The Leader of the People:*

> Comrade Kim is not only the *Protector of the political life* of the Korean people but also the *Savior of their physical life...His love makes sick people well* and gives them new life, like the rain in spring which gives a drink to the Holy Land [Korea]...
>
> The physical life ends. The political life is eternal.
>
> Communism is the highest ideal of the human being.

Some Korean sailors died in the Indian Ocean. *Kim took action and the sailors experienced the joy of being Born Again...*

He sacrifices his Sleep and Rest for the people to give the proletariat Courage and Power...The highest aim of the Korean people is to honor Kim and be loyal to him.

[Kim's son states to his father] "Forever, where you will go I will follow, the Son says to the Father."[47]

The motorcade for Kim Il Sung's funeral proceeds through Pyongyang's Arch of Triumph (1994).

Kim Il Sung's adaptation and transformation of Marxism-Leninism into the Juche religion resulted in a remarkably tight unity unprecedented in any other Communist regime. Not content with the Stalinist image of being only the "iron-willed, ever-victorious commander," Kim Il Sung used Juche to carefully craft his domestic image into the "respected and beloved Great Leader." Under Juche, he became both "the supreme brain of the nation" and the "head and heart" of the body politic. Excerpts from Korean Workers' Party newspapers from 1981 demonstrate Kim Il Sung's Confucius-like benevolent image:

> Kim Il Sung...is the *great father* of our people...Long is the history of the word father being used as a word representing love and reverence...expressing the *unbreakable blood ties between the people and the leader*. Father. This familiar word represents our people's single heart of boundless respect and loyalty...
>
> The love shown by the *Great Leader* for our people is the love of kinship. Our respected and beloved Leader is the *tender-hearted father* of all the people...Love of paternity...is the noblest ideological sentiment possessed only by our people ...His heart is a traction power attracting the hearts of all people and a centripetal force uniting them as one...Kim Il Sung is the *great sun* and great man... thanks to this great heart, national independence is firmly guaranteed.[48]

President Kim Il Sung poses with An Tal Su, Chairman of the Management Board of the Sowon Cooperative Farm, on a field path (1976).

Paternal and familial terminology became even more widely used when Kim Jong Il's designation as heir apparent was publicly announced at the Sixth Party Congress in 1980. Kim was the Father of the nation. The Korean Workers' Party was referred to as the "Mother" party. Kim Jong Il was the faithful son. "Blood ties" terminology has also been used to invoke the loyalty of the masses to serve the ever "fatherly" leader. Under the Juche umbrella and Kim Il Sung's leadership, the country had been transformed into one big happy "family." Through a "chicken in every pot" publicity campaign, Kim Il Sung promised the people refrigerators, washing machines, and televisions as well as stew with meat in it. As his new society began to emerge in the 1960s and early 1970s, particularly for Pyongyangites, the people were encouraged to respond to the paternal, devoted, and benevolent god-man with loyalty, obedience, and mutual love. Kim Il Sung's deification was so advanced by the 1990s that, in 1991, Professor Pak Mun Hoi told American scientist Jeremy J. Stone that "our President never lied."[49] Kim Il Sung told the people he was God, and they believed him.

This "god incarnate" view of Kim Il Sung continues beyond his death. Today, even amid catastrophic famine, disasters, and intense hardship, North Koreans are told:

> *President Kim Il Sung has resolved all the problems* independently and creatively in conformity with the specific conditions *of our country from the Juche-based stand in the whole period of his revolutionary activities*, carried out the anti-imperialist, anti-feudal democratic revolution and socialist revolution successfully and in a unique way and accelerated socialist construction to perform feats for the century in building socialism of Juche on this land where independence, self-sustenance and self-reliance in national defense have been definitely realized [*DPRK*].

Kim Il Sung worship continues as each year millions in Pyongyang celebrate Kim's April 15 birthday, now called "Sun Day." Ongoing prayers for his immortality and the institution of the "Juche Era" calendar in 1997 invoke pagan sun god imagery:

> *The Juche era is a symbol of the eternal harmony of the Korean people with the President*. With its institution, our nation and humankind can always live in Kim Il Sung's era, in the history of the sun. It is an immortal milestone symbolic of the immortality of the era of Juche created by the President [*KCNA*].

The use of Juche Era with 1912 as the first year, a year when President Kim Il Sung, the *greatest genius of the 20th century*, a prominent international activist and the founder of the Juche idea, was born is a great event in history...We welcome the *resolution on the eternal memory of Comrade Kim Il Sung, the great leader of the cause of independence of the people on the globe,* and express willingness to actively help propagate and disseminate it in every way [*KCNA*].

Such Kim Il Sung worship continues to be an integral part of the Juche religious faith of North Koreans.

During the last three years of Kim Il Sung's life, he was visited twice by the Reverend Billy Graham, possibly the greatest evangelist of the 20th century. Despite claims in Graham's autobiography that his 1992 and 1994 trips to North Korea were solely for preaching the gospel, his translator, Steven Linton (great-great-grandson of Reverend Eugene Bell, an American missionary to Korea), stated:

American evangelist Rev. Billy Graham poses in front of President Kim Il Sung's native home at Mangyongdae.

> The Graham policy has not been to go there and make converts, but to be constructive in a way that raises the prestige of the Christian community generally.[50]

Along these lines, Graham made a strong effort to build a bridge of understanding with North Korea. His initiatives included lecturing on Christianity during his two visits to Pyongyang and inviting North Korean representatives to the 1993 and 1994 National Prayer Breakfasts in Washington, D.C. In addition, Billy Graham paved the way for former U.S. President Jimmy Carter's 1995 visit to Pyongyang. Graham noted in his autobiography,

> I had just been to Pyongyang and had spent several hours with President Kim Il Sung. President Kim had been very warm to me personally, despite our differences in background, and *I felt that he sincerely wanted to move forward in establishing better relations.* I told Mr. Carter this and urged him to go.[51]

However, upon being asked about Billy Graham's interactions with Pyongyang, John Akers, a Graham advisor, stated, "I'm not sure who's using whom."[52]

When Dr. Graham presented the gospel to Kim Il Sung on January 29, 1994—less than six months before the dictator's death—Kim remained non-responsive. Billy Graham recorded:

> When reminded about Kim's mother's faith, Kim acknowledged that she had taken him to church sometimes as a boy, although he admitted with a smile that *he always wanted to go fishing instead.* He listened respectfully to what I said but made little comment.[53]

Since the precious blood of Jesus Christ is able to wash away the sins of even the greatest sinner, Billy Graham's motives and witness to Kim Il Sung are consistent with Jesus' love and His desire to extend salvation to everyone.

Billy Graham's role as peacemaker also paved the way for former President Jimmy Carter and then President George Bush's negotiators. In 1994 at Geneva, Switzerland, the Bush administration along with the South Koreans negotiated with the North Koreans and agreed to help them build nuclear reactors. Through this Korean Peninsula Energy Development Organization (KEDO) deal, Carter believed that U.S. diplomatic initiatives had averted an imminent war on the Korean Peninsula. But had they? Moreover, without impugning their altruistic motives, why did these Americans come under criticism from some elements of the Christian community? Had Graham, Carter, Bush, and others been duped into helping America "make a deal with the devil"?

North Korea's propagandists quickly put a Juche interpretation on these events. From their perspective, the U.S. and South Koreans "owed" them the reactors. Following Billy Graham's visit, North Korean propaganda featured illustrated articles quoting the American's alleged support for Juche's 10-Point Program of national reunification. Pyongyang's propagandists used seemingly innocuous remarks by Dr. Graham (such as, "The whole of the trip to the DPRK has been a wonderful experience and I'll never forget being among the people of this country") as proof that he approved of the Korean Christian Federation, the Juche cause, and Kim Il Sung's totalitarian rule [*DPRK*].

Before dismissing the controversial aspect of the prominent personages and their peacemaking initiatives, one should pause to consider the other side of Kim Il Sung's hologram portrait. For example, Christian missionaries note that Communist dictator Kim Il Sung destroyed over 1,500 churches. Today, only three churches are allowed to remain open for tourists to see North Korea's "religious freedom." They maintain that when people, especially Christian leaders, look at North Korea, they should recall Hitler's "final solution" to exterminate Europe's Jews and remember to ask, "Why has the entire North Korean church seemingly disappeared?" Thus, it is not surprising when they exclaim, "When Billy Graham spoke with Kim Il Sung, did he realize that he was witnessing to the man who was presiding over the ongoing murderer of all Christians in North Korea?"

Who was this man who, as a boy, avoided going to church with his deaconess mother and preferred to go fishing instead? From a cursory glance, one might conclude that Kim Il Sung had rejected the Christian faith of his mother and replaced it with the surrogate gospel of Communist atheism. Yet, Kim Il Sung's autobiography, *Reminiscences With the Century*, portrays his mother as a non-Christian churchgoer. Consider the following excerpt:

> When she [his mother] was exhausted, she would go to church with my aunt. In Songsan, where the Military University is now situated, there was a Presbyterian church. Many Christians lived in Nam-ri and its vicinity. Some miserable people thought they would go to "Heaven" after death if they believed in Jesus Christ.
>
> When parents went to church their children followed them. In order to increase its congregation, the church frequently distributed sweets and notebooks to the children. The children liked such gifts, so they went to Songsan in groups every Sunday.
>
> At first I, too, was interested in the church and sometimes went to Songsan with my friends. But I became tired of the tedious religious ceremony and the monotonous preaching of the minister, so I seldom went to church.
>
> One Sunday, as I ate some bean toffee made by my grandmother, I said to my father, "Father, I won't go to church today. Attending worship is not interesting."
>
> "Do as you please," he said to me, who was still too young to know the world. "In fact, there is nothing in the church. You may not go. You must believe in your own country and in your own people, rather than in Jesus Christ. And you must

make up your mind to do great things for your country."

After that, I stopped going to church. When I was a schoolboy in Chilgol, too, I did not go to church, although the pupils who did not were under suspicion. I believed that the Christian Gospel had nothing in common with the tragedy which our people were suffering. The Christian doctrine preached humanism, but the call of history for national salvation was more pressing to me who had been anguishing over the destiny of the nation.

My father was an atheist. But, because he had once attended Sungsil Middle School where theology was taught, he had many friends who were Christians, and I had many opportunities to meet them. Some people ask me if I was much influenced by Christianity while I grew up. I was not affected by religion, but I received a great deal of humanitarian assistance from Christians, and in return, I had an ideological influence on them.

I do not think the spirit of Christianity that preaches universal peace and harmony contradicts my idea advocating an independent life for man.

Only when my mother went to church in Songsan did I go. She went to church, but she did not believe in Jesus Christ.

One day, I asked her quietly, "Mother, do you go to church because you believe in God?"

She smiled, shaking her head.

"I do not go to church out of some belief. What is the use of going to 'Heaven' after death? Frankly, I go to church to relax."

I felt pity for her and loved her all the more. She often dozed off during prayers. When everyone else stood up to say amen at the end of the minister's prayer, she would wake up with a start. When she did not wake even after the amen, I would shake her to tell her that the prayer was over.[54]

It is noteworthy that South Korean sources describe Kim Il Sung's mother, Kang Ban Sok, as definitely a Christian. Thus, Kim Il Sung's above characterization of her as a non-believer may simply be another case of revisionist history. Nevertheless, the youthful Kim Il Sung became disillusioned with Christianity, rejected the gospel, and chose the way of communism, instead.

Like many other aspiring young foreign national leaders, Kim spent the World War II years studying Communism in the Soviet

Union in preparation for establishing totalitarian socialist states in their homelands after the anti-Fascist war. During that time, he rose to the rank of battalion commander of the 88th Special Independent Guerrilla Brigade of the Soviet Army. The main task of Kim Il Sung's unit, which was based near in the Vyatsk (Vyachkra) forest near Khabarovsk (Habarovsk), Siberia, was to gather military intelligence in Manchuria and Korea. After the war ended in 1945, Kim resurfaced in now Soviet-occupied Korea and, with Stalin's approval, seized the reigns of power north of the 38th parallel.

Since 1945, Kim Il Sung has killed, imprisoned, and literally exterminated any outward form of belief other than belief in himself. Kim, who remembered the Christian typology of his youth, presented himself as "God" to the Korean people. Kim used Juche to set up his son, Kim Jong Il, as a surrogate Jesus Christ. In June 1950, Kim unleashed a war on the Korean peninsula in which millions died. In the aftermath, Kim's rhetoric of Juche and radical Hermit Kingdom isolation only served as a mass deception to cover the fact that Pyongyang was propped up by everyone from the USSR in the 1950s to Western banks in the 1970s. None would ever be repaid. Kim doggedly remained in control of North Korea by initiating frequent purges of political opponents, inventing the Juche religion, and enacting tough isolationist policies. He justified his hard-line approach as being the reason that North Korea had survived while most other Communist-style regimes had long since either collapsed or softened their approach. Kim eliminated all his domestic critics until the only voice that remained was his, proclaiming guaranteed victory through uncompromising adherence to the purity of Juche. In the process of this "arduous struggle" of Juche, Kim Il Sung has wrought untold hardship, misery, and death upon his own people.

Kim Il Sung's true nature was far from being the irrational madman that many outsiders have surmised. The fact that, at his death, Kim Il Sung was the longest ruling dictator on earth gives us a hint of his tenacity in retaining domestic power. A more rounded view of Kim shows that he was a shrewd and calculating political tactician who expertly used isolationism, raw power, religion, education, and propaganda to shape and control the North Korean society. Meanwhile, he deftly used a "brinkmanship" foreign policy, whose elements included isolationism, terrorism, propaganda, and alternating confrontation and con-

President Kim Il Sung poses at the Mt. Paektu's "secret camp" with Kim Jong Il Peak in the background. The Mt. Paektu monuments and associated revisionist history are a grand hoax to propagate faith in Juche's Su-ryong.

ciliation, to further Juche's goals through international negotiations. In retrospect, Kim Il Sung succeeded in achieving a degree of economic development while avoiding becoming too close of a satellite of Moscow. However, his true legacy is to have bequeathed to his people the mass confusion of being blinded to the gospel and brainwashed into the idolatry of Juche. As long as North Korea continues to reject the gospel and pursue the idolatry of Juche, darkness remains on North Korea's horizon under Kim Il Sung's son, the Dear Leader.

Kim Jong Il: "The Dear Leader"

Where there is love, there is hate.[55]

KIM JONG IL

Now we'll take a look at Kim Jong Il, dictator of the Democratic Peoples Republic of Korea since 1994 and son of the deceased Communist dictator Kim Il Sung. North Korean propagandists depict Kim Jong Il as a man of benevolence. However his generally expressionless face gives the impression that he is harsh and merciless.

Kim Jong Il

North Korean propagandists create an entirely different impression of Kim Jong Il. They portray him both as Kim Il Sung reincarnated and as a genius in all fields. For example, at official meetings, it is stressed that in his role as Supreme Commander of the KPA, Kim Jong Il is a military genius. Likewise, Pyongyang's news media reports to North Koreans and the world that:

> Comrade Kim Jong Il is an outstanding thinker and theoretician, a great statesman and an ever-victorious iron-willed brilliant commander who is leading our party and people and the revolutionary armed forces to victory...The high authority and honor of our party is being demonstrated thanks to comrade Kim Jong Il, the great leader of socialism in the present times.[56]

Kim Jong Il, the first son of Kim Il Sung and Kim Jong Suk was born on February 16, 1942, in Siberia. In 1945, at the age of three, Jong Il came to Korea for the first time with his parents. He received his primary, secondary, and college education in

North Korea. At the age of eight, Jong Il briefly lived in both China and the former Soviet Union while U.N. forces occupied much of North Korea during the Korean War. After graduating from Pyongyang's Kim Il Sung University, Kim Jong Il spent several years authoring the lengthy epic movie, *The Birth of a Nation*.

In 1972, when he was informally nominated as the de facto successor to Kim Il Sung, Kim Jong Il began to be revered by new titles such as the "Center of the Party," then, "Dear Leader" (1975), "Ryongdoja" (guiding leader) (1983), "Great Ryongdoja" (1986), "Unprecedented Great Man" (1994), and recently, "Outstanding Su-ryong" (leader) (1997).[57] Today, Kim Jong Il is openly worshipped as God, Father, Great Teacher, and the Eternal Sun:

> *The Korean people absolutely worship, trust and follow the General as god…The General is the mental pillar and the eternal sun* to the Korean people…They are upholding him as their *great father and teacher, united around him in ideology, morality and obligation.* So, their life is a true, fruitful and precious life without an equal in history [*Rodong Sinmun*].

Kim Jong Il rose to power immediately upon the death of Kim Il Sung in July 1994. Given his already firmly established place in both the Party and the Juche pantheon, Kim Jong Il's succession was a foregone conclusion to North Koreans. However, among outsiders, rampant speculation reigned whether or not he would succeed his father as ruler. Part of the speculation was due to Kim Jong Il's decision not to assume all of his father's titles until after a three-year mourning period. During this time, he was best known as the Supreme Commander of the Korean People's Army, holding the rank of "Field Marshall." Most foreign analysts did not recognize the important fact that Kim was already the Su-ryong who guided the Korean Workers' Party even while awaiting the formality of his coronation as its General Secretary in the fall of 1997. When October 1997 rolled around, Kim Jong Il finally assumed all of his father's remaining titles— including that of General Secretary of the Workers' Party of Korea.

Before assuming the reins of power, Kim Jong Il had dabbled in domestic film-making. He was also reported to be a gambler, villain, womanizer, addicted to "bourgeois pleasures," and much worse. However, such "negatives" were not—and are not—permitted to be written about or discussed in the totalitarian state. Personality-wise, Kim Jong Il is generally considered to be more

*The dear leader Comrade Kim Jong Il gives on-the-spot guidance to the dairy cow
work team at the Sonbong County Integrated Farm (1975).*

reactionary and less rational than his father. Jong Il also lacks the
charisma of his father. Kim Jong Il speaks in a high-pitched voice
that reflects a man who is easily excitable. Despite Kim Jong Il's
university education, his choice of words and use of grammar are
suggestive of someone who has little education. However, such
fine points may be as meaningful as comparing the relative man-
eating capabilities of two forty-foot Great White Sharks.

Some Western diplomats have characterized Jong Il as being
paranoid. They note his reclusive behavior and general dislike
for giving speeches. Other observers question his experience in
international affairs and note that Kim Jong Il's only trip abroad
as an adult was in 1983, to China. For example, *Time* international columnist James Walsh comments:

> What is reputed about Jong Il—known as the Dear Leader
> —is itself a mass of contradictions: terrorist and warmonger,
> or would-be economic reformer and peacemaker? A pam-
> pered, pouting sorehead indifferent to responsibilities, or a
> relatively shrewd go-getter who has mastered much state
> craft? The weight of opinion holds that this candidate for the
> first dynastic succession in the dwindling communist world can-
> not hold a candle to his father.[58]

Kim Jong Il remains a mysterious figure to the outside world. To foreign analysts, who generally do not appreciate Kim Jong Il's expected role as god in the Juche religion, he remains as unpredictable as his father—if not more so. The Dear Leader's continuation of his father's use of brinkmanship in international relations fuels ongoing speculation. Jong Il's critics voice alarm that his "lack of exposure to the outside world" might cause him "to gamble disastrously on the nature of his adversaries and his chances of winning a war." Such comments tend to focus on Kim Jong Il's personality and background rather than on his role as god of the Juche religion to fulfill his sacred duty to reunify Korea. However, viewing him through his role as the god of Juche provides a more meaningful way of looking at Kim Jong Il. To put it succinctly: "It's not a matter of politics—it's the religion!"

On the home front, Kim Jong Il has stubbornly refused to reform his nation's centralized heavy industrial economy, even amid steady economic decline. This refusal to reform is because the economy is of secondary consequence in a totalitarian society. For example, during a seemingly strange speech in December 1994, Kim Jong Il admitted that North Korea's economy was going downhill, but noted his determination to continue with Kim Il Sung's direction to give the Party and the army priority over the economy.

Analysts from the U.S. and other countries tend to ignore the Kim Jong Il, god of Juche, in favor of trying to reckon with Kim Jong Il, the statesman. Former U.S. ambassador to Seoul, Donald Gregg described Kim Jong Il as "a short, unprepossessing kid following a tremendously charismatic, long-tenured father, desperately trying to live up to him." Likewise, former Secretary of State Lawrence Eagleburger noted that Jong Il's accession to power "adds uncertainty at precisely the time we don't need it." He noted that Jong Il will find it to be extremely rough trying to follow in his father's footsteps. Senior analyst Norman Levin, of the Rand Corporation, said, "If Kim Il Sung said white is black, he could make it stick. No one now has that sort of authority."[59]

Not surprisingly, U.S. Secretary of State Madeleine Albright also espouses the economy-driven view of North Korea. On February 22, 1997, while visiting a heavily fortified outpost on the unstable border between the Koreas, Albright said that the success of Korean peace talks "basically depends on how much the North Koreans are hurting and whether they are willing to realize that a peaceful solution to this division is the way to go."[60]

None of these assessments show any appreciation for the massive impact of a quarter century of intense god-making propaganda, purges, and power brokering that have gone on within North Korea. Kim Jong Il's totalitarian power is backed not only by the political force of the Party, but by the moral authority of Juche. Under the Juche religious system, white is definitely black and black is definitely white, if and for as long as Kim Jong Il says so. Kim is god, and what he says is divine.

Kim Jong Il's divine role includes, according to the Pyongyang press, mysterious power over nature. The flowers go into bloom out of season and the sun bursts through the fog when he arrives. The following propaganda, which was not in the comic section, is one of many ongoing examples:

> *Mysterious natural phenomena* were witnessed on September 28, when...Secretary Kim Jong Il in a car arrived at the entrance to the unit, *the fog cleared off and the sun shone bright in the blue sky. Two apricot trees on either side of the road to the unit had 28 and 26 blossoms* respectively. Seeing the mysterious natural phenomena, the unit servicemen said that *Secretary Kim Jong Il is the famous general produced by heaven* [*KCNA*].

One of the current propaganda goals is to transition Kim Jong Il's reputation from being the filial devoted son into the archetypal father figure that Kim Il Sung enjoyed. To accomplish this, propaganda must portray Kim Jong Il as the quintessential Confucian servant-leader who is devoted above all else to the people (whom he ruthlessly exploits).

> The dear leader Comrade Kim Jong Il, the successor to the great leader Comrade Kim Il Sung's ideology of *"The people are my God,"* judged that if the people so wish, a flower must blossom even on a stone, and took this as his motto from the days when he first gave a lead to the Party [*DPRK*].

In response to Kim Jong Il's fond devotion, protection, and leadership, the Korean people, and in particular the Party, are expected to respond with trust, loyalty, worship, and eternal devotion:

> During 30-odd years of revolutionary activities, *Secretary Kim Jong Il has strengthened the Party and boundlessly exalted it as the Party of President Kim Il Sung. Since the General led the party and the revolution, the cause of the Juche-based Party building has*

developed on to a new higher stage... He also has thoroughly applied the idea of believing in the people as in heaven and further strengthened the relations between the Party and the people *sealed in blood... He enjoys absolute authority as the great master* of Party building in our era for these feats [*Rodong Sinmun*].

In September 1997, Korean Workers' Party conferences were held throughout the nation to recommend that Kim Jong Il assume the title of Party General Secretary. A lengthy speech at one of these conferences, by WPK Central Committee politburo member Ri Jong Ok, shows both the formality and the high degree to which Kim Jong Il mythology has permeated "politically correct" Juche terminology. Ri Jong Ok's speech included statements such as:

Comrade Kim Jong Il with literary and military accomplishments, talent and virtues has perfect qualities and qualifications as the people's leader. For a long time, he has wisely led the general affairs of the Party, state and army, together with the president, waged energetic revolutionary activities and performed immortal feats in *carrying forward the Juche revolution.*

It is thanks to his leadership that our party has become famous as a revolutionary party of Juche, the wholehearted unity of the leader, the Party and the masses has been consolidated, the driving force of the revolution has been strengthened in every way, the foundation for the independent economy has been cemented and a revolutionary change has taken place in literature and arts.

He has given personal guidance to more than 300 units in the province and important instructions to the province on more than 6,700 occasions. [Accounts from North Korean propaganda of Kim Jong Il's personal on-site guidance vary widely. For example, less than six months later, the *KCNA* reported that Kim Jong Il "had provided on-site guidance to more than 2,100 units on more than 3,693 occasions."]

Recommending him as General Secretary of our Party reflects the wishes of our revolutionary forerunners who laid down their lives *for the victory of the Juche revolution,* the *purest conscience of our people* and rising generations *determined to achieve eternal prosperity in a reunified country* and the unanimous desire of the progressive people to create a bright future *under the banner of socialism* [*KCNA*].

If we can believe the North Korean press, then all North Koreans were quite ecstatic over Kim Jong Il's assumption of the Party General Secretary title. Consider the following example:

> All the Koreans are happy that their ardent desire will soon be realized. Resolutions on recommending Secretary Kim Jong Il as the General Secretary of the Workers' Party of Korea were adopted with unanimous approval... *Over the past 30-odd years Secretary Kim Jong Il has guided all the affairs of the Party, the state and the army and performed imperishable feats in carrying forward and accomplishing the revolutionary cause of Juche*... The election of Secretary Kim Jong Il as WPK General Secretary is the earnest desire of the Korean revolutionary martyrs who dedicated their lives *to the victory of the revolutionary cause of Juche*—it is *an immovable will of our people and younger generation who will work for eternal prosperity of a reunified country.* At the significant historic time when the desire and will of the people will soon be realized the whole country is vibrating with a new enthusiasm [*KCNA*].

The repetitious claim in these speeches—that "Over the past 30-odd years Secretary Kim Jong Il has guided all the affairs of the Party, the state and the army and performed imperishable feats in carrying forward and accomplishing the revolutionary cause of Juche"—is particularly amusing considering Kim Jong Il's total avoidance of any responsibility for the sad state of affairs in North Korea. One has to wonder what Kim Il Sung was doing during most of those years! Also comical are the roughly weekly propaganda announcements of Kim Jong Il's ongoing inspections of KPA units. Every time Kim Jong Il conducts a military inspection, he presents the unit with the same gifts: "a machine gun, an automatic rifle and a pair of binoculars as souvenirs" [*KCNA*]. He also poses for a picture with them so the unit can continually be reminded of their personal allegiance to their Suryong. A non-North Korean could even get the impression that Kim Jong Il was on the political campaign trail for reelection. However, these regular inspections of military units are intended to sustain Kim Jong Il's totalitarian power base.

On a more serious note, notice in the above propaganda that Juche, the de facto religion, is inseparably linked to the sacred cause of "a reunified country." Such language should be considered more than mere hype. The build-up of propaganda is quite similar to mass Nazi rally speeches of the late 1930s in which Hitler called for a new generation of young Germans to restore the Fatherland to its divine manifest destiny of glory.

During this October 1997 time frame, Pyongyang's propaganda machine went into overdrive to sample the unbiased international response to Kim's election as well:

> S. Mukherjee, Chairman of the Central Control Commission of the Central Committee of the Communist Party of India (Marxist)...described it as a great event the world has waited for that the Party conferences are held in succession to recommend Secretary Kim Jong Il, a great statesman recognized by the world, as General Secretary of the WPK, the revolutionary Party. The distinguished leader Secretary Kim Jong Il has made great contributions to the Korean revolution and the world revolution...and reflects the unanimous desire of all the people fighting for justice, peace and socialism [*Rodong Sinmun*].

Of course, fellow Communists like the Indian representative above would not ask probing questions such as, "Why were there no other candidates?" or make embarrassing comments like, "Was the 'unanimous' election ever in doubt?"

As time continues, propaganda progressively elevates Kim Jong Il as a god of Juche. Toward that end, the term "Great Leader" has now been applied to Kim Jong Il. Previously, this term was reserved exclusively for Kim Il Sung, while Jong Il was called "Dear Leader." For example, a 1998 *Rodong Sinmun* article proclaimed:

> *It is the noblest ideological and spiritual traits of the Korean people to fight indefatigably, believing in the Great Leader General Kim Jong Il as the eternal mental pillar and savior of their destinies* ...They live and struggle with their destinies entrusted wholly to the General. They deeply revere and follow him, singing the song *"We believe in the General as in heaven."* This is because the song fully *represents the noble ideological and spiritual world of the Korean people, who cannot live even a moment separated from him.* They uphold his ideas and lines with loyalty. They know well how he turns misfortune into fortune and adversity into a favorable condition with his rare ideological intelligence and veteran and tested guidance. "When the Party is determined, we can do anything." This is a slogan reflecting the loyalty of the Korean people, who are working hard to implement the

Party's lines and policies, cherishing their validity deep in their hearts. They are always optimistic about their future. The General is symbolic of the bright future for the Korean people. *They firmly believe that although they are experiencing hardships at present, the day will certainly come when they will live a happy life because he guides them* [*Rodong Sinmun*].

Subsequent state ceremonies, accompanying the September 1998 celebration of the 50th anniversary of North Korea, confirmed that Kim Jong Il had now become, like his father before him, a "Great Leader." As the process of Kim Jong Il's self-deification continues, one of the latest developments has been the elevation of his long-deceased mother, Kim Jong Suk, to goddess status.

Kim Jong Suk: The Goddess of Juche

Mother Kim Jong Suk remained loyal to President Kim Il Sung and performed undying feats in the sacred struggle for the Juche revolution and made it possible for the Korean people to be blessed with illustrious leaders generation after generation. She is immortal in the hearts of the Korean people and the progressives of the world [KCNA].

VICE MARSHAL JO MYONG ROK,
DIRECTOR OF THE GENERAL POLITICAL DEPARTMENT
OF THE [NORTH] KOREAN PEOPLES' ARMY

Kim Jong Suk (1917–1949) was born in Hoeryong, North Hamgyong Province of what is now North Korea.[61] In 1935, she joined Kim Il Sung's revolutionaries and served as a cook, seamstress, and food gatherer. Eventually, she became Kim Il Sung's wife. As Juche legend relates, she also was a spy and guerrilla fighter. Kim Jong Suk was captured by the Japanese in 1937 and then released after a year. In 1942, Kim Jong Suk gave birth to Kim Jong Il while living in the former USSR where Kim Il Sung's Communists were being trained. In September 1949, a year after her second child drowned in Pyongyang, Kim Jong Suk died at the age of 32 while giving birth to her third child. Given Pyongyang's track record of rewriting history (including the above), how much else that is attributed to Kim Jong Suk is unclear. Most contemporary North Korean accounts of Kim Jong Suk are most probably Juche-idealized fantasies. Yet, even apart from the historical Kim Jong Suk, a discussion of the reinvented Kim Jong Suk is important toward understanding contemporary Juche thought.

Since Kim Jong Il does not have any basis for being god, deifying Kim Jong Suk adds to his credibility. The concocted lore of Kim Jong Il being born on Mt. Paektu of Kim Il Sung (a god) and Kim Jong Suk (a goddess) recalls the ancient Tangun legend of the first Tangun king's birth on Mt. Paektu. Thus, the recent reinvention of Kim Jong Suk is, at its core, the calculated use of the Juche religion to bolster Kim Jong Il's legitimacy as a despot-god.

Pyongyang's propaganda on the occasion of what would be Kim Jong Suk's 80th birthday on December 24, 1997, clearly shows the use of her glorification to legitimize Kim Jong Il:

> She was *a great mother of Korea* who brought the sun of guidance for the 21st century who would carry forward the Juche revolutionary cause [*KCNA*].

Kim Jong Suk's many new titles include "indomitable communist revolutionary fighter," "outstanding revolutionary woman activist," and "the mother of the revolution and children." She is also ascribed to have been a "woman general" possessing the "spirit of Mt. Paektu" and "the spirit of defending the leader." Today, Kim Jong Suk is proclaimed as an example for revolutionary soldiers to "safeguard General Secretary Kim Jong Il as human bombs and shields in any adversity." Remarkably, Kim Jong Suk, who died years before Juche was systematically shaped as a religion, is also praised for her "great contributions to the Juche revolutionary cause."

Many millions of dollars have been invested by the North Korean government in the late 1990s to create a Juche-correct composite image of Kim Jong Suk. This goddess image is promoted in books, songs, movies, essays, plays, paintings, museums, names of prominent institutions, and through the incessant barrage of Juche propaganda. For example, Pyongyang's "three-revolution exhibit" in December 1997 featured 100 newly published works of mother Kim Jong Suk. The exhibit also displayed hundreds of Kim Jong Suk's photos, 160 paintings, and over 300 books, reminiscences, and documents detailing her revolutionary exploits.

Under today's Juche religion, the "new and improved" Kim

Jong Suk is considered superior to all other women in history and a role model for allegiance to the dictator.

> The revolutionary life of *mother Kim Jong Suk* was a glorious life…She is a distinguished great woman produced by our nation, who is highly revered by all people because she brilliantly adorned the history of great men of the 20th century *by performing exploits which are too great to be compared with the combined achievements of heroines and famous women praised by history.* By modeling ourselves on mother Kim Jong Suk, who set a great example in defending the leader [Kim Il Sung], we will fully prepare the…ranks of loyalists and death-defying defenders who absolutely believe in and follow only Kim Jong Il in any adversity [*KCNA*].

One of these books, published in 1997 by The Workers' Party of Korea Publishing House, is entitled *Comrade Kim Jong Suk, Outstanding Revolutionary Woman Activist.* Chapters in the book's two parts, which typify the flavor of the Kim Jong Suk deification craze, are shown in Table 2-5.

TABLE 2-5. Chapter Titles for a Book on Kim Jong Suk

PART I	THE MOST LOYAL SUBJECT OF PRESIDENT KIM IL SUNG
Chapter 1	– Extraordinary ideological propagandist who absolutized the leader's revolutionary idea, made it her faith and actively propagandized it
Chapter 2	– Outstanding political activist who faithfully assisted the leader's guidance
Chapter 3	– Peerless lifeguard who defended the leader at the risk of her life
PART II	THE NOBLEST TRAITS OF THE WOMAN
Chapter 1	– Great communist revolutionary fighter
Chapter 2	– Woman general with spirit of Mt. Paektu
Chapter 3	– Noble human being

Pyongyang's Korean Art Gallery now features pieces of pro-Kim Jong Suk Juche-correct paintings such as "The General Is Waiting For You," "As Real Parents Of Bereaved Children," and "On Unforgettable New Year's Day." Similarly, a collection of poems entitled "Three Generals" lauds Kim Jong Suk alongside

Kim Il Sung and Kim Jong Il. Its 73 poems include titles such as "Home Dear To Heart," "Kimjongilia," "Native Home at Foot of Osan Hill," and "Always With Us." Kim Jong Suk is now praised in song as well. A sample list of ballads telling of her real or imagined exploits is shown in Table 2-6.

TABLE 2-6. Sample Titles of Songs Glorifying Kim Jong Suk [*KCNA*]

"Kim Jong Suk Is Our Mother"
"Kim Jong Suk Whose Feats Are Shining"
"Retrospection Of Native Home"
"Unforgettable Echo In Lake Samil"
"We Will Follow Mother's Loyalty"
"Looking Up To Mother Kim Jong Suk"
"I Will Come Back With General"
"Azalea"
"My Mother"
"Korea, Let Me Embrace You Again"
"Warmest Love Of Woman Fighter"

All of these gentle, fervent, and easy-to-sing songs praising Kim Jong Suk are framed with the intent to:

> …carry the Korean people's will to hold only General Kim Jong Il, successor to the Juche revolutionary cause, forever in high esteem, following the exemplary loyalty of the woman fighter who devoted all her life to President Kim Il Sung [*KCNA*].

The [North] Korean Film Studio also continues to produce feature-length films glorifying Kim Jong Suk. Recent releases in which Kim Jong Suk is the heroine include: *On the Road to Loyalty, Bloody Marks I* and *II*, and *Forest Rustles*. Likewise, the [North] Korean Documentary Film Studio released the three films *Gun Shot by Mother Will Be Everlasting, The Bodyguard*, and *Wait for Us*. All of these films portray her ardent anti-Japanese struggle while overcoming famine, disease, and evil imperialist forces.

The legends surrounding Kim Jong Suk—mostly generated by Pyongyang's propaganda machine—are as colorful and plentiful as those surrounding Kim Jong Il's childhood. Of particular interest is the praise of Kim Jong Suk for her patronage of North Korea's garment industry, and for being a role model for hungry North Koreans to eat the thin semi-digestible layer that lies just underneath the bark of pine trees. Highlights of Kim Jong Suk's alleged exploits are shown in Table 2-7.

TABLE 2-7. Kim Jong Suk's Alleged Exploits [*KCNA*]

ALLEGED EXPLOIT	SUMMARY
Nursed soldiers	Without medicine or medical instruments, Kim Jong Suk treated sick guerrillas' wounds and gave her food to them.
Pine-bark gourmet	Kim Jong Suk prepared cakes flavored with pine bark for soldiers while she subsisted on a thin gruel of pine endodermis.
Mended clothes	Kim Jong Suk gave up sleep to mend the uniforms and shoes of guerrillas. She gave up her only cloth to make a suit for a soldier.
Daring guerrilla	Kim Jong Suk broke through Japanese lines to rescue the rifle that a guerrilla recruit had lost in battle.
Guided factories	After North Korea's independence in 1946, Kim Jong Suk implemented Kim Il Sung's guidance to garment factories.
Revolutionary spy	In June 1937, Kim Jong Suk obtained information regarding the military movements of "the Japanese imperialists." This information helped the guerrillas win a battle at Jiansanfeng.
Aided guerrillas	Kim Jong Suk obtained enough cloth to make 600 guerrilla uniforms and built a tailor shop and photography studio.
Party organizer	Kim Jong Suk started various anti-Japanese guerrilla groups and built up revolutionary party organizations.
Total devotion	Kim Jong Suk devoted her whole life to the victory of the Korean revolution through her boundless loyalty to President Kim Il Sung and raising of Kim Jong Il.

Kim Jong Suk's special glorification under the evolving Juche religion by far eclipses any of the other revolutionaries honored by busts at the Revolutionary Martyrs' Cemetery on Mt. Taesong. Her December 24th birthday is now a national holiday and a Juche holy day. Meetings have been held throughout all of North Korea's provinces, cities, counties, and industrial complexes to honor her. Celebrations of Kim Jong Suk's 80th birthday included a wreath-laying ceremony at her bust at the cemetery, gatherings at various Kim Jong Suk statues, an art performance ("Woman General of Korea"), an "accession ceremony" of the Korean Children's Union, a sports tournament for the Osandok Prize, pilgrimages to the Sinpha Revolutionary Site in Kim Jong Suk county, and the convening of a mass national meeting at the Pyongyang Indoor Stadium. Juche propaganda also includes museums and new statues of Kim Jong Suk. Pyongyang has even named a military academy after her.

Other clear signs of the deification of Kim Jong Suk include the proclamation of her immortality, homage before her statues, and Juche prayers for her immortality. Propaganda that accompanied the wreath-laying ceremony at the cemetary proclaimed:

> A solemn ceremony...was held at the Revolutionary Martyrs' Cemetery on Mt. Taesong on December 24 to *pay homage to the communist revolutionary fighter mother Kim Jong Suk* and pledge loyalty...Vice Marshal Jo Myong Rok, Director of the General Political Department of the KPA, addressing the ceremony, said: "Mother Kim Jong Suk remained loyal to President Kim Il Sung and performed undying feats *in the sacred struggle for the Juche revolution and made it possible for the Korean people to be blessed with illustrious leaders generation after generation. She is immortal in the hearts of the Korean people and the progressives of the world."* ...Written on the ribbon hanging on the wreath are the letters "exploits of the great communist revolutionary fighter comrade Kim Jong Suk will be immortal"! [*KCNA*]

Another telltale sign of the deification effort is the sudden discovery of slogans written by Kim Jong Suk on Mt. Paektu's trees. One of these slogans, which typically praise Kim Il Sung, reads, "The Commander Star is out over Mt. Paektu. The Commander Star on Mt. Paektu shines over three thousand ri [villages]" [*KCNA*]. Floral-basket worship ceremonies before statues of Kim Jong Suk throughout North Korea and various international ceremonies honoring the new North Korean goddess rounded out the deification picture.

As our journey into the realm of Juche continues, the central importance of the gods of Juche becomes more clear when we consider the spiritual dimension of Juche.

CHAPTER 3

The Spiritual Dimension of Juche

When I say there is no complete revolutionary, I do not have in mind the height to which the ordinary man cannot climb, but rather the high demand and humble character [of] a communist [who] does not feel satisfied in his spiritual and moral training.

KIM JONG IL[1]

The sacrifices of pagans are offered to demons, not to God, and I do not want you to be participants with demons.

1 CORINTHIANS 10:20

Juche's spiritual dimension permanently sets it apart from non-religious philosophies. As the introductory quote shows, even Kim Jong Il speaks openly about the spiritual aspects of Juche. However, despite mounting evidence to the contrary, the Juche faithful prefer to view Juche as a "revolutionary new atheistic philosophy" while avoiding discussion of its spiritual content. In his autobiography, evangelist Billy Graham alluded to the contradiction between North Korea banning "all religious activity" while proclaiming itself "the first completely atheistic nation on earth" and maintaining Juche to be a "non-religious ideology."[2]

Nevertheless, the elevation of Kim Il Sung and Kim Jong Il to god status demonstrates that Juche is a irreversible departure from classical atheism. Juche mandates that adherents worship the Kims. Moreover, the Juche religious system refuses to tolerate spiritual competition for the hearts, minds, and souls of the North Korean people.

Lest one be tempted to arbitrarily dismiss the spiritual dimension of Juche, it is worthwhile to consider the spiritual roots of

Marxism-Leninism upon which it is based. Like Juche, Marxist-Leninists profess to be "atheist." Yet, though Karl Marx officially professed to the world that he is was an atheist, Sir Lionel A. Luckhoo presents ample evidence in his book *The Devil and Karl Marx* to suggest that Marx was, in fact, a satanist. Likewise, Voice of the Martyrs founder Richard Wurmbrand points out in his book *Was Karl Marx a Satanist?* that Marx's writings are filled with satanist terms. In *The Player*, for example, Marx wrote: "The hellish vapors rise and pell the grain, till I go mad and my heart is utterly changed. See this sword? The prince of darkness sold it to me." Marx, who was a devout Christian as a young man, became one of God's most ardent opponents. In a November 7, 1837, letter to his father, Marx wrote, "A curtain had fallen. My holy of holies was rent asunder and new gods had to be installed." Later he wrote, "I wish to avenge myself against the One who rules above." In *The Pale Maiden*, Marx confessed, "Thus Heaven I've forfeited, I know it full well. My soul, once true to God, is chosen for hell." Marx's hairstyle and beard were patterned after those of the disciples of Joanna Southcott, a Satanist priestess, who considered herself to be demonized by the spirit "Shiloh." Wurmbrand even observes that Karl Marx's letters from his son were addressed to "my dear devil." Such evidence suggests that Marx's Communist totalitarianism is not from the mind of man but rather originated from the pit of hell.[3]

If one can admit the possibility that Marxist Communism has demonic roots, then the reality of the spiritual dimension of Juche certainly merits investigation. The discussion that follows examines this spiritual dimension of Juche in more detail including the spiritual principality of Juche, Juche religious worship practices, Juche mystery and occult phenomena, the inability of Juche to deal with the inner man, and finally, Pyongyang's strategy to subvert other religions to promote Juche.

The Spiritual Principality of Juche

We do not wrestle against flesh and blood, but against principalities, against powers, against the rulers of the darkness of this age, against spiritual hosts of wickedness in the heavenly places.

EPHESIANS 6:12 (NKJ)

Any discussion of Juche's spiritual dimension must begin with a mention of the evil behind this mass deception wrought upon approximately 23 million people. Once Christians know what they are up against in the spiritual realm, they will be able to fervently intercede in prayer. The following discussion describes the nature of the unseen spiritual forces behind the visible Juche religious system endemic to North Korea.

Every New Testament book and seven of the Old Testament books of the Bible teach of the existence of Satan. Jesus Himself acknowledged and taught the existence of Satan (Matthew 13:39; Luke 10:18; 11:18). Satan is a created spiritual being who is called by many other names in Scripture, including devil, Lucifer, Beelzebub, Belial, evil one, tempter, ruler of this world, god of this age, prince of the power of the air, accuser of the brethren, serpent, dragon, and angel of light. Satan is a murderer (John 8:44), liar (John 8:44), confirmed sinner (1 John 3:8), accuser (Revelation 12:10), and an adversary (1 Peter 5:8). A biblical biographical sketch of the devil shows that he was cast out of his original position in heaven (Ezekiel 28:16), was cursed by God in Eden (Genesis 3:14,15), was judged at the cross (John 12:31), will be confined to the abyss during the millennium (Revelation 20:2), and will be permanently cast into the lake of fire at the end of the millennium (Revelation 20:10).[4]

Table 3-1 reviews what the Bible says about Satan's sins in Isaiah 14:13,14, shedding light on the spiritual origin of Juche religious teachings regarding Kim Il Sung, Kim Jong Il, and Mt. Paektu (the sacred mountain of Juche).

TABLE 3-1. Satan's Sins Recorded in Isaiah 14:13,14

SATAN'S STATEMENTS AS RECORDED BY THE PROPHET ISAIAH
– "I [Satan] will ascend to heaven."
– "I will raise my throne above the stars of God" (could mean actual stars or angels).
– "I will sit also upon the *mount* of the congregation, in the sides of *the north*" (KJV).
– "I will ascend above the tops of the clouds; I will make myself like the Most High." (Satan wanted to be possessor of heaven and earth. His sin is called pride in 1 Timothy 3:6, and it may be characterized as counterfeiting God.[5])

These biblical statements help to identify the fingerprints of Satan, which are critical to understanding Juche's satanic nature. For example, Juche ideology claims that Kim Il Sung and Kim Jong Il are God, that Mt. Paektu in Korea's "far north" is the "sacred mountain of Juche," and that one of Kim Jong Il's pseudonyms is "lodestar of Mt. Paektu." The Juche religion attempts to dethrone God by making war upon the underground church, killing the saints, and glorifying Kim Il Sung and Kim Jong Il. Given many such parallel observations, the Christian can be confident that Satan is head over the spiritual principality of Juche.

The Bible also reveals the goals of Satan in North Korea through Juche. Some of these goals include using people to thwart the work of Christ (John 8:44; Matthew 16:23); deceiving people (Revelation 20:3); tempting people to commit immorality (1 Corinthians 7:5); blinding people's minds (2 Corinthians 4:4); sowing sons of the evil one among believers (Matthew 13:38,39); and inciting persecution against Christians (Revelation 2:10). All of these goals are inherent parts of the spiritual kingdom behind the Juche religious system. No treaty, diplomacy, or revisionist regime will change this kingdom. Only prayer and action in the name of the Lord Jesus Christ will tear down this satanic stronghold.

It is important for believers to remember that Satan has his limitations. For example, since he is a created being, he is not omniscient or infinite. Also, Satan can be resisted by the Christian (James 4:7). Moreover, God places limitations on him (Job 1:12). No power that Satan has can stand up against the blood of Jesus Christ, the power of the Holy Spirit, or the Word of God.

The Bible's Old and New Testaments also teach that Satan has established spiritual principalities over the earth (e.g., Daniel 10:13; Ephesians 6:12). These principalities must be torn down by saints through the power of the Holy Spirit for the gospel to go forth. The Bible assures the Church that the Holy Spirit will indwell, fill, and empower believers as they venture forth to proclaim the gospel in obedience to the Great Commission (e.g., Acts 1:8).

Though Juche teachings deny or ignore the existence of spiritual forces, Korean shamanist religious beliefs have always recognized the reality of the spirit realm. For example, Korean shamanism is unique among East Asia's traditional religions in that there is a purely Korean name for God. From ancient times, Korean people have believed in "Hanunim, the Creator of earth and sky." Koreans recognized Hanunim as a good spirit. While they did not profess to know anything about him, Koreans never attempted to represent Hanunim with an idol or picture.[6]

In light of the spiritual dimension of Juche, future missionaries to North Korea should not make the mistake of viewing North Korea as a "secular state," but should be aware of the spiritual forces that oppose their work. The Bible records Jesus teaching that any such secular vacuum cannot long exist (Matthew 12:43–45). Jesus also taught that "from the days of John the Baptist until now, the kingdom of heaven has been forcefully advancing, and forceful men lay hold of it" (Matthew 11:12). Thus, spiritual warfare is required to tear down the demonic forces behind Juche.

Juche Religious Worship

And God spoke all these words: "I am the LORD *your God, who brought you out of Egypt, out of the land of slavery. You shall have no other gods before me."*
EXODUS 20:1–3

The dictator Kim Jong Il and the deceased dictator Kim Il Sung are worshipped as God incarnate in the Juche religion. Consider some of the recent samples of North Korean propaganda that describe Juche worship:

> Use of the Juche era meets the cherished desire of the Korean nation and *reflects their ardent worship for President Kim Il Sung,* their desire for his immortality and their determination to exalt the history of the leader, the sun, for all ages, holding him in high esteem for all ages [*Rodong Sinmun*].

> The south Korean *people's firm faith is based on absolute worship for President Kim Il Sung and Secretary Kim Jong Il. We regard the leader Kim Jong Il, who is identical to President Kim Il Sung in idea, leadership and virtue,* as their mental support and they believe that independence and reunification will be achieved under his leadership. *We believe in the leader Kim Jong Il, who is the savior of nation and lodestar of national reunification.* Despite fascist rampage, the fatherland will be certainly reunified and eternally prosper as it is led by him, *the sun of the nation* [*Kuguk Jonson*].

> Under the banner titles "to defend great comrade Kim

Jong Il is firm faith of revolutionary armed forces" and *"absolute trust in and worship for great general Kim Jong Il,"* papers carry words...recommending Secretary Kim Jong Il as General Secretary of the WPK...Printed in *Rodong Sinmun* is an article titled "People Extend Glory to Our General." *Minju Choson* runs an article titled "General Kim Jong Il is Our Destiny" illustrated by a picture of Secretary Kim Jong Il, waving to the cheering million people in a parade [*KCNA*].

We should have absolute worship for and unshakable faith in the leader and follow him with a noble sense of conscience and obligation. *Even if we die while resolutely safeguarding the General, it is glory* [*Rodong Sinmun*].

The above excerpts are just a small taste of one month's batch of North Korean propaganda. However, they serve to show the all-encompassing intent of Juche worship to uplift and glorify the Dear Leader Kim Jong Il. Each of them presents Kim Jong Il as the object of worship as god, savior, benefactor, eternal sun, and glory. In terms of their religious implications, such words easily eclipse the claims to glory of other modern dictators.

Worship of the Su-ryong under Juche includes standard religious practices such as homage, prayer, and unquestioning allegiance on a nationwide scale. In addition, worship practices also take the form of a harem-like system of "pleasure teams." These Juche pleasure teams use a religious veneer to institutionalize the sexual exploitation of women by an elite social group of men. Each of these Juche worship practices is discussed in more detail below.

Homage

The great leader comrade Kim Jong Il...visited the Kumsusan Memorial Palace today, the 52nd anniversary of the WPK, to pay homage to the great leader President Kim Il Sung. Comrade Kim Jong Il, together with senior Party, State and military officials, made respects to the statue.

KOREAN CENTRAL NEWS AGENCY
OCTOBER 10, 1997

Ceremonies and symbolic acts designed to pay homage to Kim Jong Il and the deceased Kim Il Sung are an important part of Juche worship. Juche homage by North Koreans is, of course, the established routine in the state-controlled society. In addition, visits and speeches by foreign visitors and tourists are regularly used to show the preeminence of the Juche faith through North Korean propaganda magazines and bulletins.

Make no mistake: homage to the statue of the deceased Kim Il Sung is a key worship ritual of the Juche religion. By extension, homage to Kim Il Sung's statue and nearby tomb also represent homage to the current dictator Kim Jong Il. This customary Juche worship ritual usually includes the laying of floral baskets and flowers before the Statue of the President. Official North Korean propaganda even uses religious terms such as "holy," "sacred," "immortal," "homage," and "prayer," associated with this and other Juche rituals. Also, the North Korean use of the term "service" carries definite religious overtones. For example:

> On July 8, 1997, the workers' party and people of Korea held a National *Memorial Service* in Pyongyang three years after the death of President Kim Il Sung to come out of mourning. At the *service* all the people renewed their will to trust and follow only General Kim Jong Il and carry on the revolution, rallied closer around him, true to the President's behests [*KCNA*].

In addition to homage at the great statue and the tomb, Juche homage permeates the entire North Korean culture. For example, between 1992 and 1994, over 300 poems and 400 songs were published in North Korea praising Kim Jong Il.

In the Korean culture, language and customs regarding honor are much more formal than in the West. With the Juche system superimposed on the North Korean culture, objects of honor should be approached cautiously or an action may be misinterpreted. For example, all foreign guests are obligated to visit North Korean cultural and historical sites. Along the way, the typical visitor will undoubtedly be invited and pressured to pay homage to the massive statue of Kim Il Sung on Mansu Hill. Someone who naively thinks he is on a sightseeing tour to the Korean version of Mount Rushmore may not realize that laying a wreath at the statue of Kim Il Sung is a blatant act of idolatry—worshipping a false god. If one does not desire to partake in this Juche religious worship, then one should consider a graceful way of declining. Likewise, an American diplomat who presents a gift to Kim Jong Il may be thinking he is being courteous according to

North Koreans gather to worship before the great statue of Kim Il Sung (1994).

established Western cultural norms. However, such a gift may be interpreted by the North Koreans as homage to Kim Jong Il as well as an endorsement or accommodation of Juche. The religious, political, and cultural implications of such actions should be carefully considered in advance.

Prayer

> *They prayed for the immortality of Generalissimo Kim Il Sung and wholeheartedly wished Secretary Kim Jong Il a long life in good health for the accomplishment of the revolutionary cause of Juche.*
> RESOLUTION OF THE GENERAL ASSOCIATION OF [NORTH] KOREAN RESIDENTS IN JAPAN (CHONGRYON)
> *KOREA CENTRAL NEWS AGENCY*

The Juche doctrine of prayer, though poorly defined, includes praying for the immortality of the deceased dictator Kim Il Sung, and for him to live in their hearts. Juche prayers are routinely offered in front of the statue of Kim Il Sung, particularly his great statue on Mansu Hill in Pyongyang. Prayers by foreign delegations for North Korea's leaders or in repentance for anti-Korean acts in history are also welcomed since they serve to promote Juche. Nature is also thought to "pray" for Kim Jong Il through the occurrence of mysterious phenomena which always seem to coincide with special state or Party occasions. Prayers to anyone other than Kim Il Sung—or even to heaven on behalf of Kim Il Sung, Kim Jong Il, or Kim Jong Suk—are unthinkable under the Juche religion.

To people influenced by a Judeo-Christian worldview, the Juche concept of prayers in the present tense for the future immortality of a ruler who died in the past sounds strange. The traditional Korean belief is that deceased family members remain within the family circle, in spiritual form. For this reason, the most important concern of the family is to produce a male heir to carry on the family line. He is called on to perform ancestral rituals in the household and at the family grave site. The Juche religion has incorporated this spiritual aspect of ancestor worship into its theology of prayer.

Below are some examples of the Juche concept of acceptable prayer:

> *Prayers to the statue of Kim Il Sung on Mansu Hill:* The visiting delegation…paid [homage to] President Kim Il Sung. *The delegation expressed deep respects to the Statue of President Kim Il Sung* and then entered the hall where he is preserved in state…Then *they held a meeting to pray for the immortality of the President in front of his statue on Mansu Hill*…Shizue Araya read out [loud] a "letter of prayer for the great President Kim Il Sung"… *The letter prayed for the immortality of President Kim Il Sung and Mrs. Kim Jong Suk* amid the eternal blessings of the people… *Then floral baskets and flowers were laid before the Statue of President* [KCNA].

> *Flowers pray to Kim Jong Il:* On September 9 marking the 49th anniversary of the founding of the DPRK, a 15-year-old white apricot, which grows *by the building of the Kaesong municipal land and environmental management bureau,* put out 24

beautiful flowers. What is all the more mysterious is that all
these flowers have come only from tree branches *facing the
north*... [Working people] said that it seemed the flowers commemorated the significant day when the use of the Juche era
has begun, *praying for the immortality of President Kim Il Sung
with deep reverence for him* [*KCNA*].

*North Korean residents in Japan pray for the immortality of Kim
Il Sung:* Meetings of local headquarters and organizations of
the General Association of Korean Residents in Japan (Chongryon) have been held to warmly support resolutions...
recommending Secretary Kim Jong Il as General Secretary of
the WPK... *They prayed for the immortality of Generalissimo Kim Il
Sung* and wholeheartedly wished Secretary Kim Jong Il a long
life in good health for the accomplishment of *the revolutionary cause of Juche,* the independent and peaceful *reunification*
of the country,... and *the victory of the cause of global independence* [*KCNA*].

Allegiance

*Today the Korean peoples live and work in the revolu-
tionary spirit of soldiers... in the spirit of accepting
and carrying out the Supreme Commander's order absolutely and unconditionally and in the revolutionary
spirit of self-reliance and strenuous efforts.*

KOREAN CENTRAL NEWS AGENCY
JANUARY 16, 1998

Unquestioning allegiance to the Su-ryong (who is now Kim
Jong Il) is a key element of Juche worship. Understanding this
dualistic religious-political nature of Juche allegiance is extremely
important. Without such an understanding, many casual observers of North Korea draw improper conclusions by applying a
Western cultural paradigm that separates the political from the
religious. Such a separated concept is totally foreign to the Juche
mindset shared by 23 million North Koreans.

Loyalty to Kim Jong Il is considerably more than mere nationalism in North Korea. Since the lines separating religion and politics are virtually non-existent under Juche, allegiance to Kim
Jong Il is both a sacred religious and a political concept. Pyongyang's Juche architects inculcate voluntary unconditional allegiance to the Su-ryong through the "loyalty spirit" teachings.

These Juche allegiance teachings have resulted in the formation of the "Theory of the Immortal Socio-Political Body." According to this theory, the Leader, the Party, and the masses are integrated into one immortal body through comradeship and the "spirit of unity." The Juche "spirit of unity" works to make all North Koreans blindly act together like ants or automatons. Of course, the brain or center of this body is the Su-ryong.

Since the 1980s, North Korea's people have been urged to safeguard the Su-ryong with a "do-or-die" spirit. For example, a recent article in a North Korean magazine, entitled "By Founding and Leading the Party," provides an example: "Our people will uphold the leadership of the dear leader Comrade Kim Jong Il with loyalty, changing sorrow at the loss of the fatherly leader into strength and courage" [*DPRK*]. Each February 16th, on Kim Jong Il's birthday, Pyongyang's Kim Il Sung Stadium is packed to capacity as the young vanguards and other Party groups take an oath of personal loyalty to the Dear Leader. A more recent propaganda statement by the former Chondokyo leader, O Ik Je, also mentions this central principle of loyalty to the person of Kim Jong Il:

> The leader Kim Jong Il is indeed the center of great national unity who is leading all the members of the nation, who have different ideologies, political views and religious beliefs, to unity. *I will devote myself to the sacred cause of national reunification, remaining loyal to him* [*KCNA*].

The critical importance of allegiance as a foundational religious pillar of Juche becomes clear when we realize that North Korea is described as "perhaps the most militarized society on earth." Until the early 1970s, it was thought that North Korea's military had about 400,000 personnel. However, in 1970, North Korea changed its way of keeping census statistics from recording the total male population to recording the total male civilian population. Calculating the figures revealed that the "missing [non-civilian] male" population was 1.25 million people. By 1987, it was estimated to have been even higher. This level of national mobilization (ratio of soldiers to civilians) exceeds that of Saddam Hussein during the Desert Storm war in the Mideast and is about the same as that of the United States during World War II in 1943.

The extreme emphasis on allegiance is reflected in "the revo-

Personal allegiance to Kim Jong Il is a sacred duty of the Juche religion.

lutionary spirit of soldiers" terminology that is equally applicable
to civilians and military personnel alike.

> Today the Korean peoples live and work in *the revolution-
> ary spirit of soldiers*. This spirit is the source of strength of
> Korea, *which turns adversity into favorable condition, misfortune
> into fortune,* and is also a powerful weapon of struggle. It is
> the heroic stamina of Korea breaking through difficulties.
> The spirit was created by soldiers of the Korean People's
> Army... [whose] servicemen overcame inconceivable difficul-
> ties and hardships in the spirit of accepting and *carrying out
> the Supreme Commander's order absolutely* and unconditionally
> and in the revolutionary spirit of self-reliance and strenuous
> efforts...Now seen at workplaces of Korea are slogans and
> posters reflecting the firm determination to live and work in
> this revolutionary spirit of soldiers [*KCNA*].

The above propaganda clearly suggests that "the revolutionary spirit of soldiers" is a deceptive spirit that not only promotes
blind allegiance, but lies to the North Korean people by telling

them that misfortune is fortune—evil is good.

Upon visiting Pyongyang, one American journalist described the amazing emphasis on allegiance in North Korea:

> It was an awesome experience to see the total obedience of the people to the "Great Leader." Even though he is gone, his pictures were everywhere, his thoughts were everywhere. Everyone wore a badge bearing Kim Il Sung's face.[7]

Yet, this Juche religious principle of allegiance to Kim Jong Il as god directly contradicts the first of God's Ten Commandments given to Moses at Mt. Sinai:

> "I am the LORD your God, who brought you out of Egypt, out of the land of slavery. You shall have no other gods before me" (Exodus 20:2,3).

Given God's clear commandment against idolatry, the father and son Kims have committed exceedingly great sins by trying to rule over the North Korea as demigods, spurring the people to worship them, and persecuting those who do not obey the order. Many Christians believe that North Korea is undergoing the judgment of Almighty God because of their worship of Kim Jong Il—the false god of Juche.

The Juche religion makes allegiance to Kim Jong Il a hallmark virtue. For a North Korean not to bear allegiance to Kim Jong Il would be tantamount to committing religious blasphemy as well as fomenting an act of political sedition. For foreigners, the offense might be attributed to mere ignorance of the fact that Kim Jong Il is the true god. But, in North Korea, the offense quite easily could be punishable by immediate execution or by slow death in a reeducation (concentration) camp.

Juche's radical totalitarian allegiance is properly considered within this discussion of worship because, under Juche, there is no higher allegiance than to the Su-ryong. The biblical view of divided religious and political authority is, by comparison, decidedly different. When acting within proper biblical authority, the Bible views civil rulers, magistrates, and law enforcement officials to be God's ministers of righteousness just as clergy are. Similarly, rulers and clergy who operate outside of their proper biblical authority are admonished or condemned. Yet in North Korea, the dictator does not act within such proper authority because he views himself as God. Thus, under the Juche system, Kim Jong Il

is accountable to no one. Under such a totalitarian system, no
form of censorship or self-criticism is available within the society.

When early Christians encountered similar circumstances,
where allegiance to Rome constituted worship, Christians resisted
Roman totalitarian idolatry through civil disobedience. Civil disobedience meant that Christians by the thousands had to lay down
their lives for the principle that "Jesus is Lord," which supersedes
the idolatrous notion that "Caesar is Lord." Christian philosopher Francis Schaeffer noted:

> If there is no final place for civil disobedience, then the govern-
> ment has been made autonomous, and as such, it has been put in the
> place of the Living God, because then you are to obey it even
> when it tells you in its own way at that time to worship Caesar.
> And that point is exactly where the early Christians performed
> their acts of civil disobedience even when it cost them their
> lives.[8]

Jesus told the Roman ruler, Pontius Pilate, "You would have no
power over me if it were not given to you from above" (John 19:11).
This and many other Old and New Testament passages set bounds
on the proper authority of civil governments (e.g., Deuteronomy
17:16–19). Thus, one may view the claim of Jesus' kingship and
the Jews' response to this claim as a crucial factor in Pilate's decision to send Him to the cross (see John 19:15,16).

The pagan notion of emperor-god rulership was practiced in
ancient times as well as in contemporary North Korea:

> In most pagan cultures, church and state are or were one.
> The king was not only head of the state but also head of the
> church, with no distinction in these offices. The unity of the
> state was founded on a common religion, and the king was fre-
> quently considered to be either a demigod or a descendant of
> a god or a god himself. Emperor-worship and state-worship
> were the order of the day.[9]

However, absolute emperor-worship and state-worship were
particularly true in ancient Rome. Luther Hess Waring notes in *The
Political Theories of Martin Luther*:

> In the history of Rome there was a time when the word
> Caesar was the law and the worship of Caesar was the religion
> of the world. As *Pontifex Maximus* he was the high priest of
> the national religion. He held control of both church and state

in his own person. Indeed, in a large sense, he was the state, and he was the church.[10]

Thus, under Juche, allegiance means much more than just token assent. All North Koreans must have multiple pictures of Kim Il Sung and Kim Jong Il prominently displayed in their homes. Civilians and military personnel alike are enjoined to have such allegiance to Kim Jong Il that they are willing to give their lives to protect against imperialist aggressor forces.

Even years after his death, the spiritual dimension of Juche allegiance shows that Kim Il Sung's "spiritual" legacy lives onward through the totalitarian bondage that continues to enslave North Korea's people. However, the worship of Kim Il Sung and Kim Jong Il as gods does not end with homage, prayer, and allegiance.

Pleasure Teams

Able persons should be found in the masses.
KIM JONG IL

I acquired men and women singers, and a harem as well—the delights of the heart of man . . . I denied myself nothing my eyes desired; I refused my heart no pleasure.
ECCLESIASTES 2:8,10

One of the aspects of Juche worship that is kept at a fairly low international profile is that, in addition to Kim Jong Il having a wife and three children, he also maintains "pleasure teams." Pleasure teams are a harem of women who provide services for Kim Jong Il and his top associates at each of the ruler's specially prepared villas. Since Kim Jong Il is a god, according to the Juche religion, then he must have every possible whim and fancy met by the North Korean people. Since whatever Kim wants is, by definition, morally correct, then Kim Jong Il gets what he wants—pleasure. The pleasure team provides this aspect of ritual worship of Kim Jong Il.[11]

The pleasure team phenomena is symptomatic of the greater problem that the State has robbed women of their gender and their identity as mothers and weakened the function of the family. All children, and especially all orphans, are seen primarily as wards of the state. For decades, North Korean boys and girls have been taught from an early age that they are supposed to give their loyalty and even their very identity over to Kim Il Sung and now Kim Jong Il. Normal childhood songs are replaced by hymns to the dictator with lyrics such as:

> I'll throw myself into the bosom of the chieftain if I were to be born and re-born a hundred times...ensconced in the bosom of the father chieftain this daughter is overwhelmed with his love.[12]

In the 1980s, the outside world learned of the existence of pleasure teams when North Korea kidnapped a number of young women from Macao, Hong Kong, and various Middle Eastern nations to augment the pleasure team. The pleasure team is divided into three components: *the satisfaction team* (performs the duty of providing sexual pleasure), *the happiness team* (provides a massage service), and *the dancing team* (performs singing and dancing).

The 5th Section of the Party Organization and Guidance Department recruits pleasure team members through a nationwide network. Annually, the 5th Section orders its provincial branch officers and the Party's city-level officials to select a quota of beautiful candidates from among female senior high school students. The number of candidates is 100 times the required quota of new pleasure team members. The Namsan Medical Clinic located at Munsu-dong in Pyongyang is the site of the next phase of recruitment. There, about the top one-tenth of candidates undergo physical examinations. From among these, fifty are sent to Kim Jong Il for "final examination."

The pleasure team selection guidelines used by local officials are classified as confidential. The guidelines read in part:

> The project designed to help Kim Il Sung and Kim Jong Il enjoy longevity is *a holy duty* all Party members must abide by.[13]

Given that North Korea considers the mission of the pleasure team to be a "holy duty," it is not an exaggeration to categorize their mission as an act of worship. The guidelines charge all responsible secretaries of county and city Party chapters to be ever vigilant for prospective pleasure team candidates. In this way, they can always be ready to provide a candidate to higher ranking officials when so ordered. To meet their quotas, local Party officials routinely canvas senior high schools each term in search of candidates. Once a candidate is selected, Party officials in the local schools are ordered to take special care of them while they await subsequent screening.

Upon acceptance, the candidates go through six months of technical training pertaining to the area of specialization decided by the Party authorities. Upon completion of this training, they are commissioned as 1st Lieutenants in the Korean People's Army (KPA). Pleasure team members serve until age 25, at which time they are discharged from the KPA. Juche's institutionalized sexual exploitation of women is typical of many false religious systems throughout history.

The Spirit of Human Bombs

The soldiers of your unit have turned your naval port into an impregnable fortress and become brave sailors ready to defend your leader with your lives as human bombs and make suicidal attacks.

KIM JONG IL
MARCH 12, 1998 [*KCNA*]

Probably one of the most sobering aspects of the spiritual dimension of Juche is the emergence of "human bombs." The following paragraphs will consider the origin and implications of this spiritual belief.

Beginning in 1993, Pyongyang's propaganda has contained an increasing number of articles, particularly since 1997, that urge the Party faithful, KPA, and masses to defend Kim Jong Il "in the spirit of human bombs." During 1997 and 1998, when Kim Jong Il has inspected KPA units, the soldiers have chanted, "Human bombs! Human bombs! Human bombs!" and pledged themselves to prove their allegiance to him to the death. The 1998 New Years editorial also included such references. These New Years editorials in three major newspapers take on a greater significance than in years past because they replaced the traditional New Years message of the supreme leader. New Years editorials of 1996 and 1997 featured "Red Flag" terminology. Red Flag ideology calls on the people to embrace the spirit of self-reliance, the revolutionary struggle and spirit, and to become *"bullets"* and *"human bombs"* to protect the Leader. For example, the 1998 Joint New Years editorial declared, "We should firmly defend General Secretary Kim Jong Il and guarantee his absolute authority in every way in the spirit of defending the leader at the risk of life and *the spirit of human bombs"* [*Rodong Sinmun*]. The following 1997 propaganda article links "the spirit of human bombs" with "Red Flag ideology" while omitting the term Juche:

> The Korean people are determined to become an impregnable fortress and shield to safeguard the General at the cost of their lives. Their firm determination is to share their destiny with the General forever, upholding him as the supreme leader of the Party and the revolution. *Holding this red flag, our people are defending the idea of the leader* most purely with resolute revolutionary principles and uncompromising struggle they are most resolutely safeguarding the safety of the leader *in the spirit of human bombs* and they are highly exalting the absolute authority of the leader through their devoted struggle. *If we are to defend the red flag of the revolution, the banner of defending the leader, we should have absolute worship for and unshakable faith in the leader* and follow him with a noble sense of conscience and obligation.
>
> Even if we die while resolutely safeguarding the General, it is glory. It is the unbreakable faith of the Korean people to become an impregnable fortress to safeguard the General at the cost of their lives and *deal telling blows to the enemy* [*Rodong Sinmun*].

The topic of Red Flag ideology can await discussion in Chapter 10. However, the implications of the presence of "the spirit of human bombs" invite immediate discussion.

"Bushido" Incorporated into Juche

Less than sixty years ago, and roughly six hundred miles to the East, *the Japanese used exactly the same "spirit of human bombs" terminology* the North Koreans are now using in conjunction with their World War II suicide campaign. Like today's North Koreans, the Japanese used "the spirit of human bombs" in the context of radical allegiance to and worship of a god-king. The Japanese framed this radical allegiance within the concept of the ancient samurai code of "Bushido" (the chivalric code). A review of the Japanese precedent is helpful to more fully understand the implications of the North Korean's recent adoption of "the spirit of human bombs" terminology.

Certainly the notion of self sacrifice is a part of any nation's view of wartime heroism. Numerous nations award posthumous decorations to those who chose, either through premeditation or in the heat of combat, to sacrifice themselves to save a friend or destroy an enemy. However, the recent history of East Asia tells us "spirit of human bombs" is something more than mere self-sacrificial bravery.

The Japanese initiated an entire military campaign that featured deliberate suicide with religious emperor-worship overtones as a standard military tactic. Suicide with special honor had long existed in Japanese samurai mythology and history. These traditions included the "hara-kiri" or seppuku (ritual suicide to atone for dishonor or defeat). Japan transformed such ancient traditions into modern religious norms for the Japanese military. On January 8, 1941, almost a full year before Pearl Harbor, Japanese Minister of War General Tojo Hideki ordered that the "Senjinkun" (Battle Ethics) be distributed throughout the Imperial Japanese Army. The similar "Gunjin chokuyu" (imperial teachings to servicemen) were also distributed throughout the Japanese armed forces.[15] These orders made the unwritten code of the samurai the required conduct of all Japanese servicemen:

> The quick falling cherry blossom,
> That lives but a day and dies
> 　with destiny unfulfilled,
> Is the brave spirit of Samurai youth,
> Always ready,
> 　his fresh young strength
> To offer to his lord.
> 　　—Ancient Japanese Poem[14]

> A sublime sense of self sacrifice must guide you throughout life and death. Think not of death as you push through with every ounce of your effort, fulfilling your duties. Make it your joy to do everything with all your spiritual and physical strength. Fear not to die for the cause of everlasting justice. Do not stay alive in dishonor. Do not die in such a way as to leave a bad name behind you.[16]

As the tide of war turned strongly against Japan in 1944, voluntary kamikaze suicide attacks began at the Battle of Leyte Gulf in the Philippines. Then, early in 1945, the Japanese Imperial General headquarters issued an order that all armed forces should emphasize suicide tactics. These tactics included not only the much publicized attacks by kamikazes and Baka bombs, but also suicide weapons platforms such as midget submarines with underwater fins, explosive motorboats, human torpedoes, human mines, suicide frogmen, glider-bombs, "crawling dragons," and a small submarine about thirty feet long which would attach explosives by suction or magnets to enemy ships.

We should keep in mind that, given the religious aspects of the missions, all of these "human bomb" programs had tens of thousands of volunteers—certainly more than enough. The religious "on a mission for god" character of these missions carried with them the unbearable social stigma of shaming one's family should a serviceman refuse a suicide mission. It is entirely meaningless to split philosophical or psychological fine points as to whether the individual soldiers or sailors willingly or unwillingly "volunteered." The result was the same. In practice, no real man ever wavered. In the tradition of the Bushido code, young men instead spoke of the glory of death, saying, "I go to die for my country. It fills me with humility to have been selected by the emperor."[17]

In 1945, Lieutenant General Kawabe, Deputy Chief of the Japanese Imperial General headquarters, said:

> The pilot did not start out on his mission with the intention of committing suicide. *He looked upon himself as a human bomb* which would destroy a certain part of enemy fleet for his country. He considered it a glorious thing...we had no shortage of volunteers.[18]

After World War II, the United States Strategic Bombing Survey concluded that, by war's end, the "volunteers" were more reluctant. However, the extent of the opposition of those selected was largely limited to statements of lament. One kamikaze pilot, who was saved from flying his mission only by Japan's surrender, said that he "saddened to tears at receiving the death sentence [although]...it is unmanly to say so." Such sentiments did not result in any large-scale refusal by Japanese servicemen to attempt their missions as ordered.

Though the terminology differs slightly, North Korea has accomplished the same thing through the sacred teachings of Juche, Red Flag ideology, and a personal oath of allegiance to Kim Jong Il. Kim Jong Il's loyalty oath, like Tojo's Senjinkun, adds the cultural force of morality and honor (as misguided and warped as they may be) to suicidal allegiance. Through this allegiance oath, the Juche religion, and Red Flag ideology, Kim Jong Il is systematically indoctrinating North Korea's military with the suicidal spirit. For example, Kim Jong Il tells his people that, "A human being must know to respect and love his friends, share in their sorrows as his own, and sacrifice himself for them."[19] The response to Kim Jong Il in one war veteran's letter stated, "All our people, more than 20 million, have firm faith and will, ready to become human bombs for your sake" [*KCNA*].

The Spiritual Roots of Suicide Tactics

As we consider the possibility of the reintroduction of mass suicide tactics in East Asia, it is helpful to consider how the "suicide spirit" came to "the land of morning calm." To answer this question, let's turn the clock of history back more than seven centuries and go instead to "the land of the rising sun."

The year is 1281. Just seven years ago, a Mongol invasion force of 40,000 warriors had landed on Japan's beaches, besting the Japanese samurai with their unconventional warfare tactics, which included clouds of deadly arrows. However, the Mongols withdrew without conquering Japan after part of the Mongol fleet had been wrecked in a storm. In recent months, Kublai Khan, having conquered China, sent ambassadors to Japan demanding their acquiescence to Mongol rule. Japan answered these overtures by killing and mutilating the Mongol envoys. Thus, the Khan is quite displeased. Now, Kublai Khan, ruthless ruler of most of the Eurasian land mass, is determined to launch a major Mongol invasion of Japan and subjugate the samurai once and for all.

As the story goes, the Japanese Bakufu (Shogunate) is more than a little bit concerned. So the Bakufu summons all the sorcerers of Japan and asks them which god is the strongest; that is the one he will turn to for Japan's deliverance. The sorcerers advise the Bakufu that the sun goddess is the strongest—so the Bakufu asks all the Buddhist temples and Shinto shrines to pray and chant spells to invoke the sun goddess' protection and repulse the Mongols.

As expected (and as provoked), Kublai launched an invasion force of approximately 140,000 undefeated veterans in a Mongol armada composed of thousands of small ships. However, the Japanese altered their tactics. For several weeks and with suicidal ferocity, the Japanese attacked the Mongol ships by night as they lay at anchor. Small Japanese boats, with 12 to 15 men each, ferried teams of skilled samurai warriors to the Mongol ships. On the dark confined spaces on the decks of the Mongol ships, the samurai were able to use both their superior swords and superior swordsmanship with telling effect. The decks ran red with Mongol blood.

Then, after four weeks of holding the Mongol fleet at bay with such tactics, a typhoon sprang up, seemingly out of nowhere, and destroyed over 4,000 Mongol ships. Japanese historians of the day called this miraculous storm the *kamikaze* ("divine wind"). Mongol casualties were estimated at well over 100,000, though there is no way of knowing for sure. However, the invasion was repulsed. Few of the Mongol attackers survived the debacle. Though he desired to, Kublai Kahn never mounted his intended third invasion of Japan.

Grateful for Japan's salvation, the Bakufu entered into spiritual intercourse and union with the sun goddess through the Daijosai ceremony. This is the origin of the Japanese emperor being worshipped as a god-king by the Japanese people (and why the sun appears on the Japanese flag). Every Japanese emperor through Hirohito (who renounced his divinity in 1945) has entered into the Daijosai ceremony.[20] Though this understanding of Daijosai is held by a minority of Japanese historians, a Christian may view the ceremony as the invocation of demonization by Japan's ruler on both an individual and corporate/national level.[21]

The Link: Japan's Spiritual Influence on North Korea

Having noted the Japanese origins of "human bombs," let us now look at the link: Japan's spiritual influence on North Korea. From a spiritual history perspective, there is more to "the spirit of human bombs" than an idle academic comparison between similar "human bombs" statements out of two possibly unrelated cultures. In fact, Korea has been under Japanese domination for most of the first half of this century.

Much of the 1904–1905 Russo-Japanese war took place in northern Korea in the Pyongyang area. Japanese armies established bases on the Korean peninsula and defeated the Czar's armies in a campaign that culminated in their decisive victory at Port Arthur. By 1910, the Japanese forced the abdication of the Korean king and annexed the entire Peninsula as a Japanese territory. To reduce the risk of revolt, the Japanese began systematically reeducating the Korean people. Shinto idolatry was enforced while Christians were persecuted. The Japanese abolished Korean language education in public schools and instead taught children Japanese. Korean cultural traditions were forcibly replaced by their Japanese equivalents. Korean Christian churches and church schools were the last holdouts against these Japanese policies until they finally capitulated in 1938. Thus, an entire generation of Koreans was forced to partake in Shinto baptism and bow before Shinto shrines.[22] In a spiritual sense, the act of Christians worshipping Shinto idols during the Japanese occupation made the Korean nation vulnerable to the full spectrum of Japanese godless influence...including "the spirit of human bombs."

Elements of the modern Juche religion recall elements of ancient Korean sun god worship that bear a striking resemblance to Japanese Shintoism. For example, Samguk yusa (Memorabilia of the Three Kingdoms) records that the first ancient Korean king, Tan'gun Wanggom (Tangun) (c. 2333 B.C.) was conceived when Hwanung (the king who had descended from heaven), the sun god/son-of-the-Creator had intercourse on Korea's sacred mountain (Mt. Paektu) with a woman who had previously been transformed into a human from a she-bear.[23] (Recall the similar ancient Daijosai Japanese myth from c. 700 B.C.) Today, Kim Il Sung, his wife Kim Jong Suk, and their dictator son Kim Jong Il are referred to, in Juche revisionist history and current propaganda, as "the three generals of Mt. Paektu."[24] In a manner reminiscent of the Japanese occupation, Kim Jong Il, like his father before, requires every Korean home to prominently display their pictures. Additionally, all North Koreans must bow and render homage before Kim Il Sung's statue. Moreover, the North Koreans under Juche are even more radically anti-Christian than the Japanese ever were.

Currently, the Kim Jong Il regime has instituted a full-scale campaign throughout North Korea's military calling for the death-defying protection of the Su-ryong through suicide tactics in "the spirit of human bombs." On January 28, 1998, North Korea directly associated "the spirit of human bombs" with suicide air attacks:

> The KPA [Korean People's Army] officers and men have been firmly imbued with the *spirit of human bombs* under the slogan "Let us safeguard the headquarters of the revolution

headed by General Kim Jong Il with our lives." Among them are *hero Kil Yong Jo who sacrificed himself for the safety of the head-quarters of the revolution by piloting his plane, not bailing out of the plane when it was out of order*...in defense of the authority of Supreme Commander General Kim Jong Il...The KPA is a model of society in all aspects including spiritual and moral traits, fighting spirit, cultural and emotional life [*KCNA*].

Similar propaganda articles call for the use of suicide land and maritime tactics. For example, a North Korean training film shows officers gathered around a model of a U.S. aircraft carrier. The context of the film suggests that the North Koreans view the carrier as a both a target and a symbol of "American imperialistic oppression." This photo suggests that aircraft carriers are likely to be potential targets of suicide attacks.

A September 1998 report out of South Korea's civil defense program indicates that the North Koreans are already proceeding from theory to practice with "the spirit of human bombs." The report stated:

> North Korea is training up to 140 suicide bomber pilots to plunge into key South Korean targets if war breaks out on the divided peninsula...The new unit appears to be fash-ioned after the Japanese kamikaze pilots of World War II, the high-ranking official said on condition of anonymity...North Korea set up the suicide squads earlier this year to use its out-dated Soviet-designed MiG-15 and MiG-17 jets, the official said. The new air unit appears to be under the direct com-mand of North Korean leader Kim Jong Il.[25]

Despite the foregoing observations and analysis, is the "spirit of human bombs" cause for alarm or merely speculation? Future world events will ultimately answer the question.

Mystery and the Occult

A miracle is not an accident given by Heaven, but a necessity given by the people.[26]

KIM JONG IL

Juche, as with many false religions, has a shroud of mystery and the occult associated with it. As a later chapter will show, there are definite occult worship implications associated with the Juche holy sites. How much more of Juche involves the occult remains uncertain. However, the existence of occult practices at the top of the Juche hierarchy would not be a surprise.

North Korean propaganda states outright that Kim Jong Il has special occult powers.

> Kim Jong Il has the *occult power* of finding out links of complicated things in a moment and the key points, superb intelligence of seeing the large through the small, the extraordinary from the ordinary, the speed and boundless width of thinking like lightning [across] Korea and the world, [in] the past, present and future, and the outstanding analysis capacity of penetrating thousands of things from one and making them intensive—this is his intelligent great personality [*Rodong Sinmun*].

Ongoing Juche propaganda also caters to the superstitions of the people of North Korea by regularly noting the frequent supernatural phenomena accompanying Kim Jong Il. These stories relate how nature bows down to Kim Jong Il through blossoms appearing and flowers blooming out of season, fishermen catching rare sea cucumbers, sunbeams breaking through foggy skies, and a white owl flying around in a government building [*KCNA*].

The Japanese Socialist Workers Party commented on these mysterious natural phenomena in the October 1997 issue of its journal, *Petrel*. They noted, in particular, that the North Korean "owl phenomena" was patterned after the Japanese tradition from the Nara era that "a white pheasant appears and it bodes well when the emperor ascends." The article continued:

> Why is such a foolish as mere child's play necessary? If his is winning the support of the people and has the conviction, he will not need the story like such a concoction. In that sense, this will teach the weakness of the powers of Kim Jong Il, will [it] not? Anyway, this new leader seems to have neither confidence nor belief in the meaning of the truth.[27]

With his alleged clairvoyant intelligence and command over nature, it is surprising that Kim Jong Il cannot stop nature's floods, droughts, excessive erosion, and abnormal tidal waves. In other countries, such articles would be printed in sensationalist tabloid newspapers along with articles titled "Baby Born With Two Heads" and "Elvis Sighted in Argentina." The mysterious flowers coming into bloom out of season at the agricultural college and experimental agricultural science buildings are particularly laughable. As Kim Jong Il's introductory quote would suggest, these "supernatural phenomena" are most probably horticultural hoaxes rather than credible anomalies. However, even if they were real, Kim Jong Il's mysterious power over nature seems to be narrowly limited to flowers, blossoms, catches of exotic fish, indoor bird droppings, and a few sunbeams. Enough information is not yet available to determine the full amount of occult activity that surrounds the Juche religion.

Dealing with the Inner Man

If one knows oneself, one becomes a revolutionary; if one does not know oneself, one becomes a slave.[28]

KIM JONG IL

The fool says in his heart, "There is no God." They are corrupt, and their ways are vile; there is no one who does good.

PSALM 53:1

According to Juche, the inner man is a matter-energy-chance concept of reality that is limited to the present life and this life's deeds. Though shamanism and other spiritist practices were known in North Korea before the end of World War II, this belief system has been replaced in entirety by over 50 years of intense religious indoctrination that denies the existence of an afterlife. The following excerpt from an interview with Li Yang Su, Vice Editor-in-Chief of the *Korean Central News Agency*, provides an illustration:

> *Question:* Within the philosophy of Juche, are the faithful followers of Juche and the Korean Workers' Party thought to have an eternal spirit after they die?
> *Answer:* Well, if human being dies, it's all. But, as you know, [the] great musician Beethoven died many years ago. But people of the world everyday play his great works. So his spirit is eternal. Physically everyone dies, but his exploit or deed remains forever. You may understand "eternal spirit" like so.[29]

Dr. Pak Song Duk, a professor at Pyongyang's Social Science Institute's Juche Idea Division, provides an explanation that clarifies the limited Juche concept of eternity:

> The source of the individual's life lies in the life of the

social community and the two lives are interlinked. Men, the social beings, are combined socially to form a social community and advance endlessly along the road of development from the old society to a new society. A man cannot live in isolation. He can only survive as a member of a social community. Irrespective of his subjective intention, a man is born and lives as a member of society that changes and develops endlessly. In this sense, the life of [the] social community is the individual's life.

The life of [the] social community is immortal, whereas an individual's life is limited. An individual's life is related to his life span whereas the life of [the] social community is related to the social community which undergoes constant socio-historical change and development. Social community is not an arithmetic sum total of [the] individual persons who formed it; it is an organic whole of many generations who enter social relations and carry them forward historically. Organic combination of individual lives gives birth to the life of a community with immortal vitality which is different from limited individual lives.

The Juche idea requires that man live and struggle with the collectivist view of life... *Therefore, although his life ends, his cause and exploits will be everlasting* with the continuation of the cause of his community and the community's love for, and trust in him, will remain forever in the hearts of the people from generation to generation. *This is the only true way to realize man's desire for immortality.*[30]

Thus, unlike the individual emphasis of Western atheism, Juche places a major cultural emphasis on the moral necessity for the collective will of the masses to follow the will of the Su-ryong and the Party. The Juche view of eternity is important to keep in mind when North Korean propaganda uses such words as "heaven," "eternity," "immortal," "spirit," and "hell-bent." When outsiders read or hear these words in North Korean propaganda, they must be careful to apply the limited Juche definition rather than a foreign "religionist" paradigm.

One of the Juche religion's problems with their limited theology of eternity is that it does not adequately deal with sin and the inner man. Instead, Juche focuses almost exclusively on controlling the thoughts and conduct of its adherents, while denying the fact that sin exists. For example, Professor Pak Song Duk comments:

The reality of our country eloquently proves that the socialist society alone is the most advantageous and vital society
in which people *know no social evil*, love and trust each other,
and advance, in single-hearted unity, towards a bright future.[31]

Yet, crucially, Juche's threefold denial of sin, God's existence,
and man's need to be redeemed by God means that the Juche
concept of man is also inadequate.

Through the Juche denial of God, who is the final reality,
Juche's materialistic concept of eternity is limited to what eternity is not. Likewise, the Juche concept of man is limited to what
man is not. According to Juche ideology, man is seen only as an
arrangement of molecules, made complex by chance. Instead of
seeing man as the Bible does—significant even in his sin—Juche
thinking reduces man to even less than his already finite existence. Since Juche's concept of man is mistaken, the North Korean concept of society and law is, by extension, mistaken.

Since memories, propaganda, monuments, and history record men's exploits, then, because memories fade, history can be
revised to make one's eternity into whatever the Su-ryong or the
Party wants it to be. Grasping this Juche concept of eternity helps
to explain the major emphasis on education, propaganda, and
monuments. Additionally, such an understanding helps explain
why North Koreans pray in the present tense for Kim Il Sung's immortality. Juche's hereafter is very much a present tense eternity.

The Bible devotes an entire book (Ecclesiastes) to the self-
reliant lifestyle's futility and inability to deal with the inner man.
The "live for today" mentality, notoriety, pride, luxury, wealth,
sex, and power associated with self-reliance are viewed as "a chas-
ing after the wind" (e.g., Ecclesiastes 4:16). Numerous compar-
isons can be made between the "vanity under the sun" worldview
presented in Ecclesiastes and the Juche religion under Kim Il
Sung, Juche's "eternal sun." In contrast, the Christian worldview
calls believers to live their lives on a higher plane, by faith, as citizens of heaven through spiritual rebirth in Jesus Christ.

The North Korean government's claim that, under Juche, there
is no crime problem in North Korea illustrates this policy of
denial. Admitting crime would admit the failure of Juche in the
same way that admitting that North Korea requires food aid
would. These shortcomings highlight the fallacy that a "paradise
on earth" has been achieved through comprehensive Juche "self-
reliance." However, many visitors who return from the standard

Pyongyang guided tour—including Christians—report that the people of North Korea are so "innocent." Unknowingly, they swallow part of the Juche lie. Even the American evangelist Dr. Billy Graham unwittingly remarked that he found "no crime" during his visit to Pyongyang. In sharp contrast, the members of North Korea's underground church claim that North Korea, itself, is a crime. In fact, "all have sinned and fall short of the glory of God" (Romans 3:23), even in North Korea. Yet, since Juche has no answer to the sin problem, sin under Juche officially does not exist.

Regardless of propaganda, the North Korean society must deal with the reality of sin even if they deny its existence. In 1866, the French agnostic writer Renan wrote, "If Rationalism wishes to govern the world without regard to the religious needs of the soul, the experience of the French Revolution is there to teach us the consequences of such a blunder." Alexander Solzhenitsyn echoed Renan's conclusion, while reflecting on how Soviet World War II war criminals were never punished. Solzhenitsyn pointed out the classical problem that arises in a totalitarian system when crimes go unpunished. He wrote, "From the most ancient times justice has been a two-part concept: virtue triumphs and vice is punished." Yet Solzhenitsyn concluded that in totalitarian Russia, "Young people are acquiring the conviction that foul deeds are never punished on earth, that they always bring prosperity." He added, "It is going to be uncomfortable, horrible, to live in such a country!" Everywhere the Communists have attained power, the story has been the same. Will and Ariel Durant, who collaborated to write the voluminous *Lessons of History*, concluded: "There is no significant example in history, before our time, of a society successfully maintaining moral life without the aid of religion."[32] North Korea, where there are few vestiges of moral restraint, is no exception. Under the Juche religion, nothing apart from raw power exists to deter crime.

North Korea's shattered economy and endemic starvation are driving the rate of crime steadily upward. One defector recently reported how more and more ordinary workers, farmers, and common people are being driven to crime:

> Mr. Kim [Hyong Tok] says, the impoverished state didn't always provide enough supplies, so he and his men raided farmers' homes for wood, cement and other materials needed to fulfill their work quotas. Mr. Kim's superiors turned a blind eye, until 1993, when he broke into the home of a senior

North Korean official and stole a Sony video camera and other valuables. Mr. Kim was given a 10-month sentence in a "re-education camp." He was subjected to hard labor with little food and regular beatings.[33]

Another report out of the underground church told of a case where a thief broke into the home of an underground church member. While stealing belongings, he found a Bible. The thief reported the family to local Party officials. The family was sent to a concentration camp to die while the thief received praise. Anyone caught possessing a Bible in North Korea is subject to a fifteen-year prison sentence in a reeducation (concentration) camp. Such examples illustrate the morally bankrupt nature of the Juche religion, which is sustained by calling evil good and good evil.

Widespread bribery is another symptom of the inability of the Juche religion to deal with the reality of sin. In order to survive, everyone in North Korea, regardless of class, is involved in some sort of money-making activity on the side. Bribery is a prevalent form of the corruption that permeates this society where fear of God is no longer a factor. It is particularly common for Party and other officials to unscrupulously abuse their power to extract bribes from ordinary people. For example, it generally requires a bribe of 300 to 400 *won* (Korean currency) to obtain a rail pass to travel outside one's village or town. Those who do not have a rail pass are fined. Even with a rail pass, one still runs the risk of being robbed of any food or other goods. Finally, one also may be robbed by the police themselves, who routinely tell their victims, "A commercial transaction is the first step to capitalism."[34]

With the collapse of the domestic economy, the value of foreign currency has risen dramatically. The official exchange rate of one U.S. dollar is 2.15 North Korean won. On the black market, where prices are generally ten times higher than government prices, the U.S. dollar exchanges for 70–100 won. Similarly, one Chinese won officially exchanges for 0.25 North Korean won, while on the black market it exchanges for 18–22 North Korean won. Given such noteworthy differences, it is not surprising that since the early 1990s, U.S. dollars have become the favorite bribery item among North Korea's populace.

In the past, those interacting with tourists and other foreign nationals used to pocket their U.S. dollars for personal use. For example, Jeremy Stone noted during a 1991 visit to Pyongyang:

Later that day, at a hard currency store large numbers of Koreans, as well as foreigners, were buying up foreign goods including short wave radios, which have been sold there since the store opened in 1986. Apparently, [only North] Koreans working abroad or getting foreign currency from foreign relatives can come there and, with no questions asked, purchase items not available on the open market. Consequently, the urban populations at least are not aware that North Korean goods are not the best in the world.[35]

However, now the foreign currency is used openly for trading within North Korea's black market economy. Bicycles, television sets, radios, refrigerators, sewing machines, tape recorders, electric cooking pots, and much more are bought and sold via the black market since they might not otherwise be available. The growing popularity of U.S. currency within North Korea's black market also suggests an independent cottage counterfeiting industry may exist in addition to probable government-sponsored counterfeiting operations.

The growing black market, in turn, has given rise to the evil of loan-sharking or usury. Usurers, who are able to take advantage of the expanded "foreign exchange earning businesses," prey upon their fellow countrymen by loaning money and, in return, exacting astronomical interest rates:

Usurers include mainly returnees from Japan who are able to obtain economic support from their relatives in Japan, and Chinese businessmen residing in North Korea. These people are reluctant to deposit their money in banks due to low interest rates and, moreover, because of difficulties in withdrawing money from banks on time. Those who borrow money are North Korean businessmen engaged in "foreign exchange earning businesses" and they use the debt at the interest rate of 10 to 20% a month.[36]

North Koreans' false pride is another symptom of the inability of Juche to adequately deal with the sin problem of inner man. One example of this pride (coupled with paranoia and suspicion) is the North's cancellation of shipments of free food, in 1997, to their starving nation if the shipping was "off schedule." Another example of this misplaced pride occurred in 1991 when United Nations and Western experts in rice growing, soil, tidal land reclamation, and computer-integrated circuit technology approached North Koreans to share information. Conversations gave the foreign experts the impression that the North Koreans naively thought that Juche methods were more advanced in each of these areas than in the rest of the world. Even when North Koreans do recognize foreign technology as more advanced, they somehow reject the decidedly non-Juche use of it on the basis that it is the "common property of mankind." False pride also shows forth in North Korean officials as they maintain, despite widespread famine and hardship, that North Korea is satisfying the basic needs of the populace and that "there is no serious malnutrition even in rural areas."

The growth in the acceptability of divorce is another symptom of the moral decline of North Korea. Before Juche, most marriages in North Korea were arranged and divorce was extremely rare. Now, a growing number of Koreans choose their own mates. Simultaneously, Juche teachings have superseded previous Korean cultural traditions that viewed divorce as a disgrace. The result is that North Korea's divorce rate is steadily growing, particularly among the educated urban "core" group.

Under Juche, however, such changes cannot be acknowledged. One example of this "see-no-evil, hear-no-evil, speak-no-evil" stance is the reaction of a Pyongyang television executive when, in 1994, journalist Dan Wooding showed him a Christian video of a couple who experienced marital problems, divorced, and later reconciled and remarried. The North Korean executive responded:

> We couldn't show that in our country. We have no divorce
> or problems in our country. We believe that the family is like
> a cell.[37]

The Juche religion's ongoing inadequacy in dealing with the sin problem of the inner man highlights its fundamentally flawed man-centered theology. Apart from the self-government that arises from fear of and faith in one true God, North Korea is unable to sustain a society whose citizens are capable of governing themselves in a righteous manner. Totalitarian works-based righteousness, even to the glory of Kim Jong Il, can never satisfy the deepest heartfelt needs of the inner man. However, the gospel of Jesus Christ does adequately address the fundamental spiritual need of North Koreans. As a result, the Church has been Juche's spiritual nemesis from Juche's inception.

Use of Other Religions to Promote Juche

No one may use religion as a means by which to drag in foreign powers or to destroy the state or social order.[38]

ARTICLE 68,
DPRK CONSTITUTION
(1992 REVISION)

Although religious freedom is technically guaranteed by the North Korean government, non-Juche religious activity is strongly discouraged. In fact, under Juche, the terms "religion" and "religionist" tend to be exclusively used in either a condescending or derogatory sense in state-censored literature. Given the negative meanings of these words, North Korean officials, quite understandably, might object to Juche being called a "religion." A token amount of non-Juche religious activity is officially permitted by the North Korean government. This activity is allowed both for its propaganda value in bolstering Juche reunification efforts and to advertise to the outside world that North Korea has freedom of religion. Religions that are permitted such token representation include Buddhism, Chondokyo, Confucianism, and Christianity.

In one sense, the imposition of the Juche religion upon North Korea's masses represents a radical departure from the Korea of a half-century earlier. Before World War II, Koreans were traditionally pragmatic and eclectic in their religious practices. Their religious outlook was not conditioned by a single, exclusive faith but by a combination of indigenous beliefs and creeds, such as Confucianism, Taoism, and Buddhism. In another sense, the strong degree to which religion has always been an intrinsic part of the Korean people's culture helps to explain why Kim Il Sung's regime needed to create a surrogate religious system. History shows that Koreans have always believed in a world inhabited by spirits. Thus, traditional Communist atheism did not fit Korea's situation. The high degree to which religion was embedded into pre-World War Korean culture helps to explain both the creation of Juche and its incorporation of selected Confucian, Buddhist, and Christian themes.

Unlike non-totalitarian societies, North Korea's Constitution does not provide the force of law. Most North Koreans have never heard of it or read it. Despite the Constitution's limited application, a brief look at North Korea's changing constitutional provisions for non-Juche religions serves to highlight both its internal contradictions and stark contrast with reality. According to Article 14 of the 1948 Constitution, "Citizens of the Democratic People's Republic of Korea shall have the freedom of religious belief and of conducting religious services." However Article 54 of the 1972 Constitution stated, "Citizens have religious liberty and the freedom to oppose religion" (also translated as "the freedom of anti-religious propaganda"). In the 1992 Constitution, Article 68 grants freedom of religious belief and guarantees the right to construct buildings for religious use and religious ceremonies. The article also protects the Juche religion by stating, "No one may use religion as a means by which to drag in foreign powers or to destroy the state or social order."[39]

Some observers argued that the 1972 constitutional provision for persecuting other religions occurred because political authorities thought they no longer needed the support of the much-weakened organized religions. Already, in the decades leading up to 1972, Kim Il Sung's regime had killed nearly 200,000 Christians alone and declared that all Christians had been wiped out. So this constitutional update might be more correctly viewed as an after-the-fact provision to legalize the persecution that had already been occurring for decades.

Over the last five decades, many of the existing churches and temples not destroyed during the Japanese occupation have been taken over by the state and converted to secular use. Under the Juche system, some of these sites have been designated as "national treasures" to appreciate the creative energies of the Korean people in the past. Two such sites are the Buddhist temples located at Kumgang-san and Myohyang-san.

For all of the isolation associated with the Hermit Kingdom, Pyongyang has gone to great lengths to attempt to dupe visitors and sway world opinion about the extent of its blatantly anti-Christian Juche religion. Over the years, North Korea has created and continued to allow token religious organizations such as the Korean Buddhists' Federation, the Korean Christian Federation, and the Chondokyo Youth Party to promote the Juche reunification effort and present the international community with the illusion of religious freedom through limited domestic and international activities.

For example, discussion at a March 1998 meeting of the Korean Religionist Association primarily focused on promoting the

Juche national reunification agenda. The topics included enlisting the support of South Korean religious groups to reject "domination and interference by outside forces" and denounce South Korea's "National Security Law" and "Agency for National Security Planning." There was absolutely no mention whatsoever in the North Korean press of any spiritual discussion at this "religionist" conference [*KCNA*].

None of these government-sanctioned "religionist" groups have ever proclaimed that there is any authority higher than Kim Il Sung and now Kim Jong Il. In fact, every government-sanctioned religious leader within North Korea is first screened for adherence to Juche religious ideology (including national reunification) and primary allegiance to the Su-ryong. In the pages that follow, we will consider the present religionist role of Buddhism, Chondokyo, Confucianism, and Christianity under Juche.

Buddhism

Buddhism is a superstitious and false doctrine designed to paralyze the people's class consciousness and to protect the interests of the ruling class.[40]

THE HISTORY OF KOREA
(NORTH KOREAN TEXTBOOK)

Buddhism roots in Korea date back to its introduction from China around the fourth century. The Buddhist religion dominated Korea during the Silla Dynasty (668–935) and reached its height under the Koryo Dynasty (918–1392). Afterwards, Buddhism suffered a decline. To some extent, Buddhists were even persecuted during the Chosun Dynasty. The combination of the Japanese occupation, allied bombing, severe anti-Buddhist religious persecution, and two generations of Juche indoctrination have significantly reduced Buddhism's influence on North Koreans.

North Korea has significantly reduced or eliminated the practice of Buddhism by subordinating the weakened Buddhist adherents under the Juche faith. Only a token number of Buddhist temples are permitted to emphasize Juche's respect for Korea's ancient historical roots. The Korean Buddhists' Federation, like those for Chondokyo and Christianity, serves to provide a endorsement by "religionists" for Kim Jong Il's sacred Juche cause of national reunification. However, one would be mistaken to think of North Korean Buddhism as equivalent to the traditional Buddhism practiced in lands such as Thailand. Buddhist monks are not allowed to worship at North Korean Buddhist temples and one Buddhist "monk," upon questioning, could not even name Buddha's birthday (May 14). Instead, Pyongyang's surrogate form of Buddhism serves as a front to promote the Juche program for national reunification.

For example, in 1997, the propaganda newspaper *Rodong Sinmun* released a statement by the Chairman of the Central Committee of the Korean Buddhist Federation in support of Secretary Kim Jong Il's work "Let Us Carry Out the Great Leader Comrade Kim Il Sung's Instructions for National Reunification." This statement by the nation's leading Buddhist describes Kim Jong Il's essay as *"a great scripture* for reunification the Buddhists should regard as *a guideline"* [*KCNA*]. Another 1998 propaganda release also shows how Buddhist worship in North Korea, as with all religions other than Juche, must focus on national reunification:

> *Buddhists* held masses on *Jan. 6* to mark the day of Buddha's attainment of great wisdom at temples across the country. The speakers at the masses expressed their firm will to redouble efforts for the sacred cause of *national reunification* ...to further strengthen unity and solidarity with the Buddhists in South Korea and abroad. They expressed the belief that the country will be certainly reunified as it is led by General Kim Jong Il, the great sun of the nation. They evinced their vows to vigorously advance [and] to *speed up the day of reunification* [*KCNA*].

Like Christianity, unchecked Buddhism represents a spiritual threat to the religion of Juche. Buddhists believe in transcendent principles of good and evil and practice spiritual worship of someone other than the Su-ryong. In contrast, Juche teaches that the determination of what is good and evil is up to the Su-ryong, who is unquestionably gifted with such great intelligence that it surpasses that of the Party, the masses, and Buddha. Also, Kim Jong Il's Buddhist leader teaches that Buddhists should work to promote Kim Jong Il's "earthly paradise" [*KCNA*] whereas Buddha taught that one should be more concerned with the afterlife.

As with the state-sponsored puppet Christian Church, a token amount of Buddhism is also permitted. This includes the establishment of an academy and some Buddhist temples which are allowed to conduct religious services. Other Juche-approved concessions to Buddhists include the publication of a twenty-five-volume translation of the Korean *Tripitaka*, or Buddhist scriptures. These scriptures had been carved on 80,000 wooden blocks stored at central North Korea's Myohyang-san temple. However, the primary purpose for the tolerance of the limited practice of Buddhism is to support the sacred Juche cause of national reunification.

Two significant links between Juche and Buddhist teachings are the concepts of ancestor veneration and of a spirit-enlightened man. Elaborate rituals of ancestor veneration, originating with Confucianism and Buddhism, have played an important part in the traditional religious life of Koreans. Aside from these links, Buddhist spiritual concepts have been replaced with Kim Il Sung-ism and Kim Jong Il-ism. Traditional Korean Buddhist and neo-Confucian philosophers developed concepts of the spirit world, the cosmos, and humanity's place in it. These concepts were fundamentally religious rather than philosophical. Pyongyang's concerted efforts have uprooted most of these indigenous animist beliefs. By the early 1990s, the practices of shamanism and fortune-telling seem to have all but disappeared.

Kim Jong Il's highly advertised three-year mourning period (later extended to four years) after Kim Il Sung's 1994 death suggests that ancestor veneration has been incorporated into Juche. Likewise, numerous propaganda that attributes clairvoyant powers, special wisdom, and enlightenment to Kim Jong Il present him as a modern surrogate Buddha of sorts. Similarly, the *Korean Central News Agency*'s characterization of Kim Il Sung being an immortal and eternal spiritual father, in conjunction with regular worship at his statue, frequently casts the former dictator in this surrogate Buddha role as well. However, the Juche religion's practice of borrowing ideas from, and attempting control of, other religions is not limited to Buddhism.

Chondokyo

I will devote myself to the sacred cause of national reunification, remaining loyal to him [Kim Jong Il].

O IK JE
(CHONDOKYO LEADER WHO DEFECTED
FROM THE SOUTH TO THE NORTH IN 1997)
KOREA CENTRAL NEWS AGENCY

Chondokyo (also translated Chondoism, Chondonism, Chundogyo, and Ch'ndogyo), "the religion of the heavenly way," is another competing religious movement that North Korea's leaders have attempted to control and reinvent to suit the needs of the Juche religious system. Chondokyo is a Korean syncretistic religion that emerged from the Tonghak (Eastern Learning) Movement of the mid to late 1800s. It draws from the teachings of shamanism, Buddhism, Taoism, Confucianism, and Catholicism to emphasize the divine nature of all people.

Recent North Korean propaganda have highlighted the 1997 defection of O Ik Je (leader of the Chondoist movement in South

The great leader President Kim Il Sung inspects the renovated Tomb of King Tongmyong.

The *"Monument to the Renovated Tomb of King Tongmyong"* bearing the handwriting of the great leader President Kim Il Sung.

Korea) to North Korea. *Korean Central News Agency* accounts have included the presentation of O Ik Je with the "National Flag First Class" (a high award), proclaimed his concurrence with the Juche agenda for national reunification, and noted that he paid homage to the great leader through speeches, praise, and gifts. North Korea had already heavily publicized the alleged discovery of Tangun's tomb and skeletal remains in September 1993. However, O Ik Je's 1997 defection became the propaganda bonanza that added impetus to Pyongyang's effort to show that the truest Chondoists should give preeminence to Juche, which emphasizes the divine nature of Kim Jong Il. Kim Jong Il had succeeded in persuading O Ik Je to proclaim him to be the modern leader who will restore the ancient Tangun nation of Chondokyo. In return, O Ik Je has been given positions, titles, and privileges within North Korea's elite in return for portraying Chondokyo as being naturally subordinate to Kim Jong Il and the Juche religion, including the recent deification of Kim Jong Suk.

Kim Il Sung and Kim Jong Il's control of Chondokyo now seems so complete that the native religion seems to be tolerated as an ancient form of the Juche religion. For example, on February 11, 1998, O Ik Je stated in a letter to Kim Jong Il:

> With the soul of the nation, General Kim Jong Il enhanced the dignity of the independent state and wisdom of the Korean nation as high as Mt. Paektu, as wished by President Kim Il Sung. Though only six months have passed since I settled in the north, now I can tell the rightness from the wrongness in the history of nation. *Here, only in the north, are the holy land of the Tangun nation and the orthodoxy of the nation* [*KCNA*].

The subversion of Chondokyo serves to build the sense of Kim Jong Il's legitimacy by enabling him to take on both the new title "the great leader of the Tangun nation" and the aura of Korea's more recent 10th century Koryo kings.

Artist's sketch of the plan for the restored Tomb of Tangun.

After the North Koreans completing the restoration of the tomb of Tangun, the North held a great "National Foundation Day" celebration in Pyongyang on October 3, 1997. After this event, Kim Jong Il sent a letter to Ahn Ho Sang, head of Daejonggyo (a religious group in the South that upholds Tangun), asking him to collaborate with the North to achieve national reunification.

These national reunification overtures to indigenous Korean religious groups help to explain why Kim Il Sung and Kim Jong Il have refurbished Korea's archeological sites from the Tangun era, such as the Tangun monument and the royal burial mounds of the Koryo kings. For example, 1998 New Years propaganda postcards distributed throughout South Korea featured:

> ...a picture of President Kim Il Sung with a bright smile on the face against the background of the Kumsusan Memorial Palace and written under it were the red letters *"President Kim Il Sung is the eternal sun of Juche produced by the Tangun nation. Let us all pray for the immortality of President Kim Il Sung in humble reverence"* [*KCNA*].

Thus, Kim Jong Il continues to use elements of Chondokyo beliefs to legitimize both the worship of Kim Il Sung's statue, and the worship of himself as the ruler of the modern reunified communized Koryo Republic (Democratic Confederal Republic of Koryo) and the modern Tangun nation.

Confucianism

The traditional Confucian five relationships in the North were... [transformed] into one relationship, Kim, as Confucian father-ruler exemplar at the top and the people as children loyal to him at the bottom.[41]

DR. THOMAS HOSUCK KANG
PRESIDENT, CENTER FOR DAO-CONFUCIANISM

The Juche religion is a significant departure from the Korean people's strong adherence to the teachings of the Chinese philosopher Confucius (555–479 B.C.). Juche doctrine maintains that Juche is superior to all other systems of human thought, including Marxism and Confucianism. Juche anti-Confucian policies and propaganda have reduced Confucian influence on North Koreans over the last few decades. Unlike Buddhism,

Chondokyo, and Christianity, there does not seem to be an official North Korean Confucianism organization. Nevertheless, some Confucian teachings, such as those that emphasize subservience to authority and social harmony, have been adopted by the Juche religion to add to its legitimacy.

No detailed determination has been made of the full extent to which Juche has changed Confucian values of the Chosun Dynasty. Opportunities for observing everyday life in North Korea remain extremely limited by the government's highly restrictive regimen of "revolutionary tourism." Revolutionary tourism requires that those few people allowed to visit the country generally are taken on scripted tours of monuments to Kim Il Sung, revolutionary theatrical performances, model farms and factories, modern apartment complexes, and scenic splendor. Virtually no opportunity exists for private one-on-one conversations to hear what people really think or feel. Despite these limitations, various sources including essays, speeches, and propaganda provide some valuable insights into the selective censorship of Confucian values under the Juche religious system.

One of the notable signs of Confucian influence is the clear male dominance within Korean society. The Korean family focuses on the male to the extent that sons are more valued than daughters. There is a clear hierarchy by age in the Korean family. Moreover, there is great respect and care for elders within the Korean culture. Respect for parents and ancestors is paramount since Koreans traditionally believe they owe their parents everything.

If you take North Korean propaganda at face value, North Korea's press leads one to believe that the present Juche regime values its Confucian heritage. For example, one article stated that Koryo Songgyungwan University's ancient curriculum of Confucianism, criminal jurisprudence, arithmetic, and writing remains unchanged after six centuries [KCNA]. However, significant evidence does exist that the systematic Juche education system has resulted in major changes in how the average North Korean thinks.

Juche indoctrination has made strenuous efforts to replace thought patterns typical to Confucianism that might threaten the Juche totalitarian system. Over the last five decades, Confucianism has been officially condemned as a philosophy because of its counter-Juche history of class exploitation and cultural subservience to a foreign state. For example, all North Korean youths are instructed by school teachers to turn their parents in to the state

Juche propaganda portrays Kim Il Sung as the surrogate Confucian-like "Father to the People."

for reeducation (a death sentence in a concentration camp) if they practice religious beliefs other than Juche. Such teachings promote loyalty to the state while serving to eradicate the Confucian principle of filial loyalty to the parents. One book written to North Korea's youth by Kim Jong Il even states, "Young people should become the faithful, filial sons and daughters of the Party and the leader (Su-ryong)."[42]

The Juche education system of brainwashing, which begins at the preschool level, systematically replaces allegiance to family with allegiance to the Party and the leader. Meanwhile, parents, who typically have heavy work schedules, have only a limited amount of time to spend with children. Thus, from an early age, parental authority is subordinated to that of the state and the Party representatives. To be sure, some degree of filial piety remains in contemporary North Korea culture. For example, the state-controlled media teaches children to respect their parents. There is no doubt that, under Juche, such family loyalty now clearly plays a secondary role compared to loyalty to the state and Kim Jong Il.

At the same time, those aspects of Confucian thinking that facilitate Juche have been retained and incorporated into the Juche religion by the Pyongyang regime. Retained aspects of Confucianism include its more authoritarian and hierarchical themes. These themes have been transformed to serve as a means to make the population more receptive to the Juche personality cult of Kim Il Sung and Kim Jong Il. Another example of a Confucian principle that has been approved by Juche is the emphasis on social harmony.

Additionally, the Juche mythology surrounding the Kims has carefully incorporated traditional Confucian virtues in an effort to bolster the legitimacy and appeal of Juche to Koreans. This quasi-Confucian Juche teaching that the ruler is divinely benevolent is evident in state propaganda:

- Kim Il Sung *warmed his mother's frozen hands every winter day* after she returned from work...he gave up the childhood joy of playing on a swing to avoid possibly tearing his pants and making more work for his mother. As a youngster, he always responded by running, bowing and waiting for instructions whenever a parent or other adult called for him.

- When Kim Jong Il was five, *he faithfully guarded his father from evil imperialists* with a toy wooden rifle at a secret revolutionary camp on Mt. Paektu.

- Kim Jong Il personally arranged for life-style improvements for lighthouse keepers and their families on a remote island... [who] shed tears of gratitude to the Secretary for *his warmhearted care for them*" [*DPRK*].

- Kim Jong Il ordered workers to build a "bridge of love," in a remote area in order to allow thirteen children to cross a river so they could go to school. Propaganda emphasized that the bridge had absolutely "no economic merit."[43]

North Koreans are taught that they owe a debt of gratitude for such benevolence and that Confucianism teaches they must repay that benevolence with unquestioning loyalty and devotion to Kim Jong Il.

Christianity

But they [the Jews] shouted, "Take him away! Take him away! Crucify him!" "Shall I crucify your king?" Pilate asked. "We have no king but Caesar," the chief priests answered. Finally Pilate handed him over to them to be crucified.

JOHN 19:15,16

Since the unrestrained practice of true Christianity would result in the downfall of the false religion of Juche, North Korea permits only enough of a facade of Christianity to perpetuate the myth of religious tolerance and to further the Juche cause of national reunification. The government-approved Korean Christian Federation (KCF) presents itself as the presiding body representing "North Korea's Protestant and Catholic churches." However, their obeisance to Kim Il Sung as God constitutes pagan idolatry according to the Bible. Meanwhile, North Korea's true believers in Jesus Christ continue to be hunted down, sent to concentration camps, and killed.

Pongsu Church is one of three Pyongyang puppet churches built to propagate the myth of North Korea's religious tolerance.

It would be presumptuous to claim that everyone in North Korea's official Christian church was apostate. However, it is certainly an accurate observation that North Korea's Christian organization was created and exists to promote the Juche agenda, not the kingdom of God.

The following excerpt from a North Korean propaganda piece posted on the Internet illustrates the function of the Korean Christian Federation (KCF).

Question: What is the main work of the Korean Christian Federation?

Answer: *The most important task of the federation is to lead Korean Christians to work for the construction and reunification of our country.* In order to promote the reunification, we maintain close relations with many organizations including the World Council of Churches and Christian associations in foreign countries to ensure their support for the peaceful reunification of the Korea Peninsula. As the solidarity of the whole nation is the only way to realize a lasting peace in our country, Christians in north and south Korea and overseas should be united first.[44]

The above question and answer, and others like them, were provided by Hwang Shi Chon and Kim Nam Hyok, Director of the International Department and Deputy Director of the Organizational Department, respectively, of the KCF's Central Committee. Other questions and answers served to convince inquirers that freedom of religion to practice Christianity exists in North Korea as it does in many other nations in the world.

Even the Korean Christian Federation's own brochure states that the organization really serves as a political organ of the state. Consider the following excerpt:

> [The] Korean Christian Federation was founded on November 28, 1946 in Pyongyang. It has set it as its programme to endeavor for the prosperity of the country with patriotism upholding the constitution and the policy of the Republic government...It makes positive efforts to educate Christians in national independent consciousness [Juche] and patriotism and to promote the socialist construction and *national reunification.*[45]

The following *Korean Central News Agency* bulletin further illustrates the KCF's apostate nature and Juche religious goals (national reunification):

> *"Even Christians worship Kim Jong Il as God."* Chairman Kang Yong Sop of the Central Committee of the Korean Christian Federation Monday released a statement in support of Secretary Kim Jong Il...The religionists are determined to turnout as one in a *sacred struggle for reunifying the country* in hearty response to the noble patriotic intention of the General with firm belief that he is identical to President Kim Il Sung and is *god of the Korean nation,* he said. To the Christians, *his work is a great bible* which indicates the way of *saving the nation,* the path of *national reunification...*All the Christians in the northern half of Korea will regard the General's idea and line concerning *national reunification as the great bible*

and strengthen the activities for solidarity with the Christians in south Korea and abroad to achieve great national unity and to reunify the country under the banner [*KCNA*].

The North Korean "official" church's replacement of the gospel of Jesus Christ with the counterfeit gospel of national reunification under Juche is reminiscent of the error of many German churchmen in the 1930s who confused political salvation in this world for salvation in an unseen life to come. For example, in early 1934, Julius Leutherser, one of the many duped pro-Nazi German pastors, proclaimed:

> Christ has come to us through Hitler...through his honesty, his faith and his idealism, the Redeemer found us...we know today the Savior has come...we have only one task, be German not Christian.[46]

As with other religious official religious organizations that are permitted by the state, government-sanctioned "Christian" church services have absolutely nothing to do with promoting the gospel of Jesus Christ or preaching from the Bible. Instead, the three puppet churches serve as an arm of the totalitarian state to promote the national reunification agenda of the Juche religion. For example, below is a propaganda press release describing the Christmas Day, 1997, worship services at Pyongyang's Pongsu Church:

> *"Christmas Marked"*: Christians here worshipped on Dec. 25 to mark Christmas Day at Pongsu Church. Visiting overseas compatriots and foreign believers joined them. Chief priest Ri Song Bong in his sermon said that the way out for the Korean nation suffering from national division for over 50 years is to put an end to the division of the nation and reunify the country. He stressed that they should further strengthen contacts, dialogue and solidarity of Christians in the north, south and abroad to realize reunification by means of confederacy with the great unity of the whole nation based on patriotism and the spirit of national independence... Christmas services were held across the country [*KCNA*].

Note also the policy of presenting an air of normality in the above news bulletin's announcement that "Christmas services were held across the country." Such a statement is patently false. Meanwhile, anti-Christian persecution continues unabated.[47]

Despite their open support for the supremacy of Juche and idolatrous worship of Kim Jong Il and the deceased Kim Il Sung, North Korean KCF representatives at overseas conferences continue to claim that there is no contradiction between Christian beliefs and the veneration of the Great Leader or Juche philosophy. Some compare this compromise with idolatry to that of the larger Japanese Christian community before and during World War II. During that era, the Japanese Christian community officially acknowledged the divine status of the emperor. However, the comparison is not necessarily valid, since the KCF was founded in 1945 as a counterfeit Christian organization to further the ends of the Communist revolution in North Korea.

In the late 1980s, it became apparent that North Korea was beginning to use the Christian religion to establish contacts with Christians in South Korea and the West. Such contacts were deemed useful for promoting the regime's Juche agenda, with particular emphasis on national reunification. In 1988 the state built the Protestant Pongsu Church and the Catholic Changchung Cathedral in Pyongyang. In June of the same year, a new association of Roman Catholics was established. In October 1988, Roman Catholic Church papal representatives were invited to attend the opening of the Changchung Cathedral. Despite North Korea's refusal to let Rome's leadership have any official oversight over the Changchung Cathedral, North Korea did send two North Korean novice priests to study in Rome. More recently, on December 22, 1992, the government erected North Korea's third church, the Chil Gol Church, as a religious monument to Kim Il Sung's mother, Kang Ban Sok. In Kim Il Sung's youth, Kang Ban Sok was a Christian deaconess and her father, Kang Don Uk, was a Christian elder at the original Chil Gol Church which had been destroyed long ago.

Though Pyongyang's KCF "Christian" clergy are scrutinized for primary loyalty to Kim Jong Il, many of the laity at Pyongyang's three churches may very well be bona fide believers. A "Catholic" priest at the Changchung Cathedral told a visitor:

> To build the church had cost 300,000 won of which 100,000 had been a loan from [the] Government. [In other words, about 200 families had put up a year's income each.][48]

With such an allegedly high degree of involvement by the laity in financing the building, one might conclude that Pyongyang had a committed Christian community. However, given North Korea's ongoing campaign to exterminate all Christians, applying a Western church-building paradigm to this situation in a totalitarian state may lead to a dubious conclusion.

In November 1988, KCF representatives held an International Seminar of Christians of the North and South for the Peace and Reunification of Korea in Switzerland. The following year, a North Korean Protestant pastor attended a meeting of the National Council of Churches in Washington, D.C. There, he reported that his country had 10,000 Protestants and 1,000 Catholics who worship in 500 home churches. Eight years later, 1997 propaganda set the figure at 30,000. However, in a Juche system where statistics can be manufactured out of thin air, such numbers are entirely meaningless. Only the most naive observer would conclude that North Korea's anti-Christian government would willingly agree to a threefold increase in Christianity.

In both 1992 and 1994, evangelist Billy Graham visited North Korea. He met with then dictator Kim Il Sung, toured monuments, and was permitted to preach to selected audiences at the state churches and an auditorium at Kim Il Sung University. North Korea's limited openness to Billy Graham may have been due, in part, to Graham's wife, Ruth Bell Graham. In 1932, Ruth had attended the Pyongyang Foreign School, a Christian school in Pyongyang. The school was shut down in 1940 during the Japanese occupation of Korea. While the Great Leader declined to receive Jesus Christ as his personal Savior in private, the North Korean press used the occasion to demonstrate publicly the Great Leader's "openness" to Christianity.

Any appearances of state-sanctioned Christianity remain as a cultural facade to fool international observers. North Korean officials desire tourists and visitors to depart Pyongyang with the image of genuine churchgoing religiosity, that many expect to see, indelibly imprinted in their memories. However, the thin veneer is fairly easy to detect. For example, one recent American visitor made some interesting observations when he attended both Catholic and Protestant church services during his stay. Signs that these services were staged for tourists and visitors included the Bibles in the pews being brand new and the Pyongyang churchgoers being unfamiliar with their hymnals. Moreover, many of the same people who attended the "Catholic" church also filled the pews at the "Protestant" church service. They were actors.

Another source confirms that those in the pews of the "Christian churches" are drafted and coached into acting like regular churchgoers. Despite such appearances, there are no regular weekly services at these churches. Instead, church doors are opened for scheduled visits by outsiders and for state purposes only. Also, "churchgoer" actors are not allowed to attend too many such services, particularly "when state officials detect genuine tears in their eyes."[49]

CHAPTER 4

Juche's Spiritual Archenemy: The Church

It has been reported that Christians are persecuted in North Korea. The fact is the contrary. A Christian minister saved Kim Il Sung's life and Kim was always respectful to Christianity. Kim read the Bible in prison.[1]

LEE WHA RANG

Religion is superstition. All the religions, be they Christianity or Buddhism, belong in essence to the same superstition. Historically, religion has always been the tool of the ruling class who want to deceive, suppress and exploit the working class for the benefit of their interests. In the modern age, the imperialists have been using religion as an ideological tool to invade the underdeveloped countries.[2]

KIM IL SUNG

Despite a steady stream of propaganda to the contrary (such as above), the Church remains Juche's spiritual archenemy. The word "archenemy" here is intended in a spiritual context, not a political one. However, from a North Korean Juche worldview, where political and spiritual practices have been inseparably linked, the Church is a political enemy of the state as well as a spiritual one.

In sharp contrast to Juche, the Christian worldview distinguishes between the spiritual kingdom of God and the political kingdoms of this world. Jesus taught his disciples to worship God alone, proclaim the gospel, obey God's Word, love their enemies, abstain from idolatry, feed the hungry, and love those that hate and persecute them.

These conflicting agendas have resulted in both the accommodation of humanitarian aid by Pyongyang and the ongoing war against the true Christian Church, driving it "underground" (into hiding). The war against the Church continues in North Korea because of the many true Christians who would rather accept crowns of martyrdom than ever bow to worship the Juche gods of Kim Il Sung and Kim Jong Il. Despite Juche's anti-Christian theology, many international Christian groups view North Korea's starving masses as those who need Jesus' compassion. At the same time, Christians, particularly in South Korea, are engaged in concerted prayer against the evil that dominates North Korea's spiritual life. Other international groups are engaged in the risky business of providing underground believers in North Korea with spiritual food in the form of smuggled Scriptures.

The War Against the Church

If power is combined with trust, we can overcome even Heaven.[3]

KIM JONG IL

From its birth to the present, there has been an ongoing war against the North Korean church. The following discussion provides highlights of events leading up to its birth, persecution and compromise under the Japanese occupation, and North Korea's ongoing war against the church.

Forerunners of the Indigenous Church (1628–1866)

Dutch seamen made the first Protestant Christian contact with Korea in the seventeenth century. In 1628, three sailors, all members of the Dutch Reformed Church, were shipwrecked on the Korean coast and made the country their home. In 1653, another Dutch ship, *Sparrow Hawk*, shipwrecked on Cheju Island in southern Korea. Twenty-eight of the sixty-four crewmen drowned; the thirty-six survivors were captured by island authorities and sent to Seoul and elsewhere in southwestern Korea. In 1666, eight of the captives escaped after a fourteen-year imprisonment. Though there are no documented conversions of Koreans to Christianity from these contacts, one may infer from the writings of Hendrik Hamel, the *Sparrow Hawk*'s bookkeeper, that Koreans likely took note of Christianity. Hamel's 1668 book, *An Account of the Shipwreck of a Dutch Vessel off the Coast of Qelpart, Together with a Description of the Kingdom of Corea*, also introduced Western Christians to the existence of this far-off land.

In 1784, Korean scholar Yi Sung Hun converted to Roman Catholicism while studying in Peking (Beijing). In 1785, the same year the first Roman Catholic missionary entered Korea, King Chongjo outlawed Christianity. Nevertheless, in 1794, the first Catholic priest arrived in Korea. Despite harsh persecution of Roman Catholics that began in 1801, the Catholic Church steadily grew to about 23,000. In light of neighboring China's experience with Western powers, Korean leaders generally formed a negative impression of Westerners and opposition to Korean Catholics continued throughout the rest of the century.

The next Protestant contact with Korea occurred in 1832, when German missionary Reverend Karl Gutzlaff came to Korea while serving as interpreter for the British ship *Lord Amherst*. The Korean royal court refused to enter into a commercial trade agreement with England. Though Gutzlaff did not document any conversions during his month-long stay, he did give the Koreans some tracts and a Chinese translation of the Bible he had obtained from Robert Morrison, the first Protestant missionary to China. As Gutzlaff departed Korea, he wrote:

> In the great plan of the eternal God, there will be a time of merciful visitation for them. While we look for this, we ought to be very anxious to hasten its approach by diffusing the glorious doctrine of the cross by all means in our power …The Scripture teaches us to believe that God can bless even these feeble beginnings. Let us hope that better days will soon dawn for Corea.[4]

In 1860, Taesinsa founded the militaristic and anti-Western Tonghak, or "Eastern Learning," movement that espoused agrarian reform, equal rights for all, and man as God. Then, in 1863, amid such prevalent anti-Western sentiment, Taewn Gun (also translated Taewongun and Taewon-gun), the regent and father of the Yi Dynasty's then boy-king, Kojong, prohibited the propagation of Christianity. Taewn Gun instituted a hard-line closed-door policy that effectively isolated Korea from the outside world. These edicts were accompanied by the Korean regent decreeing the eradication of all Catholics. Over 8,000 converts and nine French priests were executed. This harsh persecution virtually obliterated the Korean Catholic Church.

As a result of Taewn Gun's massacre of Catholics, France sent their Indochina squadron, under the command of Admiral Pierre G. Roze, to Korea's western coast off of Kanghwa Island at the mouth of the Han River. On October 13, 1866, French troops landed on the island. However after capturing a fort, their landing party was repulsed by Korean forces, and the French fleet withdrew. Several years later, a U.S. Marine Corps officer wrote:

> The French came three years ago to avenge their priests, who had been murdered, when they skinned a French doctor, and crucified him on the beach under the eyes of the Frenchmen who had been driven off, and who were unable to help their friends.[5]

Taewn Gun considered the French withdrawal a Korean victory. Following the failures of the American *General Sherman* (described later) and the French punitive naval expedition attempts to "open" Korea, the Choson regent had stone tablets erected throughout Korea that warned:

> The barbarians from beyond the seas have violated our borders and invaded our land. If we do not fight we must make treaties with them. Those who favor making a treaty sell their country.[6]

These "successes" encouraged Taewn Gun to think that he could hold out indefinitely against external pressure. Korea closed its borders and resisted all foreigners. Thus, Korea came to be known as the "Hermit Kingdom."

Amid this anti-Western sentiment within Korea, Western powers, including the British, Russians, and Prussians, continued to insist that the Choson Dynasty enter into commercial relations with them. For example, in 1866, the Prussian merchant Ernest J. Oppert twice requested trade with Korea, but was refused.

Probably the most notorious of these attempts to establish trade was the infamous *General Sherman* incident, which occurred near Pyongyang during August and September of 1866. In August 1866, the *General Sherman*, an American trading schooner under lease by a British company, sailed up the Taedong River past the port of Nampo in open violation of the Hermit Kingdom's isolationist foreign policy. One of the *General Sherman*'s passengers was a man named Robert J. Thomas.

Thomas was a young missionary from Scotland. After he was ordained on June 4, 1863, the London Missionary Society sent him to Shanghai, China, where he remained for several years. After his wife died in Shanghai in 1866, the Reverend Thomas heard about the upcoming voyage of the *General Sherman* which, laden with a cargo of European merchandise, would seek to establish trade relations between Korea and the United States. Thomas secured free passage in return for his services as an interpreter. In August 1866, as the *General Sherman* proceeded upriver toward Pyongyang, Thomas tossed gospel tracts to Koreans along the riverbank. Despite official warnings to immediately depart, the American schooner continued upriver until she ran aground on a shoal and stuck fast in the muddy river bottom. The situation went from bad to worse. Local Koreans appeared along the riverbank waving long machete-like knives at the strange-looking foreign vessel. Then, Pak Kyu Su, the Governor of Pyongyang, initiated attacks against the grounded ship. As the Koreans attempted to board, Americans opened fire. Over the next two weeks, the Americans held off repeated attacks killing twenty Koreans and wounding many others. The Koreans finally set fire to the ship and killed the crew as they came ashore.

Among the knife-wielding Koreans who attacked the *General Sherman* was a plain peasant named Kim Ung U. He was the father of Kim Bo Hyon, who later had a son named Kim Hyong Jik. He, in turn, was the father of Kim Il Sung. Since no crew members survived, the historical account of the *General Sherman's* fate is incomplete. Accounts vary. One account alleges that the American crew had intended to pillage the tombs of Koryo dynasty kings. Another recounts that the local Koreans allegedly cut up the corpses, pickled them, took them in the interior and set them up as curiosities![7] However, Harry Rhodes, the first American missionary to Korea, gave one of the more believable versions of the incident:

> At Sook-Syum, Preston, the owner of the ship, and his Chinese interpreter went ashore and met the governor of Pyongyang and the commander of the garrison. The commander and three of his men went out to visit the ship. The ship's crew asked to see his insignia of office, which had been given to him by the King, and refused to give it back. Then the four men were forced into the ship's long boat and taken up the river. The Koreans on the shore offered a large reward to anyone who would rescue their comrades. A man by the name of Pak Choon Kwun rowed out in a scull to the

"long boat" which was having difficulty getting up the rapids...The Koreans attempted to jump into the scull. The general and one of his men were saved but the other two were drowned...Firing from the ship continued off and on for two weeks, during which time twenty Koreans were killed and a large number wounded. Meanwhile the ship was hopelessly grounded in the mire and the crew began to sue for peace. They sent a man and an interpreter to make apologies to the governor. The men were bound and ordered to send for the rest of the crew if apologies were really meant. But this order was suspected to be a ruse and as soon as a note on paper was sent back, firing from the ship resumed. The Koreans now determined to burn the *General Sherman* and sent down against the ship a large scow loaded with pine branches of fire, on September 3, 1866. The crew in attempting to escape, jumped into the water and were killed as they came ashore.[8]

Once ashore, the Reverend Thomas exclaimed, "Jesus, Jesus" in Korean and offered his Korean Bible to a Korean man. The man refused. When Thomas knelt to pray, the man cut off Thomas' head and threw it into the river. The young missionary's life had been cut short—and to what end?

Thomas' legacy did not end. The Korean man who killed him was quite convicted in his spirit that he had killed a good man. So, he took the Bible home. The man used the pages of the book to wallpaper his guest house and later became a Christian. In 1891, a quarter-century later, an American visited the area and asked the proprietor about the unique wallpaper in the guest house. The owner told how, over the years, people had come from far and wide to "read the walls." In the years that followed, the killer's nephew graduated from Pyongyang's Union Christian College and served as part of a team that revised the Korean Bible. The Word had come to Korea at the price of a martyr's blood.

The Birth of the North Korean Church (1867-1893)

In the decade following the *General Sherman* incident, Protestant Christian witness to Koreans began to increase. In 1867, Alexander Williamson, who had given Robert J. Thomas Bibles to take to Korea, journeyed to northeastern China to her border with Korea. There at "Korea Gate," Williamson sold Christian books to Korean border merchants. In 1873, two Scottish Presbyterian missionaries, John Ross and his brother-in-law, John McIntyre, preached the gospel to Koreans living on the Chinese side of the border. In 1876, McIntyre baptized his first Korean converts. Five years later, Ross baptized another 85 Koreans in Manchuria. In 1884, he baptized several more.

In 1882, during these years of work with the Koreans in China, Ross and McIntyre obtained the help of Korean language teachers to translate the Gospel of Luke into Korean. By 1887, they succeeded in translating the entire New Testament into the Korean language. One of these language teachers was an itinerant medicine merchant named So Sang Yun. On one of his trips to northeastern China, he became ill and was cared for by McIntyre. McIntyre's great compassion so moved Sang Yun that the Korean merchant assisted in the task of translation. During the course of their work, So Sang Yun and his brother, So Kyong Yun, were converted. After completion of the New Testament, So Sang Yun and his brother returned to Korea and settled in Sorae on the west coast of Hwanghae Province. There, where they established a Presbyterian church, So Sang Yun became one of the first Protestant, Korean-ordained ministers. However, he most likely was not the first.

Several years before, after the Gospel of Luke had been translated, three Korean scholars, who converted to Christianity while studying in China, headed back home. These men requested and received Bible scrolls so that they could proclaim the gospel of Jesus Christ in their homeland.

As one of the three neared the border, he had a vision of scrolls made into ropes. So, he unrolled his precious Gospel of Luke and twisted and braided it into a rope. Then, in obedience to the vision, he used the rope to tie his belongings to his back. When he arrived in Korea safely, he learned that his two friends' copies of the Scriptures had been confiscated at the border.[9] Afterward, this remaining scholar unrolled the rope and shared the gospel with his fellow Koreans. And thus, the Korean church was born at the price of the blood of martyrs. When Western missionaries arrived during the next decade, they were surprised to find a small community of established Christians already present in what is now North Korea. Though missionaries helped strengthen and disciple the Korean believers, North Korea is distinct from most other nations, in that a native Korean first brought the gospel to his own people, not a foreigner (like the Ethiopian in

Acts 8:27). Ross and McIntyre laid the foundation for Korean Protestantism in northeast China. But it was Koreans, converted in China, who first penetrated the Hermit Kingdom with the gospel. In the decades that followed, the rapid growth of Christianity in Korea had an increasing impact on the nation as she emerged from the politics of isolationism.

In 1871, only five years after the *General Sherman* incident, U.S. ships again appeared off of Korea's western coast. This time it was five Navy warships that exchanged fire with shore batteries on Kanghwado Island. The U.S. marines then landed, capturing some ports on the island but having to withdraw due to stubborn resistance from the Chosun Dynasty's forces. A sharp contrast existed between foreigner and Korean views during this era. For example, in 1871, U.S. Marine Corps Captain McLane Tilton recorded in his diary on May 16 that the Americans did not anticipate hostilities because:

> ...our mission being a peaceful mission, and for the purpose only of exacting a reasonable promise from the Korean government that Christian seamen wrecked on their coast may be treated humanely.[10]

However, they did end up engaging in hostilities accompanied by the following unexpected response from the Koreans, who rejected their seemingly reasonable overtures:

> Today [June 4] we got a communication from the Head Man at the fort...who stated...he didn't see why we wanted to come so far to make a treaty. They had been living 4,000 years they said, without a treaty with us, and of course they couldn't see why they shouldn't continue to live as they do![11]

In the decade that followed, such gunboat diplomacy influenced the Chosun Dynasty to reluctantly depart from its hardline Hermit Kingdom policy through the signing of treaties with Japan (1876) and the United States (1882). With the signing of the Treaty of Peace, Amity, Commerce, and Navigation (the "Shufeldt Agreement"), the United States was the first Western power to establish diplomatic relations with Korea. In the years that followed, Korea also established treaties with Great Britain (1883), Germany (1883), Russia (1884), and France (1886). The U.S., in particular, helped to build Korea into a modern industrialized nation. In addition, the establishment of diplomatic relations was quickly followed by many U.S. missionaries entering Korea. Many

Korean scholars also traveled to the United States to study at American colleges and universities. However, the publication of William Elliot Griffis' 1882 book, *Corea: The Hermit Kingdom*, strongly influenced Western opinion to the view that Korea was not capable of self-rule.

In 1884, R. S. Maclay obtained permission from Great Britain's Queen Victoria for British Protestant missionaries to go to Korea. These missionaries gained unexpected favor after Dr. Horace Allen, the first Western missionary to Korea, saved the life of a royal prince injured in the December 1884 pro-Japanese Kapsin Coup that was put down by Korean and Chinese troops. That same year, Dr. Horace Underwood, Henry G. Appenzeller, Samuel Moffatt, W. J. Reynolds, and others began strengthening the new Korean church. Protestant missionaries also had the benefit of learning from the mistakes of the Catholics. As a result, they focused on education and health care to reach the hearts of the Korean people for Jesus Christ. These missionaries, who included doctors and teachers, established schools, hospitals, and orphanages throughout Korea. For example, Methodist missionary Henry Appenzeller founded the first missionary school, Paichai Haktang. Later missionaries founded both Yonsei and Ewha universities. Their proclamation of the gospel in word and deed would later result in tens of thousands of Koreans becoming Christians. Typical life for these early Korean Christians included Bible study, prayer (including frequent 4:00 a.m. prayer meetings), self-support, and a heavy emphasis for all believers to win souls to Jesus Christ.

Persecution and Compromise Under the Japanese (1894-1945)

In 1894, just ten years after Christians were allowed into the country, Chon Pong Jun, a Tonghak leader, initiated an anti-government rebellion. The Tonghaks opposed government corruption, confiscation of land, foreign imperialism, and Christianity. Though King Kojong quelled the four-month rebellion with promises of reform, the short-lived bloodshed was followed by a larger conflict when war broke out between China and Japan over Korea. Japan's decisive military victory in 1894–1895 Sino-Japanese War shifted the regional balance of power in East Asia and ended Chinese dominance over Korea. By 1894, Protestant missionaries had won almost 250 people to Christ, mostly in the ruling class. In the decade that followed, the Church in Korea grew slowly in size as well as in self-sufficiency. Then, in 1904, Russian activities in the North sparked a new conflict, this time between Japan and Russia.

Much of the Russo-Japanese War (1904–1905) took place in what is now North Korea, especially around the Pyongyang area. During the war, the growth of the Korean Church accelerated. American missionaries did not flee the Korean war zone but instead continued to strengthen the Korean Church. In January 1907, the Korean Church experienced a great revival that coincided with revivals elsewhere around the globe, such as South Africa, China, and Los Angeles, California. Korea's revival started in Pyongyang. Thousands of people confessed their sins and a wave of repentance spread over the entire country. This revival was followed by a great spiritual awakening resulting in the Million Souls Movement of 1909–1910. As the Korean Church grew to over 26,000 believers, Pyongyang came to be called the Jerusalem of the East.

The Japanese, who had taken control of Korean foreign relations, in 1910 further extended their dominance by forcing the abdication of Korea's king. Then they formally annexed Korea as part of the Japanese Empire. To reduce the risk of revolt, Japan shifted its objectives toward spiritual and cultural dominance over Korea. During the three-and-a-half decades that followed, elements of Korean culture were outlawed and replaced by similar Japanese traditions. The Korean language was replaced by Japanese as the official language in all business, government, and educational institutions. Koreans were forced to adopt Japanese names, 800,000 Koreans were forced to serve in the Imperial Japanese Army (during World War II), the best Korean artisans and craftsmen were taken to Japan, and Korea's crops, fishing industry, raw materials, and national treasures were plundered by the Japanese. As the occupation continued, Korean national pride gave birth to a weak resistance movement.

Many Koreans looked to Christianity and Christian missionaries for hope during this time of national crisis. The fact that many of the foreign Christian missionaries did not support the Japanese helped the Church to grow rapidly. By 1914, the Church quadrupled in size to almost 100,000 believers. Missionaries imparted a biblical Great Commission focus to the growing Korean

Church. As a result, Korea's General Evangelical Council formed the Federal Council of Missions. Korean churches began sending missionaries to Shantung in China, Siberia in Russia, and elsewhere.

During the First World War and its aftermath, the embers of nationalism within the Korean people burst into flame and anti-Japanese resistance increased. Christian, Confucian, Buddhist, and Ch'ondogyo leaders jointly decided in favor of a non-violent popular independence movement. The climax came on March 1, 1919, when, during a period of mourning for the recently deceased Emperor Kojong, 33 Korean patriots, 15 of whom were Christians, publicly issued a Declaration of Independence at Seoul's Pagoda Park. Japanese retaliation against these "criminals" was swift, ruthless, and bloody. Japanese occupation forces slaughtered between 4,000 and 8,000 Koreans and injured many thousands more. The Japanese soon came to see that the Church was the centerpiece of the resistance movement. Japan initiated new persecution and harsh policies specifically aimed at Christian hospitals, schools, universities, and churches. For example, Canadian missionary F. W. Schofield records that on April 15, 1919, Japanese troops ordered about 30 villagers at Suwon, Kyonggi-do province to assemble in a Christian church, nailed the doors shut, and then set the building ablaze. All the people, including women and infants, perished in the five-hour inferno. The Japanese soldiers then proceeded to burn 31 houses in the village and 317 others in 15 nearby villages.

Atrocities, torture, and persecution continued during the 1930s. Yet the Church in Korea continued to grow, with an estimated 168,000 believers by 1935. In Pyongyang alone, over 50,000 residents were Christians. Additionally, most of the Korean church programs were totally self-supporting.

Meanwhile, the Japanese were looking for a way to break the power of the Korean churches—and they found it. Since the beginning of Japan's occupation, the Japanese had required Koreans to bow before their Shinto shrines as a political statement of allegiance to Japan's emperor. However, this also had a spiritual significance. These Shinto shrines commemorated the spiritual union between the Japanese sun goddess, Amaterasu Omikami, and the Japanese emperor-god. This meaning clearly marked both the goddess and emperor as pagan deities and the associated shrines as religious idols. Thus, any Korean who bowed before a Shinto shrine was engaging in an act of worship.

Although the Japanese had made Shinto worship a high priority in Korea, in 1937 they began to systematically enforce mandatory Shinto idolatry for all Koreans. For example, all students at Christian schools were ordered to worship at Shinto shrines. The Roman Catholic, Methodist, and Holiness denominations submitted to the Japanese directive in the face of Japan's brutal enforcement measures. They rationalized their acquiescence to Shintoism by calling the blatant idolatry a "cultural rite." The Presbyterians were an exception. Rather than submitting, their denomination's leaders opted to close all of their Christian schools.

Not satisfied with their significant success against most of the Christian denominations, the Japanese intensified their persecution of the Korean churches. In 1938, the Japanese issued a decree that all Christians had to pay homage to Amaterasu Omikami at a Shinto shrine before attending any church service. In addition, every village that did not have a Shinto shrine had to erect one on church grounds. These tough measures split the church leadership. Many missionaries and church leaders felt convicted that they were being ordered to worship idols, and they refused. Others continued to rationalize Shinto worship rituals as merely Japanese cultural events of no spiritual significance. Since most Christian leaders did not categorically oppose Shintoism as complete idolatry, many believers gave in to the Japanese pressure. They bowed.

On September 9, 1938, the leadership of the last holdout denomination—the Presbyterians—met to discuss the crisis. Two weeks prior to the meeting, Pyongyang's chief of police summoned the Presbyterian missionaries and warned them that they would be required to pass a motion stating that it was right to worship at Shinto shrines. No debate would be allowed. Any "no" vote against the motion would be interpreted as an insult to the emperor. The Japanese gave the 400 General Assembly members the options of attending the meeting or going to prison. Many opted to go to prison. In his book *Gold in Korea*, American missionary William Blair describes how, when the General Assembly convened, over 50 armed Japanese policemen and other officials took control of the meeting. The Japanese prevented any debate on the shrine motion. Blair, over the protests of the Japanese, records that he loudly exclaimed, "I demand that my name be enrolled on the minutes as protesting this action as contrary to the laws of God and of our church." Nevertheless, the moderator, under coercion from armed Japanese police on either side of him, declared the motion "passed." On the following day, the Japanese police sent out word to all the churches, "Now that the General Assembly has taken this action, no further objection will be tolerated."[12] Thus, all Christian congregations throughout Korea were directed to bow to idols as part of their civic duty.

That decision marked the darkest day in the history of the Korean church. The sole remaining denomination had succumbed to institutionalized idolatry, and the Korean churches unanimously abdicated their spiritual stewardship. In the spiritual realm, this defeat both crippled the influence of the Korean church and increased Korea's vulnerability to demonic influence. In the aftermath of this tragic decision, spiritual darkness engulfed most of Korea.

The Japanese further increased their persecution of Korean Christians by pressing the people to participate in other Shinto rituals. Korean Christians were induced to renounce faith in Jesus Christ and receive Shinto baptism. As the situation continued to decline, most foreign missionaries left the country. By late 1941, the Japanese were quite convinced that the power of their sun goddess was far greater than this Christian God. Thus, from a spiritual viewpoint, the Japanese initiation of war against the United States was motivated—at least in part—by the belief that they were invincible because of their Shinto gods. The events that followed proved their reasoning to be faulty. After nearly four years of warfare in the Pacific, the U.S. decisively crushed the Japanese empire and forced Japanese Emperor Hirohito to publicly renounce his claim to deity.

North Korea's Ongoing War Against the Church

Church: An organization that spreads poisonous anti-government ideas to take the people's rights away, disguised as a religious activity.[13]

DEFINITION TAKEN FROM A
NORTH KOREAN DICTIONARY

With Japan vanquished and missionaries returning, the unresolved rift within the Korean Church resurfaced. Those who had bowed to idols and those who had not were unable to reconcile, leading many of the latter to move south. Most of those who had bowed remained in the north. This rift in the church became manifest in the physical realm as the major powers arbitrarily divided the Korean peninsula at the 38th parallel. No Korean was happy about the division of their land by the Soviet and American superpowers. However, most recognized that communism and Christianity could not peacefully co-exist in Korea. When negotiations for general elections broke down in the North, after three years of Soviet-sponsored Communist control, the northern half of Korea officially became a Communist totalitarian state on May 1, 1948. Shortly thereafter, the southern provinces became the independent Republic of Korea.

In the Communist-controlled North, Kim Il Sung rose to power with the backing of the Soviet Union. Pyongyang, home of more than a hundred churches, became the capital of the North. From the beginning, Kim Il Sung and the Communist authorities targeted "religionists" as "bad elements" deserving of persecution and extermination. For example, Kim Il Sung's early writings reveal the Communist justification for their program of persecution:

> Whether one believes in Christ or Buddha, [religion] is essentially a superstition. Religion has historically been [used] in the service of the ruling class in deceiving, exploiting, and oppressing the people; in recent times it has been used as an ideological tool of imperialists for aggression against backward peoples.[14]

In 1945, the Communist Korean Workers' Party began the massive anti-religion campaign by systematically destroying about 2,000 churches and 400 Buddhist temples. Countless atrocities and murders were committed against the 50,000 Catholics and 300,000 Protestants who became the first ideological targets of the new totalitarian regime.[15] For example, in Yusoo, a Communist brutally murdered the two sons of Sohn Yang Won, pastor of the Wilson Leprosarium, because they had been witnessing about Jesus to others. Remarkably, Pastor Sohn forgave the Communist, led the man to the Lord, and began discipling this future pastor. However, not long afterward, Pastor Song was killed by other Communists. By 1946, the Communists had also purged all Nationalist and Christian leaders from the governing coalition in the North.

In the three years that followed the 1948 Communist takeover, approximately five million refugees left their homes. Most fled to the South to start over again in poverty. Communists brutally killed thousands of these refugees as they tried to flee.

This Bible was buried for fifteen years in North Korea.

Countless others died of starvation. Many of the Christians who remained in the North were hunted down, summarily accused of treason, and slaughtered—often en masse.

When the Communists came to power, one of the ways they persecuted Christians was through their children. Children found to have been "indoctrinated" in the Christian faith were forcibly removed from their families and enrolled in regimented Communist youth training camps. Their parents were either killed outright or sent to a slow death in concentration camps. This common government practice placed Christian parents in the quandary of having to decide whether or not to teach their children the gospel of Jesus Christ.

To search for remaining Christians, Communists had another way of using children against their parents. In about 1988, forty years after one such event, a North Korean woman still vividly remembered the incident from her youth:

> One day the teacher told us that we would not have the normal homework today, rather the students were to participate in a special game. The students were delighted and cheered. School was strict and it was a special day not to have the usual homework, and the game intrigued us.
>
> The teacher went on to reveal the special homework she

had for us. She began to whisper as she walked among us telling us about a special book that our parents may have hidden in our homes. We were to wait until Mommy and Daddy went to sleep and search for this book and bring it to school the following day.

All of the children were excited because the teacher said we would receive a special surprise if we found this book. We asked her how we would know what the book looked like. The teacher told us that the book usually had a black cover and our parents often read the book after we went to bed. We were not to tell our parents about this homework or we would forfeit our surprise.

I went home that afternoon and immediately began searching for a black-covered book. I couldn't wait for my parents to go to bed. I was anxious to complete my assignment.

The next day I was one of 14 children who brought the black book, a Bible, to class. We were all lined up at the front and had a bright red scarf placed around our necks. All of the students clapped as the teacher paraded us around the room.

I ran home that afternoon and yelled, "Mommy, Mommy!" I was so excited to tell her how I had won the red scarf at school.

My mother wasn't in the house so I ran to the barn, again yelling, "Mommy, Mommy!"

I waited for my mother to come home. Hours passed and I didn't understand where she could be. My father didn't come home either and I was beginning to become afraid. I was hungry and it was quickly becoming dark outside. I fell asleep in a chair, hoping that, at any moment, my parents would come home and carry me to bed. I began to feel sick inside.

The next day police officers were at my door and informed me that I was now in the care of the government and would be placed in a home with other children. I never saw my parents again.[16]

In June 1950, Kim Il Sung had 150 Roman Catholic priests rounded up and executed. Protestant pastors were hunted down and executed as well. In other incidents, whole congregations of North Korean Christians were herded off the side of bridges to drown in the icy rivers and reservoirs below. Amazingly, the Communist propaganda blamed the American soldiers for the atrocities of their anti-Christian holocaust.

Those Christians who were not immediately executed were locked into cells that were so overcrowded there was no room to

미제 승냥이들은 1,000여명의 녀성들을 이곳 서원저수지에 빠드려 학살하였다.

Communists blamed Americans for their slaughter of Christians. The caption reads: "Barbarous U.S. imperialists threw more than 1,000 women in this Sowon Reservoir to kill them."

even sleep. They were beaten, tortured, denied medical care, underfed, used for forced labor, and eventually starved to death. During the Korean War, countless other Korean Christians were slaughtered by North Korean soldiers. The following eyewitness account provides one example of the atrocities of this period:

> Shortly after the war broke out, communist soldiers overtook a small town outside PyungYang [sic]. During the takeover, 190 Christians were apprehended. Among them was their pastor, Reverend Kim. "Is it really worth dying for Jesus?" Pastor Kim was asked. "I can save your life only if you will say, 'I don't believe Jesus.'" Pastor Kim would not deny the Lord. He was hung on a cross, amidst a slow-burning fire to prolong his agony. The soldiers turned to the 190 and said, "Those who still believe in Jesus: Come forth!" To their surprise, all 190 stepped forward.
>
> The soldiers marched the 190 into an old, abandoned mine, and threw sticks of dynamite inside. They were left for dead. Hours later, one man awoke. He felt the blood of others on his hands, and, realizing he had survived, was filled with remorse. "Why, Lord?" he asked. "Why didn't you take me to heaven?"
>
> Later, realizing the Lord had kept him for a purpose, he

종교의 탈을 쓰고 조선에 기여든 미국침략의 서루병들

*In this "hate America" museum in North Korea, the first missionaries are vilified.
The phrase under their photo says, "The American intruders with the religious
facemasks who have come to take over the land."*

spotted a small light coming from the end of the mine tunnel. With his hands, he dug his way out, though it took several days. When he emerged from his tunnel, he discovered all
his fingers [were] missing, and his hands swollen and bloody.

Eventually, he found the son of Pastor Kim, and stated,
"The Lord saved me to tell you how your father and his flock
died. They did not deny Jesus," he concluded. "I must go
now, and tell their families."[17]

By 1953, roughly half of the 200,000 North Korean Christians
had fled south before the highly fortified "Demilitarized Zone"
(DMZ) border between the North and South became virtually
impassable. Most of the rest were hunted down and butchered by
the Communists. In 1962, North Korea's President Kim Il Sung
declared:

> Through court trials, *we have executed all Protestant and
> Catholic church cadre members* and all other vicious religious
> elements have been sent to concentration camps.[18]

In the South, the church grew rapidly to about 1.25 million believers, due to both the influx of Christian refugees and many new
converts.

In the 1990s, Communist propaganda continued to portray Christianity as a tool of America imperialism rather than as faith in the risen Savior of all mankind. Kim Il Sung declared:

> *Christianity must be annihilated* because it has become the tool of the imperialists led by the U.S. to paralyze the independence consciousness of the people, to spread anti-Communist thoughts and to destroy national liberation movements among the people of newly emerging nations.[19]

Kim Jong Il, like his father, has continued the crackdown against Bibles and all of Christianity. North Korea's anti-Christian stance has so penetrated the culture that even "Christian" definitions found in North Korean dictionaries are anti-Christian, as shown in Table 4-1.

TABLE 4-1. "Christian" definitions from a North Korean dictionary[20]

WORD	DEFINITION
Church	An organization that spreads poisonous anti-government ideas to take the people's rights away, disguised as a religious activity.
Bible	A book written of the false Christian religion to deceive.
Heaven	A false world created to trick or lie that a person will live better after death.
Jesus	An idol of this faith who is proposed to be the Son of God.
God	Falsified One who said that He created nature, society and destiny.
Cross	A wooden symbol that resembles the grace and love that the uncouth believers of Jesus use.

Thus, to be caught or even accused of being a Christian means almost certain death in a concentration camp for oneself and one's family. Aside from the persecuted underground church, only three phony "showcase" churches exist. These churches, all located in Pyongyang, are allowed by the government to provide an illusion of religious freedom to foreigners.

North Korea's Underground Church

"Now, holy communion." All eyes turned to the corner of the room. The voice belonged to a woman who had been baptized before the Communist takeover. The elderly

For fifty years, the Christian community has been rigorously persecuted in North Korea and the open practice of the Christian faith has been banned. Recent reports from missionaries in contact with North Korea's underground church indicate that it is both alive and growing. In North Korea, the true Church does not exist as denominations or in buildings. Believers must gather secretly as early Christians once did when persecuted by Roman emperors such as Nero. One source reported that there are at least 30,000 underground church believers. In December 1997, The Voice of the Martyrs (VOM) estimated the number of true Christians to be about 60,000. Then in February 1998, VOM revised its estimate to "60,000–100,000 Christians worshipping secretly in North Korea." Though no exact accounting is possible, projections from more accessible areas indicate that there may be over 100,000 true believers in Jesus Christ in North Korea.[22] In 1994, the Reverend Dr. David J. Cho,[23] from the Institute of Korean Studies at William Carey International University in Pasadena, California, estimated the size of the North Korean underground church to be about 200,000 believers.

For the last half of the 20th century, the true church in North Korea has consisted of individuals or pockets of believers who have secretly maintained their faith under constant fear of persecution. Under what was, until recently, a constitutional right to persecute "religionists," Christians were hunted down, whole families sentenced to die in concentration camps, and their relatives permanently designated as belonging to the "hostile group" of the Juche caste system. During the early 1990s, North Korea modified its consti-

A hand-copied Bible from the North Korean underground church opened to the Book of Acts.

tution to promise that "citizens will have freedom of religion." However, the revised language also includes a provision that "no one can bring religion from the outside, or use it against national security policies." Despite the rewording, religious freedom remains non-existent and the persecution of Christians continues.

On one occasion in the late 1970s, a group of Christians were martyred in Gok San village about 155 miles outside of Pyongyang. The saga began with workers building a special paved road, so Kim Il Sung could drive to the remote village for an agricultural inspection. The Great Leader's fear of flying meant that his travel was confined to surface transportation. As the workers were demolishing a building on the outskirts of Gok San, they stumbled upon an underground catacomb. The catacomb served as the home and meeting place for a group of 27 Christians pastored by Kim Tae Yong. The workers promptly called the police and the Christians were rounded up. Then the 30,000 inhabitants of Gok San were assembled and the Christians were dragged out before them. A Voice of the Martyrs account relates what happened next:

> Under orders from Pyongyang, the police gathered the Christians and, in the presence of all 30,000 inhabitants of Gok San, they were told: "Deny Christ, or lose your lives!"
>
> The congregation refused. Cruelly, the officials separated four children from their parents and prepared to hang them unless the church recanted. Fondly, the parents told their children, "We will see you in Heaven soon."
>
> Afterwards, the adults were told: "Reconsider, or you will be placed under a steamroller." The believers refused to deny Christ.[24]

Then the workmen proceeded to kill these Christians, one at a time, by slowly crushing them with a steamroller. They were crushed feet first to maximize their agony. As onlookers watched the executions, they heard Pastor Kim's flock singing:

> More love to Thee, O Christ.
> More love to Thee!
> Hear Thou the prayer I make on bended knee:
> This is my earnest plea,
> More love, O Christ, to Thee.
> More love to Thee,
> More love to Thee![25]

Only one Christian boy out of the group escaped to tell what actually happened. Pyongyang's labor newspaper, however, gave a quite different account, which concluded by announcing the cessation of "all forms of heresy or superstition" throughout North Korea.

For decades, Christians in North Korea have been fearful of witnessing to even members of their own families. Parents cannot even trust their own children since the Juche primary education system indoctrinates all children to turn in their parents for anti-revolutionary religionist activities. Such activities include possessing a Bible, praying, witnessing, or participating in any religious praise, music, or worship. A lot of the witnessing that does occur is "deathbed witnessing" where a dying parent passes on faith in Christ to family members. The following account shows both the power of the gospel and the degree of fear associated with its propagation as the underground church continues to grow:

A few years ago, a North Korean government official was dying of tuberculosis. "You only have a few months to live," his physician told him.

Mr. Park decided to pay his final respects to his relatives in Manchuria (Northeast China). One evening, while visiting a relative, Mr. Park overheard a Gospel radio broadcast, originating from South Korea. An American evangelist, aided by an interpreter, gave a message on healing.

"I cannot come to you," the evangelist concluded, "but if you believe God, He *will* heal you!..." Mr. Park did not know what a Bible was, and asked his relatives for a Bible. He was handed a Bible, which he placed upon his chest. Echoing the broadcast's prayer, Mr. Park ended with a hearty 'Amen,' though ignorant of its meaning.

Weeks passed, and the incident was forgotten. Mr. Park returned to North Korea. Months later, Mr. Park realized that he was still alive. Puzzled, he visited his physician. "I don't understand," his doctor concluded, "but your health is normal!" Instantly, Mr. Park recalled the radio broadcast, the prayer and the Bible.

Requesting a leave of absence, Mr. Park hurried back to Manchuria to re-visit his relatives. He burst out that he had been dying, and that he had been healed. Word grew silently among the village believers, and they rejoiced. Laying their hands on him, they prayed, saying, "We are sending a missionary into North Korea!"

Upon his return, Mr. Park was bursting to share the Good News. Was it safe? Who could he tell? After much prayer, he told his mother. As Mr. Park shared his testimony, she broke out in tears, sobbing, "Son, please forgive me. Before the War, I was a church deaconess. Your grandmother was a senior deaconess. However, I was afraid to tell you about Jesus. I feared you would report me to the Communists as others who had turned in their parents. Surely the Lord allowed this sickness that you might find Him and be saved!"

Turning to the Lord, the elderly mother sank to [her] knees in gratitude: "Oh, Lord, forgive me," she wept, "Thank you for saving my son, and returning the Gospel to our family."

Tearfully, mother and son earnestly prayed for guidance. Subsequently, an underground church was formed. Imagine, a North Korean Church! The fellowship numbers 80 members.[26]

One Christian lady has prayed secretly every day for years in a small closet. Since she had to pray quietly so as not to arouse suspicion, she expressed her deep emotion while praying by repeatedly pivoting her feet to the left and right during prayer. After years of secret prayer, the wooden floor was indented from her long hours of fervent prayer. Her greatest prayer and dream is that someday she will be able to sing the praises of her Savior publicly, without fear.

Bibles are relatively rare among North Korea's underground believers. Over the last twenty years, thousands of Bibles have been smuggled into the country through a variety of means, so they are becoming

North Korean reading a new Bible.

more plentiful in the underground church. However, a Bible is still considered to be such a treasure to persecuted Christians that many are meticulously hand-copied in secret.

Over the years, The Voice of the Martyrs, Cornerstone Ministries International, and other ministries have launched thousands of Scripture balloons into North Korea, smuggled in tons of Bibles, and financed radio broadcasts on behalf of the underground church. These ministries have also sent containers of food and warm clothing to the spiritually and physically starving people of North Korea.

The Scripture balloons (bright orange balloons covered with Bible verses), in particular, cause a lot of problems for the North Korean authorities. The first Scripture balloons in 1969 were simply thin plastic American-made shopping bags with the open end left uncut at the factory. At the cost of only pennies apiece, current balloons are printed with a Gospel tract entitled "How to Know God." The balloons also include 49 pages of Scriptures explaining the good news of Jesus Christ. Random launches of these helium-filled balloons have caused the Korean People's Army to mobilize large numbers of troops near the North Korean border to try to gather all the balloons to prevent anyone from reading them.

Given such diligent measures by the North Korean authorities to intercept them, how effective are these Scripture balloons?

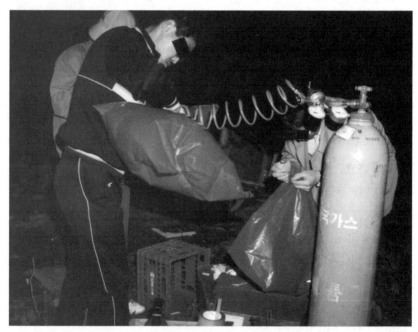

One of thousands of Scripture balloons is filled with helium for a
night launch into North Korea.

Underground church members gather to read a Scripture balloon.

Apparently, the balloons work quite well. A recent defector from the North tells of a little girl who brought a brightly colored balloon to her nearly blind grandmother. The grandmother felt it and called her daughter and said, "Come and tell me what this is." As the daughter read the Scripture balloon in its entirety, the grandmother joyfully exclaimed, "Oh, I thought they had forgotten us!" The balloon had arrived in their village 120 miles away from its launch site.[27]

More conventional means are also used to propagate the gospel in this anti-Christian environment. While in a hotel restaurant, some couriers to North Korea noticed a woman who had a kind face waiting on tables. After praying, they slowly began eating while watching the waitress. When she passed nearby, they showed her some gospel booklets. Then the lady went out of sight for a few minutes. The couriers did not know what to expect, so they simply trusted God and continued to eat. A few minutes later, the waitress reappeared carrying a North Korean newspaper. While passing by, she discreetly slid the Christian literature into the newspaper and continued walking on by. The Word of God had been planted.

Another interaction with an underground believer is revealed in account from 1990:

A Christian visitor to North Korea met a 17-year-old youth who risked his chance by repeatedly tracing the impression of a cross in the palm of the visitor. Some days later, the teenager again approached the visitor and asked: "When is Jesus returning?" The young man continued, "Persecution is severe. How I so desire to be with Jesus." When asked for personal requests, the young man did not ask for freedom, food or the reunification of Korea. Instead he said, "I have a job. And I have saved up money, but I have no place to give my tithe. Where can I send it?" The young believer concluded by mentioning his heartfelt desire to be baptized, for communion and the breaking of bread.[28]

Such accounts demonstrate that sound biblical doctrine has endured within the North Korean underground church through over a half-century of brutal persecution.

Cornerstone Ministries International recently published the following account of a Korean missionary's secret encounter with the North Korean underground church:

> As the young Korean missionary departed for the North, he was handed a gift. "What is it?" he inquired. "It is from Israel," explained his benefactor. "Open it in North Korea. You will know when the proper moment has come."
>
> Disguised as a businessman, the minister was assigned a guide. As days passed, the State official believed the visitor was solely on business. Carefully guarding his tongue, avoiding political or ideological debate, the minister put the guide at ease.
>
> In time, the official became relaxed, taking short naps. On the day of the minister's departure, the guide had been drinking heavily and fell into a deep sleep.
>
> The missionary was approached by the villagers. "You must baptize us!" they pleaded. The young man, a newly ordained minister, had never conducted a baptism! Knowing he must confirm each individual's commitment, he was bewildered, "Lord! What should I ask them?" he prayed. "The Holy Spirit will lead you," came the inward response. As the ceremony unfolded, he prayerfully confirmed each believer's testimony.
>
> The next problem arose: There was no bathtub or tank of water. There were no...gowns or white gloves. The brethren were attired in soiled clothes. Without hesitation, the young minister asked for a bowl of water. Then, facing the group,

he asked, "Are you prepared to die for Jesus?" All nodded declaring, "Our greatest desire is to live for Him." Sobbing in gratitude, the assembly began praising their Savior.

"Now, holy communion." All eyes turned to the corner of the room. The voice belonged to a woman who had been baptized before the Communist takeover. The elderly sister had remained faithful to Jesus, although many of her relatives had been martyred.

As Communion began, the assembly of saints broke a rice cake. "Where is the wine?" someone asked. Suddenly, the young minister remembered the package he had carried from the West. Discerning the Lord's timing, he opened it. To everyone's surprise, it was a bottle of wine. He poured the wine into a plastic bowl, and they drank in remembrance of Christ's remission of their sins.

Speechless, the brethren could only burst forth in gratitude. "Oh God, thank you!" they wept openly. "After 40 years, thank you Lord." "We must disperse again," whispered the visiting minister. "If someone…Someone might report us if we stay too long."

As the missionary prepared to leave, the villagers were deeply saddened(they didn't know when their next communion would be held. A few days later, believers from other towns arrived and bitterly wept for having missed the blessed event. As they left for their homes, they pounded their fists to the ground. "Oh God," they agonized. *"We have waited so long! We have waited so long!"*

Please remember our brethren in North Korea. As you partake in Communion, take it for those who have waited five decades to openly break bread.[29]

Reliable reports out of North Korea state that not only does the persecuted Church exist, but it continues to grow! The continuing existence of the Christian Church in North Korea is an ongoing testimony that the gates of hell shall not prevail against the Church.

Accommodation of Christian Humanitarian Aid

North Korea's strong sense of self-sufficiency [Juche] prevented them from admitting that they had a severe famine…until the problem became too big to handle internally.
DR. RALPH PLUMB
PRESIDENT, INTERNATIONAL AID

Why, one might ask, do North Korea's leaders accommodate Christian humanitarian aid given their opposition to the gospel and continuing persecution of the underground church in North Korea? Actually, given the extreme "self-reliance" aspect of Juche, the North Korean move to accommodate any foreign humanitarian aid was a tough decision for their leaders to make. Juche's emphasis on the material realm probably has led North Korea's leaders to be convinced that the military and political threat to their Juche system is more serious than the spiritual one. Moreover, their experience with the puppet Korean Christian Federation gives them the impression they can control the propagation of the gospel through restrictive policies.

Yet, even given the low view of Christianity from a Juche perspective, North Korea opened their doors only slightly for humanitarian aid following the natural disasters (floods, droughts, and tidal waves) that have battered their nation since 1995. Despite significant relief efforts, countless people are dying. Signs of growing starvation are everywhere. International Aid's President, Ralph Plumb, commented; "North Korea's strong sense of self-sufficiency prevented them from admitting that they had a severe famine...until the problem became too big to handle internally." Plumb added, "Getting beyond their position of self-sufficiency was difficult for them, but they saved face because of the natural disasters." According to the United Nations' Food and Agriculture Organization (FAO), North Korea's Public Distribution System, on which 80% of the population relies, ran out of food in May and June 1997. One North Korean official accurately summarized the situation: "We are out of food."[30]

Protracted starvation has resulted in both general malnutrition and a massive death toll among the people. One journalist from *Asia Week* noted:

> We found out from one study that women begin to menstruate anytime from 18 years to 21 years. What this suggests is very low nutrition. Also there is tremendous bleeding associated with childbirth, showing that the women do not have enough iron. In addition, their low nutrition is resulting in very low birth rates. Women also have high rates of tuberculosis, ulcers, tension, which also add to the low birth rate.[31]

In January 1998, China's Xinhua News Agency quoted Cha Limsok, Deputy Director of the Farm Produce Bureau of the DPRK

Children at a nursery in Pyongsan County, South Hwanghae Province. Signs of malnutrition are evident in the swollen faces, enlarged heads and emaciated necks (1997).

(North Korea) Agricultural Commission, as having stated that "2.8 million North Koreans have already died of 'natural calamities.'" Cha reported:

> Because of summer's serious drought, the amount of food per person in the Democratic People's Republic of Korea from October 1997 to September 1998 is a mere 180 grams [6 ounces] a day.

Cha Limsok's statements marked the first time that North Korea revealed the full extent of the ongoing famine. If his remarks are accurate, then 2.8 million deaths meant that over 12% of North Korea's population had already starved to death by the beginning of 1998. In February 1998, a North Korean diplomat to Italy, who defected with his family to South Korea, reported the situation he witnessed in Pyongyang during December 1997:

> I visited Pyongyang in December. The children are dying. There is basically no food. The situation is at its worst. On the way to work in the morning, bodies of children who have starved to death can be seen in front of the train station.[32]

The relief agency World Vision reported that all the pets in North Korea have long since been eaten by the starving people.

So many people are dying that there are not enough coffins to bury the dead. Andrew Natsios, World Vision's Vice President, estimates that the death toll already may have reached 15% of the population. Clearly, what has been called the "slow-motion famine" has picked up considerable speed. On September 29, 1998, *CBN News* reported that the death toll in North Korea's largely self-inflicted holocaust had risen to 25% of the population—nearly six million people. On February 5, 1999, *London Times* reporter James Pringle wrote this account of the famine:

> This week I witnessed and heard scenes of human suffering with virtually no parallel. Through my binoculars, looking across the frozen Tumen River, I was able to see firm evidence of a society that after years of starvation has descended into medieval barbarism. According to refugees, three million North Koreans have died of famine out of a population of just 20 million, the result of a Stalinist regime that prefers to see children die rather than open its impoverished country to the world. While the privileged ruling class and military leaders are looked after in the capital Pyongyang, often fed from overseas aid, nothing is getting through to this remote border province that famine has gripped for four years. One of the few signs of life are the ox carts picking up the bodies of the dead, not unlike those that took away victims of the Black Death in Europe.[33]

Meanwhile, the North Korean government tells its people that Juche self-reliance will solve these minor problems in their utopian world and "the arduous march" must continue.

Attempts to improve matters by stimulating economic growth have proved unsuccessful. Though North Korea's government invested millions of won into developing the Rajin-Sonbong Free Economic and Trade Zone (FETZ) in the Northeast, the resulting level of international investment was disappointing. North Korea initiated what ended up becoming a bungled submarine incursion at Kangnung while the 1996 Free Trade Zone conference was being hosted in the Rajin-Sonbong area. This submarine grounding incident on South Korea's coast politically sabotaged Pyongyang's own requests for foreign investment. However, from a Juche perspective, the act of limiting foreign investment was very consistent with the Juche teaching that reliance upon foreign aid has been the very thing that resulted in the collapse of other modern Communist socialist states around the world. Nevertheless, North Korea continues to enact trade laws to make it "possible to fix the achievements in foreign trade by law and develop it in keeping with the demand of Korean [Juche] socialism."

Food aid from other nations such as the United States, Japan, China, and South Korea has generally been sporadic, in part due to North Korea's "brinkmanship" foreign policy. Some analysts have interpreted North Korea's recent cries for help as a new opportunity to change the course of this dangerous renegade nation. A more realistic view is that the North's leaders will cling to power by whatever means possible for fear of losing their Juche system and privileges. These means include the use of thinly veiled threats of nuclear war to extract financial and diplomatic concessions. Conversely, foreign governments often request human rights or political concessions along with their proposed famine relief. Just when an agreement seems imminent, North Korea's caustic propaganda and periodic volatile border or terrorist incidents often create an international political climate where politicians withhold aid due to public outcry against North Korea. One of many such recent incidents occurred in 1997 when North Korea repeatedly threatened to blow up South Korea's Seoul-based *Choson Ilbo* newspaper for publishing an article that called for Kim Jong Il's resignation.

Another issue that has obstructed food aid is Japan's well-documented allegations of North Korea abducting Japanese citizens. North Korea flatly denied the Japanese claims. When North Korea subsequently rushed to capitalize on former U.S. President Jimmy Carter's March 1998 attempt to "depoliticize [Japanese] food aid," not surprisingly, Japan did not rush to change its position.

> Former U.S. President Jimmy Carter urged the Japanese government to grant more active food aid to the DPRK…On March 12 [1998], he told the Committee of the Foreign Policy and Defense Affairs of the House of Councilors of Japan that he was disappointed by Japan's insufficient food aid to the DPRK and said that the Japanese government was too hesitant. He urged Japan to grant active food aid to the DPRK, saying that the assistance would be a favorable move for laying foundations for DPRK-Japan relations and normalizing diplomatic relations between them as well as from the humanitarian point of view…He said Japan "has not even been generous" and "there is a stinginess about it that really

This woman, herself malnourished, recently lost her husband, and her two children were also showing distressful signs of malnutrition (1997).

concerns me."...Carter said that the "international community was taking advantage of the famine as a means for 'political extortion,'" adding that "I think it's an inhumane way to address the real crisis that exists in North Korea" [*KCNA*].

In contrast to political aid, food aid from parachurch Christian organizations has been offered with no political strings attached. International Aid's Dr. Jack Henderson notes, "Christian relief organizations are providing food for starving North Koreans while governments sort out politics." Henderson continues, "Christian relief must focus on the needs of the people because other food aid is too dependent on political process."[34]

Most Christian leaders involved in providing famine relief are well aware of North Korea's opposition to the proclamation of the gospel. One missionary commented that North Korea is "a land under a curse—the judgment of God."[35] Yet, he and other Christians are motivated by the Bible's teaching that God's compassion through the gospel of Jesus Christ extends even to God's enemies. Christians are bound by Jesus' teachings to love their neighbor and enemy, and to feed the hungry as well as proclaim the gospel to all nations.

North Korea's leaders do not seem to feel too threatened by

this genuine heartfelt motivation of love. Dr. Dale Kietzman of the Center for American(North Korean Understanding (CANKU) explains, "While the famine is making the North Korean government officials more open…concessions being made do not yet constitute an opening for preaching the Gospel freely, but the more Christian presence in the land, the better." [36]

As with the former Soviet Union, the North Korean government has no criteria or motivation to distinguish between receiving aid from orthodox Christian groups and cult organizations. From the North Korean government's standpoint, the matter is simple: food is food.

Thus, though North Korea remains wary of any foreign aid, famine has forced them to compromise. From a Juche perspective, no-strings Christian humanitarian aid seems to be the lesser evil among various other alternatives. Ultimately, North Korea's leaders feel that they can take advantage of short-term humanitarian aid from naive international "religionists" because they truly believe that Juche can dominate and will ultimately triumph over the church.

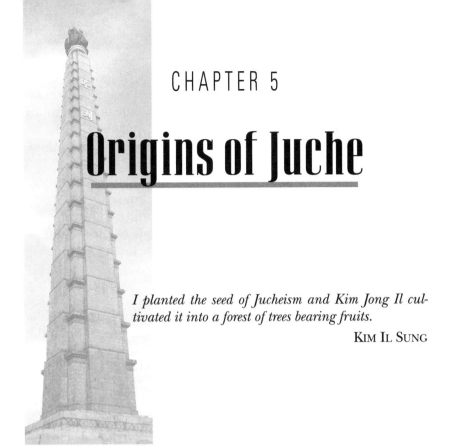

CHAPTER 5

Origins of Juche

I planted the seed of Jucheism and Kim Jong Il cultivated it into a forest of trees bearing fruits.

KIM IL SUNG

On May 1, 1948, Kim Il Sung, with the backing of the USSR, defied United Nations plans for a plebiscite throughout the entire Korean peninsula and established the Democratic People's Republic of Korea north of the 38th parallel. Though there is unmistakable evidence of Marxist Communist influence on Juche ideology along with Japanese, Chinese, and even pseudo-Christian influence, the spiritual roots of Juche probably date back to ancient Korea.

Did Kim Il Sung invent the Juche religion? Answers to this question by North Korean writers vary. Some maintain that the Great Leader Comrade Kim Il Sung, the "Father of Juche," originated the idea. Another slightly different answer dismisses the notion that Kim Il Sung was influenced by Marxist-Leninist ideology and maintains that Juche's origins are entirely North Korean. This line of reasoning considers Juche as a total break from all past philosophies. Otherwise, a contradiction would arise between Juche's "self-reliance" and its origins "dependent" on foreign ideas. A third view is articulated by Lee Wha Rang: "Does

Jucheism sound like representative democracy, Marxism, Christianity, Confucianism, and Chondokyo rolled into one? Nothing is created from a vacuum. Jucheism draws its ideas from many sources."[1] Though Lee Wha Rang is an outspoken advocate of Juche, his conclusion is probably the most accurate among these differing views.

This chapter considers Juche's spiritual origins as well as its historical origins. The historical progression presents two divergent views of the growth of Juche from its origin to its development into a full-fledged religion. This analysis of the origins of Juche culminates in the historical failure of Juche in practice.

Juche's Spiritual Roots

Juche represents a powerful evil in the spiritual realm. While it is essential that Christians love people who are caught up in the Juche faith, we should not be ignorant about the evil associated with Juche idol worship. As believers in our Lord Jesus Christ, Christians must unite in prayer against Juche until we see its unholy influence over North Korea defeated.

Much evidence exists to show that modern spiritual forces have influenced the development of the Juche religion. However, the ancient Korean roots of Juche should not be overlooked.

The ancient spiritual history of Korea originates with the Tangun dynasty, which North Korean historians estimate was established around 3,000 B.C. Such dates are approximate. Biblical creationist scholars would date the Tangun dynasty as sometime after the great flood of Noah's era. From the Tangun dynasty onward, the occupants of the Korean peninsula proved to be a fiercely territorial people culturally distinct from the Chinese to the west, Manchurians to the north, and the Japanese to the south and east. Nevertheless, for long periods of their early history, all or part of the Korean peninsula came under foreign domination, due to its geographical location as an East Asian crossroads.

Within the last millennium, ancient Korea was often divided among the three warring kingdoms of Kokuryo (37 B.C. – A.D. 668), Paekche (18 B.C. – A.D. 660), and Silla (57 B.C. – A.D. 935). The Kokuryo kingdom was located in northeast Korea and, when not under Chinese control, in northwest Korea. The Paekche kingdom occupied southwest Korea. The Silla kingdom, in southeast Korea, often tended to be a Japanese vassal state. The fierce independent spirit of the Koreans was evident as the Kokuryo kingdom repulsed five major Chinese invasions between A.D. 611 and 647. The Silla kingdom achieved autonomy from foreign rule between A.D. 670 and 740. Wang Kon, the first minister of Latter Koguryo, conquered Latter Paekche in A.D. 934–935, Shilla in A.D. 936, and founded the Koryo Dynasty (A.D. 935–1392), the name of which is derived from Koguryo.

In the 10th century, the kingdom of Koryo was established in west-central Korea, with its capital in Kaesong. The North Koreans have made highly speculative use of the Koryo history in their attempt to rationalize and legitimize the Juche religion. Even so, the spiritual influence of Korea's ancient dynasties on the development of modern Juche ideology should not be arbitrarily dismissed.

In particular, Korea's history shows evidence of the extreme isolationism that is characteristic of Juche. For example, although Korea's Yi Dynasty maintained its tributary relationship to Manchu China, instituting a policy of national seclusion had a generally stagnating effect on Korea's culture and economy.

Juche's spiritual origins also reflect much of classical Communist ideology. A continuous ideological lineage can be traced from European Free Masonry of the post-Renaissance period to the Enlightenment philosophers, to Karl Marx and the early Communist revolutions in Europe, to the former Soviet Union's Josef Stalin and China's Mao Zedong. Stalin and Mao, in turn, influenced Kim Il Sung, while Marxist and Leninist teachings inspired young Hwang Jang Yop in the late 1940s and early 1950s. Many of the characteristics of Juche originated from this stream of philosophy. Juche's occult symbology, concept of a godless man-centered utopia, brutal internal totalitarianism, and so on, all have their origins in classical Communism as shown in Table 5-1.

The modern spiritual history of Korea parallels that of the biblical Israel and Judah, whose disobedience to God resulted in conquest by foreign enemies. In 1938, Korea's disobedience resulted from spiritual compromise by church leaders as they allowed Shinto idols in Korean Christian homes during the Japanese occupation. However, the spiritual seeds of Juche were planted long before.

By typological comparison, the seeds of Israel's post-Solomonic oppression were planted during the reign of David. The Bible provides an account of Israel's disobedience against God's instructions for warfare. For example, compare God's commands in Deuteron-

TABLE 5-1. Selected Historical Landmarks in the Development of Communist Ideology[2]

YEAR	EVENT
1780	*"Communism" (utopian society context):* Paris journalist and author Restif de la Bretonne envisioned a master race of "Spartan people" living in "equality and union," "the most perfect sociability" and having all possessions in common ownership. He wrote: "All must be in common among equals. Each must work for the common good. All must take an identical part in work" (similar to Juche socialist ideology).
1780s	*Man-centered utopia apart from God:* During the Age of Enlightenment, humanists proclaimed the autonomy and infinity of human reason. They turned to man as beginning from himself and rejected the Bible's claims of God's existence, creation, and salvation in Jesus Christ. The French philosopher Voltaire typified Enlightenment thinkers in proposing that a utopia could be realized apart from God (similar to Juche).
1794	*Glorification of "nature" (apart from God):* In Paris, Robespierre proclaimed that the "true priest" of France's revolution was "nature": "its temple, the universe; its cult, virtue; its festivals, the joy of a great people…renewing the sweet bonds of universal fraternity" (similar to Juche view of nature).
1795	*Single leader / "Day of the People":* Revolutionary journalist François Noël Babeuf stated that the means of ending *the spirit of domination* was to obey an elite hierarchy, and the way to avoid *the tyranny of factions* was to accept a single leader. The miraculous move to popular sovereignty was to take place on a springtime *Day of the People"* (similar to North Korea's annual "People's Greatest Day" holiday/holy day).
1831	*"The people are my god":* French historian Jules Michelet popularized the mythical idea of "the religion of the people." Subsequent writers followed suit with *Reign of the People* and *Gospel of the People* and a popular song of the era which proclaimed "the people…is God" (similar to current Juche saying).
1848	*"Communist dictator":* Marx chastised French revolutionaries for failing to impose a dictator.
1850	*"The permanent revolution":* Marx introduced the term "dictatorship of the proletariat." The aim of the dictatorship is to overthrow all the privileged classes, subjugating them to the dictatorship of the proletariat by sustaining "the permanent revolution" until the realization of communism, which has to be the final form of human society (similar to Juche concept of permanent revolution).

TABLE 5-1. *(continued)*

YEAR	EVENT
1920s •	*Ruthless internal measures:* In Vladimir Lenin's book *The Lessons of the Paris Commune,* he concluded that the French had been defeated in 1871 because they had not killed enough of their enemies. When Lenin came to power in Russia he set up the machinery of oppression to ensure that he did not make the same mistake. Similarly, all Communist regimes have had to function through the imposition of rigid internal oppression (similar to North Korea's ongoing Reign of Terror).

omy 20:10–18 with the conduct of David's army in the war against Edom (1 Kings 11:14–17). Israel's sins planted seeds of judgment that emerged a generation later. Among the reconstituted enemies of Israel were Hadad the Edomite and Rezon the Aramean. The Bible specifically says that God raised up these adversaries:

> Then the LORD raised up against Solomon an adversary, Hadad the Edomite, from the royal line of Edom (1 Kings 11:14).

> And God raised up against Solomon another adversary, Rezon…Rezon ruled in Aram and was hostile toward Israel (1 Kings 11:23,25).

As in the biblical account of disobedience, seeds of idolatry and oppression are also sown in the preceding generation. In 1912 and 1920, two men were born in North Korea who would wreak spiritual havoc throughout the Korean peninsula in generations to come. Their evil influence would affect countless others around the world as each of them, in their own way, deceived millions to believe that they were god incarnate. These two men later even became close friends. Surprisingly, these men were not raised in Buddhist, Taoist, or Chondokyo homes. They were raised in Korean Christian homes. Who were they?

One of them, of course, was Kim Il Sung. At the time of his death, Kim Il Sung was the longest reigning dictator in the world. The other was a man named Yong Myung Moon ("Shining Dragon Moon"). In 1946, Moon changed his name to Sun Myung Moon ("Shining Sun and Moon"). Sun Myung Moon eventually founded the Unification Church, which like Juche, uses "obvious, widespread and forceful psychological pressure on members to

conform and remain loyal to the group at all costs."[3] What influences existed in the Korean Church of the 1920s and early 1930s
that may have resulted in these two bright young men turning
against Christianity?

Kang Ban Sok, Kim Il Sung's mother, is generally recognized
by scholars to have been an "ordinary Christian woman." However, as noted in Chapter 2, Kim Il Sung claims in his autobiography that she did not have faith in Jesus Christ. Kim's openly
atheist father, Kim Hyong Jik, also had a profound spiritual influence on him in the male-dominated Korean culture. The young
boy watched year after year as his father thought little of the
Christian faith. While Kim Il Sung's mother was an unbelieving
churchgoer for a season, his father devoted his energies toward
the anti-Japanese revolutionary activities. During these formative
years, the Church may have had an opportunity to shape Kim Il
Sung through its program of Christian education. Yet, in the
final analysis, the church had little influence on his spiritual
growth as a youth. Years later, Kim Il Sung, possibly in a reflection of his mother's insincere faith in Christianity, would erect a
few token church buildings—the empty shells of feigned respect.

What about the young Shining Dragon (the future Sun Myung
Moon)? Myung Moon was extremely bright and as a young man,
he was even allowed to teach Sunday school in the Korean church.
But at age 16, Myung Moon started dabbling in spiritism and had
a vision of (a false) "Jesus Christ." This vision was a key turning
point in this life. Whatever the case, Sun Myung Moon and Kim Il
Sung rejected the gospel.

If the youthful experiences of Sun Myung Moon and Kim Il
Sung are any indication, then Korea's Church in the 1920s and
1930s tolerated serious compromises of the Christian faith with
syncretism and gnosticism from the surrounding spiritual practices of the region.

Two Versions of Juche's Early History

Having noted some of the ancient spiritual origins of Juche,
let us now consider some of the more modern events in the history of Juche. The modern historical origins of Juche stem from
Korea's experience during both the Japanese occupation of the
late 1930s/early 1940s, and the Soviet installation of a Communist regime following World War II in 1945. Korea was subsequent-

"Our people rose up in the just Fatherland Liberation War for freedom and independence of the country against the U.S. imperialist aggression."

ly engulfed in the War for National Reunification (Korean War) from 1950 to 1953. However, the Juche version of history paints an entirely Kim Il Sung–centric view of North Korea's origins. North Korean history maintains that:

From the first days of paving the way for the cause of Juche, President Kim Il Sung put it forth as the most important task to defeat the Japanese imperialists and liberate Korea, and put it forth as an important task to build a powerful sovereign and independent state after the liberation [*KCNA*].

This revisionist teaching hints at how the Juche version of history has radically skewed the thinking of 23 million people. To gain a better understanding of the Juche worldview, we will consider the North Korean version of history followed by a factual account of North Korea's early history.

This is a typical North Korean version of Juche's origins:

Kim Il Sung, a convert to Communism at age 14, was greatly troubled by the petty internecine rivalry and ideological bankruptcy of the old Communists in China. He wrote in his memoirs that "the Communists and nationalists who professed themselves to be engaged in the national liberation movement of Korea were divorced from the people; many top personalities spent much time shouting empty slogans and quarreling among themselves, instead of mobilizing the people to an effective revolutionary movement."

The great leader Kim Il Sung making a report to the Inaugural Congress of the Worker's Party of North Korea (August 29, 1946).

Kim Il Sung learned a bitter lesson from his Communist cadres during his days in China and wrote: "We emphasize that the people are the masters of revolution. If we step up the revolution of our own country by our own efforts pragmatically and intelligently, whether or not recognized by foreigners, we are bound to gain sympathy, recognition and assistance from other countries in due course of time."

Kim Il Sung's June 30, 1930, report, "The Path of the Korean Revolution," presented at a meeting at Kalun (China), was his first attempt at formulating Jucheism. He said: "The leaders of the movement must go among the masses and awaken them politically, so that they themselves wage the anti-Japanese struggle." Kim was fighting a partisan war at the time and his "Jucheism" was more or less along Mao's famous dictum that guerrillas must operate amongst the people like "fish in water."

Kim Il Sung's anti-Japanese guerrilla war was indeed a difficult fight. Kim had to operate in China where anti-Korean sentiments ran high, for so many Koreans in China worked for the Japanese. Korean nationalism was virtually non-existent among the working poor of Korea. His political war among the populace was much more arduous than his military operations against the Japanese. It is interesting to note that one sees 'Jucheism' here and there in the US CIA manual on partisan warfare.

In 1945, Kim Il Sung was put in charge of North Korea by Stalin. Kim was surrounded by Soviet advisers; 2,000-plus Soviet Koreans loyal to Stalin ran the country. Kim (in his early 30s and with grade-school education) had no prior experience in running a nation. In fact, his power was quite limited until the Red Army pulled out in 1947–48.[4]

The Korean War fiasco fortified Kim's resolve to be self-reliant. He had to kiss Stalin's rear-end for scraps of discarded Soviet weapons. He took insults from Peng Duhay, the Chinese Volunteers Army commander, who was not shy about fingering Kim's limited generalship. For example, Peng blamed Kim Il Sung for the failure of the Communist Armies to annihilate the 200,000+ UN troops trapped in the Hamhung valley in December, 1950. Kim's troops failed to carry out their assigned task of blocking MacArthur's Big Bug-out from Hungnam.[5]

The following rendition of North Korea's early history presents a more accurate account:

> Korea's liberation from Japan in 1945 left the South under the control of United States forces while the North was under the control of the Soviet forces. The North had about 2/3 of the land and 1/3 of the people, and most of the mineral and industrial resources of the nation. Even before the division of the nation was formalized with UN-sponsored elections in the South in 1948, the Soviet imprint was firmly planted in the North, with Kim Il Sung in charge and nationalization of industry and collectivization of agriculture beginning from 1946.[6]

At the time Korea was liberated from Japanese rule on

August 15, 1945, Kim Il Sung, an army captain belonging to the Soviet Union's 88th Special Brigade (a combined unit of Chinese and Koreans under a Chinese commanding officer), was picked up by the Far East Command of the Soviet Union's State Security Commission (NKVD, the predecessor of the KGB) to become a puppet to represent the Soviet's interests in Korea. He returned to Korea through Port Wonsan on September 19, 1945, aboard the Soviet warship Pugachev, with no political base at all inside the country. However, backed by the Soviet Army, Kim Il Sung organized the Workers' Party of Korea (October 10, 1945), and established the regime (September 9, 1948) following the foundation of the People's Army (February 8, 1948).

Kim Il Sung acted as the proxy of the Soviet Union's Occupation Troops in Korea to help turn North Korea into a Soviet satellite state. On February 17, 1947, Kim set up the North Korean People's Assembly (with himself as chairman) as the supreme legislative organ. He also set up the North Korean People's Committee (again, with himself as chairman) as the supreme administrative organ. These acts set the stage for the division of the country into the South and the North.

Subsequently, the (North) Korean People's Army was founded, and thereafter Kim Il Sung had the "Democratic People's Republic of Korea" (DPRK) established, boycotting the United Nations proposal to form a unified government through a free general election in both South and North Korea. On June 25, 1950, Kim Il Sung attacked south across the 38th parallel against the lightly defended South. A bloody three-year Korean War (1950–1953) followed. At the start of the war, the United Nations, including the United States, intervened on behalf of the South. Then in late November 1950[7], the People's Republic of China intervened on behalf of the North to prevent North Korea from being overrun by United Nations forces. By 1953, the front lines had stabilized into trench warfare which closely approximated the original 38th parallel line. An uneasy armistice followed.

In an effort to strengthen his power base, Kim Il Sung undertook bloody purges against opposition factions and potential enemies. There were, for example, the purge of elements originating from the Workers' Party in the South immediately after the truce of the Korean War (July 27, 1953), purges of the pro-Chinese faction and the pro-Russian faction in the late 1950s, and also a purge in the military in the late 1960s. Because of the vulnerability of the legitimacy of the North Korean regime, North Korea needed to fabricate a heroic image for Kim Il Sung in order to make up for the lack of legitimacy. As a result, Kim Il Sung was depicted as if he personally led all anti-Japanese struggles beginning in 1925, when he was merely 14 years old (born in 1912).[8]

Party, Purges, and Power: The Development of the Embryonic Religion

Juche did not become a religion overnight. North Korea's Juche Idea was devised in the 1950s as a means to purge Kim Il Sung's political rivals. After North Korean forces were defeated in the fall of 1950, Kim Il Sung's regime was saved by the intervention of millions of Chinese troops, Soviet money and arms, including Russian-piloted MiG aircraft. Upon Stalin's death in the aftermath of Korea's War for National Reunification, Vladimir Lenin's volatile de-Stalinization movement started to rage within the Soviet Union.

Since Stalin had helped Kim Il Sung seize power, criticism of Kim Il Sung was growing within North Korea because of Kim's failure to win the Korean War. His post-war political image was critically weak. Stalin's death on March 5, 1953, added a heightened sense of instability to Kim Il Sung's rule. So, Kim invented the Juche Idea to justify a series of brutal purges to cut off excessive Soviet and Chinese influence and eliminate political rivals. In addition to Kim's motivation to retain power, evidence exists that his early Juche philosophy was also motivated by personal anti-Soviet and anti-Chinese reactions. This view is reflected in North Korean historical statements that "Kim Il Sung had to beg for outdated equipment" and "the Chinese were critical of his generalship."[9] Thus, Juche began as both a means to justify Kim retaining power and a reactionary philosophy against Soviet and Chinese domination. A general chronological overview of the formation of the Juche ideological system is shown in Table 5-2.

Juche did not become a religion, or even a prominent ideology, overnight. From 1945 through 1955, Marxism-Leninism unquestioningly served as the reigning dogma of the land. During this decade, Korean nationalism was sublimated in deference to North Korea's close ties to the Soviet Union and China. However, by the mid-1950s, Juche had gained respectability as a "creative"

TABLE 5-2. Formation of the Juche Ideological System

NEW IDEOLOGICAL CONTENT	EVENT / DATE OF CHANGE	HISTORICAL BACKGROUND
Juche ideology	Propaganda agitation meeting, December 28, 1955	– Stalin's death – Purge of the domestic faction
Economic independence	Central Committee plenary meeting, December 11, 1956	– External aid reduced (problems with 5-year plan) – Anti-Kim Il Sung movement high within the Party
Political independence	Central Committee plenary meeting, December 5, 1957	– Resistance against rising power of one person – Yenan and Russian faction overthrown
Military independence	Central Committee plenary meeting, December 10, 1962	– China/Soviet struggle worsens – U.S. and Soviets explore coexistence – Military coup in South Korea
Independence in foreign policy	Second meeting of party leaders, October 5, 1966	– China/Soviet struggle spreads – Development of non-aligned movement
Comprehensive systemization	16th meeting of the Fourth Central Committee, June 28, 1967, and Fifth Party Congress, December 11, 1970	– Kim Il Sung's dictatorship established – Expansion of Kim Il Sung's personal victory
Kim Il Sung-ism	Sixth Party Congress, December 6, 1980	– Solidification of father/son hereditary line

application of Marxism-Leninism. Kim Il Sung carefully walked a fine line through a philosophical minefield to contend that Juche was a Korean outgrowth of Marxist-Leninist doctrine. Kim explained that his practical Juche ideology was the only authoritative interpretation of Marxism-Leninism that was appropriate to the revolutionary environment in North Korea.

The following remarks by Kim Il Sung provide the dictator's view of the mid-1950s. These statements show that the dictator was struggling to shape his own ideology in the face of both internal ("sectarianists and dogmatists") and external pressures ("foreign forces").

Our Party in 1955 adopted a policy to oppose dogmatism and to establish Juche-oriented principles in all sectors of life, and since then we have been struggling hard to realize this policy. Our Party has directed concerted efforts to unmasking the dangers of dogmatism prevailing among Party cadre officials, and has been conducting indoctrination programs to encourage them to study thoroughly the Party's policy line, which is designed to apply Marxism-Leninism creatively to the realities of our country, and to call upon them to carry out all projects in accordance with the Party's line. Modern revisionism has begun to raise its head in the wake of an international communist movement, so under these conditions, our struggle to oppose sectarianism and dogmatism has naturally come to collaborate with the movement to oppose this modern revisionism. Revisionism made inroads into our country through sectarianists and dogmatists...

An attack on our Party by the opportunists had reached its peak in 1956–1957. At that time a few sectarianists and dogmatists within the Party have tried in collaboration to attack our Party, under support from foreign forces and based on the revisionist idea. They not only criticized our Party line but also tried to overthrow the leadership of the Party...In the 20 years of our Party's history, the "Fatherland Liberation War" [Korean War] was a fierce struggle to oppose imperialist invasion as well as counter-revolutionary forces within the country, and the post-war struggles to oppose the opportunists were bitterest struggles aimed at removing the enemies within the communist movement. Through these struggles, our Party has grown stronger and attained precious lessons ...Our Party has been able to crush decisively all sectarianists, thus to achieve unity among members. Our Party has been successful in opposing modern revisionism and establishing our own Juche-oriented form of Marxism-Leninism.[10]

Juche ideology continues to celebrate the link between Juche and Marxism. For example, the following propaganda excerpt shows North Korea's view of the link between Karl Marx and Juche:

Karl Marx is an author of the doctrine of scientific communism and a great teacher of [the] international working class. His greatest achievement is that he expounded the materialistic dialectics for the first time and, basing himself on this, gave an exposition of the inevitability of the downfall of capitalism and [the] inevitability of the victory of communism so as to change utopian socialism into a scientific one and indicate the way of class liberation.

Great changes have taken place in the international arena in more than one hundred years since the appearance of Marxism and the looks of the world have changed fundamentally. President Kim Il Sung founded the Juche idea to develop from a new angle and consummate the revolutionary theory of [the] working class. General Kim Jong Il is making a new history of the human cause of independence, the cause of socialism. The imperialists and renegades of socialism try to hamstring the truth of the revolutionary idea of [the] working class, the doctrine of scientific communism. They are now raising a hue and cry over the "eternity" of capitalism and "end" of socialism. The truth of revolution that socialism emerges victorious and the law of social development can never be changed, though socialism is suffering turns and twists temporarily. Marx's revolutionary exploits are immortal along with the great advance of the time towards independence of the whole world [*Rodong Sinmun*].

Once his one-man rule was firmly established, Kim Il Sung began to develop Juche into a personality cult to strengthen his authority. Kim Il Sung's biography as a protégé of Stalin was weak by Korean Confucian standards. So, Kim and his entourage created stories that his forefathers were anti-Japanese fighters. These fabrications culminated in Kim declaring himself to be divine. Kim's proclamation of his own deity meant he had taken Juche across the spiritual Rubicon. He had irreversibly committed himself to the transformation of Juche from a Marxist-Leninist ideology into a new embryonic world religion.

Our look at Juche's origins continues into the 1950s and 1960s, where there are again two divergent views of North Korean history. The Juche version of these decades resounds with the praises of Kim Il Sung and Kim Jong Il while hinting at bloody internal purges:

> During the Cultural Revolution in China, the Red Guards of Beijing accused Kim Il Sung of waltzing the nights away in a snow-white field-marshal's tunic while the citizens of Pyongyang and the Chinese Volunteers were being napalmed by the Americans. This insult apparently revived Kim's anti-Chinese sentiment caused by the killings of Korean anti-Japanese par-

tisans by the Chinese Communists.

At the Workers Party Congress in 1955, he openly criticized several top Party leaders of dogmatism, formalism and flunkeyism and demanded their purge. He told the Party followers that "all ideological work must be subordinated to the interests of the Korean people (and not of any foreign powers)."

The basic idea of Jucheism is to think on your own and not copy-cat foreign ideas. Kim told the Party ideologues to be more creative and original. In China, Mao initiated his "Let One Hundred Flowers Bloom" campaign, which he had to terminate because it created more factionalism by dogmatists and opportunists than any creative ideas by true believers.

In May 1967, Kim Il Sung lashed out at the Party ideologues. He said: "Recently, while studying documents of the Party Conference some scholars and others responsible for ideological work have put forward diverse opinions on the questions of the transition period and the dictatorship of the proletariat. These issues must be solved from the Party's Juche viewpoint and that they should neither cling to propositions of the classics (Marxism-Leninism) and try to settle the questions dogmatically nor be enthralled by the ideas of flunkeyists and try to interpret the issues as others do."

Kim wrote in "For Carrying Forward and Accomplishing the Cause of Socialism" published on March 13, 1992 that: "In responding to the requirement of our revolution and the demand of the people leading their lives in the new independent era, I brought forward Jucheism and have led our revolution and construction in conformity with its requirements. However, I have not particularly thought about systematizing the philosophical principle of Jucheism. This was taken care of by Comrade Kim Jong Il. Based on his thorough study of the fundamental principles of Jucheism, Comrade Kim Jong Il formulated our Party's guiding idea as an integrated system of ideas, theory and methods."

Kim Jong Il studied Marxism-Leninism in 1960s at Kim Il Sung University. He continued his study of Communism for three more years after his graduation from the University. Kim Jong Il formulated Kim Il Sung-ism based on his understanding of Jucheism and Communism. Kim Jong Il concluded that Jucheism is a new philosophy originated by Kim Il Sung.[11]

The actual account of what happened inside North Korea during this period shows how Kim Il Sung used Juche ideology to justify his ruthless consolidation and retention of power.

After the Korean war leveled the country, north and south, Kim Il Sung proclaimed the "Juche" economic and political philosophy that still appears to rule North Korea. Juche, which has no real equivalent in English but is usually translated as self-determination, self-reliance and the like, preaches the primacy of the Labor Party, the North Korean Communist party, an independent line between the then Soviet Union and China, and totally self-sufficient economic development.

Juche was proclaimed in December 1955, when Kim underlined the critical need for a Korea-centered revolution rather than one designed to benefit, in his words, "another country." Juche is designed to inspire national pride and identity and mold national consciousness into a potentially powerful focus for internal solidarity centered on Kim and the KWP.[12]

According to Kim, Juche means "the independent stance of rejecting dependence on others and of using one's own powers, believing in one's own strength and displaying the revolutionary spirit of self-reliance." Juche is an ideology geared to address North Korea's contemporary goals—an independent foreign policy, a self-sufficient economy, and a self-reliant defense posture. Kim Il Sung's enunciation of Juche in 1955 was aimed at developing a monolithic and effective system of authority under his exclusive leadership. The invocation of Juche was a psychological tool with which to stigmatize the foreign-oriented dissenters and remove them from the center of power. Targeted for elimination were groups of pro-Soviet and pro-Chinese anti-Kim dissenters.[13]

Juche ideology in 1955–66 had been a mere political catch phrase to support political campaigns designed to prevent the influence of the de-Stalinization movement from infiltrating into North Korea, to spur the people to harbor the spirit of self-reliance in coping with the economic difficulties after the suspension of aid from the Soviet Union, and then to justify Pyongyang's stand to conduct equidistant diplomacy toward Beijing and Moscow, while the two allies were engaged in disputes. At the same time, North Korea began to use the catch phrase to intensify the personality cult of Kim Il Sung and to justify his monolithic leadership.[14]

Kim's practical ideology was given a test of relevancy throughout the mid-1960s. In the late 1950s, Kim was able to mobilize internal support when he purged pro-Soviet and pro-Chinese dissenters from party ranks. During the first half of the 1960s, Kim faced an even more formidable challenge when he had to weather a series of tense situations that had potentially adverse implications for North Korea's economic development and national security. Among these were a sharp decrease in aid from the Soviet Union and China; discord between the Soviet Union and China and its disquieting implications for North Korea's confrontation with the United States and South Korea; Pyongyang's disagreements with Moscow and apprehensions about the reliability of the Soviet Union as an ally; and the rise of an authoritarian regime in Seoul under former General Park Chung Hee (1961–79).

These developments emphasized the need for self-reliance—the need to rely on domestic resources, heighten vigilance against possible external challenges, and strengthen domestic political solidarity. Sacrifice, austerity, unity, and patriotism became dominant themes in the party's efforts to instill in the people the importance of Juche and collective discipline. By the mid-1960s, however, North Korea could afford to relax somewhat; its strained relations with the Soviet Union had eased, as reflected in part by Moscow's decision to rush economic and military assistance to Pyongyang.

Beginning in mid-1965, Juche was presented as the essence of Kim Il Sung's leadership and of party lines and policies for every conceivable revolutionary situation. Kim's past leadership record was put forward as the "guide and compass" for the present and future and as a source of strength sufficient to propel the faithful through any adversity.[15]

The early ultra-nationalist quality of Juche served Pyongyang well during the Soviet-Chinese rivalry. As Beijing and Moscow tried to woo Kim Il Sung, he expertly played them against one another. The Juche economy of the 1970s prospered as well. In terms of per capita GNP, North Korea out-produced South Korea until the early 1970s. According to U.S. estimates, 1977 was the last year that North and South Korea's GNPs were roughly equivalent. South Korea's export-oriented economy then began to experience rapid growth, and the economic gap has since turned into a deep chasm.

By 1998, the "have" South out-produced the "have not" North by a 14-to-1 ratio.

Despite Juche's transition into a religion upon the deification of Kim Il Sung, Marxist-Leninist creeds remain embedded within the Juche worldview. For example, the April 1972 issue of *The Worker* referred to the Korean Workers' Party as "a Marxist-Leninist Party." This designation was presented within the context that "the only valid policy for Korean Communists is Marxism-Leninism." The author called for "its creative application to our realities."[16]

Since 1974, Pyongyang has proclaimed Juche to be an entirely separate ideology from Marxism-Leninism. The new Juche ideology emphasizes that Juche is:

> ...the only scientific revolutionary thought representing our era of Juche and communist future and the most effective revolutionary theoretical structure that leads to the future of communist society *along the surest shortcut.*[17]

This new "surest shortcut" emphasis was based on the contention that a different historical era, with its unique sociopolitical circumstances, also requires a new revolutionary ideology. These revised teachings contend that Juche is the new philosophy for a new era. While Marxism and Leninism were valid in their own time, contemporary Juche ideology views them as the philosophical dinosaurs of an age gone by.

In the years since the 1970s, references to Marxism and Leninism have been steadily purged from Party literature. By 1980, the two terms practically disappeared from the pages of *The Worker*. A March 1980 editorial in *The Worker* proclaimed:

> Within the Party, none but the leader Kim Il Sung's revolutionary thought, the Juche ideology, prevails—*and there is no room for any hodgepodge thought contrary to it.*[18]

When the time for the Sixth Party Congress rolled around in October of the same year, Kim Il Sung's address did not contain a single reference to Marxism-Leninism. Kim's October 1980 report proclaimed:

> The whole party is rallied rock-firm around its Central Committee and knit together in ideology and purpose on the basis of the Juche idea. *The Party has no room for any other idea than the Juche idea,* and no force can ever break its unity and cohesion based on this idea.[19]

This was a remarkable shift from his many references to North Korea's Marxist-Leninist heritage in his November 1970 speech to the Fifth Party Congress.

One of the current trends in post-Kim Il Sung Pyongyang is to replace technocrat leaders with military leaders thought to be more loyal to Kim Jong Il. Such a falling-from-grace replacement typically results in a non-assignment, which often leads to the person's disappearance from the usual social circles. However, replacement also can mean the official is destined for "re-education" in a concentration camp. In some cases, such a falling out of favor can even result in one's execution if some act of rebellion or defection is suspected or alleged. In one such recent purge, Kim Jong Il removed over 40 high ranking military and political officials just prior to the July 27, 1998, elections. Thus, the purges that have gone on throughout a half-century of totalitarian rule continue to occur.

The Juche religion of today has become so glorified that it has been transformed within North Korea as an end unto itself. This idolatrous religion is so powerful that it serves as a galvanizing framework that unifies 23 million North Koreans and permeates their entire culture. Even amidst severe famine and economic woes, Juche ideology reinforces the Party's policies through its incessant demands for Spartan austerity, sacrifice, discipline, and unswerving dedication to Kim Jong Il. With his new proclamation of the advent of "the Juche Era," Kim Jong Il's prophesies of the downfall of imperialism and the worldwide victory of socialism and Communism resonate with the jihad-like quality of a present-day Islamic Mahdi.

Practice Falls Short of Theory: Departures from Self-Reliance

The practice of Juche started falling short of theory in the 1970s as the Hermit Kingdom veered from economic self-reliance. With a sluggish economy, North Korea strayed from the purity of Juche by seeking international investors, loans, and economic and technical aid from Japan, West Germany, Sweden, and other countries. Then, in 1976, North Korea ruined its international credit when Pyongyang defaulted on its $1.3 billion worth of international loans from Western banks. In 1984, North Korea passed its first legislation permitting foreign investment and enabling small-scale export-oriented joint ventures. North Korea's overhaul of foreign investment laws in the 1990s, along with the creation of the Tumen River area's Rajin-Sonbong Free Economic and Trade Zone in cooperation with Russia and China, demonstrate yet other departures from truly self-reliant Juche.

Kim Jong Il, since assuming rule in 1994, has turned the ideal of North Korean Juche-style socialism into a caricature of begging for food at the backdoor of the international community while proclaiming itself "self-reliant" at the world's front door. However, Kim Jong Il's Juche "class consciousness" mandates that no blame may be attributed to the Juche system itself. Thus, the Juche prohibition against self-criticism eliminates the possibility of any meaningful social or economic reforms apart from a wholesale replacement of the Juche religious-political system. Though Pyongyang is aware of the need to open its doors to bring about economic recovery, North Korean leaders are obsessed by the fear that such openings will weaken their totalitarian grip on the state.

Recognition of this philosophical contraction is highly important. Note that from an orthodox Juche standpoint, virtually any dealings with foreigners represents a potential philosophical contradiction with Juche religious ideology. Such a contradiction explains North Korea's sporadic derailment of the Korean Peninsula Energy Development Organization (KEDO) Light Water Reactor (LWR) project and initiation of the Kangnung submarine sabotage mission while hosting the September 1996 Rajin-Sonbong Free Trade Zone Conference. Nevertheless, following a December 1996 apology by North Korea for the submarine incident, U.S. Secretary of State Madeleine Albright and South Korean Foreign Minister Yoo Chong reaffirmed support for the 1994 KEDO agreement. This agreement is to provide over $5 billion in light water nuclear reactors to North Korea in return for Pyongyang freezing its nuclear program.

The threat is very real that North Korea might use chemical and/or biological weapons (also called "poor man nukes") within the East Asian area. However, the thought also arises that North Korea's much publicized "nuclear weapons program" might be a $5 billion hoax on the United States and South Korea. Hwang Jang Yop maintains, even after his 1997 defection, that he knows of no North Korean nuclear weapons program. Six years earlier, in 1991, North Korean Professor Pak Mun Hoi told Jeremy J. Stone that, given the failure of the North's scientists to build a nuclear power plant, he could not believe they could build a bomb. Pak further stated, "Everything would become clear when there is an [IAEA[20]] inspection." Pak told Stone that "Stalin blew up 100,000 tons of dynamite once to create the impression that he had a nuclear weapon." (The complexity of fusing large quantities of munitions would make the difference between a conventional and nuclear explosion readily detectable by sensitive seismometers.) However, when Stone asked Pak, "Would it be Juche to have nuclear weapons in the sense of their providing strength and independence?," Pak replied:

> Yes, of course, but if all people think and act in the same way, it is stronger than an atom bomb. One can't consolidate the system with atom bombs alone.[21]

The formation of the "second economy" (black market) is another important aspect of the failure of Juche in practice. The second economy in socialist states refers to "all private economic activities which are excluded from the state-run distribution channel."[22] In August 1958, North Korean cabinet decree No. 140 replaced rural markets with government-run markets. Since then, farmers were given the privilege of cultivating a small plot of vegetables, limited to 100 square meters, for private use and sale. Growth and exchange of grain on and from these plots was strictly forbidden. According to Juche ideology, these private plots would someday disappear "when socialism attains a high degree of development in which the people are supplied with sufficient commodities, and the cooperative ownership system is replaced by the people's (national) ownership."[23] However, since the 1980s, these farmers' markets have gradually grown into huge black markets in which contraband goods are sold. The importance of the second economy in the former Soviet Union suggests the importance of this North Korean counterpart:

> Soviet farmers on cooperative farms in 1977 had been able to meet about 72% of their demand for meat, 76% for milk and almost all potatoes and eggs with the products from private farming and stock breeding. It was also reported that 25% of total agricultural products in the Soviet Union at that time came from this private land, which accounted for only 3% of the total arable land. [24]

In the 1980s these rural markets were allowed to be open only ten days per month. As the economic situation worsens, they have now become open daily. In 1992, the North Korean authorities tried unsuccessfully to restrict the growth of these markets. Since 1993, even grains such as corn and rice are openly sold on these markets in many areas.

As the border trade between North Korea and China expands, ethnic Korean peddlers from China have crossed the border to ply their trade. Their products include Chinese-made industrial goods which they barter for Korean antiques and marine products. These peddlers have opened the eyes of many North Koreans to capitalist ideas, which are heretical according to strict Juche "self-reliance" religious ideology.

From a philosophical standpoint, Juche's origins in foreign Marxism-Leninism also represent a departure from self-reliance. If Juche arose out of Marxist-Leninist roots, then, like Kim Jong Il's birthplace, Juche was born in Russia as well. This embarrassing contradiction explains the campaign to recreate Kim Jong Il's birthplace to Mt. Paektu and purge any references to Juche's Marxist-Leninist origins from the collective memory of the Party and masses.

From a religious standpoint, the Juche concept of a god-king lacks originality as well. Ancient rulers in Babylon, Egypt, Assyria, and Rome—just to name a few—proclaimed themselves to be gods. A more recent self-proclaimed messiah was China's Hong Xiuquan, the "younger brother of Jesus Christ." In the 1860s and 1870s, in neighboring China, Hong Xiuquan instigated the failed Taiping rebellion that resulted in over 20 million—possibly even higher than 100 million—deaths. Thus, Juche's origins and implementation represent an ongoing self-contradiction. Given this persistent problem of practice falling short of theory, Pyongyang's propaganda and policies are aimed at "damage control" to protect both the domestic and international illusion of the purity of Juche.

CHAPTER 6

Juche Holy Sites

King Nebuchadnezzar made an image of gold, ninety feet high and nine feet wide, and set it up on the plain of Dura in the province of Babylon.

DANIEL 3:1

While there are literally thousands of monuments, parks, schools, roads, and edifices dedicated to the gods of Juche, four stand out as particular sacred places in the Juche religion: the tomb of Kim Il Sung (also called Kumsusan Memorial Palace and the Temple of Juche); the giant statue of Kim Il Sung (and Kim Il Sung Square); the Tower of the Juche Idea (and the Tower of the Juche Idea Square); and Mt. Paektu, the sacred mountain—the birthplace of Juche. The first three of these Juche holy sites, located in North Korea's capital city of Pyongyang, hold a religious significance that is comparable to the holiest sites of other major world religions. The fourth site, Mt. Paektu, is located in the northern part of the country, not far from the border of the People's Republic of China.

The Temple of Juche

Officers and men of the Korean People's Army visited the Kumsusan Memorial Palace on Tuesday to pay homage to President Kim Il Sung... The visitors expressed deep

185

*reverence up to the Statue and went upstairs to make bows
to the President who lies in state.*
                                    KOREAN CENTRAL NEWS AGENCY
                                    SEPTEMBER 10, 1997

When Kim Il Sung died on July 8, 1994, North Korea's leaders had his body mummified and interred in an elaborate coffin at Pyongyang's Kumsusan Memorial Palace. Pyongyang's leadership seized this highly emotional moment to initiate a propaganda campaign declaring that Kim Il Sung is "immortal and imperishable." The inscription on Kim Il Sung's memorial captures this Juche version of immortality: "The great leader comrade Kim Il Sung will always be with us."[1] Formal dedication of the Kumsusan Memorial Palace/tomb complex occurred in July 1997 on the three-year anniversary of Kim Il Sung's death. Each year, North Korea's government spends about $2 million for the special gasses used in Kim Il Sung's coffin to keep him looking alive.

The mummification of Kim Il Sung is not a unique idea within Communist cultures. The Communist version of this ancient practice started in 1924 when Josef Stalin ordered Vladimir Lenin's remains to be preserved and displayed for future generations. George Washington University's Peter Reddaway explains:

> Stalin wanted to set up Lenin as an icon of the alternative Bolshevik religion...Lenin was to be a Christ-like figure.[2]

This form of leader veneration is also practiced in China and Vietnam. The mummified bodies of China's Mao Zedong and Vietnam's Ho Chi Minh are virtual holy sites in these lands. A deep level of sentiment is associated with the worship of these mummified leaders.

However, Juche elevates classical Communist leader veneration to the extreme of religious worship. In North Korea, foreign and domestic visitors alike are expected to bow with the deepest reverence to this god of Juche and pray for his immortality. Along with bowing and praying at the site, worshippers also frequently lay floral wreaths and floral baskets at the tomb.

The statue inside the Temple of Juche depicts Kim Il Sung seated on a throne at the top of a series of stairs (very similar to the Lincoln Memorial in Washington, D.C.). However, this statue is the "Holy of Holies" of the Juche religion. Propaganda highlights North Korean worship inside the temple, while the masses and foreigners are generally depicted to worship outside in Kim Il Sung Square before the great statue on Mansu Hill. However, unlike Judaism's ancient temple in Jerusalem, or particularly sacred Islamic holy sites, non-Juche adherents are permitted to go inside the Kumsusan Memorial Palace. The following North Korean propaganda excerpt speaks of the religious significance of this Juche holy site:

> Party members, soldiers and working people visited the Kumsusan Memorial Palace on Friday to pay respects to the great leader President Kim Il Sung... *They renewed their firm faith and will to uphold the President as the eternal sun of Juche,* exalt his revolutionary life and great exploits for all ages and complete the Juche revolution under the leadership of the great comrade Kim Jong Il, cherishing the great national pride of having the peerlessly great man at the head of the WPK [*KCNA*].

In particular, Kim Jong Il's visits to the Temple of Juche for key holy days[3] cast him in the role of the High Priest of Juche as he enters the temple to perform worship on behalf of the nation. For example, at the stroke of the 1998 New Year, Kim Jong Il, along with an entourage, entered the Temple of Juche to worship Kim Il Sung:

> Kim Jong Il, General Secretary of the Workers' Party of Korea visited the Kumsusan Memorial Palace at 00:00 on January 1, the New Year Juche 87 (1998). Laid before the Statue was a basket of flowers in the joint name of the WPK Central Committee and Central Military Commission and the DPRK National Defense Commission, Central People's Committee and Administration Council. General Kim Jong Il, together with senior party, state and army officials, paid deep respects to the Statue. Then he went upstairs to the hall where President Kim Il Sung lies in state and bowed to the President in humble reverence [*KCNA*].

The Statue of Kim Il Sung

They came in waves to stand before the gigantic bronze statue of Kim Il Sung, the late "Great Leader" of North Korea...Twenty-four hours a day, they just kept coming.[4]

DAN WOODING
CHRISTIAN HERALD
NOVEMBER 19, 1994

The gigantic bronze statue of Kim Il Sung, the father of Juche, was erected in 1972 in celebration of President Kim Il Sung's 60th birthday. It looks down from Pyongyang's Mansu Hill upon Kim Il Sung Square where, throughout the year, crowds of upwards of 2 million North Koreans gather to worship Kim Il Sung, Kim Jong Il, and celebrate their common Juche faith. This giant statue is the most famous of the more than 30,000 monuments to Kim Il Sung.

Its religious significance is comparable to the biblical account of the great statue of Nebuchadnezzar in Daniel chapter 3. As with the biblical account, the penalty for North Koreans who refuse to bow before the Great Statue is death. When one foreign businessman visited the statue, he noted that he sensed the same spirit of idol worship before the Statue of Kim Il Sung as he felt in Japan while observing the Japanese bow to their Shinto idols. When directed by his North Korean guide to bow before the Great Statue, this man refused to bow on the grounds that he was a Christian. The guide immediately escorted the visitor away from the Great Square. Not surprisingly, he was not taken to Kim Il Sung Square by his guides on subsequent business trips to North Korea. Remarkably, Kim Il Sung's 30-meter (98.4-foot) tall statue is almost exactly the same height as Nebuchadnezzar's 90-foot-high gold statue in the Bible.

It is understandable, given the North Koreans' view (like the Babylonians of old) that Kim Il Sung is god, that they believe everyone should worship, honor, respect, and pay homage to his image. To more fully appreciate the significance of the image, one must keep in mind the Pyongyang-centric Juche worldview. In a theoretical sense, the Juche world figuratively emanates in concentric rings from Mt. Paektu. Indeed, a giant mural of Mt. Paektu flanks Pyongyang's great statue of Kim Il Sung on Mansu Hill. However, in a practical sense, the great statue of Kim Il Sung is the focal point of the Juche religion.

In September 1994, American journalist Dan Wooding reported on the ongoing phenomena of Juche worship before the image:

> They came in waves to stand before the gigantic bronze statue of Kim Il Sung, the late "Great Leader" of North Korea, to observe a one-minute silence, place flowers before "him" and bow and weep. Twenty-four hours a day, they just kept coming to his shrine in the center of Pyongyang... "The people have lost their father and keep on wanting to mourn his

death," the North Korean guide explained.[5]

Frequently, North Korean propaganda uses the occasion of foreigners (knowingly or unwittingly) paying homage to North Korea's god to validate and promote Juche. In particular, North Korean propaganda seems to put the spotlight on foreign ambassadors and diplomatic emissaries from Vietnam, Indonesia, Iran, Cuba, Japan, Guinea, Nepal, India, and elsewhere who pay homage at Mansu Hill. These foreign visitors pray to and bow before the great statue. Their worship also includes laying floral baskets and wreaths before the giant idol of Juche.

Nations and people should carefully consider whether to render spiritual or religious homage before the great statue of Kim Il Sung. Make no mistake, this statue is not North Korea's version of America's Mount Rushmore in South Dakota. It is the idol of idols in a land where Kim Il Sung is genuinely believed to be god. In a very rough comparison to the ancient temple of Jerusalem, this great statue presides over Kim Il Sung Square which, along with the Tower of the Juche Idea Square, forms sort of the "Court of the Gentiles" of the Juche religion. All North Koreans are expected to show reverence for the great statue—including even the

North Koreans fill Kim Il Sung Square during Kim Il Sung's funeral.

reigning Su-ryong, the Dear Leader Comrade Kim Jong Il. From a Juche viewpoint, failure to render proper respect to the great statue approaches blasphemy.

North Korea has unwittingly set the stage for a contemporary repeat of the Bible's Shadrach, Meshach, and Abednego incident (see Daniel 3). Considering that the devil has not changed over the last 26 centuries, people should not be too shocked if they hear one day soon that Pyongyang has decreed that all who do not bow to Kim Il Sung's image, regardless of nationality, will be subject to a high-profile public execution!

The Tower of the Juche Idea

Then they said, "Come, let us build ourselves a city, with a tower that reaches to the heavens, so that we may make a name for ourselves and not be scattered over the face of the whole earth."

GENESIS 11:4

The Tower of the Juche Idea was built in 1982 in Pyongyang, the capital of North Korea. The tower is situated along the Tae-dong River opposite Kim Il Sung Square and the Tower of the Juche Idea Plaza. At a height of 170 meters (over 550 feet), the Tower of the Juche Idea looms over Pyongyang as a religious "high place" and a constant reminder of Juche's dominion over the capital.

The book *An Earthly Paradise for the People* provides Pyongyang's view of the tower:

> The immortal Tower of Juche Idea soars high in the heart of Pyongyang. It is symbol of the greatness of the Juche Idea. *The tower, which is a token of the people's burning loyalty to the great President [Kim Il Sung] and His Excellency, dear Kim Jong Il,* can be seen from any part of the city, day and night.[6]

The Tower of the Juche Idea overlooks several annual celebrations attended by half a million to two million North Koreans who praise their Juche god, Comrade Kim Jong Il. A 1997 propaganda account relates how a massive crowd gathered near the tower and:

> ...extended highest glory to comrade Kim Jong Il on his election as WPK General Secretary with absolute support and trust from the Party members, servicemen and all other people and hardened their resolution to complete the Juche revolution under his leadership [*KCNA*].

The Tower of the Juche Idea on the bank of Pyongyang's Taedong River.

According to the North Koreans, the tower's height was derived from the number of stones used, which is based on the number of days Kim Il Sung had lived up until his 70th birthday (April 15, 1982)—the date on which the tower was dedicated. Since the tower's construction, high officials have gifted more than 600 high-quality commemorative stones to be mounted on this monument to the Juche religion. The following account from North Korea's *DPRK Magazine* explains the meaning of these stones:

The prominent figures in many countries have donated stones of superior quality to the Tower of the Juche Idea *as a token of reverence and praise* for the great leader President Kim Il Sung who has founded the Juche idea and applied it in the revolution and construction and the dear leader Comrade Kim Jong Il who has clarified the Juche idea as the guiding one in the era of independence and developed and enriched it constantly [*DPRK*].

Visitors look out over Pyongyang City from the observatory of the Tower of the Juche Idea.

The Pyongyang propaganda journal continued by giving an account of one donated stone:

> The Director of Naomi Trading Company in Hong Kong surveyed famous stone production centers to pick a rare natural stone and processed and engraved it with the letter reading "Long Live Great Juche Idea of Kim Il Sung and Kim Jong Il!" and sent it to the tower [*DPRK*].

The long list of organizations donating these stones includes Party, state, and government leaders, political parties, public organizations, public figures, international organizations, and Juche study groups from over 90 countries.

From a biblical perspective, the Tower of the Juche Idea, like a giant Ashtoreth pole (see 2 Kings 23:13), represents the chief spiritual high place of Pyongyang.

Mt. Paektu, the Sacred Mountain: Birthplace of Juche

> *Mt. Paektu... is the great home of the revolution where the precious revolutionary tradition was formed... The revolutionary spirit that rose in flames in the thick forests of Mt. Paektu is the most precious asset which should shine in this land from generation to generation, and is the immortal banner which guarantees the boundless prosperity of the Korean nation.*[7]
>
> KIM JONG IL

From a height of just over 9,000 feet, the majestic snow-capped peaks of Mt. Paektu look down over the Korean peninsula to the south. Mt. Paektu (also translated Mt. Paekdu and Mt. Baekdu), located in Samjiyon County of North Korea's Ryanggang Province, is part of a 744-mile-long mountain range. The name Paektu, which may be translated literally as "White Head" or "white headed," originates from the white pumice stones that covered the mountain after volcanic eruptions. About 500 yards below the mountain's summit is a beautiful, crystal-clear volcanic lake named Ch'onji, which means "heavenly lake" or "pond of heaven." The mountain belongs to the coldest zone on the Korean peninsula and the weather is prone to sudden changes. The headwaters of both the Amnokkang (Yalu River in Chinese) and the Tumangang (Tumen River in Chinese), which form the frontiers between North Korea and China, flow down from the thickly forested mountain.

For centuries, Mt. Paektu has had a special spiritual significance as Korea's ancestral mountain. The Juche religion has captured this ancestral spiritism by teaching that "the Juche idea was rooted in Paektu Mountain, which symbolizes the spirit of the Korean people."[8] Even South Koreans generally believe Mt. Paektu is a holy mountain. Juche's architects have capitalized on ancient Korean traditions by designating Mt. Paektu as "the holy mountain of the Korean revolution" [*KCNA*]. For example, the DPRK Ministry of Post and Telecommunications issued memorial stamps on February 16, 1998:

> Printed in the upper part of a sheet of stamp are letters "56th birthday of the great leader comrade Kim Jong Il" and in the lower part is his native home in the secret camp of *Mt. Paektu, a holy place*, against the background of the sky above Jong Il Peak, with fizzling firecrackers [*KCNA*].

Before we consider the Juche significance of Mt. Paektu in detail, it is important to be able to distinguish between truth and propaganda myths. For example, the historical truth is that Kim Jong Il was actually born in the Khabarovsk region of Siberia, not on Mt. Paektu. Evidently Juche's image makers did not think it was appropriate for the future god of North Korea to be born in the Soviet Union. However, the Juche view of the past is that history is only what the collective consciousness of the people actually remembers. So Juche propagandists have totally rewritten North Korea's history to teach that Kim Jong Il was born in a "milyong" (a secret camp) on Mt. Paektu. For example, at a March 1998 art show featuring Mt. Paektu art, Kim Jong Il commented, "Mt. Paektu and its vicinity have [been] turned into a school for education of Party members, working people and students in the revolutionary tradition established by President Kim Il Sung" [*KCNA*]. This multi-million dollar nationwide hoax of Kim Jong Il's birthplace and idyllic childhood continues to be propagated through the curriculum at all primary and secondary schools and the "Kim Jong Il Department" of each of North Korea's universities. People throughout North Korea are encouraged to make an annual visit to the milyong at Mt. Paektu. The "secret camp" has now officially been designated as Juche sacred ground.

Along with the revisionist history surrounding Kim Jong Il's childhood and youth, Mt. Paektu is also home of Comrade Kim Jong Suk, the goddess of Juche. Juche history records that "Dear

Mt. Paektu is the sacred mountain of North Korea's Juche religion.

Comrade Kim Jong Il grew up under the care and revolutionary education of the great leader General Kim Il Sung and Comrade Kim Jong Suk, an indomitable communist revolutionary fighter" in a secret camp beneath the shadow of Mt. Paektu. Given the known Mt. Paektu fabrications about Kim Jong Il's birth and childhood, the Juche record of Kim Jong Suk's exploits and other "history" surrounding Mt. Paektu also becomes highly suspect. For example, in the 1930s and early 1940s, Kim Il Sung, Kim Jong Suk, and little Kim Jong Il were living in the Soviet Union and had little or nothing to do with the anti-Japanese resistance. Also, Kim Il Sung was not a general back then, but still a junior officer holding the rank of captain. Moreover, it is unlikely that the Japanese considered Mt. Paektu to be of much military value during their occupation given its lack of strategic or economic importance. No major battles were ever fought in its vicinity during the 1930s and 1940s.

In contrast, Pyongyang teaches its people that:

> The great leader General Kim Il Sung set up secret bases around Mt. Paektu to lead the Korean revolution as a whole from the latter half of the 1930s to the first half of the 1940s during the anti-Japanese armed struggle. In Mt. Paektu's secret camp there is the Command of the revolution where General Kim Il Sung lived. There is a log cabin in which dear Comrade Kim Jong Il was born. It was here that dear Comrade Kim Jong Il, great successor to the revolutionary cause of Juche, grew up, going through crucial stages in the anti-Japanese struggle. Comrade Kim Jong Suk, an indomitable communist revolutionary fighter, came to Mt. Paektu in September 1936 and

took part in the building of secret camp. She worked hard to implement General Kim Il Sung's plan and line for national liberation.[9]

The secret camp, which is on display, features a very new looking Davy Crockett–styled "humble log cabin in *its original shape.*" This little cabin allegedly simultaneously served as the headquarters of the entire revolution, was home of General Kim Il Sung, a barracks for guerrillas, and was the place "in which dear Comrade Kim Jong Il was born."[10]

The following propaganda gives a brief hint of the extensive "history," "battlefields," archeological digs, and lore that have sprung up around Mt. Paektu:

> Mt. Paektu is Korea's ancestral mountain with 1,200-kilometer-long ranges. The sunrise seen on the mountain is the most magnificent view loved by the Korean people. The people are deeply fascinated by Mt. Paektu, Lake Chon on the mountain and the sunrise viewed on the top of the mountain. The sunrise is associated with the enduring feats of three generals who liberated and glorified the country…President Kim Il Sung…comrade Kim Jong Suk…and Secretary Kim Jong Il, who was born as lodestar of Mt. Paektu…*Especially, the indomitable spirit of Secretary Kim Jong Il, the spirit of Mt. Paektu, is mirrored in the sunrise* [*KCNA*].

> When he [Secretary Kim Jong Il] mounted Mt. Paektu, the time-honored place of the revolution, he evinced his determination to glorify it…and said that he would take it as his lifelong motto to give joy and satisfaction to the President [*KCNA*].

> Secretary Kim Jong Il was born with distinguished gifts… He cultivated his traits more admirably through the building of a new country…With such distinguished gifts, *he has become the greatest man of Mt. Paektu type* and a brilliant commander [*KCNA*].

The Mt. Paektu chronicles have been officially incorporated into the "Juche-speak" terminology. For example, recent public speeches by Pak Song Chol, North Korea's Vice President, and Kim Man Yong, an official from the Korean Writers Union, both incorporated Mt. Paektu mythology in a factual manner:

> *Pak Song Chol:* The DPRK Government, under the wise guidance of President Kim Il Sung and the respected General

Kim Jong Il, has firmly preserved the Juche character...Un-shakable is the Korean people's faith and will to *accomplish the revolutionary cause of Juche started in Mt. Paektu forests,* holding Secretary Kim Jong Il at the head of the revolution...in the struggle for global independence [*KCNA*].

Kim Man Yong: The great comrade Kim Jong Il's election as WPK General Secretary is a product of the firm will of the Korean people to hold in high esteem *the great man produced by Mt. Paektu* and accomplish the sun's cause generation after generation as well as of the unanimous desire of the revolu-tionary people of the world...A powerful Kim Jong Il's Korea will be built on this land [*KCNA*].

As if the legends surrounding Mt. Paektu were not enough, nearby Jong Il Peak has been dedicated by Kim Jong Il in everlast-ing memory of himself:

The Jong Il Peak, 1,797 meters [5,896 feet], is situated in the Sobaeksu Valley with the secret camp on Mt. Paektu. In August 1988 words "Jong Il Peak" were carved on granite rocks in three tiers, each weighing over 100 tons. The rock contain-ing the character "Jong" depicts the Changgun Peak in Mt. Paektu; the rock with "Il" portrays a mirror; and the "Peak" rock a flower basket.[11]

Far from being humorous, it is important for political, mili-tary, and spiritual strategists to grasp the meaning of Mt. Paektu. From a military targeting standpoint, a few precision-guided wea-pons could quickly obliterate the central Juche worship sites in Pyongyang. However, such destruction would not break the spiri-tual grasp of the Juche religion over the hearts and minds of the Korean people. Unlike the manmade Juche religious structures in Pyongyang, Mt. Paektu cannot be erased off of the map of North Korea by conventional or even nuclear weapons. Given this un-derstanding, the political analyst should conclude that, without a fundamental change in the people's belief in the Juche religion, any imposition of a solely political-military end state, with or without the use of military power, would not result in lasting change. In Chapter 11 we will discuss the biblical significance of Mt. Paektu, and describe what action is required to bring about a lasting change in North Korea.

CHAPTER 7

The Juche Worldview

Juche has made clear the philosophical principle that man is the master of everything and decides everything... the philosophical principle of Juche is not a mere view of life but a principle which makes clear its worldview. Juche philosophy elucidates a human-centered worldview, a Juche-oriented worldview.[1]

KIM JONG IL

The Juche worldview is radically different from that of the typical American. It is characterized by extreme nationalism coupled with a deep distrust of the outside world. This xenophobia has been nurtured both by Korea's pre-1945 colonial experience and by its ongoing struggle to survive as a Communist nation.

A worldview is a comprehensive frame of reference through which an individual or people view the world around them. For example, the American and North Korean worldviews are so far apart that, without one temporarily suspending one's own cultural paradigm, one truly cannot understand the other. Ultimately, the Juche worldview provides that framework for North Korea's foreign policies and attitudes toward nations.

Cross-cultural communication can be considered as having seven dimensions, one of which is *worldview*. Different cultures have varying cultural distances between them in any given dimension. Table 7-1 shows an estimate of the differences between the U.S. and the North Korean ("DPRK") and South Korean ("ROK") cultures in terms of these dimensions.

TABLE 7-1. Cultural Distances Among the U.S., North Korea, and South Korea[2]

CULTURAL VARIABLE	CULTURAL DISTANCE									
	1	2	3	4	5	6	7	8	9	10
Worldview	US						ROK			DPRK
Cognitive Process	US						ROK			DPRK
Linguistic Form	US									ROK DPRK
Behavioral Pattern	US					ROK				DPRK
Social Structure	US					ROK				DPRK
Media Influence	US				ROK					DPRK
Motivational Resources	US				ROK					DPRK

From a quick glance at the above table, it's apparent that there is more to the cross-cultural gap than the fact that North Koreans are simply "Korean." The concept of the worldview spans all dimensions of culture. Under North Korea's totalitarian system, all of these dimensions of culture are shaped by Juche religious ideology.

How important is an understanding of North Korea's worldview to those unfamiliar with the Hermit Kingdom? Without a basic understanding of the Juche worldview, foreign policy makers, international organizations, and businesses are apt to have unrealistic expectations in their dealings with Pyongyang. For example, North Korea's national interests are guided by the Juche worldview. Though these interests have never been officially stated, they may be summarized in three objectives: (1) safeguard "our style of socialism" (Juche totalitarianism) from destruction by any outside aggression; (2) improve the people's material living conditions; and (3) achieve national reunification of the peninsula under a Communist system.

Yet, most outsiders lack any appreciable grasp of Juche ideology. This ignorance is reflected in a "maybe they'll change" sentiment, expressed in the following press release from South Korea and the United Nations:

> Recent cries for help tempt the world with *a chance to buy influence* in the course of a country that has been a dangerous renegade for decades. Flooding and food shortages have

forced increasingly isolated North Korea to diverge from its ideology of Juche, or self-reliance, and seek aid from its worst enemies. "You could see this as North Korea opening its doors a bit," said Ola Almgren, who led a U.N. team that visited recently to assess damage from summer rains that the North said were the worst in 100 years. "It is an opportunity for the international community to improve its relationship with that country."[3]

The following discussion considers how the Juche worldview impacts North Korean attitudes, policies, and actions toward South Korea, Japan, the United States, China, Russia, and other nations.

South Korea

The [North Korean] nation will curse forever the criminal behaviors of the South Korean war maniacs who have been hell bent on war preparations, not interested in dialogue.

KOREAN CENTRAL NEWS AGENCY
JANUARY 14, 1998

North Korea's national goal is to unify the South through revolutionary means. In order to create a revolutionary atmosphere in the South, the North has turned loose its propaganda experts to prepare the South's populace for reunification North Korean-style.

Since the 1990s, the North has begun to employ nationalism-oriented propaganda activities in conducting a political offensive against Seoul: the North's propaganda machines have been trying to implant in the minds of all people in the South with the belief that the government in Pyongyang is the only legitimate one on the Korean peninsula, saying that the North Korean form of socialism is designed to regard the nation first and that the Korean nation was founded in the northern part of the peninsula.[4]

North Korea's ongoing hostility toward South Korea will never change as long as the Juche religious system remains in power in North Korea. Reunification on the North's terms is a sacred intrinsic part of the Juche religion. The anti-South Korean attitude is so entrenched that North Korean Juche-speak does not permit the use of "South Korea," "Republic of Korea," or even capitalizing "South" in most of their English translations of speeches and writings. Instead, terms are used such as "the illegitimate regime of the south," "hell-bent war maniacs" and, during brief respites, just "the south." According to Juche teachings, the people of the south remain in bondage. Their land is an impoverished colony of American imperialistic aggression. The following December 1997 North Korean propaganda article provides an example of this viewpoint.

> The world people say that South Korea is the *"worst backward country in politics"* at the end of the 20th century. Above all, this is illustrated by the fact that South Korea is *the last colony when the 20th century is coming to an end...*Worse still, the prerogative of *the supreme command of its army is in the possession of the U.S. forces.* Its political backwardness finds its expression in...one-man and one-party dictatorships and clan government...Its political backwardness also finds its expression in *...fascist, murderous and repressive politics.* The "Agency for National Security Planning" in South Korea is empowered with supra-constitutional privileges...
>
> *In South Korea, barbaric tortures and murder, the worst human rights violations of medieval type, are institutionally inspired and tolerated by law.* The Kwangju massacre[5] 17 years ago and the August 15 bloodshed of last year[6] are anti-people crimes without an equal in the world, which concentrically reveal the anti-people, facist and barbaric nature of the South Korean ruling system...It is only too natural that the world people brand South Korea as a politically underdeveloped country without an equal in the world, a "political infant" and a "society below third class." It is the historical truth that the government based on absolute power and corrupt politics...will never last long and its ruin is inevitable [*Rodong Sinmun*].

Kim Jong Il's pledge to carry forth his father's Juche revolutionary strategy against "the illegitimate regime of the south" makes it impractical to anticipate any meaningful deviation from this stance. North Korea's "holy grail" to communize the South remains a sacred mainstay of their Juche religion.

Though the United States generally stations fewer than 40,000 combat troops in South Korea (compared to over a million troops in the North Korean army), the continuing presence of these U.S. military forces represents the key obstacle that restrains the North from initiating another "war for national reunification." Consequently, most diplomatic interactions with North Korea generally include some sort of demand for the withdrawal of all U.S. military forces from Korean soil as a precondition for any meaningful progress. Given Juche religious ideology and reunification fervor, a U.S. withdrawal of its forces would likely trigger an immediate invasion of the South. This fervor would transcend any "one state, two systems" or other "peaceful reunification" diplomatic agreement. Following a U.S. withdrawal, such an agreement most probably would not be worth the paper on which it was written.

Along with continual demands for the removal of U.S. troops in the "south," other major demands include removal of the concrete wall across the Demilitarized Zone (DMZ), repeal of South Korea's National Security Law (NSL)[7], and disestablishment of the South Korea's National Security Planning Agency (NSPA). These demands were renewed in the 1998 Joint New Years editorial, which is roughly equivalent to the President of the United States' annual "State of the Union" speech.

In a joint editorial carried Thursday in the *Rodong Sinmun* and *Peoples Army* newspapers, North Korea stressed economic development *and demanded that the new South Korean government should embark on a reconciliation policy with Pyongyang* …The editorial did not mention Kim Dae Jung, but said that *the change in government in South Korea did not necessarily reflect a change in policy.* It demanded that Seoul move towards a policy of reconciliation, the removal of the concrete wall on the DMZ and the scrapping of the national security law and the National Security Planning Agency (NSPA). Commenting on politics and society it stated that even though the world has changed, the country will not waiver from its path of socialism under Kim Jong Il and that the secret of its economic recovery lies in the spirit of the revolutionary soldier.[8]

Though these demands are made in the name of "independence, peaceful reunification and great national unity," their aim is to weaken the South for its planned communization by force. The sacred Juche belief in reunification—and communization—forms a filter through which Pyongyang views its policies regarding the South.

Other nations invoke the displeasure of the North's propaganda machine if they form an alliance with the South or otherwise provide them with notable assistance. In the following example, even Russia was censored for a small 1998 arms shipment to the

South. However, given the importance of Russian–North Korean relations, the main target of the article was the South.

> The South Korean authorities have become overheated with the purchase of weapons from Russia...including Russian-made 10 combat armored vehicles by early next month...We take a serious view of the fact that the [South Korean] authorities are openly purchasing arms behind the curtain of "four-way talks." No one will give credit to their call for "relaxation of tension" and "confidence building" at the talks. Their misdeed will only result in hampering the smooth progress of the talks. *The nation will curse forever the criminal behaviors of the South Korean warmaniacs who have been hell bent on war preparations, not interested in dialogue* [*KCNA*].

The North has backed up its steady stream of decades of anti-South rhetoric with intermittent border provocations, threats, sabotage, terrorist incidents, and brinkmanship. One such incident occurred in 1995 when Kim Jong Il responded erratically to Kim Young Sam's generous shipment of 150,000 tons of free rice. When the South Korean ship arrived pierside at the North Korean port of Wonsan, the North detained the ship's crew thereby creating an international incident.

Nevertheless, the South's overtures to the North continue under South Korea's new President, Kim Dae Jung (elected in February 1998). Kim Dae Jung's friendly "Sunshine Policy" toward North Korea recalls an Aesop's fable where warm sunshine is more effective than a strong wind in getting a man to take off his coat voluntarily. The three basic principles of this new policy are: (1) no toleration of any form of provocation by the North; (2) denial of any effort to absorb the North; and (3) reconciliation and cooperation. This policy, based on the "principle of separating economics from politics," is intended:

> ...as a carrot to help the North overcome pending economic difficulties, thus to induce it to come closer to Seoul's policy objectives.[9]

Despite their Sunshine Policy, the South Korean government officially regards North Korea's current food shortage as primarily a manmade crisis. While this view is highly accurate, the South sometimes minimizes the extent of the devastation in the North, regardless of who or what caused it. For example, as of 1999, the

ROK's U.S. embassy website stated that "there is so far no indication that mass starvation has already begun in North Korea."[10] Yet, even when the extent of the famine in the North is fully admitted, the North's unabated hostility toward the South poses constant problems for Seoul's periodic humanitarian aid initiatives.

The North's initial response to Kim Dae Jung was propaganda that denounced the new leader and questioned his sincerity. In addition, from April 11 to 17, 1998, the North's negotiators stuck to their standard haughty attitude during fertilizer negotiations in Beijing.

The North's actions since Kim Dae Jung initiated the new policy have also included a renewed series of infiltration attempts, lessening the likelihood that the Sunshine Policy will work. For example, on June 22, 1998, a North Korean midget spy submarine was captured off South Korea's east coast. The nine North Koreans inside were already dead from an apparent murder-suicide. Three weeks later on July 12, 1998, the dead body of a North Korean commando and a submersible tow were found washed up on a beach on South Korea's eastern shore. Then, on July 24, 1998, the South Korean newspaper *Seoul Sinmun* reported that the North was training over 20,000 elite commandos at six locations.[11]

International press and political commentaries generally reflect a pervasive ignorance of the significance of the Juche religion on current and future East Asian events. One such article deemed the North's policies as "crazed" while expressing hope that South Korea would continue to "woo" the North toward peace. Many of these commentaries, and possibly the "sunshine" hopes as well, are based on a misapplication of the German reunification paradigm and neglect to consider the Juche religious factor. For example, in January 1997, the *Korean Central News Agency* specifically declared the German reunification paradigm did not apply to Korea:

> General Kim Jong Il is the symbol, future and sun of the nation. Our dream and desire to build an independent, democratic and reunified country will certainly be achieved despite the collapse of socialism in East European nations because we are led by General Kim Jong Il [*KCNA*].

Some policy analysts from South Korea view the North's policies to be a function of Kim Jong Il's leadership and his insincere attitude, rather than seeing their hardline policies as predominantly motivated by Juche religious beliefs. From Pyongyang's viewpoint, the Juche religion makes any Korean reunification plan other than under their god, Kim Jong Il, an untenable proposition.

Nevertheless, South Korean commentators continue to generate a steady stream of political analysis that fails to grasp the irreconcilable core differences between Juche totalitarianism and the South Korean system. Some of these analysts split philosophical hairs by distinguishing between arms control and arms reduction. Others major on the minors by advocating "confidence-building measures" to influence the North. For example, one South Korean analyst commented:

> So far Seoul's policy toward the North has been based on a concept that the South must provide the North with economic support in order to help promote reconciliation between the two sides. In fact, the two-way trade volume between the two sides has been steadily expanding for the past 10 years, registering more than $300 million in 1997.[12]

However, a basic understanding of Juche suggests that confidence-building measures and economic statistics are fundamentally invalid metrics. Such sophisticated-sounding analysis may amount to nothing more than wishful thinking.

The "hawk" view that a North Korean attack is imminent merits careful scrutiny. Unlike the "sunshine" view, proponents of the "hawk" view note that another invasion by the North would be totally in accord with Juche ideology. Though Pyongyang maintains the pretense of being willing to achieve national reunification peacefully, its policies remain openly hostile to South Korea and her allies. South Korea perceives the North's offensive doctrine and numerical superiority in soldiers and weapons—including a sizable chemical weapons arsenal—as a continuing threat to her national security. Along with the world's fourth largest army, the North has the third largest stockpile of chemical weapons in the world—approximately 1,000–5,000 tons. In addition, North Korea is reported to be fully capable of producing an additional 5,000 tons of chemical munitions each year. North Korea also maintains a 2-to-1 military advantage in terms of tanks, artillery, and infantry over the combined South Korean and U.S. forces. In addition, they have regional missiles and possible intercontinental ballistic missiles, and have already prepared numerous well-constructed tunnels[13] under the demilitarized zone in preparation for their sacred war of national reunification. In light of the North's extensive preparation and their Juche ideology, Juche's architect-defector, Hwang Jang Yop, warned that South Korea must continue to take seriously the North Korean military threat.[14]

Even so, the constant fear in Seoul of a repeat of the 1950 invasion may be overrated. The North's forces and logistics might achieve short-term gains in a "Battle of the Bulge" scenario. However, the best conclusion they could hope for would be military defeat followed by a Saddam Hussein-style cease-fire with Kim Jong Il remaining in power. Aside from high-profile border incidents and predictably abrasive propaganda, North Korea is in no shape to fight a sustained offensive war against the South. Without renewed Chinese military intervention—which Kim Jong Il does not want—any invasion would be a short-lived affair. Instead, the following analysis argues that continuing brinkmanship is the more likely scenario.[15]

The Juche religious teaching that the North is a paradise while the South is a desolate impoverished wasteland also makes it unlikely that Pyongyang and Seoul will establish any Beijing–Taipei style cultural exchange program. One South Korean writer noted the impact of this paradise-in-the-North/wasteland-in-the-South teaching:

> Their [North Korea's] media are filled with a tremendous amount of lies about the rest of the world. Perhaps the most dominant lie of the moment is that everybody in South Korea has AIDS. People are afraid to shake hands with each other because they will catch AIDS. I have witnessed this great fear with defectors and others that have come from North Korea.[16]

In contrast, China and Taiwan share a large-scale exchange between families, churches, athletes, and businesses. The key difference between the two Chinas and the two Koreas is that the two Chinas share a common economic motivation without a fundamental religious barrier. Any similar exchange between the two Koreas would expose the paradise-on-earth myth to be a lie. Any revelation that the South is a better place to live would weaken the credibility of Juche's god, Kim Jong Il. Thus, any sizable North-South exchange is extremely unlikely. Given such considerations, it makes perfect sense that the North's leaders continue to declare they will never deal with "the illegitimate regime of the south."

Japan

*...no amount of penitence of Japan is enough to resolve
the pent-up grudges of the [North] Korean nation.*
KOREAN CENTRAL NEWS AGENCY
OCTOBER 3, 1997

North Korea's Juche worldview is intrinsically anti-Japanese. It is difficult for most Americans to fathom the deeply ingrained hatred by many Koreans of the Japanese people. However, North Korea's Communists have tapped into this undercurrent of hatred, which is largely rooted in the 1910–1945 Japanese occupation of Korea.

In his autobiography, *Reminscences With the Century*, Kim Il Sung relates a visit, when he was six years old, to see his father who was imprisoned by the Japanese:

> Even in such an atmosphere, my father was smiling as usual. He was delighted to see me, and praised my mother for having taken me with her. The gaunt face of my father, who wore prison clothes, defied instant recognition. His face, neck, hands, feet and all the rest of his body were scarred and wounded. Despite his condition, however, he was worrying about the safety of his family at home. His imposing and dignified bearing inspired me with an irresistible feeling of pride, mixed with a grievance and hatred for the enemy.
>
> "You've grown up. Obey your elders at home and be good at your school work!" he said to me in his usual tone of voice, calm and composed, without so much as glancing at the warden.
>
> The sound of his voice brought tears to my eyes. I said in a loud voice, "Yes. Please come home soon, father." He nodded with satisfaction. He asked my mother to help the brush-sellers and comb-sellers who might occasionally come to visit her. By these he meant his comrades in the revolution.
>
> His indomitable image that day left a lasting impression on me...Until that time, I had not really experienced the atrocities perpetrated by the Japanese army and police...But never had I seen them inflicting such appalling wounds upon an innocent person.
>
> The wounds remained in my mind throughout the period of my revolutionary struggle against the Japanese. The shock I received on that visit still has a strong effect on me.[17]

A year later, in the autumn of 1918, the release of Kim Il Sung's father from prison reinforced the lasting impression of hatred within young Il Sung.

With wounds from his beatings all over his body, my father tottered out through the prison gate. My grandfather, trembling with indignation, told my father to lie down on the litter.

"I will walk. How can I be carried on a litter under the eyes of the enemy? I will walk to spite the enemy," my father said walking boldly forward.

Back home, my father said to his brothers, "In prison I even drank as much water as I could out of my determination to survive and fight to the end. How can I leave unpunished the Japanese who are the worst of living creatures? Hyong Rok and Hyong Gwon, you, too, must fight the Japanese. The enemy must be made to pay for our blood even if we must die."[18]

One can also capture a sense of this deep-seated anti-Japanese sentiment from a look at the Revolutionary Martyrs Cemetery, situated on the scenic Chujak Peak on Mt. Taesong to the northeast of Pyongyang. According to North Korean literature, the cemetery was built in 1975 to "convey through generations the lofty revolutionary spirit of the revolutionary martyrs and their everlasting exploits."[19] In 1985, the cemetery was expanded to include massive granite sculptures, obelisks, 110 copper busts of heroes, and a monument with Kim Il Sung's autograph. Numerous statues vividly portray North Koreans throwing off the yoke of Japanese slavery and oppression:

They portray the fighters renewing their revolutionary determination to fight on, remembering the beloved fighters who laid down their lives heroically in the struggle for the liberation of the country and the freedom and emancipation of the people.[20]

North Korea spared no expense to revise its history to transform a few strategically insignificant and largely ineffective remote guerrilla actions into an "arduous march" and "decisive battles."

Meanwhile, the North Korean version of history either minimizes or ignores that it ultimately took American blood in the titanic struggle in the Pacific War to end the Japanese occupation of Korea in 1945. Instead, revisionist history proclaims that

The Revolutionary Martyrs Cemetery features 110 copper busts of anti-Japanese "revolutionary martyrs," with a red flag in the background.

North Korea single-handedly threw off the yoke of Japanese oppression. Remarkably, Juche propaganda continues to portray Japan as an imperialistic aggressor nation relentlessly bent on reinstating the Greater East Asian Co-Prosperity Sphere.

North Korea's distrust of Japan runs particularly deep. Compounding Pyongyang's attitude is the prevalent view by Japanese that the Korean people are fundamentally inferior. This well-entrenched belief adds a racist dimension to the ongoing tension. Meanwhile, the Juche educational system, museums, and propaganda tout the anti-Japanese origins of Korea's "arduous struggle," and insist that Japanese repentance and reparations are required to compensate for Japanese atrocities during the 1930s and 1940s. Yet, the DPRK's high-stake negotiation style in demanding Japanese reparations is not limited to the era of the occupation. The North Koreans are also seeking reparations for the years since 1952 for Japan's lack of normalized diplomatic relations with North Korea.

Despite this anti-Japanese undercurrent, there is a sizable Korean ethnic minority community in Japan. In 1980, North Korea established a Juche organization called the Chongryon. The Chongryon is chartered as "a patriotic organization loyal to the General's idea and leadership and [to] further strengthen and develop the movement of Koreans in Japan into a truly patriotic movement serving the Juche cause" [*KCNA*]. North Korea also operates the

Kim Il Sung's inscription at the Revolutionary Martyrs Cemetery: "The noble revolutionary spirit of anti-Japanese revolutionary martyrs will live forever in the hearts of our Party and our people. Kim Il Sung, October 10, 1985."

international arm of the *Korean Central News Agency,* including its propaganda website (www.kcna.co.jp), out of its office in Tokyo, Japan.

Pyongyang's hyper-nationalistic view of history strongly opposes the "flunkeyism" exemplified by their Japanese colonialist experience. Kim Jong Il, who is depicted as an avid student of Korean history in his youth, was said to have called the great general Kim Yushin of the Silla Dynasty (668–935) a "flunkeyist" rather than a national hero. Yushin was a "flunkeyist" because he enlisted support from China's Tang Dynasty (618–907) to defeat Koguryo and Paekche to unify the country. Ultimately, the lasting legacy of Japanese colonialism is that any meaningful North Korean–Japanese rapport would run counter to the Juche religious "anti-flunkeyism" ideology.

As the North Korean press surrounding the Japanese "religionist" delegation shows, Japan is considered "hell-bent" along with the United States and the "illegitimate regime of the south" (South Korea):

> *The Japanese reactionaries are now hell-bent* on infusing militarism into people. In Japan events are held undisguisedly to laud as "patriots" and "heroes" those who were killed in the past overseas aggression war, and attempt to revise history textbooks is being made under Government direction to bury the Japanese imperialists' history of aggression in oblivion. And ultra-right reactionary organizations are preaching revanchism while news media are extensively agitating for war among people, allegedly for Japan's "security," the paper points out, and says: The purpose of such moves is as clear as day-

light. The Japanese reactionaries are persistently seeking to realize the old dream of *"Greater East Asia Co-prosperity Sphere"* the predecessors failed to bring into practice in the past [*Rodong Sinmun*].

Propaganda surrounding a recent visit by an apparently non-Christian Japanese religious delegation reveals the depth of Juche animosity toward the Japanese. The peaceful delegation visited Pyongyang in October 1997 amid ongoing controversy between Japan and North Korea. North Korea was demanding Japan provide reparations for atrocities of the 1930s and 1940s while Japanese had leveled various charges against North Korea, including international kidnapping and exporting counterfeit money. Propaganda shows that North Korea thought it totally appropriate that the Japanese visited sites of Japanese atrocities in North Korea and worshipped at the great statue of Kim Il Sung. However, there was nothing in the Juche religious philosophy to accommodate the concept of repentance when the Japanese openly expressed their remorse, guilt, and a desire for peaceful international reconciliation. The following excerpts provide highlights from North Korea's press coverage:

> The visiting delegation of Denchishokyo of Japan led by its leader Shizue Araya held a ceremony…aimed at repenting of and liquidating the unhappy past between Korea and Japan on behalf of the Japanese nation, who left deep scars and pains in the hearts of the Korean nation. A rite was held and a prayer was read. The prayer expressed hope that the wounds of the miserable past will be healed with the approach of the 21st century, *although no amount of penitence of Japan is enough to resolve the pent-up grudges of the Korean nation* [*KCNA*].[21]

> …*Japan, however, is still branded as enemy state and is not willing to atone for its unethical, anti-historical unheard-of crimes.* Japan aims to become a political power, exercise privileges, act in an arbitrary way and establish militaristic domination in the international arena by becoming a permanent member of the UN Security Council. At the UN General Assembly Session, the Japanese official said Japan's contribution to the UN is nearly as much as that of the United States and that Japan would have to reduce its contribution considerably if it does not become a permanent member. This means that Japan asks to buy the seat of a permanent member with money [*Rodong Sinmun*].

Along with North Korea's branding of Japan as an "enemy state," the North Koreans continue to emphasize historical issues that magnify the existing regional tension. For example, the North Koreans recently placed their propaganda spotlight on a book written by Japanese professor Nakatsuka Akira of Nara Women's University. The book, entitled *Correcting the Fraud in History*, presents the argument that newly uncovered Japanese historical documents prove that the Japanese initiated the Sino-Japanese War two days before its officially recognized July 25, 1894, start by committing the premeditated military occupation of the Korean Royal Palace in Seoul. Previously, Japan's "official reason" for stationing Imperial Japanese Army troops in Korea was to protect Japanese nationals from rioting Korean farmers. However, Nakatsuka's book states that documents now reveal the Royal Palace incident and military occupation was a naked act of aggression. North Korean propagandists used this news to reinforce their people's anti-Japanese worldview:

> ...this incident is just another example of how Japan is an aggressor nation and [how] the Japanese people came to have a perverted outlook to the world [*People's Korea*].

North Korea continued in its unrelenting hateful policy toward Japan by denouncing Japanese Prime Minister Obuchi's apology to South Korean President Kim Dae Jung for the 1910–1945 period of forced Japanese rule over Korea.

> North Korea Sunday slammed an invitation by South Korean President Kim Dae Jung for the Japanese emperor to visit South Korea, saying the reconciliation gesture was "a petty act." Calling the Japanese Emperor Akihito "a descendant of the special-class criminal who committed immeasurable crimes against the Korean people," the North's official Korean Central News Agency said a visit by the Japanese emperor would "hurt the national feelings of the Korean people."...North Korea said Kim's invitation was "a petty act of a person who has no iota of self-respect and dignity."[22]

North Korea's consistently anti-Japanese rhetoric, coupled with its August 1998 launch of a three-stage rocket over Japan (see Chapter 10), have made the Japanese increasingly on edge about the threat of North Korean missiles. Even so, opinions regarding North Korea vary considerably among Japanese analysts. For example, Professor Yoshida Yasuhiko, who teaches international relations at Saitama University and has made several trips to the DPRK, states:

> The line of the U.S. is that North Korea is unpredictable, that Kim Jong Il is an enigma, that you don't know what he has in mind—I don't think so. They are very logical and clear... their agenda: Preserve the long-term survival of the Kim regime, gain access to food and economic assistance, and negotiate diplomatic recognition from the U.S....I went to Pyongyang last fall [1998] and every day I was treated to luxurious food, the food of the elite. They don't care about people starving in the countryside.[23]

Sato Katsumi, one of Tokyo's experienced North Korea watchers, advocates that the U.S. opt against lifting economic sanctions and maintain a tough stance toward the DPRK. Mr. Sato says that lifting sanctions:

> ...would only make North Korea happy. The U.S. doesn't know Kim Jong Il. They don't know what Kim is capable of. The best [strategy] is to apply militaristic pressure so an internal breakdown takes place.[24]

Japan, which is already an economic superpower, is determined to play a more assertive role in regional and international affairs. Japan's most immediate security concern is the direct threat posed by North Korea's ballistic missile program. North Korea's anti-Japanese Juche rhetoric adds to the ongoing uncertainty and tension. The well-entrenched religious and ethnic aspects of Juche's anti-Japanese worldview make it unlikely to expect any notable thawing of North Korean–Japanese political relations past limited cultural and economic ventures.

The United States

> *On the Korean Peninsula—where nearly 40,000 Americans patrol a militarized fault line—the prospects of reconciliation are matched by the danger of miscalculation.*[25]
> BILL CLINTON
> PRESIDENT OF THE UNITED STATES

Juche ideology continues to sustain North Korea's consistently anti-U.S. rhetoric and harsh anti-American policies. North Korea blames the United States for a divided Korea, their economic woes, and their famine. Pyongyang's prevailing view is that any food or other assistance that is given to North Korea is owed by the U.S., and is given to assuage America's feelings of guilt over years of anti–North Korean foreign policies.

Given Juche religious teachings, the United States foreign policy objective for a permanent peace treaty, through mutual recognition of the two Koreas as separate states, seems quite naive. A more accurate assessment of "Kim country" would be to recognize it as a land where Kim Jong Il is god, and politics and religion are inseparably linked. Kim's monolithic theocentric Juche state is designed to keep him in power. Without reunification along Juche guidelines (Kim Jong Il reigning over all of Korea), "the arduous struggle" of the "Juche revolution" continues.

Sadly, the Juche religious system requires such continuing conflict to survive. Without an ongoing frenzied struggle against enemies foreign and domestic, the fundamentally false Juche regime cannot continue to exist. For example, North Korea's ill-fated submarine incursion into South Korea in September 1996, while hosting an international economic conference and preparing for international peace talks, were symptomatic of her seemingly schizophrenic foreign policy of brinkmanship. Brinkmanship reflects a fundamental paranoia that improved international relations will undermine Kim Jong Il retaining power.

North Korea's Anti-U.S. Worldview

One of the U.S. important policies for "new world order" is to bring into submission and dominate other countries and nations with [a] strong arm...in disregard of the progressive mankind, the United Nations and international law. Its rulers now try to revive [the] "Monroe Doctrine" and "Marshall Plan"....It is part of its moves intended to establish American laws and order in the world and thus Americanize the world.

RODONG SINMUN
MARCH 22, 1998

North Korean stereotypes of Americans differ from those of South Koreans. South Korean behavior toward Americans is influenced by the popular stereotype that the United States is the

North Korean anti-American propaganda cartoon.

land of riches. However, North Korean attitudes toward Americans continue to be shaped by the long-standing anti-American ideology and Juche propaganda by DPRK's totalitarian government. All North Koreans have been told for over a half-century that the United States is a savage, imperialist, capitalist, hell-bent, barbarian-invading empire that "occupies" the south, maintains it as "a colony," and ultimately aims to conquer the North. These attitudes have repeatedly surfaced over the years. One such unprovoked international incident occurred on August 18, 1976, when two U.S. army officers were brutally hacked to death by 30 axe-wielding Communist guards in the Joint Security Area of Panmunjom.

U.S. deterrence-minded foreign policy provides abundant fuel for the anti-American stereotypes of Pyongyang's propaganda presses. The following propaganda article provides a typical example. (Note the lowercase "s" in the abbreviation for South Korea, which is quite intentional by the North's editor.)

> The spokesman for the National Democratic Front of South Korea (NDFSK) made public a statement on September 24 *denouncing the United States* and the Kim Young Sam group for more frantically building up armaments these days, reported the Seoul-based radio *Voice of National Salvation*...The arms buildup in south Korea, *a colony*, clearly shows that, against its vociferous advertisement about "relaxation of tension" and "peace" on the Korean Peninsula, *the United States is the very one who seeks only aggravation of tension and war*...For the present, all the pro-democracy, pro-reunification patriotic forces should turn out resolutely as one man in the struggle against the arms buildup of *the U.S. aggressors*...The United States must clearly see the will of our people for the independent and peaceful reunification, stop the criminal arms buildup at once and immediately withdraw from south Korea its troops

and military equipment whose existence cannot be justified, feeling its due responsibilities for the division of the Korean Peninsula [*KCNA*].

The above anti-U.S. propaganda was fairly mild by Juche standards. For example, North Korea's 1997 New Years Message used characteristically harsh anti-American language:

> In case the enemies unleash war, *our army will strike and wipe out the U.S. Imperialist aggression forces* before anyone else and uproot the source of war on the Korean peninsula [*Rodong Sinmun*].

In an even more remarkable example, the next propaganda release from May 3, 1997, actually declared war on the United States!

> The U.S. bellicose elements recently said that the danger of war is imminent on the Korean Peninsula and that it is necessary to build a powerful force to deter war. Their remarks are a vicious provocation against and a challenge to the Democratic People's Republic of Korea.
>
> The *U.S. war maniacs* are describing the DPRK as a source of war danger, misleading public opinion to cover up their true colors as the bellicose elements. Their crying for a "powerful deterrent force" coincides with arms buildup and reckless military maneuvers in and around south Korea. They are trying to stifle the DPRK by force of arms, rendering the situation on the Korean Peninsula strained.
>
> The U.S. sincerity for the improved relationship with the DPRK can be proved only through the adoption of a trustworthy measure. The U.S. hawks try to threaten and stifle the DPRK by force of arms. The DPRK, therefore, is compelled to take a countermeasure. *The DPRK and the U.S. are in a state of war.* Nobody knows when the war racket of the U.S. hawks turns into a real war. We are in full preparedness to cope with the case of emergency and keep a close eye on the reckless moves of the U.S. bellicose elements. The *U.S. war maniacs* should put an immediate halt to the foolish and reckless moves to stifle the DPRK and look into the realities with reason [*Rodong Sinmun*].

At first glance, it seems remarkable that this "state of war" announcement was issued in the same week that North Korea acknowledged receipt of a major humanitarian food aid shipment from the United States. Apart from an understanding of the Juche

*North Korea's Juche worldview merges radical anti-Americanism
with radical anti-Christianity.*

religion, such contradictory announcements seem to be like those from the pages of the novel *The Mouse That Roared.* In this classic novel, the mythical "Duchy of Grand Fenwick" declares war on the United States in hope of a quick surrender to obtain the benefits of generous American post-war reconstruction.

However, the humor of the comparison fades when one considers both that North Korea has a million-plus man army and does not share the "Duchy of Grand Fenwick's" materialistic motives. Instead, from a Juche religious standpoint, anti-Americanism is truly as much a part of being North Korean as baseball and apple pie are American. As long as the Juche demi-god and accompanying religious system are in place, no promise, speech, or treaty is likely to result in any fundamental change to North Korea's hard-line anti-American stance.

While, from an American viewpoint, Christian missionaries and U.S. foreign diplomats make unlikely co-conspirators, Pyongyang views the distinction as artificial. From their perspective, Christianity is a religion emanating from America. Christianity opposes Juche. Washington opposes Pyongyang. Both are viewed as part of the same American anti-Juche threat.

Although Kim Jong Il seeks to normalize relations with the United States, Japan, and other "capitalist nations," these foreign policy objectives may easily be misconstrued if they are not viewed from within the context of Juche. This context includes Kim Jong Il's convictions which: (1) oppose the world tendency of post–Cold War era "globalism"; (2) oppose "imperialist reactionary policies and trends" of international labor division, supra-nationalistic capital investment, and other internationalization phenomena; (3) oppose any notion that capitalism and socialism are potentially compatible; and (4) oppose the introduction of any capitalistic "Western style" reforms of the existing Juche totalitarian system.[26]

Kim Jong Il's views, like those of his father before him, are directly reflected in North Korea's propaganda. Key themes, elements, and adjectives remain consistent within North Korea's anti-American propaganda. First, one can readily note that North Korean propaganda generally has a caustic tone toward the United States. Second, the U.S. is consistently painted in ignominious terms. Count on it. Examples of these and other anti-American elements that consistently appear in North Korean propaganda are shown in Table 7-2.

TABLE 7-2. Consistent Elements in North Korea's Anti-U.S. Propaganda

ELEMENT	PROPAGANDA EXAMPLE
U.S. is "hell bent"	The U.S. broadcasting of *Radio Free Asia* aiming to infuse…American-style democracy to disintegrate Asian nations… *The United States is hell bent on ideological and cultural offensive through the radio* [*Minju Choson*].
Lowercase letters "u.s."—not "U.S." Anti-U.S. hatred is justified	…if the u.s. and the South Korean authorities dare to invade…the KPA will deal an annihilating strike to the enemy with strong combat power they *cultivated for scores of years and with bitter hatred* [*KCNA*].
Exaggeration of any U.S. military news to be a grave provocation	The United States is seeking the reform of the U.S. 8th Army Command in South Korea…We view this military step as [a] *very dangerous move* to put the South Korea-based U.S. troops in *war posture*…with the situation being brought to *the brink of war* [*Minju Choson*].
The very presence of U.S. forces in the South is viewed as a threat to the North's sovereignty	It is a fixed will and unshakable faith of the Korean people and People's Army to mete out a merciless punishment to *those who encroach upon the sovereignty of the DPRK* and to defend the anthropocentric [Juche] socialism of Korean style impregnably. If the U.S. warhawks try to place the U.S. Forces in South Korea under wartime system, ignoring our warnings, we cannot but take countermeasures and the U.S. will be held responsible wholly for the consequences arising therefrom [*KCNA*].
Mythical U.S. military build-ups alleged U.S. insincerity assumed	The *United States has escalated [its] military threat to the DPRK*, touching off KPA's vigilance and enmity. What we cannot overlook is that the United States has continued the military threat *behind the curtain of the talks*. It indicates that the united states is calling for dialogue overtly, but seeking to stifle the DPRK by force of arms covertly…
References to revisionist history	In dealing with the enemy's invasion, it is merciless and determined. The escort craft, *Pueblo*[27] ship, *EC-121* reconnaissance plane[28] and helicopter incidents are some of the good examples… [*Rodong Sinmun*].

TABLE 7-2. *(continued)*

ELEMENT	PROPAGANDA EXAMPLE
More references to revisionist history	The controversial ban on the use of anti-personnel mines…was produced by the U.S.… *It occupied South Korea militarily and divided Korea…*
A U.S. intent to start a war of conquest against the DPRK is assumed	*Since it was defeated in the three-year Korean war in the early 1950s, the United States has resorted to every conceivable means and method to ignite another Korean war…All facts prove that the final solution to peace*
Continuous demands for the pull-out of U.S. troops	*and stability and the mine problem of the peninsula depends on the pullout of the U.S. troops from South Korea [KCNA].*

North Korea's Anti-U.S. Strategy and Tactics

With the united states trying to attack the DPRK with military force, we can never sit with folded arms. We do not reject dialogue and negotiations. But we cannot allow them to be used as a means of testing and stifling us. If the U.S. warhawks attempt to play a military gamble behind the scene of talks, we will cope with it with greater strength.

RODONG SINMUN
MARCH 1, 1998

Many commentators have interpreted various North Korean actions and declarations as intending to drive a diplomatic wedge between the United States and South Korea, presumably because it considers the ROK government as an American puppet.[29] Yet, North Korea has an international agenda that may be even more significant. Propaganda consistently reveals that Pyongyang has been hard at work building strong relationships with non-aligned nations, Arab states, and dictatorships around the world. These nations range from Peru to Madagascar to Libya to Cambodia. Having established these relationships, North Korea has systematically translated this growing influence to advance their policy agenda in the United Nations General Assembly. For example, consider the following North Korean propaganda release from December 1997:

The 30th UN General Assembly Session adopted a resolution *calling for the dissolution of the "UN Command" and pullout of all foreign forces stationed in south Korea under the UN flag.* It says: The "UN Command" was framed up under pressure from the United States. Through the "UN Command" the United States and its forces have threatened peace and increased the danger of war on the Korean Peninsula. *We call for immediate implementation of the resolution on the dissolution of the "UN Command" and the withdrawal of the U.S. forces from south Korea.* We believe that the UN will soon deal with the issue [*KCNA*].

Another example of North Korea's progress in their international agenda was when their diplomats succeeded in influencing the United Nations to chastise South Korea for "human rights abuses" because of the South Korean National Security Law. From the Juche "class consciousness" view, hypocrisy concerning human rights is not even an issue, much less a policy consideration. The long-term goal of North Korea's foreign policy strategy is very straightforward: influence the United Nations to call for the U.S. to withdraw her forces from South Korea.

The Juche view of negotiations with the U.S. is that what is North Korea's is theirs and what is the United States' is negotiable. North Korea teaches its diplomats that "the diplomatic activity is a struggle to achieve revolution, and negotiations are the means to be employed for the struggle."[30] Some examples of North Korean negotiation tactics—all approved by dictator Kim Jong Il —are provided in Table 7-3.

North Korea's consistent use of these negotiation tactics guarantees a highly volatile complexity that comes free with the price of admission to U.S.–DPRK negotiations. Behind this façade of negotiations lies the reality that, under Juche ideology, North Korea can never sign a peace accord or recognize South Korea as a nation. However, it is easier for North Korea to hide behind unacceptable demands for a full U.S. troop withdrawal from the South as a precondition for a peace accord. An additional tactic is for North Korean negotiators to make frequent note of objections to U.S. proposals by mythical North Korean "military hardliners." This ruse induces quite a few Western scholars and specialists on North Korea affairs to believe in the unconfirmed existence of "moderates" within North Korea's monolithic Juche leadership. U.S. advocates of support for "unconfirmed moderates" within North Korea's leadership reveal their general lack of understanding of the radical, one-man-centered nature of the Juche totalitarian system. "Softball" tactics tend to be ineffective when

TABLE 7-3. North Korea's Standard Negotiation Tactics [31]

THREATENING LEVERAGES	COMPROMISE-INDUCING LEVERAGES	INSIGNIFICANT OR UNVERIFIABLE CONCESSIONS
Threats of initiating a war	Stalls in high-level talks	Claims of internal reforms
Threats of the development of nuclear weapons	Use of multi-channel/back-channel contacts and invitations to influential U.S. personages	Resumption of official dialogues with Seoul
Initiation of small-scale armed border incidents	Embarrassing the other party during talks with irrational or inconsistent behavior	Participation in multinational talks
Missile development	Changing the terms of an agreement before an agreement can be signed	The return of a few remains of Americans killed during the 1950–1953 Korean War
Derailment of talks leading to a permanent peace treaty		Voluntary disclosure of alleged past nuclear achievements
		Temporary suspension of missile development, production, and/or export

negotiating with the totalitarian dictator's incessant hard-line rhetoric and demands for unilateral concessions and aid from the U.S. in pursuit of Kim Jong Il's version of Hitler's "peace in our time" Munich Pact.

U.S. Policies Toward North Korea in Light of Juche Ideology

The U.S. describes it as a "strategy of participation in expansion" ["engagement and enlargement"]... The "expansionist strategy" made by the U.S... is, in essence, to turn the world into the world of American and western style for its monopolistic domination.

RODONG SINMUN
MARCH 4, 1998

> *To think that today's North Korean leadership can be*
> *nudged toward reform with multi-billion-dollar bribes is*
> *like trying to propitiate an unreformed serial killer with*
> *an offer of parole.*[32]
>
> THE WALL STREET JOURNAL
> OCTOBER 12, 1998

The Clinton administration has demonstrated unprecedented patience with North Korea. This patience shows the United States' preference to pursue negotiation rather than confrontation. U.S. fundamental interests in East Asia centers on the prevention of the rise of any single hegemonic power in Asia-Pacific, access to the region's expanding markets, nonproliferation of Weapons of Mass Destruction (WMDs), and the promotion of democratization. These interests call for continued U.S. commitment to the region's security. Yet, critics maintain that the U.S. has already yielded too much to North Korea in its Geneva talks on the nuclear issue. Analysts note that the U.S. has given much to North Korea, while the latter has done nothing to improve South–North relations in spite of the Geneva accord.

The following contemporary analysis reflects the "cause and effect" based thinking that predominates much of the current U.S. policy decisions regarding North Korea.

> Recent giveaways of food and fuel worth hundreds of millions of dollars and the promise of nuclear reactors worth $4 billion haven't changed the North's cantankerous attitude...
>
> The West has longed *to pry open the North and draw it into rapprochement* with South Korea and the rest of a world, from which it has been estranged for a half-century. The North's leaders, fearing the loss of their system and privileges, have put up a strong resistance, using thinly veiled threats of nuclear war to extract financial and diplomatic concessions from Washington. *But now, the communist North finds itself largely dependent on generosity from Washington, Tokyo and Seoul.*[33]

This article is right on target with the statement about "The North's leaders, fearing the loss of their system and privileges." Notice, however, that the rest of this analysis did not recognize the Juche status quo worldview as the fundamental factor in Pyongyang's decision-making. Economic terms and causal terms such as "pry open," "draw it into," and "recent giveaways haven't changed ...attitude" were used. Since such analysis presupposes a Western worldview, the conclusions are flawed.

We should be careful not to impose our Western compartmentalized view, which distinguishes between politics and religion. American diplomats want North Korea to modify their political views and actions, while Christian missionaries want the North Koreans to change their spiritual views through the power of the gospel. Americans see these as different objectives. However, from the Juche standpoint—where the Su-ryong is god—there is absolutely no difference between them. To them, the only difference is that American "religionists" use one set of jargon while American "militarists" use another.

This merger of politics and religion creates a significant blind spot in North Korea's Juche worldview paradigm. Recognizing this helps explain the contradiction between the May 3, 1997, propaganda announcement that "a state of war exists" and the ongoing receipt of U.S. food aid. This blind spot exists because the Juche paradigm cannot provide a coherent explanation of the simultaneous occurrence of "anti-DPRK" and seemingly "pro-DPRK" actions by Americans. In fact, our foreign policy seems to be as mysteriously schizophrenic to them as theirs seems to us.

From 1953 until recently, United States policy toward North Korea revolved around the concept of deterrence through a policy of "containment." This policy strategy simply ignored North Korea's Juche ideology. Instead, it was built around a military solution of maintaining a sufficient force presence in East Asia. These forces, including those stationed on South Korean soil, serve to convince the North that any invasion would be futile. This U.S. view notes that lack of sufficient American presence contributed to Kim Il Sung's nearly successful overrun of South Korea in 1950.

In the 1990s, the United States has adopted a more progressive "engagement and enlargement" or "selective engagement" foreign policy that seeks to maintain an open dialogue with the North Koreans. This policy of open dialogue aims to help North Korea become less isolationist and promote stability within the East Asian region. However, this new policy tends to ignore the inherent limitations and overall impact of Juche religious ideology on every North Korean policy decision. In actual practice, Juche ideology permeates North Korean foreign policy. In virtually every negotiation with the United States since 1988, North Korea has consistently put forth the Juche principle. Thus, it is not surprising that the new U.S. policy toward North Korea has attracted critics. A growing number of critics of the Clinton administration's "selective engagement" policy tend to view it as a thinly veiled policy of appeasement. A November 24, 1998, issue of the sensationalist Washington, D.C.–based *Drudge Report* made unconfirmed charges that numerous U.S. foreign policy documents showed a long-term cover-up by the Clinton administration of a failed policy of trying to buy off North Korea from making nuclear weapons. Criticism of the Agreed Framework has been growing among U.S. Congressional lawmakers, as well, including U.S. Senator Frank H. Murkowski (R-Alaska). Such concerns remain high especially in light of North Korea's new vast underground installation 25 miles northeast of Yongbyon at Kumchangri. Colonel William Taylor, USA (Ret.), a policy analyst, recently commented, "How do you 'selectively engage' North Korea? That makes about as much sense as 'selectively engaging' a rattlesnake!"[34]

In the face of mounting pressure to take a tougher stance toward North Korea, Clinton administration supporters defend the multi-billion dollar giveaway of two nuclear reactors. Secretary of State Madeleine Albright maintains that the October 21, 1994, Geneva Agreement is "one of the best things the administration has done." In his July 1998 Senate testimony, Assistant Secretary of State Rust Deming stated that the 1994 U.S.–DPRK Agreed Framework and its associated giveaways were both the cornerstone of U.S. policy toward North Korea and a small price (bribe?) to pay for regional stability.

However, these appeasement initiatives have worked about as well as the U.S. policies to bribe the Barbary Pirates under the John Adams administration. The failed Geneva Agreement is, in retrospect, only one in a series of failed appeasement initiatives intended to obtain North Korea's agreement to refrain from building a nuclear arsenal. These U.S. appeasement initiatives and their corresponding failures include the following:

- *In 1985, North Korea signed the nuclear nonproliferation treaty.* North Korea subsequently ignored the agreement and forged ahead with its nuclear weapons program.

- *In 1991, North Korea signed a Joint Declaration with South Korea promising that it will neither seek nuclear weapons nor separate plutonium, and that it would accept nuclear inspections.*

North Korea continued its nuclear weapons program and denied access to their facilities to any international nuclear inspectors.

■ *In 1992, North Korea signs the International Atomic Energy Agency (IAEA) "Full Scope Safeguards Agreement" thereby allowing inspections of its nuclear facilities.* Based upon this agreement, the U.S. and South Korea cancel the 1992 "Team Spirit" joint military exercise. However, in 1993, North Korea refuses to allow any IAEA inspections.

■ *In 1992, North Korea and the U.S. sign the Declaration of the Denuclearization of the Korean Peninsula.* The U.S. removes its tactical nuclear weapons from Korea. Afterwards, Hans Blix, director general of the IAEA, reports that North Korea continues to develop nuclear weapons at Yongbyon.

■ *In 1994, North Korea signed the Geneva Agreement with the United States regarding nuclear non-proliferation in return for the U.S., Japan, and South Korea funding construction of two nuclear reactors in North Korea at a cost of over $5 billion.* Satellite imagery revealed that North Korea continued its nuclear weapon development even after the agreement. Once again, international inspectors were denied access to North Korea's nuclear facilities to verify compliance.

■ *From 1995 to 1999, North Korean demands for U.S. famine relief continue.* Massive shipments of U.S. food aid to famine-stricken North Korea continue. However much of the food aid is being diverted away from the needy and toward supporters of the regime and the military.

■ *In 1998, North Korea demands that the U.S. pay $500 million per year to compensate the North Koreans for not selling missiles to other countries.* The Clinton administration has argued that Congress should pay the annual ransom to avert war.

■ *In 1998, after North Korea launched a multi-stage missile over Japan in August 1998 (see Chapter 10), the U.S. Congress initially balked at funding the fuel oil shipment, but then reluctantly approved it.* The 1994 Geneva Agreement provides for the U.S. to donate 500,000 tons of fuel oil to the North Koreans until the reactor is completed.

■ *In 1999, North Korea demands the U.S. pay $300 million to inspect its facilities after U.S. Special Envoy Charles Kartman* *and National Security Advisor Samuel Berger tell reporters that the DPRK is building an underground nuclear facility at Kumchangri.* U.S. Senate majority leader Trent Lott criticizes the Clinton administration for wanting to provide millions in U.S. taxpayer dollars to the criminal regime in North Korea.

U.S. leaders still hold high "political" hopes for improved relations with North Korea, notwithstanding North Korea's solidly anti-American Juche ideology. Most U.S. foreign policy analysts continue to view North Korea as a rogue or Stalinist nation cutting against the grain of the New World Order. For example, consider General Colin Powell's view presented in his 1995 autobiography, *My American Journey:*

> ...only Marxist Cuba and North Korea still cling to a political and ideological corpse, perhaps hoping for protection under the endangered species act. But even they cannot escape the tide of history, and we must begin *to adjust our policies of Cold War isolation to hasten their integration into a new world.*[35]

General Powell's two-dimensional view of North Korea typifies that of contemporary American leaders who dismiss the spiritual dimension of Juche rather than factor it into their policies. American leaders acknowledge Christian humanitarian ministries and missionary-evangelists simply as do-gooders. However, they view them as extraneous from the non-religious compartmented foreign policies that flow from the Western worldview. For example, General Powell continued:

> Television delivers tragic scenes from these places into our living rooms nightly, and we naturally want to do something to relieve the suffering we witness. Often, our desire to help collides with the cold calculus of national interest...Our humanitarian instincts have been touched...But when the fighting starts, as it did in Somalia, and American lives are at risk, our people rightly demand to *know what vital interest that sacrifice serves.*[36]

Thus, the U.S. concept of a "soft landing" for North Korea seeks to avoid war even at the cost of the continuation of Kim Jong Il's totalitarian rule.

North Korea claims it is carrying out its Geneva Agreement obligation to freeze its alleged nuclear project.[37] However, its consistent rejection of the provisions requiring verification inspections raises the possibility that North Korea either retains an ongoing nuclear weapons program or they never had a viable nuclear program to start with. Under the fear-based Juche totalitarian system, it is doubtful that the North Koreans would ever give away or dispose of nuclear weapons if they really had them. In similar matters such as human rights abuses, biochemical weapons, and long-range missiles, the North Koreans are rigid in not granting any meaningful concessions. However, there is no way to either prove or disprove the existence of a North Korean nuclear capability.

An alternative U.S. foreign policy toward North Korea, presented in the November 23, 1998, issue of Dallas-based Stratfor, Inc.'s *Global Intelligence Update*, would be to shift away from an unenforceable Weapons of Mass Destruction (WMD)–prevention policy to a policy of comprehensive deterrence. Simply put, the United States would guarantee the utter destruction of the leadership of any nation that hosted groups who employed WMDs against the U.S. or her allies. In a manner similar to the U.S. policy toward terrorists, there would be nowhere for the host nation's leaders to hide, no negotiations, and no guarantee of rules of evidence. Thus, every nation's leaders would have a vested interest in ensuring both the existence of adequate provisions for WMD command and control and for policing groups based within their own borders.

Since the 1994 Geneva Agreed Framework, construction of the nuclear reactor began at Sinpo, North Korea, in August 1996. Construction intermittently stalled in October 1998 as claims and counterclaims between North Korea and America of Geneva violations signal the beginning of another round of North Korean brinkmanship diplomacy. *Reuters* news agency reported:

> North Korea, angered by allegations it is stepping up a nuclear weapons program, does not care if a landmark nuclear pact with the United States is broken, the *Korean Central News Agency* (KCNA) said in a report…Under the 1994 agreement, Washington promised Pyongyang it would receive 500,000 tons of fuel oil a year, as well as two light-water nuclear power reactors…South Korea urged the U.S. Congress to fund the fuel oil supplies to North Korea, saying refusal to do so could jeopardize the framework agreement. The U.S. Congress balked at meeting the fuel oil commitment after North Korea recently launched a multi-stage rocket [see Chapter 10]…and the KCNA dispatch denied the underground

structures Pyongyang was building were military:

> (North Korea) has a lot of civil underground struc-
> tures now under construction...The U.S. demands to
> verify them, claiming that they are 'underground nu-
> clear facilities.'...The allegations are an attempt to dis-
> arm North Korea and to violate its sovereignty. If the
> U.S. policy is to break the framework agreement, (North
> Korea) has no intention to keep the U.S. from doing so
> ...If the U.S. side considers the framework agreement
> [to be a] white elephant, it is free to break it. (North
> Korea) does not care about it.[38]

The United States has clearly resolved to defend South Korea
against aggression. Even so, some U.S. scholars, such as Selig
Harrison (in January 1998) and Don Oberdorfer (in April 1998)
advocated unilateral South Korean arms reduction thinking that
this would reduce North-South tension.[39] However, the lack of understanding of the Juche worldview leaves even the most diligent
of these intelligence analysts with the difficulty of working with
an imprecise model for predicting what North Korea will do
next. They find it almost pure guesswork to determine what supposed factions exist, who controls them, and what they stand for.
With no fundamental understanding of the Juche religious system, North Korea's decidedly abrasive and seemingly erratic foreign policy remains an enigma to many Americans.

China

*A fresh breeze [of cooperation in the Free Economic and
Trade Zone] may blow into North Korea from China
only as long as it is accompanied neither by flies nor by
mosquitoes.*[40]

KIM JONG IL

The Juche view of China is that China has departed from the
straight and narrow way of her socialist revolution in pursuit of
"capitalistic" economic growth and "revisionism." Kim Jong Il
resists emulation of China's ongoing economic reforms. His limited agreement to participate in the Rajin-Sonbong Free Economic and Trade Zone with Russia and China is based on his
allowing a "fresh breeze" of opening to blow into North Korea
"only as long as it is accompanied neither by flies nor by mosqui-

toes." South Korean movie director Shin Sang Ok and actress Choe Eun Hee, who were kidnapped by North Korea in 1978 and escaped in 1986, reported that Kim Jong Il refuses to open the country because he believes that doing so would allow foreign agents to spy on the North Korean military.

China, on the other hand, does not wholeheartedly underwrite the Juche religio-political version of Communism. When Kim Jong Il succeeded Kim Il Sung through the Juche hereditary system, China's Deng Xiao Ping withheld immediate approval. One Chinese analyst commented on the dynastic passing of power, "China cannot criticize, but we are not accustomed to this method." Sources indicate that in 1992 Deng had advised Kim Il Sung against the father-to-son succession. British scholar Dr. Reinhard Drifte commented on the difficulties the Chinese perceive with North Korean relations:

> The Chinese influence on the DPRK is extremely difficult to gauge because of the scarcity of open sources, but also because of a Chinese concern of losing influence over Pyongyang by pressurizing the DPRK to accept policies which the latter dislikes. However, it is evident that the DPRK is at best a difficult "friend" for China, and the diverging economic and foreign policies of both do not help. China has now recognized the ROK, and derives considerable economic benefits from the booming bilateral economic relationship.[41]

Nevertheless, in the past, Beijing has bragged that the two nations are "as close as lips and teeth."[42] Such statements have a basis in historical fact, given that Chinese emperors exercised suzerainty over the Korean vassal state for long periods of history. The contemporary legacy of Korea's history as a satellite country of China is seen in China's bilateral commitment to protect the integrity of the North Korean government. Though not understood by American leaders in 1950, this bilateral PRC-DPRK relationship was the primary motive behind the Chinese intervention in the Korean War.

China's security interests center around sustaining the current favorable economic conditions, enhancing China's comprehensive national strength, and effectively handling instability on the Korean peninsula. Officially, China believes the Korean problem is one that the two Koreas must resolve themselves. Unofficially, China may exercise her considerable influence over the activities of the North Koreans now that Beijing is Pyongyang's only ally of significance. However, the extent of Chinese influence upon North Korea's policies may be quite less than presumed.

Nevertheless, Chinese influence on North Korea should not be underestimated, either. One-third of China's foreign aid goes to North Korea. As of 1995, China provided 93% of North Korea's crude oil imports (the other 7% came from Libya). Additionally, in a May 1996 meeting with DPRK Deputy Prime Minister Hong Song Nam, China agreed to provide the North with 500,000 tons of grain per year for five consecutive years—half of it free of charge. North Korea depends heavily on Chinese grain imports. Thus, despite their core Juche beliefs against reliance on other nations, North Korea is in no position to sever its continuing reliance upon Chinese imports and assistance.[43]

Another example of Chinese influence on North Korean domestic policy is North Korea's declining birth rate. China's rigid enforcement of a "one child per family" policy found its counterpart in North Korea's "two-child norm" and "one-child only" option:

> Unlike China, North Korea's population policy is shrouded in mystery. No information about North Korea's population policy may be found in North Korea's propaganda. However, some offhand remarks by Kim Il Sung indicate that he thought it desirable that the population growth be slower. Indeed, defectors report that a "two-child norm" prevails and a "one-child only" option is encouraged. However, North Korea, unlike China may be viewed as labor-scarce—so why would the regime limit the growth of the working class? The impact of these policies between 1960 and 1980 cut North Korea's birthrate in half.[44]

Meanwhile, North Korea is careful to make efforts to stay in China's good graces. One such example was the high-profile celebration of former Chinese leader Zhou Enlai's 100th birthday on February 27, 1998. North Korea wined, dined, and honored Chinese ambassador Wan Yongxiang and other Chinese embassy officials on the 27th. The following day, North Korea's Vice Foreign Minister and Party leaders from South Hamgyong Province paid homage to a bust of Zhou Enlai with ribbon-laden floral baskets. In true Juche worship fashion, the writing on one ribbon proclaimed, "[The] precious feats of comrade Zhou Enlai, close comrade-in-arms of the Korean people, will be immortal" [*KCNA*].

Propaganda releases that followed praised the former Chinese leader at length, recalled his friendship with Kim Il Sung, and emphasized North Korea and China's friendship. Chinese officials then reciprocated by hosting a big party at Pyongyang's Koryo Hotel in Zhou Enlai's honor. Chinese officials also hosted a documentary film about Zhou Enlai's exploits.

Another diplomatic courtesy toward the Chinese quickly followed. On March 16, Kim Jong Il sent a message to Chinese President Jiang Zemin congratulating him on his reelection as President of the PRC and Chairman of the Central Military Commission. Four days later, Hong Song Nam, acting Premier of North Korea's Administration Council, followed suit by sending a message congratulating his counterpart, China's Zhjr Llan, on his appointment as Premier of the State Council of the PRC. Pyongyang's Foreign Minister, Kim Yong Nam, sent a message the same day congratulating his counterpart, Tang Jiaxuan, on Tang's appointment as Foreign Minister of China. Again China reciprocated. This time the return favor was via Ma Guidsheng, a Chinese doctoral student at North Korea's Kim Chaek University. On March 23, more than five weeks after his son's birth, Ma requested that Kim Jong Il name his son because he was born on Kim's February 16 "Greatest Day" birthday. North Korean propaganda reported:

> Receiving the letter, General Kim Jong Il named the baby Sol Gwang in the hope that he will always throw bright rays of Korea-China friendship, undaunted by any snowstorm [*KCNA*].

Of course, the propaganda article did not mention what the baby's name originally had been, since that was of no concern to the two totalitarian states.

Beijing has been wedded to North Korea even before 1950 when Kim Il Sung sent his tanks rolling south across the Demilitarized Zone to precipitate the bloody three-year War for National Reunification. With Kim's invasion, Mao Zedong embraced North Korea as a strong ally. When North Korea's forces were subsequently crushed at Inchon and its aftermath, China intervened by sending the People's Liberation Army across the Yalu River. Between late 1950 and the 1953 armistice, an estimated half million Chinese soldiers died to bail Kim Il Sung out of his debacle, including Mao Zedong's eldest son, Mao Anyang.

Today, Juche's "anti-flunkeyism" self-reliance makes North Korea reluctant to admit that it was only China's commitment of millions of troops that saved the defeated Pyongyang regime. Over the last half-century, the friendship between Pyongyang and Beijing has taken on a bittersweet quality, but the alliance stands fast.

With the growing economic disparity between the Chinese and North Koreans, Pyongyang has had to strengthen its measures to prevent defection across their mountainous border to the sizable Sino-Korean population in China. The border guards' task is complicated by having to both prevent defection and defend against Scripture balloons. These balloons are periodically launched by Christians in China and South Korea to float the gospel skyward sometimes over hundreds of miles into Korea. Additional Korean People's Army units are often mobilized to "defend" against massive drops of thousands of these orange Scripture balloons.

Out of necessity, Pyongyang has permitted a large-scale barter business to be established with the Chinese. For example, three tons of North Korean scrap metal exchanges for one ton of Chinese flour. On any given day, 200 to 300 trucks cross the Friendship Bridge over the Yalu River near Dandong, China. Southbound trucks are loaded with bags of flour, car tires, sacks of cotton, and other materials not available in North Korea. Northbound trucks are filled with scrap metal, timber, mountain herbs, and ginseng roots. These barter businesses stand in open contradiction to Juche teachings that espouse anti-capitalistic self-reliance. However, economic necessity dictates such exceptions. Meanwhile, the Chinese businesses continue to make a healthy profit off the North Korean trade.

Kim Jong Il's hard-line socialist economic stance is radically different from the Gorbachev-style "new thinking" and "perestroika" socialist market economy adopted by the former Chinese leader Deng Xiaoping. Despite China's economic successes and North Korea's economic failures, Kim Jong Il remains steadfast in his claims of the "superiority of the North Korean style of socialism." This myopic policy recalls the popular tale of "The Emperor's New Clothes" in which a vain totalitarian ruler is duped by a tailor into buying a suit of invisible clothes and walking around naked. Everyone in his kingdom was afraid to laugh. Then a child told him he was stark naked. However, no one in North Korea, including the children, may oppose Kim Jong Il's willful misrule which continues to impoverish his nation.

The Chinese liken North Korea's current Juche culture and Party slogans to their Cultural Revolution of the 1960s. Xu, who works for the Chinese railroad near the Friendship Bridge, said, "They are still at the state of chanting slogans and waving the Red Book of Chairman Mao...[but] we [Chinese] know what is really important."[45] With a booming economy, China continues to walk the delicate political line between maintaining an excellent trading relationship with Seoul and sharing common Communist ideological roots with Pyongyang. Notably, China recognizes both the North and South Korean governments. Both the DPRK and ROK have embassies in Beijing. With quiet indifference to Juche, Chinese motivation to support a reunified Korea or even a peace treaty is to increase their growing influence in East Asia. Peace in Korea would set the stage for the withdrawal of American forces from Korea. The gradual reduction of U.S. bases in East Asia continues to validate China's patient policy aimed at eventually dominating East Asia.

Despite her recent progressive economic policies, East Asian analysts should keep a wary eye on China. China has doubled her military expenditures from 1994–1998 to modernize the People's Liberation Army. To many analysts, China is the key power to watch in East Asia, more so than her tiny yet highly volatile neighbor, North Korea. Not withstanding Pyongyang's and defector Hwang Jang Yop's claims of North Korea's military self-sufficiency, China continues to provide limited food for the hungry 1.2 million member Korean People's Army. This same People's Republic of China intervened in the Korean War by ordering a secret offensive across the Yalu River against U.S. forces in 1950. In many respects, China should continue to be viewed as the protective "big brother" dragon which serves to guarantee the continued existence of the Pyongyang regime.

Russia

Moscow needs to rebuild its credibility and restore contacts with Pyongyang. Neither will prove to be an easy task. For some time to come, Russia's influence in the region will be negligible.[46]

CHUNG DOO HEE
PROFESSOR OF HISTORY
SOGANG UNIVERSITY, SEOUL

Pyongyang continues to show a respectful and cooperative attitude toward Russia in its economic policies and propaganda. North Korea's formation of the Rajin-Sonbong FETZ in its northeast region is a cooperative, though not lucrative, venture with both Russia and China. Meanwhile, given the Russian Communist Party's receptivity to Juche, propaganda continues to paint the Russo–North Korean relationship in a positive light. Notwithstanding the generally positive attitude toward the Soviets, Juche ideology continues to teach Korean ethnocentric superiority to Russia. This superiority is based on the conviction that where Russia's Communist system failed due to over-dependence on capitalist nations, the North Korean "revolution of the Juche type" will not.

Russia, in return, has a vested interest in maintaining stability on the Korean peninsula, but not an overriding one. Though the former Soviet Union was North Korea's largest trading partner during the Cold War, the annual trade volume dramatically dropped from $1.4 billion in 1990 to only $360 million in 1991 when Moscow demanded that all trade be conducted with hard currency instead of the barter system. In 1990, Moscow also strained its relationship with Pyongyong when it established diplomatic relations with South Korea and exchanged ambassadors. Russia is not particularly interested in making a substantial financial investment in the FETZ (also known as the Tumen River Delta Development Project) since most of the development stands to benefit the Chinese and North Koreans. Moreover, Russia's scarce investment capital is better served in developing her Maritime Province rather than the multilateral project which has a lower expected payoff.

Russian multilateral initiatives toward Korean reunification would probably lead to negative reactions from Japan, due to long memories, and probably from South Korea as well. Faced with complex domestic problems and a struggling economy, Russia will probably continue to play a secondary role in East Asian affairs. Thus, the cash-poor Russian government maintains an indifferent attitude toward North Korea. Denis Dragounsky, a political commentator in Moscow, noted that at least two Russian views of North Korea exist. One view is that North Korea is one of the ex-Soviet Union's remaining geopolitical embarrassments left over from the Cold War era. The other view, by remaining Bolshevik believers, views North Korea and Cuba as the last surviving bastions of the Communist revolution. Little change in Russia's indifferent policy toward North Korea is expected.

Other Nations

North Korea's overtures toward other nations are designed to continue to spread Juche religious teachings which highlight Kim Jong Il's role as champion of the world's working class—particularly in developing and non-aligned nations. Relationships between North Korea and such nations as Libya, Cuba, Yemen, Iran, Syria, and Palestine are particularly strong.

North Korea also continues to maintain a quiet, ongoing economic and diplomatic relationship with nations such as Sweden and Germany. However, these North Korean trading partners generally are not mentioned in propaganda. One notable exception was the following scathing rebuke of the German Foreign Minister who recently advocated that the German "reunification by absorption" solution be applied to Korea:

> The *German Foreign Minister* has made unreasonable utterances concerning some issues related to the DPRK, getting on its nerve. Recently, he reportedly said the DPRK, which agreed to take part in "four-way talks," used its reason and it seems that the DPRK is aware of the time when it should pull itself from international "isolation." The other day, he made such imprudent utterances over the Korean reunification issue, encouraging the south Korean puppets in their efforts for *"unifying the country by absorbing the north."* His remarks are indicative of his *wrong attitude* towards the DPRK. We are disillusioned with his *improper thinking pattern and reversed judgment*...The German Foreign Minister's utterances are really *nonsense*. International "isolation" has nothing to do with the DPRK, a dignified sovereign state which has established friendly relations with many independence-advocating progressive people around the world. The German authorities' allegation about "isolation" is only part of the anti-DPRK acts. Their behavior is apparently motivated by [what is] construed to be a foolish attempt to chill the atmosphere of the "quad talks" and derail the "talks" from its original purpose. They [Germany], who set up even a "consultative body" with the South Korean puppets for "unification by absorption," fostering military confrontation between the two halves of

Korea, are now trying to intentionally laying an obstacle to the "four-way talks," going against the trend towards peace and stability of the Korean Peninsula. People hardly understand why *Germany is unable to tell right from wrong over the internationally delicate Korean issue,* while seeking a permanent seat on the United Nations Security Council…If Germany is to win public trust, evading ridicule and denunciation, it must refrain from such a despicable act as hurting others [*KCNA*].

Despite Juche's xenophobia, North Korea's interactions with the world community aim to propagate the Juche religion of Kim Jong Il-ism. Not surprisingly, most of North Korea's dealings with other nations tend to be either out of economic necessity or to promote the Juche religion on an international level, including reunification. Pyongyang has invested considerable resources into organizing Juche study societies around the world and bringing foreign visitors to North Korea for national celebrations. For example, 4,000 foreign dignitaries were invited to attend Kim Il Sung's 80th birthday celebration. Similarly, the Juche worldview, with its own definition of morality, is useful in understanding how Pyongyang can initiate terrorist activities, sabotage, and counterfeiting operations while rejecting recurring charges of human rights abuses.

CHAPTER 8

Hwang Jang Yop: The Architect of Juche

The defection to the South by Hwang Jang Yop, the very architect who led the work of framing so-called Juche Ideology, is incontrovertible proof that North Korea's future is gloomy.[1]

KOH HU HWAN
PROFESSOR OF POLITICAL SCIENCE
DONG KUK UNIVERSITY, SEOUL

Following a high-profile defection to South Korea's Beijing embassy on February 12, 1997, Hwang Jang Yop ("the architect of Juche") and his aide, Kim Duk Hong, arrived in Seoul on April 20. Defection by high-ranking officials is a clear sign that North Koreans are disgusted with Kim Jong Il and the hellish Juche totalitarian system under which they live. In contrast to Kim Jong Il, Hwang finally concluded that the planned economy and the market economy should not be regarded as incompatible but as complementary.

Hwang Jang Yop pointed out that Kim Jong Il's theory of "Socialism is Science" reveals the total lack of any viable means of self-criticism from within the Juche totalitarian system. Hwang views the deprivation of any mechanism of self-criticism as the very cause of the collapse of Juche socialism.[2]

Hwang's defection and subsequent remarks bear special significance because of his influential status as the "godfather of Juche" and an esteemed former secretary of the North's Central Committee of the Workers' Party. In the 1990s the number of defectors from the North has been increasing. There have been defections among North Korea's diplomatic corps in Africa, among trade mission members in Europe[3], and, remarkably, even Kim Jong Il's first wife defected while she was in Russia. Yet, of the approximately 616 North Korean defectors to the South by 1996, Hwang Jang Yop is the highest ranking official to have defected from North Korea since the Korean War armistice was signed in 1953. Some liken Hwang's defection from the Juche state of North Korea as roughly equivalent to Marx or Lenin abandoning the Communist world. Other analysts maintain that Hwang Jang Yop has not been particularly influential in the Party since 1980. A third view is that Hwang Jang Yop was a neo-Juche revisionist who desired to purify Juche of nepotistic feudalism. According to this theory, Hwang fled to the South not because he liked capitalism or democracy, but rather to save his own skin.

Hwang Jang Yop's own version of his motives sounds very altruistic. In a sensationalist series of remarks, Hwang said he came to warn the South of the strong likelihood that the North would soon invade with a blitzkrieg-style offense. Though North Korea has repeatedly threatened to turn Seoul into "a sea of flames," Hwang's remarks gave the South Koreans renewed cause for concern. Hwang's chilly statements such as, "I am sure North Korea will start a war," and "North Korea will never let the South continue to prosper alone," sent shock waves through the Republic of Korea. This chapter considers Hwang Jang Yop's central role in the formation of the Juche religion, his landmark defection, and finally some of Hwang's post-defection remarks which provide an insider's view of Juche.

Visionary, Villain, Victim, or Revisionist?

Dispatches were sent by couriers to all the king's provinces with the order to destroy, kill and annihilate... and to plunder their goods.

ESTHER 3:13

Remarks from any contemporary historical figure must be carefully weighed against their motivation, credibility, and worldview. Hwang Jang Yop's remarks are no exception. Should Hwang Jang Yop be considered a visionary, villain, victim, or neo-Juche revisionist? Is he a hero become traitor, traitor become hero, or merely a highly adept and possibly corrupt political opportunist? To what extent was Hwang the mastermind behind some or all of the numerous purges and mass murders inside North Korea over the last several decades? While definitive answers to some of these questions will await the judgment of history, people should exercise extreme caution before believing all of Hwang Jang Yop's statements, including those provided herein. Hwang Jang Yop's long-standing pivotal role near the pin-

Hwang Jang Yop

nacle of North Korea's volatile power structure compels us to take a closer look at this intriguing historical figure.

Hwang Jang Yop was born on the east coast of Korea in 1925 in Ju-ul, Hamgyong Bukdo. Hwang attended Ju-ul Kyong-sung Middle School where he did not show any particular interest in communism. During World War II, Hwang lived as a scholar in Japan. Then, from 1946 to 1948, he attended the Pyongyang Commerce School. During this time, Hwang became a Communist. Afterwards, Hwang studied Marxism at Kim Il Sung University where he distinguished himself as the most ardent student of Marxism on the entire campus. He graduated in 1949. In 1950, during the Korean War, Hwang was sent to the Soviet Union where he received a doctorate degree in Marxist philosophy. Upon return to Pyongyang, Hwang Jang Yop quickly established himself as the premier scholar in Marxism. As a result, in 1954, he was appointed to the post of head lecturer of philosophy at Kim Il Sung University. By 1958, he became a member of the influential Academy of Sciences at the age of only 33.

Hwang's long career near the top of North Korea's power structure included serving as President of Pyongyang's Kim Il Sung University. With its approximately 10,000 students, it is North Korea's largest and most prestigious university. Throughout his career, Hwang Jang Yop enjoyed special power, prestige, and perks. Since 1953, he has visited China, India, Thailand, Greece, Japan, and France. Before his 1997 defection, Hwang had not traveled to Great Britain or the United States. Hwang's posts included influential positions spanning most of North Korea's history, as shown in Table 8-1.

However, Hwang was best known as the chief architect of Juche ideology. Hwang was the "brains" behind the North Korean

TABLE 8-1. Hwang Jang Yop's Influential Posts in the DPRK

YEAR(S)*	POSITION
1954	Chief Lecturer of Philosophy at Kim Il Sung University
1958	Member of Academy of Sciences
1959	Deputy Director of the Propaganda and Agitation Department of the Workers' Party
1966–1972	President of Kim Il Sung University
1970	Member of the Workers' Party Central Committee
1972–1977	Chairman of the Supreme People's Assembly (parliament)
1972–1983	Chairman of the Supreme People's Assembly (3 terms)
1977, 1980	Chairman of the Foreign Affairs Committee of the Supreme People's Assembly
1980–1993	Workers' Party Secretary for Ideological Affairs
1983–1997	Chairman of Foreign Diplomacy
1984	Co-Chief Secretary (with Kim Guk-Tae) of the Workers' Party Central Committee
1984	Vice-Chairman of the Fatherland Peace and Unification Agency
1993–1997	Secretary of Foreign Affairs

* or year first assigned

Workers' Party imposition of so-called monolithic leadership under Juche. By his own admittance, Hwang handcrafted the Juche religion for the sole purpose of sustaining the totalitarian dictatorship of Kim Il Sung and to provide an ideological basis for the hereditary succession of power to his son, Kim Jong Il.

Upon Josef Stalin's death in March 1953, the Communist world was plunged into ideological confusion and turmoil. In the Soviet Union, a radical de-Stalinization movement posed a threat to Kim Il Sung's continued rule in North Korea, since he was originally installed as a dictator at Stalin's behest. Amid this turmoil, Hwang's Moscow University education enabled him to spin a philosophical theory to safeguard Kim Il Sung's one-man rule system. Hwang, then chief lecturer of philosophy at Kim Il Sung University, called this theory "Juche," literally meaning "self-reliance." Hwang later modified this Juche system to include a hereditary succession plan to hand over power to Kim Jong Il.

Hwang first attracted the attention of the Party elite in 1956 by writing a paper entitled "Potentials for the Peaceful Unification of our Fatherland." His choice of topic was not a fluke. As chair of the Academy of Sciences History Research Institute in May 1956, Hwang noted that the "peaceful unification" theme had been a particularly hot topic at the Third Workers' Party Convention. Two months later, he presented his research paper before the Academy of Sciences. Quick to spot an opportunity, Hwang had written on the right topic with the right ideological slant at the right time.

From then on, Hwang made the transition from scholar to politician. In December 1959, he was appointed as Deputy Chairman of the Workers' Party Propaganda Section. In October 1962, Hwang became an alternate member of the Supreme People's Assembly. At about the time he was named as President of Kim Il Sung University, in October 1965, Hwang experienced his first political attack. Party comrades criticized Hwang's Moscow University doctorate thesis. They claimed that his thesis, entitled "Problems of Socialism Transition and Proletariat," deviated from orthodox Marxism-Leninism. Hwang Jang Yop withstood the challenge and managed to overcome their criticism.

From 1972 onward, when Hwang rose to Chairman of the Supreme People's Assembly, he was actively involved in foreign diplomacy. In 1983, Hwang served as Chairman of Foreign Diplomacy. He served in that post, among others, until his defection in February 1997. Hwang Jang Yop's consecutive and overlapping roles in key government positions cast considerable doubt on the notion of some that his political influence has been waning since 1980.

In 1957, Hwang Jang Yop became a key figure in the "August Factions Fighting Incident," which culminated in a Party purge. The series of events started when Hwang published the essay "Some Questions on the Conflict of Production Means and Production" in *History Philosophy* magazine's May 1957 issue. Controversy began due to this article and another in the December 1957 Party organ, *Workers*. These articles were divisive because Hwang, along with co-author Kim Hu Sin, presented the false idea that the Communist movements of the 1920s were "factionalist movements." Along with the "factionalist" label, Hwang advanced the idea that the *real* Korean Communist movement arose out of Kim Il Sung's anti-Japanese guerrilla activities in the late 1930s and early

1940s. This "factionalist" view challenged many senior Party leaders' authority. At the same time, Hwang's move catapulted him into the good graces of Kim Il Sung who was seeking to consolidate his power by ousting his would-be competitors.

At the December 1957 meetings entitled "Philosophical Debates on Socialist Foundation in Korea and Its Leadership Formation," Hwang Jang Yop, who organized the event, not surprisingly, also gave the keynote speech. In this new era of Leninism, Hwang Jang Yop's pivotal speech articulated the view that North Korea's political system was fundamentally rooted in the Marxist-Leninist doctrine of proletariat dictatorship. Then, again discounting the old-time Communist predecessors in favor of Kim Il Sung, Hwang openly declared the watershed event in Korean socialist history to be "the North Korean Provisional People's Commune" of February 1947. Who led that 1947 meeting? If you guessed Kim Il Sung, you are quite right.

Thus, Hwang Jang Yop's writings and speeches provided the impetus to purge potential rivals of Kim Il Sung such as Lee Chung Won and Song Eh Jung. Their arguments of a "Democratic People's United Dictatorship" along the Chinese Party line were denounced and they were killed. Purging these men and their respective entourages strengthened Kim Il Sung's power not only by eliminating rivals, but by reshaping North Korea's Communist ideology.

Three key elements changed in DPRK communism in the wake of this strategic purge. First, Kim Il Sung's anti-Japanese partisan movement became the accepted origin of Korean communism, not the Korean Communist movement of the 1920s. Second, the denouncement and purge of the "pro-Chinese Yanan faction" established independence of the Korean Party from excessive Chinese influence that existed in the aftermath of the Korean War. Third, "leftist" party theoreticians and leaders who studied in Japan during the occupation were replaced with new theoreticians trained in Moscow. Note that Hwang Jang Yop falls under both the *bad* "studied in Japan" and *good* "trained in Moscow" categories.

Hwang's reward for significantly contributing to the purge of the old Communist cadres was his 1959 appointment to the post of Vice Chairman of the Worker's Party's Propaganda Section. Subsequently, at the young age of 40, Hwang was promoted to President of Kim Il Sung University. By the late 1960s, Hwang was being openly lauded as a "model" scholar and theoretician.

Hwang Jang Yop continued to be a major proponent of Juche ideology as it changed and developed through the 1960s and 1970s. For example, on the 20th anniversary of Kim Il Sung University on September 30, 1966, Hwang Jang Yop's remarks included the statement:

> Loyalty to the Party and the President is the first life and glorious tradition of the University.[4]

Hwang was the first to use the catch phrase "loyalty to the President and the Party."

Hwang's work to systematize Juche culminated at the Fifth Party Congress in November 1970. There, the Workers' Party officially adopted Juche alongside Marxism-Leninism as the guiding philosophy of the KWP. The Sixth Party Congress in October 1980 revised the Party's doctrine and constitution one step farther, declaring Jucheism to be "the only guiding principle of the Party." No mention was made of Marxism-Leninism. This was a major shift away from the Party doctrine of the 1970s where Marxism-Leninism shared center stage with Juche.

During the 1980s, Juche philosophy took a new revisionist turn. Hwang was writing Marxism-Leninism out of Juche's past, just as he had erased all record of North Korea's Communist movement originating in the 1920s. Now, instead of Juche being viewed as an outgrowth of Marxism-Leninism, it was declared to be a truly new philosophy. Though Juche contained a Marxist-Leninist element, it was held to be the new philosophy of the world. This shift was required because the collapse of the Soviet bloc Communist states bankrupted Hwang's Marxist-Leninist flavored Juche of the 1970s. Juche had to ideologically distance itself from Marxism-Leninism, which had seemingly failed the acid test of history.

Those who would like to minimize Hwang Jang Yop's role within the government present an alternate view of his role during the last two decades. They argue that Hwang's fortunes were really declining from the 1970s onward. According to this view, while Hwang formulated, propagated, and canonized Juche philosophy in the 1960s, Kim Jong Il started to replace him in that capacity in the 1970s. Proponents of this view maintain that Kim Jong Il's ascent to Party Secretary in October 1973 meant Kim had replaced Hwang in his key influential role. As proof of their claim, they cite Kim Jong Il's name being listed as "author" of political essays on Juche.

However, during these years, Hwang Jang Yop continued to be Kim Il Sung's go-between for communications between Kim Il Sung and his inner circle. Moreover, Kim Il Sung discouraged Hwang from having his name listed as the author of articles so that his close friend and confidant would not come under political attack. Nevertheless, Hwang Jang Yop continued to review, edit, and probably write many of the political essays and speeches on Juche that were published in the totalitarian state. Most of these essays ended up having Kim Jong Il's name on them. Some of these essays and speeches are listed in Table 8-2.

**TABLE 8-2. Some of the Many Hwang Speeches
and Essays Attributed to Kim Jong Il [5]**

TITLE / DATE	SIGNIFICANCE
"The Brilliant Master Piece of Our Great Leader Comrade Kim Il Sung Who Created the Party's Unique System of Ideology" (October 1973)	This essay first used the term "unique system" of the Party in reference to Juche.
"On Some Issues of Conforming Our Society to Kim Il Sung-ism" (February 1976)	Kim Jong Il's speech said that Marxism-Leninism was limited both in time and geography, while stressing that Kim Il Sung-ism (Juche) was unique in that it was not likewise limited.
"10 Principles in Establishing the Party's Unique Ideology" and "On Correctly Understanding Kim Il Sung-ism's Originality" (April 1974)	These "Kim Jong Il reports" proclaim Juche to be the new trend of nationalism.
"On Jucheism" (March 1982)	This essay, allegedly by Kim Jong Il, is the definitive work on Juche.
"On Some Questions on Teaching Jucheism" (July 1986)	This Kim Jong Il speech at the Party Central Committee Leadership Conference criticized reform policies in the USSR and China.

It is quite doubtful that Kim Jong Il, with his coarse vocabulary and comparatively lesser education, was the mastermind who shaped Juche ideology during the 1970s and 1980s. Thus, the effort to minimize Hwang's influence may well be another attempt at revisionist history to lessen the impact of Hwang Jang Yop's defection.

Hwang's reputation as a theoretician enabled him to rise to

important positions within the Korean Worker's Party in the 1970s and 1980s. These were significant decades for systematizing the Juche religion and refining Party ideology. Hwang Jang Yop, in effect, became Kim Il Sung's chief expert advisor on Juche. When asked if Kim Il Sung consulted him on matters of foreign relations, Hwang responded, "Yes." Hwang said that he was consulted on virtually all decisions, because all decisions depend on Juche. North Korean professor Pak Mun Hoi told Jeremy J. Stone, "Yes, we can say so [that all decisions were considered in light of Juche ideology], because it is a guiding idea of our Government."[6]

Professor Pak also told Stone about Hwang Jang Yop's key behind-the-scenes role as an intermediary between Kim Il Sung and other government officials:

> Hwang consults with the President and then advises others what is the correct line. But, Pak said, he does not do work to make himself famous and, indeed, hates publishing books in his own name. The President likes and trusts him. For example, in 1967, Hwang wrote a paper "On the Transition from Capitalism to Socialism and the Proletariat Dictatorship." It created a great stir; scholars and professors criticized him severely. The President called him to his home and explained that such and such was right and such and such was not. Now the President keeps himself informed of Hwang's works before they are published so that this [problem of criticism] will not happen again.[7]

Yop's privileged status as one of Kim Il Sung's closest advisors means that he undoubtedly was at least privy to the dictator's ongoing series of government purges and mass elimination of "hostile group" "cadre members."[8] It is quite probable, despite his "Confucian sage" reputation, that he played a primary role in eliminating any possible domestic threat to his newborn religion.

Given Pak's close relationship to Kim Il Sung and Kim Jong Il, it was not surprising that Professor Pak told Stone that "everyone wants to be on friendly relations" with Hwang and that he also has "very good" relations with the "Dear Leader," Kim Jong Il. Pak continued:

> Indeed Kim Jong Il urged Hwang to take a holiday for a month when Hwang did not want to do so. Also, the President [then Kim Il Sung] showed his affection for Hwang by sending him to China for three months for his hoarse throat.[9]

So, Hwang Jang Yop's later defection might correctly be viewed as a 1997 reenactment of the defection of Nazi SS criminal Rudolf Hess to Britain in 1940. However, Hwang's role within North Korea might be better compared to Josef Goebbels who presided over Hitler's propaganda effort. Just as Hess's defection gave Hitler fits, Hwang's defection likewise probably enraged Kim Jong Il. On the other hand, maybe Hwang's defection was planned by Kim Jong Il and Yop himself. If this is true, then the 1997 post-Yop defection war scare in the South might just be the latest calculated "strategy of terror" in Pyongyang's ongoing psychological warfare against "the illegitimate regime of the south."

Six years before his defection, Hwang Jang Yop met with Jeremy J. Stone, president of the Federation of American Scientists, during Stone's 1991 trip to Pyongyang. Hwang's remarks were the standard Juche line with a smile. Stone reported:

> He [Hwang] made no secret that national reunification is their goal and that U.S. support of the South as a military base is for the North the major obstacle...There is, he thought, no more excuse for U.S. forces to protect against the threat from the North...He thanked me for "making an effort to improve relations," which he said they wanted. So, it was his conclusion that *all questions of improving relations really depend on the U.S.*[10]

Considering that North Korea is a rigidly totalitarian state, the international press speculation that Hwang's defection "spells the end of Jucheism" or otherwise marked the impending downfall of North Korea's dictatorship seems premature. Such opinions discount or underestimate the rigid centralized control of the totalitarian state and dictator-god religious system that Hwang Jang Yop helped to shape.

Another interesting view of the Hwang Jang Yop affair is that Hwang was about to be purged for being a "neo-Juche" revisionist who was secretly disenchanted by the hereditary succession of power. The neo-Jucheism theorists allege that Hwang wrote a 321-page paper entitled "For the Bright Future of Humanity" in March 1995 under the pseudonym "International Juche Foundation." This rather lengthy "paper" was accompanied by two abstracts, "Historical Tasks of Today" and "Mission of Philosophy." As the story goes, Hwang claimed that he secretly prepared these items with the intention of distributing them to Juche study groups throughout the world. One proponent of this "neo-Juche" theory quotes Hwang as stating in these "International Juche Foundation" writings that:

> In general, Jucheism is believed to be a mere political doctrine which was created by Korea's Great Leader Kim Il Sung and developed further by our Dear Leader Kim Jong Il …Jucheism is more than that…Jucheism was created by Kim Il Sung in order to counter Marxism-Leninism and define a path for the future of mankind. *However, the Party leaders have adulterated this theory to benefit their self-interest, used it as weapons to enhance their dictatorship, and to deceive the students of South Korea.*[11]

Proponents of the "neo-Juche" theory also point to other statements by Hwang and his adopted daughter, Park Myong Ae of Seoul. For example, Park Myong Ae stated at a December 1995 Seoul press conference that,

> I met my father prior to my visit here. He is known as the creator of Jucheism but today's Jucheism is a far cry from his Jucheism. He is very anxious to promote his Jucheism worldwide and he has been working on refining it. Some day this will be brought to light. He works on it now and then and gives me a section now and then when I visit Pyongyang.[12]

An example of a pro-capitalist neo-Juche remark by Hwang after his defection is:

> The market is a place where man's nature of self-reliance is associated with his or her creativity. Therefore, the development of the market makes enhanced creative ardors in a person.[13]

Proponents of the neo-Juche theory also point out that Hwang Jang Yop is not listed as one of the contributing authors to the mammoth 10-volume series "The Great Jucheism," published on the occasion of the Party's 40th anniversary in 1985.

From the North Korean perspective, "neo-Jucheism" would be perceived as a threat for three reasons. First, neo-Jucheism attacks the basic governing ideology of North Korea. Second, neo-Jucheism claims that a socialist central economy is inadequate and promotes capitalist market economy and value systems. Third, neo-Jucheism attacks socialist collectivism and admits individualism and capitalist views of society and people. As the neo-Juche theory goes, Hwang had to decide either to align his view with the main Juche school of thought or invent his own Jucheism. Hwang apparently chose the latter. This view is partly based on a statement made by Hwang on February 19, 1997:

> Some of the self-styled leading ideologists fail to realize that their beliefs are obsolete and refuse to accept progressive ideas. Those who blindly follow an ideology are in fact superstitious believers and will be left behind [*Donga Ilbo*].

In his post-defection remarks, Hwang Jang Yop also characterizes Juche as a "superstition" and his neo-Juche ideology as "progressive." Hwang believes that North Korea should emulate China's economic reforms.

Much of the above "neo-Juche" theory could be characterized as a mixture of half-truths, post-defection fabrication, and conjecture. Since Hwang, as the architect of Juche, was an expert as such fabrications, it is a challenge to believe that he was secretly an ardent "neo-Jucheist" capitalist without much justified skepticism. For someone who was, according to the neo-Juche theorists, a secret capitalist, Hwang continued to enjoy the high privilege of international travel throughout the 1990s. Had Kim Il Sung and later Kim Jong Il perceived even a hint of "neo-Jucheism," those privileges would have been immediately revoked. Moreover, if Hwang Jang Yop articulated such views, he would probably have quickly become a victim of the police state he helped to craft.

Throughout the 1990s, Hwang capitalized on his reputation as the premier Juche scholar and became Secretary-in-Chief for Foreign Affairs of the KWP (1993) and Chairman of Foreign Affairs, Supreme People's Council. These positions enabled him to promote Juche ideology on an international level. For example, in October 1994, Hwang went to Brazil, Cuba, and Uruguay. He went to France and Great Britain in November 1995 and Russia in January 1996. In June of the same year he went to Vietnam. And, finally, in February 1997 he went to Japan and China where he defected. Hwang's defection in Beijing was even more of a surprise because the more likely time and place for him to defect would have been during his scheduled April 1997 seminar at the Carter Center in the United States.

Another less flattering yet tenable rendition of Hwang Jang Yop's defection motives is the "take the money and run" scenario. Hwang Jang Yop would certainly not be the first nor the last tyrant to succumb to greed. This possibility will be discussed in more detail in the next section.

If all the facts about Hwang Jang Yop became public, he, like Hess before him, would probably be sentenced to prison for life. Certainly, Hwang Jang Yop's life does not testify to the fact that he was a misguided altruist. His careful crafting of the Juche religion shows a steady pattern of ruthless abuse of power and intentional deception on a massive scale. During his many decades as part of North Korea's upper echelon, Hwang enjoyed the reputation of being a profound theoretical thinker. As the architect of Juche, he presided over the development of the Juche religion during most of the last quarter-century.

Hwang's belated love affair with capitalism seems more like an opportunistic after-thought. Even after his defection, Hwang, like an ideological chameleon, seems to blend into his new surroundings and continuing to operate as an academic sage. To date, Hwang has said nothing publicly to indicate he takes any personal responsibility or has any remorse for his crimes against the Korean people.

The Landmark Defection

> *The authorities began to attack my ideology claiming that it conflicts with Kim Jong Il's ideology... They have mounted a campaign to discredit me.*[14]
>
> HWANG JANG YOP

Hwang Jang Yop and Kim Duk Hong's landmark 1997 defection in Beijing resulted in a five-week standoff that caught the world's attention. In this section we will consider this series of events as well as some behind-the-scenes allegations that did not receive much notice in the international press.

In August 1995, a year-and-a-half before the defection, Hwang is reported to have loudly exclaimed in a Chinese hotel's lobby, "My plans for my country are finished!" Possibly Kim Il Sung's death just fifteen months prior, along with the floods, energy shortages, and general economic malaise, had been weighing heavily on Hwang's mind. Nine months later, in May 1996, harsh criticism against *Juche revisionists* started to appear in North Korea's propaganda. For example, the May 10 issue of *Rodong Sinmun* stated:

> The Soviet Union collapsed because of the modern revisionists and traitors to socialism who took power upon Stalin's

death. The traitors utilized all sorts of intrigues and treachery to gain power and purged those who were true to the revolution.[15]

In a secret letter to "Mr. A"[16] (a South Korean) dated November 13, 1996, Hwang wrote:

> The authorities began to attack my ideology claiming that it conflicts with Kim Jong Il's ideology. I am being watched more closely now. They have mounted a campaign to discredit me.[17]

Details of this anti-Hwang campaign are not available. However, by early 1996 some analysts think Hwang was already in disfavor with many influential Party members. His alleged opponents included "the young Turks" educated in the Manggyongdae Revolutionary School. This elite school caters exclusively to the descendants of anti-Japanese partisans, Korean War veterans, and Party leaders. In addition, some of the remaining old guard were aligned against Hwang, including Kim Guk Tae, Yang Hyong Sup, and Kim Ki Nam.

Hwang Jang Yop's fall into disfavor may not have been entirely due to his personal political views. He allegedly formed secret organizations using assets of his aide, Kim Duk Hong: the Juche Peace Foundation and the Korean Hotel Trading Company. Hwang's position since 1987 over the Korean Social Scientist Association also provided another front for secret activities. His former student, Associate Chairman Jin Young Gul, may also have been using his position to provide special favors to foreign diplomats in return for cash or other considerations.

Also, Hwang's aide and co-defector, Kim Duk Hong, does not fit the junior "gopher" stereotype typically ascribed to aides. One source alleges that Kim Duk Hong engaged in five money-making schemes. First, Kim Duk Hong ran a hotel company that allegedly provided funds for Hwang's covert activities. Second, Kim obtained the funds from overseas Korean businessmen and even had close ties to a South Korean company. Third, Kim allegedly arranged for members of rich South Korean families to escape from the North in exchange for cash. Fourth, allegedly at Hwang's behest, Kim solicited funds from South Korean businessmen by promising they could be involved in the Wonson-Kumgangsan railroad project. And fifth, Kim, along with Hwang, allegedly received bribes from South Koreans wanting to start a business in the North. Kim Duk Hong is reported as being so affluent that he could buy an entire hotel in China.

Unconfirmed reports allege that Hwang also made sizable sums of money by using his son, Hwang Kyong Mo, and his adopted daughter, Park Mong Ae, to smuggle Korean archeological treasures from the North to the South. Chinese scholar Pyong Wijung, who met with Hwang twice each year, is also reported to have played a significant role in Hwang's covert activities. Between April and November 1996 alone, Hwang's contacts in the South allegedly provided more than $225 million to Hwang. The August 1996 "Hanchongryon Incident" and the September 1996 "Submarine Grounding Incident," enabled Hwang was able to obtain large amounts of cash. For the nine days of the August 1996 Hanchongryon Incident, 12,000 South Korean police hit 23 universities and detained hundreds in a coordinated crackdown against a radical pro-North student group infiltrated by North Korean agents. The cash payments to Hwang, allegedly funneled with the approval of the South's government, were intended to jump-start a market economy in the North. Park Myong Ae said, "What my father and I are doing is welcome in South Korea, but in North Korea, its discovery will mean the end for my father."[18]

Kim Duk Hong studied political economics under Hwang at Kim Il Sung University. Kim became a close confidant, friend, and protégé of Hwang over the course of many years. In March 1995, Hwang established the Juche Peace Foundation for the politically acceptable reason of "providing funds for foreign students of Jucheism." Hwang appointed Kim Duk Hong to be the foundation's Director of Finance. In a letter to "Mr. A." dated November 13, 1996, Hwang called Kim "my younger brother and comrade-in-arms." He requested that Kim be allowed to carry on in his place in the event of his death. Hwang also arranged for Kim Duk Hong to be appointed as the General Manager of the Korean Hotel Trading Company and Associate Director of the Material Research Section, Workers' Party Central Committee. These posts enabled Kim to not only plan the timing and location of their defection, but also coordinate the transfer of their sizable financial assets as well.

Hwang Jang Yop and Kim Duk Hong's plans may have included the formation of a North Korean government-in-exile with the intent to take the reins of power in the North upon the demise or toppling of Kim Jong Il through a coup or other event. If this is the case, it would explain why the South Korean government would permit Hwang's indirect contacts and financial transactions with the South. However, the full scope of Hwang's involvements and real motives have not been made public. Indeed, given that no "North Korean government-in-exile" has been announced since the duo defected, their motives may simply have been self-preservation and sheer greed.

In addition to Hwang's perception that his political views were under attack within the Party, Hwang alleges that the North Korean Political Security Bureau initiated an investigation into his activities in October 1996. On November 10, 1996, Hwang wrote to Mr. A:

> I have no close people here. Everyone pretends to be close to you. This is a police state. I expect personnel changes here in July. If I lose my job, I will be unable to travel abroad. I won't be meeting foreign visitors. My life won't be worth living and I don't have much time left. There is a big event in February and they will probably use me until then and purge me quietly after that. But anything can happen prior to February. I and my comrades must not be destroyed totally. You must ensure that this does not happen…I would rather commit suicide than stand trial being accused of crimes made up by the authorities and then executed.[19]

The first hint of Hwang Jang Yop's intent to defect probably occurred during a February 1995 meeting between Hwang and Paik Young Joong, a Korean-American businessman. Hwang met with Paik several times and told him, "North Korea cannot last much longer. Jucheism in not working." Hwang asked Paik to convey those words to South Korea's former National Assembly President, Kim Jae Sun. Kim Jae Sun had attended the Pyongyang Commerce School with Hwang before the Korean War. Thus, South Korea probably already had plans in place for Hwang's defection well over a year before the February 1997 incident.

In September 1996, still five months before the defection, then South Korean President Kim Young Sam reportedly met with Kim Duk Hong in Beijing to confirm Hwang's desire to defect. Afterwards, Kim Young Sam allegedly ordered South Korean government personnel to accelerate arrangements for Hwang Jang Yop's defection. When Hwang and Kim defected the following February 12, the U.S. CIA and South Korean ANSP had personnel already on standby to debrief the duo. During the 35-minute debriefing, Hwang allegedly claimed that four or five other high-ranking officials, including former Party secretary Ryu Jin Sik, might defect.

When Hwang Jang Yop and his aid Kim Duk Hong actually defected on February 12, 1997, they created a diplomatic dilemma for the Chinese government. The Chinese government wanted to offend neither North Korea, its long-time ally, nor South Korea, an important trading partner.

North Korea's immediate response to the double defection was quite negative and almost violent. They insisted that Hwang and Kim were kidnapped by South Korean agents. Pyongyang also threatened to take "decisive measures," which is a euphemism for terrorist retaliation. Furthermore, the North sent out armed personnel to surround the South Korean embassy in Beijing. This resulted in a delicate situation for the Chinese since the North Koreans had no jurisdiction on Chinese soil, where they were threatening another sovereign nation's embassy.

Inside the South's Beijing embassy, Hwang issued a statement describing his motive for defection. In his statement, he wrote:

> For the past 50 years, I have been faithful to my duty as a member of the Workers' Party. I have been in the good graces of the Party and the Leader, and therefore all I have toward the Party and the Leader is a deep sense of gratitude. Now North Korea is suffering from economic difficulties, but there can be no danger of collapse because there is firm political unity there. All the people, including my own family members, may say that I became insane when they hear that I, under these conditions, decided to defect to South Korea after abandoning all I had enjoyed in North Korea. I myself also have been beset by the thought that I am insane. But the question is am I the only man who has become insane? For over a half century, our nation has remained divided, and the people are raising their voices saying their fatherland must be unified. But they are confronting each other, calling the other sides by the name of enemy, and even threatening to turn the other side into a flame of fire. Can this be regarded as the behavior of rational people?
>
> The people used to boast that they have built an ideal society for the workers and farmers despite that they are suffering from starvation. Can you say that these people are sane? In the meantime, the people (in South Korea) are indulged in staging demonstrations, being indifferent to the reality that a great number of their brethren (in the North) are starving to death. I cannot understand these people.

After so many sufferings from worries about my nation, I decided to leave the North and come to the South to meet the people there for consultations.[20]

Outside the embassy, the Chinese had dissipated the immediate tension and a few days passed with little progress. Then, on February 17, 1997, the North Korean Foreign Ministry released the following statement:

> Our stand is simple and clear. If he was kidnapped, we cannot tolerate and will take decisive countermeasures. If he sought asylum, it means that he is a renegade and we don't mind where he is going. Pyongyang made this statement after its attempts to make forced entry into the South Korean Embassy building in Beijing where Hwang was taking refuge and was blocked by the Chinese police, and after the Chinese authorities were reported to have confirmed Hwang's will to defect to South Korea. North Korea's de facto leader, Kim Jong Il, was also quoted by Pyongyang broadcasts as saying "cowards, go if they want to go."

After five days of analysis, Kim Jong Il and his advisors must have concluded that denying the defection would be an ineffective strategy. With a significant dependence on foreign famine-relief shipments of food, North Korea could not easily afford to alienate the entire international community. Thus, Pyongyang's efforts shifted toward minimizing, criticizing, and otherwise discrediting Hwang Jang Yop's pivotal role in the formation of Juche ideology. Once again, the historical records had to be revised and the collective memories of the masses appropriately calibrated to a new truth. Hwang was dismissed as a senile fool and Kim Duk Hong's defection was basically ignored.

Initially, China asked both South and North Korea to find a solution to Hwang's incident. Then Seoul responded that it would be realistically impossible to resolve the impasse through inter-Korean talks. China then gradually specified its position on Hwang's case, noting it would handle it in accordance with international laws and practices in line with its policy of helping maintain peace and stability on the Korean peninsula. From the beginning, China wanted to send the asylum seekers to Seoul by way of a third country where they would stay for a considerable time needed to calm North Korea's anger. China, in an effort to quell North Korea's anger over the defection, wanted the duo to stay in the third country for at least a month. South Korea hoped for as little as a week. As the standoff in Beijing exceeded a month, the South Koreans finally realized that they would get Hwang to Seoul faster by agreeing with the Chinese version of the third-country plan.

Through consultation among China, South Korea, and the Philippines, Manila had agreed to allow the asylum seekers to stop off on their way to South Korea.

Having them stop in a third country is a symbolic gesture that avoids a direct trip from Beijing to Seoul, which would be seen as a snub to the North. On March 18, after five weeks of negotiations and consultation, the two defectors were permitted to leave Beijing for Manila in the Philippines. Philippine officials imposed a tight news blackout on the entire affair. Under the South Korea–Chinese agreement, Hwang and Kim would stay in Manila for the specified period before flying to Seoul.

When Hwang finally spoke publicly, he characterized Kim Jong Il as a typical Communist leader who had to initiate new policy guidelines upon assuming power. Hwang noted his defection was prompted by North Korea's totalitarian state initiating indirect attacks against his version of Juche ideology in May 1996. Hwang's concern over political surveillance was well-placed. Though people are under surveillance, the higher one's position is in the government, the stricter the surveillance. Private letters to foreigners and even telephone conversations between children are tapped. However, as already noted, other motivations may have been the main driving factor triggering Hwang Jang Yop's defection.

After a delay of almost an entire month, North Korea's propaganda finally reacted to the Beijing stand-off in Party propaganda. In a March 9, 1997, editorial in *Rodong Sinmun,* "reformist betrayers" were accused of trying to destroy the purity of North Korean socialism:

> Great Leader Kim Jong Il has pointed out that *due to the modern revisionists, socialism ran off its normal tracks,* began to be frustrated from within, and finally came to collapse due to *counterrevolutionary acts of these betrayers who tried to bring about reform.* The reform in this case was the product of the schemes of modern revisionists *who attempted to degenerate socialism and then replace it with capitalism.* They have weakened the centralized leadership of the state systematically by advocating that

the economic management system must be simplified and the autonomous function of individual enterprises must be expanded in order to stimulate the economy.

The reformatory policies also delivered a blow to the military sector. As a result, capitalist practices began to prevail in all sectors, including politics, economics, and the military. Under the name of a new thinking, they began to court the imperialists. As a result, socialism in the Soviet Union ceased to exist in 1991. History tells us that the admittance of *even minor revisionist factors in the course of carrying out socialist construction will lead to the degeneration of socialism.*[21]

Rodong Sinmun's editorial implies that one impact of Hwang's defection has been to strengthen the aspirations of Pyongyang's military and hard-liner elite. Meanwhile, reformists and economic technocrats are likely to lose their influence and even be purged. Thus, inter-Korean relations look to remain strained for some time to come.

On April 20, 1997, after slightly more than a month in the Philippines, Hwang Jang Yop and Kim Duk Hong finally arrived from Manila and set foot on South Korean soil. The high-profile defection had finally concluded. Meanwhile, all of South Korea and many throughout the world awaited to hear what Hwang Jang Yop would say next.

An Insider's View of Juche

Kim Jong Il is idolized to the extent that people regard him as God and the feudalistic ideas of loyalty and filial piety are deeply rooted in society.[22]

HWANG JANG YOP

Since his virtually unimaginable defection, Hwang Jang Yop's public remarks have provided a detailed sketch of Pyongyang's basic war plan for "National Reunification." In addition, Hwang's many statements provide an insider's view of the Juche worldview. Some of Hwang's observations are presented in Table 8-3.

In addition to making observations about the Pyongyang regime, Hwang Jang Yop also gave a speech in Seoul at a July 1997 press conference. His remarks confirm the sweeping impact that the Juche religious system has had in shaping the North Korean worldview. For example, in part of Hwang's speech, he stated:

The North government is saying that they have created a society for workers and farmers but actually the people are starving and are living in appalling conditions such as having

TABLE 8-3. Hwang Jang Yop's Insider's Look at North Korea[23]

TOPIC	HWANG JANG YOP'S INSIGHTS
On war preparations	North Koreans believe that they can win a war against the South in six months and therefore, they are reserving war materials for six months' use only. The basic strategy for a war is: In order to make an excuse for war, they use special forces wearing South Korea military uniforms to fake an invasion of the North. Then they fire missiles at Seoul for five to six minutes to turn the city into ashes. Before more American troops are sent to the South, they invade the south as far as Pusan. When the United States shows signs of becoming involved in the war, the North Koreans threaten the Americans with the destruction of Tokyo and other Japanese cities with missiles to stop their involvement. Kim Jong Il and high-ranking party officials, administration and the military believe that they can unify with the South by force if there is no outside involvement.
	People think that a war may be a better choice rather than famine. North Koreans are 100% self-sufficient in arms production. They also produce a great amount of helicopters, missiles and multiple-launch rocket systems. They believe the most important factor in choosing the timing of the war is…to take advantage of turmoil in the South and of U.S. preoccupation with conflict elsewhere in the world.
On nuclear weapons	I have not seen either nuclear weapons or any facility related to the weapons in the North. But I and other secretaries of the party came to believe that the North had some when the regime decided to quit the Non-Proliferation Treaty (NPT) after the International Atomic Energy Agency (IAEA) demanded special inspections in the North in 1992. In negotiations with the United States over the nuclear issue, Kim Jong Il issued instructions directly to Kang Sok-ju. No other organizations were involved.
On Kim Jong Il	Kim Jong Il is in good health. He is timid and easily changes his moods responding to what he likes and what he does not. So he loves people who flatter him, but soon changes his attitude if he finds anything suspicious about them… Unlike his father Kim Il Sung, he makes decisions by himself.

TABLE 8-3. *(continued)*

TOPIC	HWANG JANG YOP'S INSIGHTS
On politics	North Korea is more a modern version of a feudal state rather than a socialist state. *Kim Jong Il is idolized to the extent that people regard him as God* and the feudalistic ideas of loyalty and filial piety are deeply rooted in society. It is difficult to predict the reshuffle in the North Korean leadership after Kim Jong Il's ascension to power because of the unpredictability of Kim's character. I think economic officials will be changed on a large scale and the vice premiers who have not been active due to illness will be replaced. It is true that North Korea is facing a collapse with its economy almost paralyzed and people hungry. But it is still a mistake to believe that the North Korean system will collapse in one or two years.
On the economy	North Korea has invested much in military-related industries since 1967 and the policy has brought an imbalance between the military and civilian sectors. Kim Il Sung and Kim Jong Il have also wasted much money in erecting monuments and statues idolizing themselves…North Korea has had difficulty in obtaining raw materials. These three elements are main reasons for the current economic hardship.
On the food shortage	In Pyongyang each citizen is entitled to a 300-gram grain ration. But in local provinces, the ration ceased long ago. The shortage has been dealt with using grain imported from China through border villages. But with no other measures to cope with the problem, North Korea began to request international aid under the pretext of the flood damage.
On society	Kim Jong Il once said the international community would find fault with the North's human rights problem after the nuclear and chemical weapons issues had been resolved …Recently, people have been executed publicly across the nation. In 1995, seven people, including actors, were executed in Pyongyang before a crowd of 300,000 people for producing a pornographic film to earn foreign currency. The economic difficulties also have brought about an increase in crimes.
On defectors	The number of defectors surged to double-digits in the wake of Kim Il Sung's death (in 1994), averaging about 40–50 annually. This year (1997) has seen 46 defectors so far. The number of defectors will rise to about 100 by the end of 1997.[24]

the mountains and streams destroyed. The North system of government is an absolute dictatorship and everything in North Korea is owned by the leader, such as the government, party, army and even nationalism. The North's government are blocking the peoples' ears, eyes and mouth and demand them to think about the leader's ideology. They are strongly leaning towards a closed national isolation policy system of government because they do not want to show the reality that is happening in North Korea, and this is a criminal act which cannot be comprehended in any world. Such a personal dictatorship system should come to an end.[25]

Hwang Jang Yop's speech also included a warning of war. He noted that a DPRK-initiated war would be consistent with the radical religious nature of North Korea's "National Unification" belief. Before Hwang's defection, many South Koreans were very skeptical of the seriousness of an all-out attack from the North. For example, Kim Jin Ho, a Seoul businessman, said:

I didn't think that the Stalinist regime was so bent on a war with the South. As its economy is in shambles and the people there are starving, I thought the North was not capable of launching a war, but after hearing Hwang's warning I changed my mind and guess we need something to counter that.[26]

In particular, Kim said that he felt a chill when Hwang said, "North Korea would refuse to die without dropping a bomb or two on Seoul."[27]

In another post-defection public appearance, Hwang Jang Yop gave more details of what life is like in the North. The following remarks vividly depict both the megalomaniac pride of Kim Jong Il and the plight of the Korean people.

The confrontation between the North and the South is the confrontation not between capitalism and socialism but between capitalism and feudalism because now North Korea has nothing to do with socialism. A society where the workers, farmers, and intellectuals are dying from starvation cannot be depicted as a socialist society. Dictatorship has dominated North Korea under Soviet-style socialism, but the one-man rule system nowadays, which is the product of a hereditary succession plan, must be depicted as even more dictatorial. North Korean propaganda depicts Kim Jong Il as if he

was born as a "bright star" ordained to be the successor to his
father. North Korean personality cultists have invented various adjectives to deify the father and son Kims, but these
words were still short of glorifying them. The cultists even concocted mythologies: "when the great general is about to take
a picture, rain suddenly stops, and sky will be bright and clear,
and even the mist clears in order to safeguard the great general." The Workers' Party organ, *Rodong Sinmun*, also publishes
these myths from time to time.

The personality cult of Stalin in the former Soviet Union
has been the target of criticism, and these days democratization movements have taken place in former socialist countries.
Quite contrary to these phenomena, the movement to glorify
a person is in full swing in North Korea. The theory of the
"view on the Leader," which is designed to justify the personality cult worship of the Leader, has become an absolute
guideline for the Party to abide by in mapping out all plans
and in carrying out all projects.

Routine life in North Korea can be represented by popular acts of pledging loyalty and emphasizing filial duty toward
the Leader. This is a surprising fact. Sometimes I cannot but
doubt if the "great general" himself may be tired of hearing
such praises. In North Korea, the so-called "organized life" is
always being stressed, and every one is told to start their rou-
tines by swearing his or her loyalty toward the Leader.

The "great general" has grown to be arrogant and auda-
cious as shown by his remarks made before his associates on
December 7, 1996. His remarks were distributed to all Party
members later in printed form. He said, "Now the people are
accepting the instructions of the Party Central Committee
unconditionally thanks to my personal dignity, but not because Party members are doing their job excellently. Now no
one is correctly performing his duty to assist me. I am doing
my job alone."

"The great general" appears to be occupied by a sense of
self-admiration. He appears to be thinking he is really a genius.
He made himself a dictator, and has been forcing the people
to obey him unconditionally, and moreover, he never hesitates
to attack his associates, saying that he is assisted by no one but
he is doing his works all alone. He takes credit to himself and
lays the fault at others' door. This is his "greatness."

North Korean citizens are now suffering from the worst

living conditions. The country is short of about 2 million tons of grain, but the state spurs the people to deliver military provisions. Under these conditions, farmers are compelled to give away a considerable amount of grain from what they have stocked for their own use. Many school children fail to present themselves at their classes because they are hungry. Despite this reality, North Korean broadcasts and newspapers never cease to boast that the North is a paradise on earth and a model socialist society which the people all over the world envy, and that the Leader is the savior. The people are shouting "Hurrah! Great General!" in order to survive in this miserable land of darkness where all we can see is merciless oppression and deception.

Even in a feudalist society, popular riots can take place if the situation develops to these worst conditions. But in North Korea such a thing can never be imaginable due to a well-organized surveillance system. Under current conditions it will be impossible to expect that the North Korean citizens may be able to bail themselves out of this oppression.[28]

Dr. Kang In Duk, former Director of Seoul's Center for East Asian Studies, notes that these remarks by Hwang Jang Yop confirm that:

Juche ideology is not merely an abstract idea but it has taken root in North Korea as an absolute norm not only dominating government policies but also regulating the routine lives of the people ranging from their way of thinking to minor activities. [29]

Hwang Jang Yop's warnings, though consistent with the radical "national reunification" worldview of Juche, still pose questions for Korea-watchers. Will Kim Jong Il attempt to punch through the Maginot Line–like border between the two Koreas despite the overwhelming air power that can be arrayed against him? Is Kim Jong Il such a megalomaniac that he will believe his own "spirit of human bombs" propaganda? While these questions and many others remain unanswered, Kim Jong Il will, in the aftermath of "the Architect of Juche's" defection, continue to impose the Juche culture upon the North Korean people with his iron-fisted rule.

CHAPTER 9

Promoting the Culture of Juche

Then the face of Big Brother faded away again, and instead the three slogans of the Party stood out in bold capitals:
WAR IS PEACE
FREEDOM IS SLAVERY
IGNORANCE IS STRENGTH.[1]

GEORGE ORWELL, *1984*

F ar from being merely an abstract idea, the Juche religion has taken root in North Korea as the absolute norm. It dominates not only government policies, but also regulates every aspect of the lives of North Koreans. The Pyongyang regime continues to promote the culture of Juche by government controls over how one may think and over all aspects of Korean life even down to the most minor activities. These controls span the entire range of cultural activities and provide a Juche-correct viewpoint from which to create or judge art, literature, drama, and music. This "correct" Juche viewpoint also permeates the country's entire educational system. Anything that conflicts with Juche principles is forbidden.

Juche Holy Days

Revolutionization of [the] Family!
Revolutionization of Women!
Promotion of Women to [the] Working Class![2]

PARTY SLOGANS FOR "GENDER EQUALITY DAY"
(JULY 30)

263

Given that the Juche religious system deifies North Korea's former ruler, Kim Il Sung (1912–1994), and their current ruler, Kim Jong Il (1942–), it is not surprising that Kim Il Sung's birthday (April 15) and Kim Jong Il's birthday (February 16) are celebrated as the chief national holidays. Since both of these men are considered to be god according to the Juche religion, it seems more correct to call February 16 ("People's Greatest Holiday") and April 15 ("Sun's Day" or "The Eternal Festival of the Nation") as Juche holy days. Each year, on these two days, downtown Pyongyang looks like a remaking of the movie *Ben Hur*, as millions of North Koreans parade through the streets, celebrate, and assemble in Kim Il Sung Square to worship before the great statue of Kim Il Sung.

Kim Il Sung's birthday has taken on new religious significance in 1997 with Pyongyang's adoption of the Juche Era calendar. Kim Il Sung has taken on a "sun-god" aura and April 15 now has been declared "Sun's Day." To advertise this key Juche holy day, North Korea has sponsored their "Sun Society" operatives in the South to issue a new book entitled *Sun's Day, the Eternal Festival of the Nation*. This book features a picture of former President Kim Il Sung, the full text of the Pyongyang "Sun's Day" resolution, and an article entitled "Let us uphold President Kim Il Sung as the sun of Juche for all ages" [*KCNA*].

March 5 is Farmers' Day in North Korea. On this Juche holy day, agricultural working people celebrate by paying homage to statues of Kim Il Sung with floral baskets and bunches of flowers. They also enjoy special propaganda sessions about Kim Il Sung's "on-site teachings" and visit monuments dedicated to Kim Il Sung's revolutionary activities. Farmers are then encouraged with Juche slogans to succeed in their farming.

May 1 is the International Holiday of Workers, a traditional Communist holiday throughout the world. This Juche holiday has a particularly anti-imperialist theme. Slogans used to celebrate this holiday praise Kim Il Sung and Kim Jong Il while encouraging North Korea's working class and the working class around the world to unite, defend, and advance the cause of anti-imperialist Juche socialism for peace-loving people everywhere.

Since 1946, North Korea has celebrated July 30 as Gender Equality Day. For decades North Koreans have been chanting slogans such as "Revolutionization of [the] Family," "Revolutionization of Women," and "Promotion of Women to [the] Working Class." Yet the true purpose of these slogans seems to be to extract cheap labor from women for the socialist labor programs. Many women are often forced to work in the fields, factories, and government offices for free while also feeding their family. Despite the impressive sounding slogans, gender equality remains just another Juche myth. Thus, over a half-century of women's liberation slogans and even their own annual holiday has not released women from the yoke of gender inequality.

Other Juche holidays are based around the four seasons and 24 divisions of the lunar calendar year. These lunar calendar–based Juche holidays include January 1 (lunar New Year Day), May 5 (fifth day of the fifth lunar month), and August 15 (Harvest Day). Since the "Japanese imperialists" outlawed these holidays in the decades before North Korea's founding, propaganda presents their celebration as proof of the restoration of traditional cultural practices in the North.

Traditional Korean shamanism holds that when a person dies, the spirit floats. Thus, many Koreans engage in ancestor worship three or four times per year, such as on the August 15 Harvest Day holiday. Juche has adopted and converted some of these traditional Korean holidays into Juche holy days. For example, the mid-autumn festival (North Korea's "Thanksgiving Day") is celebrated annually on September 16 as a Juche holiday. Pyongyang's Juche rendition of this traditional Korean "Thanksgiving Day" has transformed it into a day in which Koreans are actively encouraged to give "thanks to the wise policy of the Workers' Party of Korea on inheriting and developing national heritage" [*KCNA*]. No expense is spared for these lavish events—particularly on the two Kim birthdays.

Palaces, Temples, Monuments, Statues, and Parks

It is the unwavering faith and unshakable will of the respected General Kim Jong Il to exalt Pyongyang as the eternal capital of Kim Il Sung's Korea... However difficult and vast the project may be, we should turn out as one in the honorable construction of the capital and unconditionally carry out the task assigned by the General.

KIM YUN HYOK,
NORTH KOREA'S VICE-PREMIER
KOREA CENTRAL NEWS AGENCY

Since his emergence in the 1970s as heir apparent to Kim Il Sung, Kim Jong Il has launched a major campaign to erect monuments such as the "Arch of Triumph" and the "Tower of Juche Idea." Behind the scenes depicted in truly heart-rending international press articles about North Korea's flooding, endemic famine, and malnutrition, Kim Jong Il's monument-building program continues unabated. What foreign observers generally do not report is that over 24% of North Korea's budget goes to sustain the world's fourth largest army, while at least another 4% (US $900 million per year) goes toward making monuments to the gods of Juche. Another sizable chunk of North Korea's wealth supports Kim Jong Il's personal palace-building pastime. According to South Korean officials, "If they saved just one-third of it, the food [shortage] would be solved."[3] Kim Jong Il's Juche monument construction program remains a national priority that robs other economic sectors of scarce investment capital and highlights the vain dictator's blind eye to the plight of his starving people.

The Great Leader Kim Il Sung, like his Soviet mentor Josef Stalin, initiated an intense program to memorialize himself. By the time of his death, over 30,000 monuments had been erected around North Korea to immortalize Kim Il Sung. In a like-father/like-son fashion, the expenditures of Kim Jong Il to glorify himself seem to be at least keeping pace with his dearly departed dad. Pyongyang's hosting of the 1989 "World Festival of Youth and Students" was another example of Kim Jong Il's personal fetish for grandiose expenditures. The $4.6 billion price tag for this festival cost North Korea an amount roughly equal to its total annual trade volume.

Beginning in 1992, Kim built a series of 32 mansions in various parts of North Korea. The cost: $2.5 *billion*. Several of Kim Jong Il's "lifestyles of the rich and famous" resorts are now underwater mansions. Certainly, by Juche standards, nothing is too good for the lodestar of Mt. Paektu.

In August 1988, Kim Jong Il also had a Korean-style Mt. Rushmore built for himself not too far from Mt. Paektu near the Chinese border. This nearly 6,000-foot-high mountain cliff, located in the picturesque Sobaeksu Valley, is called Jong Il Peak after its namesake. It is located not far from the "secret camp" national park/shrine of the 9,000-foot-high Mt. Paektu. Instead of having his face carved on the mountain, Kim Jong Il opted for the words "Jong Il Peak" carved on giant granite rocks. These rocks, each weighing over 100 tons, were then erected in three tiers on the side of the peak. The calligraphy on the first rock for the word "Jong" also portrays the Changgun Peak in Mt. Paektu. The second rock, with "Il" written on it, depicts a mirror. Characters on the third rock, with the word "Peak," present the image of a flower basket. North Korea's masses are encouraged to visit Jong Il Peak periodically to be inspired by "the Dear Leader's greatness."

In December 22, 1997, Kim Jong Il celebrated the 80th anniversary of the birth of his deceased mother, Kim Jong Suk, by unveiling another frivolous monument to himself at Mt. Kuwol. The monument is a set of letters, 43 feet high by 18 feet wide and a foot-and-a-half thick, that state, "Mt. Kuwol, a scenic place on the West Coast. Kim Jong Il. May 1, 1997." Kim Jong Il calls this monument an *aphorism* (a brief statement of truth) to commemorate the sixth anniversary of his election as Supreme Commander of the Korean People's Army. Given that the wording on the monument glorifies Kim Jong Il, its unveiling just prior to his mother's December 24 birthday appears to have been an opportunistic ploy.

Monuments, statues, and parks dot the North Korean cities and countryside to justify Kim Il Sung and Kim Jong Il's fabricated past. These sites include seven so-called revolutionary war sites and 34 historic sites. Over 20,000 plaster busts and more than 70 large bronze statues of the Kims have been erected throughout Kim country. In addition to the mandatory portrait of the dictator in every household, there were some 20 types of Kim Il Sung badges worn by the people on their clothes. The badge and portrait trend now continues with Kim Jong Il's regime. North Korea also boasts over 12,000 pieces of catchwood trees, catchwood documents, and monuments featuring the Kims' personal writings. In addition, countless books proclaim the revisionist history associated with these sites.

The vast sums of wealth spent by these dictators on their Juche sites of self-deification is dwarfed by the amount of money spent on the attempt to transform Pyongyang into the world's most beautiful city. Kim Il Sung and Kim Jong Il's devotion to building Pyongyang is reminiscent of Adolf Hitler's massive program to rebuild Berlin in the 1930s. In his book *Inside the Third Reich*, Albert Speer, Hitler's chief architect, describes Hitler's personal fetish for building a legacy Nazi city. Speer also notes the shocking amounts of Germany's wealth that went into Hitler's building program. Even as World War II was underway, Germany's leaders refused to fully mobilize their economy for war until late 1943 because Hitler was convinced that the war would be short and Berlin's building program had to be resumed.

Just as Hitler rebuilt Berlin after the First World War, North Korea's Kim Il Sung totally rebuilt Pyongyang following severe devastation from bombing in World War II and the Korean War. Kim Jong Il has fancied himself as sort of the Albert Speer of Pyongyang as he committed himself to the task of rebuilding the city in 1975. The North Korean press gave a recent account of Pyongyang's restoration:

> Pyongyang is the capital of the Democratic People's Republic of Korea. New streets and monumental edifices are being constructed in Pyongyang. So it looks more grandiose and splendid. This results from the outstanding architectural intelligence, extraordinary and big operations of construction and energetic leadership of Secretary Kim Jong Il. The new history of Pyongyang construction was started by Secretary Kim Jong Il from the middle of the 1970s...All this is a fruition of the energetic and meticulous leadership of Secretary Kim Jong Il, who is putting his heart and soul into the work to make Pyongyang have perfect looks as the capital of the revolution and provide the people with more cultural and stable conditions of living [*KCNA*].

Pyongyang also boasts the Ryugyong Hotel, which at 300 meters (984 feet) is among the world's tallest buildings and is the third tallest hotel. However, structural defects have delayed the completion of the 105-story rocket-shaped building.

The following excerpt from recent North Korean propaganda provides an additional description of both the heavy industry and monuments that have been erected during Kim Jong Il's rebuilding program:

> Monumental edifices showing the history of the creation and construction of the Korean people have sprung up on the [Taedong] river and its basin...Located there are the Hwanghae Iron and Steel Complex, the Chollima Steel Complex, the Taean Heavy Machine Complex, the Sungri General Motor Works, the Pyongyang Textile Combine and hundreds of factories and enterprises, which show the might of the Juche industry. And the Taedonggang Power Complex, the Pukchang

Fireworks display over Pyongyang's Arch of Triumph.
It is taller than France's L'Arc de Triomphe.

Thermal Power Complex, the Pyongyang Thermal Power Complex and other large-scale hydroelectric and thermal power stations…The Okryu Bridge, the Taedong Bridge, the Chongryu Suspension Bridge…There are many monumental edifices including the Tower of the Juche Idea, the Arch of Triumph, the May Day Stadium and grand theaters on the scenic river. Holiday homes and sanatoria have been built at scenic spots. Working people finish their daily work and spend a joyful time at parks, promenades, swimming pools, boating grounds and angling sites [*KCNA*].

On September 6, 1997, over 100,000 builders and Pyongyang-ites assembled at Kim Il Sung Square to receive Kim Jong Il's new direction to push ahead with the construction of the Pyongyang, the sacred city of Juche.

> Secretary Kim Jong Il set forth the task to more grandiosely and magnificently build up Pyongyang, the capital of the revolution, through an all-party, all-state and all-people campaign to mark the 50th anniversary of the foundation of the Democratic People's Republic of Korea…The reporter and speakers said that it is the unwavering faith and unshakable will of the respected General Kim Jong Il to exalt Pyongyang as the eternal capital of Kim Il Sung's Korea. They stressed: "However difficult and vast the project may be, we should turn out as one in the honorable construction of the capital and unconditionally carry out the task assigned by the General with the steadfast faith that we will win as led by him" [*KCNA*].

Nevertheless, if the comparison holds true between Kim Jong Il's ongoing Pyongyang building program and Hitler's Berlin rebuilding program, then the building program should be considered as a secondary North Korean priority. Despite the fact that Pyongyang's reconstruction is possibly Kim Jong Il's favorite project, the sacred Juche cause of national reunification must comes first.

Juche in the Movies and in Art

Art is the product of [Juche] thought and enthusiasm.[4]
KIM JONG IL

North Korean movies and art are expected and required to espouse Juche ideology to glorify Kim Il Sung and Kim Jong Il. For example, one recent art exhibit featured pieces that appropriately flattered Kim Jong Il, such as a painting of Jong Il Peak with beautiful flowers seen in the background and placed on the floor around the exhibit. What kind of flowers were they? "Kimilsungia" and "Kimjongilia." The art exhibit also featured scenic displays with titles such as "We Will Win Because You Are Leading Us," "The Intimate Name," and "Single-hearted Loyalty and

"Kimjongilia" Embroidery.

Filial Piety." Pyongyang's mildly biased art critics said the exhibit:

> ...depicted the single heart of the Korean people extending the highest honor to the dear leader Comrade Kim Jong Il and wishing him a long life in good health. The display presented...the highest honor and happiness of the working people and younger generation of Korea who live and make the revolution in the bosom of dear leader Comrade Kim Jong Il with him at the head of the Party and the revolutionary armed forces [*DPRK*].

Another Pyongyang art show commemorated the 80th birth anniversary of Kim Jong Il's mother, Kim Jong Suk. Over 200 pieces of fine art deemed to be of ideological and artistic value were put on display. All these pieces of art, in one way or another, glorified Kim Jong Il or "communist revolutionary fighter" Kim Jong Suk. Some of the titles showed "the brilliant revolutionary activity, undying feats and noble traits of mother Kim Jong Suk," including the two paintings, "Indomitable communist revolutionary fighter comrade Kim Jong Suk devotedly defending the head-

"Mt. Paektu"—a "politically correct" piece of Juche artwork.

quarters of the revolution" and "With the spirit of Mt. Paektu." Other artwork on display, of course, depicted "the greatness of Supreme Commander General Kim Jong Il."

In another "national fine-art exhibit," Pyongyang's Korean Art Gallery celebrated Kim Jong Il's February 16 birthday. The more than 100 works on display glorified Kim Jong Il and his parents. The exhibit included such titles as: "The great leader Generalissimo Kim Il Sung," "Comrade Kim Jong Il, Supreme Commander of the Korean People's Army," "Comrade Kim Jong Suk, anti-Japanese war heroine," and "Comrade Kim Jong Il is the greatest genius."

Some of the recurring themes in the artwork were to "show the noble greatness and leadership feats of General Kim Jong Il who makes tireless efforts for the security, prosperity and development of the country," showing Kim Jong Il visiting People's Army units and different parts of the country, and portraying "the bright smile of tender-hearted President Kim Il Sung optimistic of the future of Korea where General Kim Jong Il has been acclaimed as the successor to the revolution" [*KCNA*].

Korea's fine-art production centers also produce many posters. For example, the Mansudae Art Studio, Central Fine Art Studio, and Pyongyang University of Fine Arts have all produced a wide variety of Juche-correct posters. Some of these posters are designed "to encourage the working people in the forced march of socialism." Others are intended "to give the people confidence in the victory of the revolution and enthusiasm of struggle." Titles of some of these posters include: "Forward, everybody, in the forced march for final victory," "Let us adorn the 50th anniversary of the DPRK with a grand festival of socialist victors," "The weapons of the People's Army determine the destiny of socialism and prosperity of the motherland," and "We will take upon ourselves both national defense and agricultural production" [*KCNA*].

North Korea's theatrical and film productions maintain the same highly predictable Juche-correct content. For example, if you visited Pyongyang, you might take in a performance of "The Sun of February Shines" by the Mansudae Art Troupe at the East Pyongyang Grand Theater. You might ask, "Who is 'the Sun of February'?" Kim Jong Il—who else? Similarly, a typical recent ten-day film festival showed a large number of documentary and feature films at cinemas across the country. The film titles included: "Great Honor and Happiness of the People" (about General Kim

Jong Il's election as General Secretary of the Workers' Party of Korea), "Under the Guidance of the Great Brilliant Commander," "Comrade Kim Jong Suk, Great Communist Revolutionary Fighter and Woman General of Mt. Paektu," and "The Nation and Destiny" [*KCNA*]. The comprehensive way in which North Korea's movies and art are forced to conform to the Juche totalitarian system is just one of the many ways that the people of North Korea are under bondage.

Juche in Music, Poetry, and Writing

A single revolutionary poem can be worth ten million spears.[5]

KIM JONG IL

As I always say, songs should not be regarded as an art merely to be appreciated. Songs are weapons and a propelling force for revolution... This is why I often have you listen to music.[6]

KIM JONG IL

Juche's religious influence permeates the areas of music, hymn-writing, poetry, and other forms of written expression. As might be expected, only "politically correct" Juche views are tolerated. For example, from 1992 to 1994, more than 300 poems and 400 songs praising and glorifying Kim Jong Il were published throughout North Korea. One recent dedication of a story and a song to Kim Jong Il is shown below:

> Secretary Kim Jong Il, Supreme Commander of the Korean People's Army (KPA), enjoyed an art performance given by soldiers of a women's company of KPA unit No. 535 on Sunday... The female soldiers put on the stage the story and song "We have wished to see the General," the poem and chorus "We will defend the headquarters of the revolution with our lives" and other numbers. After seeing the performance of brave and courageous female soldiers, Secretary Kim Jong Il expressed deep satisfaction with the growth of the soldiers of the company into reliable woman revolutionaries and with their high cultural level... Brisk cultural and art activity among soldiers is an important work to increase the fighting efficiency of the unit, he said, and gave important tasks to invigorate art activities at all units [*KCNA*].

Some popular forms of Juche writing include statements, articles, resolutions, letters, and political essays. However, the "political essay" still reigns supreme as the major method of articulating the views of the Su-ryong to the Party and down to the masses. When political essays are issued, they take on the force of law, religious doctrine, and dogma. Those that are "signed" by Kim Jong Il are considered to be signed by god. They are so sacred that the Dear Leader's guidance is sometimes called "the people's bible" [KCNA]. Some examples of political essays are listed in Table 9-1.

TABLE 9-1. Examples of Political Essays

ESSAY TITLE / DATE	SUMMARY
"Let Us Carry Out the Great Leader Comrade Kim Il Sung's Instructions for National Reunification" (signed by Kim Jong Il) August 4, 1997	The essay sets forth the only great national reunification programme which indicates the path to overcome the present difficulties lying in the way of reunification and to achieve the earliest and most smooth reunification of the country all the fellow countrymen long for so earnestly [KCNA].
"The DPRK Flag" September 8, 1997	[The essay] mark[s] the national holiday of the Democratic People's Republic of Korea. The three-color flag of the DPRK is a symbol of the independent...dignified people who are advancing under the guidance of General Kim Jong Il,...who is firmly determined to make Kim Il Sung's nation an ideologically, politically and militarily powerful state forever and build an ideal paradise of humankind and a strong and prosperous country of Juche at an early date. To defend and glorify the DPRK flag, the pride and glory of our nation, means to resolutely safeguard the General, our destiny and future, and to demonstrate dignity and majesty of socialist Korea all over the world. [Rodong Sinmun].
"Cheers Rock Heaven and Earth" September 26, 1997	The essay says that the people extend warm congratulations to Secretary Kim Jong Il with pure conscience and faith to follow the road of the revolutionary cause of Juche under his leadership [Rodong Sinmun].
"Epic of Great Unity" September 26, 1997	The political essay says that the Korean people display army-people unity on the road of today's "Arduous March" [Rodong Sinmun].

One American visitor to Pyongyang in search of general read-ing material noted evidence of the stifling Juche-controlled regi-mentation in publications:

> There was nothing in the hotel bookstore other than ramb-ling accounts by and about the "Great Leader" and the "Dear Leader." Clearly, this is an intellectual desert.[7]

Since speeches by the Vice President and other high officials speak of the Mt. Paektu mythical revisionist history as if it were fact, it is not too surprising to find that, in addition to the lack of variety in literature, the line between Juche fiction and Juche non-fiction is considerably blurred.

For example, a typical book that might be at the top of *Rodong Sinmun*'s "Best-Seller List" in fiction (if they had such a list) might be the novel *Pyongyang Declares*. This book is the latest novel in a series entitled "Immortal Guidance." This series is about the life saga of former dictator-god Kim Il Sung and his successor-son, Kim Jong Il. *Pyongyang Declares* covers the period from the late 1980s to the early 1990s. As might be expected, none of Pyongyang's liter-ary critics decided to abruptly cut their careers short by giving the novel a "thumbs down." Instead, reviews sounded like this:

> It [*Pyongyang Declares*] depicts the noble traits of General Kim Jong Il who further consolidates the Korean-style social-ist system under the fast-changing situation and illumines the road of revival to the progressive people aspiring after inde-pendence and socialism. The novel eloquently proves that Gen-eral Kim Jong Il is an outstanding teacher of the international communist movement and the sun of the progressive people by portraying General Kim Jong Il who sees to it that the his-toric Pyongyang Declaration was adopted with the 80th birth-day of President Kim Il Sung as an occasion and shows deep love for communists of different countries fighting for the re-building of socialism. With a high artistic delineation, it con-firms that the socialist cause is, in essence, the cause of the leader and that socialism will certainly win only under the guidance of the leader [*KCNA*].

Not to be dismayed with the limited selection of fiction, the discriminating literary connoisseur might opt for non-fiction. For example, you might select one of more than 200 "writings" since 1960 that have been personally attributed to Kim Jong Il. Never mind that Kim Jong Il, though a graduate of Kim Il Sung University, speaks with the vocabulary of an uneducated man. Evidently, Kim has been quite a prolific writer over the last four decades, in between his never-ending inspections of military units and pleasure team performances at his many palaces. These essays, texts of conversations, speeches, and letters give some idea of Kim Jong Il's guiding policies. In his thesis "Socialism is Science," Kim Jong Il claimed that he had inherited his father's political abilities of "Politics of Indeok" (benevolent virtue) and "Politics of Kwangpok" (extensive magnanimity). Kim Jong Il's writings also reveal three recurring themes as shown in Table 9-2.

TABLE 9-2. Recurring Themes in Kim Jong Il's Writings

RECURRING THEME	EXAMPLE
Consistent resolve against either reforming or opening up North Korea to outsiders.	Kim Jong Il categorically attributed the collapse of communism in the USSR and the Warsaw-pact nations of Eastern Europe to "intrusions by winds of the bourgeois freedom" and "traitors from within" who "attempted to accommodate with pluralism under the excuse of reform, and opening-up, of socialist countries."
Consistent opposition to reform.	Kim Jong Il's writings document his opposition to "freedom of thoughts, multi-party political system and private ownership promoted in pluralistic society where survival of the fittest is a way of living based on individualism and liberalism." Kim denounced pluralism as being "incompatible" with "socialism…based on collectivism."[8]
Firm resolve to sustain the status quo.	In Kim's treatise entitled "Socialist Ideology and Revolutionary Perestroika," Kim Jong Il argues that, unlike the Soviet leader Gorbachev, and despite temporary heartbreaking difficulties, North Korea will achieve ultimate victory thanks to Juche's scientific value and truthfulness.[9]

Around the world, authors in nations that are friendly with North Korea have written books flattering both Kim Il Sung and Kim Jong Il. For example, Anil Gupta, editor of the paper *Indian and World Events*, authored the book *Brilliant Korea*. The book was released to coincide with the sixth anniversary of Kim Jong Il's election as Supreme Commander of the Korean People's Army in

December 1997. *Brilliant Korea* features a picture of President Kim Il Sung and General Secretary Kim Jong Il having a discussion. Chapters within the book are entitled "Thinking of Homeland," "Korea brilliant with victory and glory," "Korea, paradise of people" and "Under banner of Juche idea." The author, who was admittedly mildly biased in favor of Juche, wrote that:

> Korea, which had suffered an eclipse on the world map, has become a socialist country independent in politics, self-reliant in the economy and self-supporting in national defense, and is shining all over the world as the "Homeland of Juche" and the bastion of socialism under the wise leadership of President Kim Il Sung and General Secretary Kim Jong Il. Upholding General Secretary Kim Jong Il as the leader, the Korean people could have the highest pride in the world, blessed with two illustrious leaders in one generation, and the Democratic People's Republic of Korea has become a dignified country over which the sun is always bright, he emphasized [*KCNA*].

Other writings seek to make the modern version of Juche seem to be older than it really is. For example, the following article claims Kim Il Sung's Juche terminology dated back to 1928, before Kim Il Sung's sixteenth birthday.

> Korea marks the 70th anniversary of the newspaper *Sae-nal*. The newspaper was founded by President Kim Il Sung on January 15, Juche 17 (1928). The then newspaper carried a number of articles calling for holding fast to the Juche-based stand in the revolutionary struggle, increasing the driving force and awakening masses to national character and class [*KCNA*].

A fifteen-year-old starting any sort of newspaper in the Korea of the late 1920s stretches credibility.

Even if we do not take Kim Il Sung's age at the time into account, the terminology "Juche-based stand in the revolutionary struggle" attributes Communist and Juche jargon to a pre-Communist pre-Juche era. North Korea's Juche-correct authors have an unconscionable tendency to revise, bend, twist, rewrite, and otherwise redefine the truth. Thus, if by non-fiction we mean factual, then it becomes meaningless to separate contemporary North Korean literature into fiction and non-fiction categories. It is all fiction. Some is historical fiction—but it is fiction nonetheless.

Juche-correct music suffers from the same chronic affliction as Juche-correct writings. For example, on Kim Jong Il's birthday in 1998, his entourage gathered to pay him homage by singing snappy tunes like "Glory to the Dear Leader" and "We Sing of February Holiday." Later that day, foreign diplomats and embassy officials were wined and dined while brightly dressed dancers sang such the favorite pop tunes, "Moment of Sunrise," "Song of Comradeship," "Let Us Become General's Army" and, of course, "Glory to the Dear Leader." Less than two weeks later, the song and dance ensemble of the Korean People's Army serenaded Kim again with such favorites as "We Began in the Debris," "We Will Advance Confidently," "Toward Decisive Battle," "Let Us Hold High the Red Flag," "We Will Defend the Headquarters of Revolution With Our Lives," "Thunder on Jong Il Peak" and other such "world-famous songs."

North Korea's bands maintain a similar repertoire of Juche-correct favorites. What, you might ask, do bands have to do with Juche? Here is Kim Jong Il's answer:

> ...the band has a long history and tradition in that for more than 50 years it has made meritorious services through revolutionary and militant art activities of encouraging the servicemen and civilians to fight to build a new country, defeat the enemies, build socialism and implement the military line of the party. I have given the band important tasks, urging its creating staff and artists to deeply learn the Party's Juche-based idea of literature and art and conduct more brisk art activities for revolution among servicemen and civilians [*KCNA*].

Thus, at a typical band concert, you can look forward to enjoying uplifting tunes such as, "Let Us Uphold Our Supreme Commander with Arms," "Song of Coast Artillerymen" and—one of Kim Jong Il's personal favorites—"Following the Leader and the Party Forever."

Should you desire more artistic variety, you could always attend one of Pyongyang's musical shows. One such show featured choral arrangements of "The Leader Is Always With Us," "The General, Son of Guerrillas," "Let Us Hold High the Red Flag," and others. As one might expect, Kim Jong Il's review was favorable:

> General Kim Jong Il expressed deep satisfaction over the excellent performance of high artistic value full of the indomitable revolutionary spirit of the heroic KPA soldiers [*KCNA*].

Another colorful choral stage production showed a bit more variety. Musical numbers featured "We Will Become Today's Seventh Regiment," "We Will Defend the Revolution With Our Lives," and culminated with a female barbershop quartet rendition of "We Will Hold Our General in High Esteem."

One of Kim Jong Il's all-time favorite songs is "We Began in the Debris." Upon hearing this song at a 1998 performance, Kim Jong Il requested an encore of this "famous, unforgettable and precious song." Pyongyang's press noted:

> [Kim Jong Il] told officials that while hearing the song, he could hardly repress excitement, looking back upon the tireless efforts made by President Kim Il Sung all his life to build a powerful socialist country, an earthly paradise of the people, on the debris…The song was created 20 years ago. It sings of the benevolence and feats of the President who built the powerful socialist country, the anthropocentric socialist system, in this land. The song has been popular among the people. Singing the song, the Korean people look with deep emotion back on the undying exploits of the President in building the socialist country, independent in politics, self-supporting in the economy and self-reliant in national defense, pulling through difficulties after the Korean War and renew their determination to add luster to the system established by him. The song, called a song of noble memory and pledge, is now giving the Korean people optimism and confidence in the future [*KCNA*].

However, "We Began in the Debris" failed to win the annual "February 16 Art Prize," North Korea's version of the Grammy Awards. Instead, individual honors went to vocal soloists for "Fog Gathers on Jong Il Peak" and "Socialist Paradise." Top group honors went to performers who played "Song of Blood Sea," "Glow of Kangson," and "Korea is One." Musical dancing awards were awarded for performances of "Dance with a Long Korean Drum" and "Victory of Revolution is in Sight." Propaganda omitted any mention of the names of the individual artists or groups winning these awards.

Juche influence also permeates North Korea's film industry. For example, North Korea has a 42-part film series entitled *The Nation and Destiny*. This series features the life of the former Juche dictator-god, President Kim Il Sung. Its Juche-correct theme is that the will of the Korean people is "to follow the President, the hero of the nation who liberated the country, with ardent feelings of respect." Its theme song is the ever-popular favorite, "Song of General Kim Il Sung."

Should you be in the mood for a shorter series of films—or just have time for one—there are a wide variety of other Juche-correct movies at the local theaters such as: *Chief Secretary of the Taehongdan County Party Committee* (three parts), *Tranquil Forefront, 19 Fighters of Mt. Paekyang, Devote Your Sincerity, Son of the Seventh Regiment* (two parts), *My Look To Be Seen in Distant Future, World-Famous Peak,* and *Grand Paektu Range.*

The main characters of the films *Devote Your Sincerity* and *Son of the Seventh Regiment* train new recruits into loyal soldiers "equipped with the traditional trait of army-people unity and the spirit of resolutely defending the leader."

My Look To Be Seen in Distant Future imbues people with the Juche perspective on life by stressing that "one should live a mean-ingful life so that he can recollect his past without remorse." If you thought *World-Famous Peak* was about a North Korean moun-tain-climbing team scaling Mt. Everest, guess again! Instead, Pyongyang's film critics state that it "impressively shows, through beautiful landscapes, that Jong Il Peak of Mt. Paektu is the time-honored place of the Juche revolution." At the present rate, it may be several years before international films such as the *JESUS* film, international plays such as *Les Miserables,* or non-Juche films about concentration camps such as *Schindler's List* are ever shown in North Korean theaters.

Juche in Agriculture

It could be years before North Korea can reform its centrally planned agriculture and feed its 24 million people.[10]

CATHERINE BERTINI
EXECUTIVE DIRECTOR,
WORLD FOOD PROGRAM

Abysmal agriculture is one of the greatest failures under Juche. Ironically, under the Juche agricultural system, North Korea is the antithesis of self-reliance. Instead of being self-sufficient, North Koreans are totally dependent on donations, foreign purchases, and scavenged seaweed, grass, and other foodstuffs. The entire nation of North Korea, except for the very upper elite, are under-

TABLE 9-3. North Korea's Steadily Worsening Agricultural Situation[11]

AGRICULTURAL FACTOR	1991	1992	1993	1994	1995	1996
Grain demand (kilotons)	6,740	6,500	6,580	6,670	6,720	6,100
Grain production (kilotons)	4,810	4,420	4,260	3,880	4,130	3,450
Grain imports (kilotons)	1,300	830	1,090	360	1,100	1,120
Grain shortage (kilotons)	360	1,240	1,220	2,430	1,490	2,330
Daily grain ration/person (grams)	600	600	600	600	450	250

going what has been called "the slow-motion famine." The Chinese media reported that North Korea's 1997 fall harvest produced only 60% of the grain required to feed the country. According to a South Korean analyst from the Ministry of Unification, this 40% shortage is equivalent to up to 1.7 million tons of grain in 1998.

The impact of the ongoing starvation is unseen by outsiders. Out of the sight of tourists, starving beggars plead for food in the showcase city of Pyongyang. Agriculture workers are malnourished and have no energy. Out of a team of one hundred, only twenty will work at a time. The others sit on the banks, hungry.

North Korea has hardly come to admitting to its own people that it even has a crisis. The Seoul-based newspaper *Choson Ilbo* (which Pyongyang repeatedly threatened to blow up in 1997) reported the extent of the crisis:

> The Ministry of National Reunification (MONR) announced Monday that North Korea will have a food shortage in 1998 estimated at around 1 million tons as this year's production fell by 5.4% compared to 1996. A spokesman for the ministry commented that natural disasters including bad weather, flooding and droughts are the primary cause for the shortfall, in addition to shortages of fertilizers and other agricultural tools...The minimum required for survival in 1998 is 4.764 million tons and with a deficiency of 1.34 million tons, the North has less than 75% of its basic food requirements.[12]

Pyongyang's response to the crisis has been predictable. To their own people, they deny a crisis exists. After all, how could a crisis exist in paradise under Juche? Instead, "minor setbacks" are attributed to natural disasters by the government-controlled media. With a pocketful of slogans, the people are given starvation rations, if even that. Many have succumbed to foraging for roots and tree bark, emulating Kim Jong Il's mother as she is portrayed in revolutionary myths.

To the outside world, North Korea has reluctantly admitted that it needs help. For example, the following international propaganda article presents the self-contradictory Juche conviction of self-reliance along with an indirect appeal for food:

> *The Korean people have stepped up preparations for farming* from the beginning of the year with the firm determination *to solve the food problem by themselves at any cost this year.* At this time, *the World Food Program (WFP) made public an appeal again* calling for offering some 657,000 tons of food to the DPRK this year…The Korean people are…firmly determined to solve the food problem by their own efforts [*KCNA*].

Receiving such food aid runs counter to the Juche religion's "self-reliance" teaching. One 1998 propaganda release stated:

> Though the damage and its consequences are serious, we will make all efforts to fully *solve the acute food problem by ourselves* by doing farming well this year [*KCNA*].

Juche slogans emphasize the same self-reliance theme. For example,

> First Vice-Chairman Kim Chang Sik of the State Agricultural Commission vowed to properly solve the seed problem through the green revolution, do two-crop farming and do all farming as required by *the Juche method of farming under the slogan "when the party is determined we can do anything"* [*KCNA*].

At times food shipments, such as one shipment of noodles from the South, have been refused because the food was provided in packaging that indicated it was of foreign origin. As the famine deepens, fewer such restrictions are being enforced. While Pyongyang, out of necessity, will admit it has a severe food shortage, the full extent of the famine is kept from North Koreans.

Kim Jong Il is determined to continue standing behind his bankrupt system of agriculture. To him, the overriding issue is not how "arduous" the path to "final victory" is, but rather that he remains firmly in power. Thus, Kim Jong Il is left to constantly juggle between the lesser requirement for international food aid and the greater requirement of keeping the Juche religious-political totalitarian system intact during this national crisis. The result is endemic starvation.

As part of Kim Jong Il's "solution," university students are sent out on field trips to the surrounding farms to study *Juche Nongbub*, "the Juche farming method." What is "the Juche farming method"? Actually, it is a system of collectivized farming with designated quotas supplemented by special state farms worked by concentration camp inmates. Over the last few decades, "the Juche farming method" has also included creating terraced fields for crops by cutting down whole forests. This massive deforestation in many areas has resulted in catastrophic environmental erosion. Forest root systems, which once mitigated the effects of flooding, no longer exist. In one area, fields buried in over four feet of mud could not be planted for lack of heavy farm machinery. Some analysts forecast that a multi-billion dollar environmental cleanup program would be required to restore North Korea's shattered ecosystem after reunification with South Korea.

In 1996, North Korea modified the Juche farming system by creating an incentive program. Teams on cooperative farms that had previously had 10 to 25 workers were reduced to seven or eight workers. Each of these smaller teams was permitted to sell any crops that exceeded the government-assigned quota. These recent reforms give an increasingly capitalistic face to North Korea's Juche socialist method of agriculture.

Under the Juche religious system, it would be sacrilegious to blame "the Juche farming method" for any failures such as poor management and backward agricultural technology. Kim Jong Il had no tangible results to show for his "last-ditch" effort to improve agriculture during his first three years in leadership.[13] Yet, for Kim to take responsibility for this or any other failure would be an admission that sacred Juche "self-reliance" had also failed and the Su-ryong was wrong. Instead, Pyongyang continues to save face by blaming failures on natural disasters, economic reliance upon foreign aid, and scapegoats.

A prime example of such scapegoating is North Korea's 1997 execution of 72-year-old Suh Kwan Hi, its top Party official in charge of agriculture, for failing to properly implement the Juche farming method. According to Kim Dong Su, Hi was just one of dozens of youth league and Party officials executed in 1997. Kim Dong Su, the third Secretary to North Korea's mission to the United Nations' Food and Agricultural Organization (FAO) in Rome, defected on February 4, 1998, with his wife and eight-year-old son.

Meanwhile, North Korean students remain hard at work learning how to better implement the elusive, ill-defined, and constantly evolving technique:

> Kim Chun Bong, [the] work team's technical instructor, said, "In this room, we acquire knowledge of method of soil analysis, method of water control in paddy fields and others needed to implement *the Juche farming method*, learning the advanced farming method and having discussions" [*DPRK*].

Sometimes Party officials and foreign diplomats visit or, in the latter case, are led to visit the fields around Pyongyang to demonstrate their support for the Juche farming method. However, such visits do more to promote Pyongyang's image than result in any real economic value.

Under this system that promotes megalomania, Kim Jong Il must take center stage at something even as mundane as a flower exhibition. For example, the Pyongyang Arboretum's collection features nearly 3,500 plants given over the years by dignitaries of fellow Stalinist states. At the heart of the collection are two elegant orchids, called the Kim Il Sung flower (Kimilsungia) and the Kim Jong Il flower (Kimjongilia). It might not surprise you that there are many other flowers named after the two dictators, as well.

While Kim Jong Il is dawdling with having flowers named after himself and basking in the myth of having a utopian paradise, North Koreans are starving to death by the tens of thousands. In effect, Kim Jong Il is waging war against the North Korean people and causing more casualties through Juche than any actual war would inflict. Faced with this grim crisis, North Korea's population has already decreased 12–15% in some provinces due to starvation. In these provinces, empty trucks are sent into the villages each morning. Those who starved to death during the night are piled up like cord wood in the back of the trucks. Then the trucks dispose of the bodies and drive on to the next village. There, the grisly specter is repeated once more.

Propaganda and speeches by North Korea's leaders admit absolutely no linkage between recurring natural disasters such as hailstorms, drought, floods, and tidal waves and the wrath of God invoked by the haughty pride of Juche (self-reliance). Instead, Kim Jong Il blames his problems on a combination of random natural disasters and the failings of other nations. For example, in the propaganda below, notice how the United States, the collapse of the socialist market, and nuclear tensions are listed as causes of the crisis. Meanwhile, there is not even a hint that North Korea's government policies in general, and collective agricultural policies in particular, and even Kim Jong Il himself are the basic problems. Instead, North Korea views its agricultural woes as having been precipitated entirely by external causes.

> To look back, north Korea found itself landed in an unprecedented crisis: the collapse of the socialist market, the nuclear standoff, and the subsequent economic woes, including the looming famine. The loss of the socialist market adversely affected the north Korean production of grain partly because phosphor and potash were all imported... The situation was compounded by tensions with the United States and then by the successive years of natural disasters. In 1994 a hailstorm struck the key granaries of North and South Hwanghae Provinces on the West Sea coast, wiping out 1,020,000 tons of grain. The following year the same rice growing areas were inundated by the worst floods in 100 years, with some 3,000,000 tons of grain washed away. This was not the end of the story, however. The summer of 1996 saw downpours flooding the disaster areas again, causing extensive damage.[14]

The 1998 rendition of Kim Jong Il's New Year's Message, published in the *Workers' Party* and *People's Army* propaganda organs, called for the people to solve food shortages through a "green revolution." Though the continuing famine has driven even the hard-

Farmers going to the fields.

line Pyongyang government to institute some non-Juche reforms, this green revolution falls far short of abandoning the Juche religious and Juche agricultural systems altogether. North Korea's *People's Korea* propaganda paper reports that these agricultural reforms include dredging out the rivers, rehabilitating flooded farmland, producing soil fertility-enhancing bacteria, planting multiple crops per year, breeding goats, and encouraging mushroom growing, fish farming, and vegetable cultivation. Some portion of North Korea's "sixty specialized plants" that are allegedly intended for the production of helpful bacteria might also be used to manufacture biological warfare agents.

The *People's Korea*'s announcement of a landmark policy decision away from collectivized farming certainly runs the risk of being deemed to be a non-Juche/non-socialist option by Kim Jong Il. This non-Juche reform hints at the internal conflict between the religious duty to praise the failed Juche farming method and the hunger-driven need to find a better way altogether. Even with such reforms, North Korea's leaders continue to cling to Juche religious teachings that deny God's very existence, deny man's dependence upon God, and assert that North Korea can achieve agricultural and economic prosperity apart from humbling themselves before God.

The goat-breeding program is another non-Juche solution being implemented with the help of Switzerland. However, publicly giving credit to the Swiss for their generous initiative runs counter to the notion of North Korea's "self-reliance."

From a biblical perspective, there is little reason to believe that North Korea's agricultural woes will be reversed until the bankrupt Juche religion, which is the spiritual root of the famine, is abandoned entirely. Under the current system, North Koreans march out to the fields waving banners and singing songs to glorify their dictator and their own efforts. From a spiritual perspective, as long as they deny the God of heaven as the source of agricultural blessing, attempts at man-made economic reforms amount to vanity. For ex-

The great leader President Kim Il Sung talking with farmers in Chongsan-ri, Kangso County (1958).

ample, one recent visitor to Korea took a photo from a train of a skin-and-bones North Korean cow and a scrawny goat standing next to each other in the middle of a field of tall lush green grass. Both animals were starving though they were surrounded by a plentiful pasture. Such images challenge our natural understanding and invite us to seriously consider the spiritual roots of the famine.

Juche in Industry

Iron and the machine are the king of industry.
KIM IL SUNG
KOREAN CENTRAL NEWS AGENCY

North Korea's economy is in shambles.[15]
CHONG DOO HEE
PROFESSOR OF HISTORY
SONGENG UNIVERSITY, SEOUL

With North Korea's ongoing economic decline, one might guess that the adjective "Juche" would be inappropriate to describe North Korean industry. However, such logic does not apply. Instead, there is a "Juche way of doing things" in almost every aspect of the North Korean workplace. Process improvements, innovations, new technologies, and inventions are incorporated into the ever-changing Juche ideal.

As shown in Table 9-4, North Korea's economic indices show a steady decline. North Korean Gross National Product (GNP) statistics are probably lower than corresponding South Korean estimates because Seoul's calculations may include the North's separate military economic sector whereas Pyongyang's do not. However, both Pyongyang's and Seoul's GNP statistics make the Juche method of doing business seem like chronic industrial mismanagement.

In North Korea, if a particular industrial management method works (over the short term), the glory goes to Kim Jong Il and the revolution, and it is declared to be "Juche." If the method fails, then the individual or group surely must not have properly implemented the superior Juche method. These Juche "socialist-style" economic policies have some common elements which combine to paralyze the North Korean economy, as shown in Table 9-5.

Juche industrial management emphasizes "speed-up cam-

TABLE 9-4. Economic Indices of North Korea's Shattered Economy[16]

CATEGORY	ECONOMIC INDEX	1991	1992	1993	1994	1995
Per capita GNP	Report of Central Statistics (Pyongyang) ($)	753	659	543	432	239
	Estimate by Ministry of Unification (Seoul) ($)	1,038	953	904	923	957
Economic Sector	Trade volume (billion $)	27.2	26.6	26.4	21.1	20.5
	Economic Growth Rate (%)	-5.2	-7.6	-4.3	-1.7	-4.6
	Total External Debt (bil. $)	9.3	9.7	10.3	10.6	11.8
Energy Sector	Petroleum Imports (kilotons)	1,890	1,520	1,360	910	1,100
	Coal Production (kilotons)	41,000	39,000	36,000	34,000	31,000
	Power Output (billion KWH)	26.3	24.7	22.1	23.1	23.0

**TABLE 9-5. Common Elements of Juche
Industrial Management Methods[17]**

ELEMENT	IMPACT
Production units must fulfill their government-assigned quotas.	Quantity is emphasized while quality is sorely neglected.
The Party attempts to increase productivity through ideological campaigns rather than through material incentives.	This wastes the workers' energy on political meetings, rallies, and unending propaganda sessions rather than expending it on production.
Government edicts and Juche ideology are used as the criteria for the centralized distribution of raw materials.	The lack of the demand-based assignment of resources neglects the supply-and-demand market forces thus stagnating the "People's Economic Sector" (consumer goods) industries.

paigns," which emphasize Kim Jong Il's conviction that "speed is in the hearts of the popular masses."[18] Despite the best of these Juche industrial management techniques, North Korea's factory production has been steadily dropping to only about 30% of the amount of factory production at the beginning of the 1990s.

One analyst summarized the impact of Juche upon North Korean industry as follows:

> Kim's Juche asinine economic solutions, which may be compared to those of an ancient Egyptian pharaoh hooked on pyramid building, include the institution of "work harder" campaigns, "speed battles," "eat less," and "produce more with less raw materials."[19]

North Koreans are taught that their Juche methods, including those in industry and agriculture, are the most advanced in the world. This attitude is quite evident from the guides who are assigned to all foreign visitors to North Korea. The interaction between one American and his guide as they visited Nampo's West Sea Barrage[20] provides an example of this prevalent attitude:

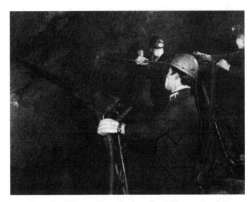

A twice Three-Revolution Red Flag winning team of coal miners demonstrates the Juche method of high-speed tunneling.

> The guide asked if I had "ever seen anything like it." Since I had not, she went away reinforced in the belief, no doubt, that North Korea was, indeed, the most advanced country in the world.[21]

Another example of this "most advanced in the world" myth is recent propaganda that claims the obsolete Kim Chaek Iron and Steel Complex, which features 45-year-old technology, is perfect.

> The Kim Chaek Iron and Steel Complex is situated in the northeastern part of Korea on the East Sea. *It has a perfect structure*; it is furnished with large and automatic equipment. It produces pig iron, steel, hot and cold rolled steel, making a great contribution to the nation's ferrous metallurgical industry …President Kim Il Sung and General Secretary Kim Jong Il visited the complex…Encouraged by their trust, the complex …is working hard to increase production full of confidence in victory and revolutionary optimism [*Korea Today*].

The Kim Chaek Iron and Steel Complex.

Most or even all credit for North Korean innovation is attributed to the amazing Su-ryong genius of Kim Jong Il. Juche propaganda holds that Kim Jong Il has mental faculties far surpassing even such great minds as Albert Einstein, Wolfgang Mozart, and Leonardo Da Vinci. Kim Jong Il maintains that "one must be an enthusiastic patriot before being a scientist."[22] Yet, even if those closest to Kim have their doubts, his inner circle is trapped within a system that must continue to promote the myth of his surpassing intelligence.

Some North Korean leaders have engaged in wishful economic doublespeak. For example, on April 22, 1996, Deputy Chairman Kim Jong-U of the North Korean External Economy Commission remarked at a Korean Peninsula Economic Cooperation Forum that "North Korea is now seeking a drastic turn of policies from the existing policy line of a self-reliant [Juche] economy." However, such words were never backed up by any move away from Juche economic policy by Pyongyang's top leadership. Not only have there been no new economic reforms, but North Korea's leaders also have failed to announce the state budget for fiscal years 1995, 1996, and 1997. Nor does it seem likely that they will approve another budget bill soon.

North Korea's industry is organized along Juche lines. The economy, which focuses on heavy industry, is designed to sustain the 1.2 million member Korean People's Army. The DPRK's five major exports, in order of monetary value (1997) are mineral oil, timber, steel, machinery, and electrical parts.[23] Consumer goods are a secondary concern. Concentration camp inmates routinely are used as a major source of conscript labor in North Korea's mines and agriculture. According to one source, the combined production by concentration camp labor produces a full 40% of North Korea's coal and farm output. The heavy reliance upon inmate labor became apparent recently when mine and agricultural production took a sharp downward turn due to guards cutting back on subsistence rations to concentration camp inmates. How could barely fed concentration camp workers out-produce well-fed Korean miners and farmers? One former concentration camp guard explained the production anomaly by saying that the inmate rationalizes his raison d'être (reason for being) to be his or her work. The inmate will remove even the smallest stone from his field, keep it weed-free, and carefully apply manure and compost. In contrast, the collectivized fields are full of rocks and leeched of nutrients. Under the collectivized system, quota-driven production by regular workers continues to promote a "do just enough" mentality.

One unusual aspect of North Korea's economy is its independent military munitions sector. This sector supplies one million troops with all of their necessary food and supplies. While the rest of the economy is reportedly failing, top priority for personnel and material resources still goes to this "royal court" sub-economy. This sub-economy is controlled by the Second Economic Committee and the Ministry of the Armed Forces. Likewise, Kim Jong Il's private luxuries are run separately from the rest of the economy out of Room 39 of the Workers' Party Central Committee headquarters in Pyongyang.

Juche ideology serves to reinforce the radical emphasis North Korea's leadership places on its independent military munitions sector. In the Fifth Party Congress (1970), Kim Il Sung called for self-reliance in military munitions. As a result, North Korea boosted heavy industrial production while stripping other economic sectors of resources. In the two decades that followed, North Korea's heavy industry accounted for two-thirds of all industrial production and 30% of the Gross Domestic Product (GDP). This level of investment was particularly enormous considering that the former Soviet Union's heavy industry was, by comparison, only 8% of their GDP.

One of Pyongyang's industrial initiatives that seems to run

counter to Juche ideology was the creation of the Free Economic and Trade Zone (FETZ) in northeast North Korea near the border of China and Russia. North Korea's December 28, 1991, cabinet decree and the January 31, 1993, "Law on the Free Economic and Trade Zone" designate the Rajin-Sonbong area along with the port of Chongjin as a FETZ. North Korea seeks to attract multinational industries to invest in the FETZ to boost its economy. However, the response by international investors in this remote area has, not surprisingly, been meager. Most of the foreign capital investment in the FETZ has come from the Korean minority community in Japan.

Recent leadership of North Korea's centralized socialist economy has sounded an uncertain trumpet regarding economic reform. For example, Kim Jong Il's response to North Korea's crumbling economy is to remain locked into continuing his Juche collectivized "heavy industry first" strategy. Like Kim Il Sung before him, Kim Jong Il considers the development of heavy industry, and in particular heavy industrial machinery, as the foundation for technical progress in the Juche-oriented revolution. Industry-related propaganda generally features slogans such as "They will certainly win as they are led by General Kim Jong Il," and highly questionable claims of increases in production by North Korea's starving workers. At times, such industry-related propaganda may also seem contadictory. For example, within a single *Rodong Sinmun* article on January 15, 1998, heavy industry was named as "the most important task," while mention was also made of the Party's "light industry first" policy.[24]

The assignment of Kim Gyong Hi, a woman, to direct the Light Industry Department in 1993 is another example of the lesser importance of light industry in the overall scheme of the North Korean economy. North Korea's leadership elite has been a distinctively male-dominated aristocracy over the last fifty years. While the nepotism of assigning Kim Jong Il's sister is duly noted, the assignment of a woman to direct this sector signifies its relative unimportance. In 1995, Kim Gyong Hi was promoted to Director of the Economic Policy Inspection Department. Her promotion, despite North Korea's declining light industrial output during her tenure, was possibly a timely move to prevent Kim Jong Il from having to blame his sister for the sad state of the light industrial sector of the economy. Now, in her new position, she can help her dictator-brother assign the blame for the ongoing economic nightmare.

The secret financial wildcard for the DPRK economy may be the newly discovered likelihood of massive offshore oil deposits off of both North Korea's eastern and western coasts. London-based analyst Alex Stewart, of North Asia Research Associates, noted in a January 4, 1999, article in the *Oil and Gas Journal* that international firms have already been quietly signing contracts with the DPRK to obtain exploration and production licenses and concessions. If North Korean oil deposits, estimated by Pyongyang at six to eight billion barrels, are not sheer fantasy, then a trans-Korea oil pipeline and a rags-to-riches story could be in North Korea's economic future. However, non-Juche foreign investment would have to be attracted and permitted on a massive scale for this vision to become a reality.

The future outlook for North Korea's industry and economy will remain bleak given the country's consistent declaration that it will stick to its Juche methods and isolationist ways that resist foreign capital investment. A September 1998 article in *Rodong Sinmun* declared:

> It is foolish to daydream to try to revive the economy by introducing foreign capital, not relying on one's own strength.[25]

A similar September 1998 article in *Kurolla* stated:

> We will...set ourselves against all attempts to induce us to join an "integrated" world. We have nothing to "reform" and "open.",...Under Kim Jong Il, the country will revitalize its economy "one sector after another as ants gnaw a piece of bone."[26]

Juche in Education

> *Even if parents are revolutionaries, their children will not necessarily be revolutionaries...If we delayed even a step the education of the next generations, the advance of our fatherland will be delayed ten steps.*[27]
>
> KIM JONG IL

The Juche educational system is the most automated and structured system of mass brainwashing in the world, bar none. State-controlled education is the mainstay of totalitarianism. Article 39 of the North Korean Constitution stipulates:

The state, based on the principle of socialist pedagogy, nurtures the rising generation into devoted revolutionaries who will carry out struggles for the benefit of society and the people, and into new communists equipped with intelligence, virtue and physical fitness.[28]

The Juche view of education agrees with Abraham Lincoln's observation that "the philosophy of the school room in one generation will be the philosophy of government in the next." Germany's Adolf Hitler gained control of the minds of millions of young Germans in this manner by eliminating all Christian schools in 1936, adopting a racist curriculum, and then two years later making it unlawful for teachers to have any religious affiliation. Compared to the Juche educational system, Hitler's system was quite mild.

Kim Jong Il's statements about the importance of Juche-style education highlight the critical role of education in winning the nation's youth to Juche ideology:

> Comrade Kim Il Sung said that training young people to be ideologically and morally sound is the greatest proof of love for them. When modern revisionists were creating illusions about imperialism and corrupting the rising generation both ideologically and morally, he put all his efforts into intensifying anti-imperialist and anti-revisionist education as well as revolutionary education, so that our children were not infected by evil ideas and trends.[29]

> Our youth must be proud of Juche-oriented socialism in our country and hold a firmer conviction in its superiority and invincibility...All our young men and women must have a firm belief in our socialism of Juche...They must sharpen their vigilance against infiltration by all manner of anti-socialist ideas and bourgeois modes of life, reject them categorically and staunchly defend the socialist ideology and our socialist system from the abuses, slander and subversive moves of the enemies of socialism...in all spheres of work and life.[30]

Under Juche, like the Nazi system, the children are considered to be wards of the state, not the Korean family. Compulsory Juche indoctrination begins at age three in North Korea's pre-school and continues through the tenth grade. These educational programs are specially designed to teach children to worship the father and son Kims. Annual primary school education includes 304 hours of

Members of the Korean Children's Union pledge themselves to grow up resolutely into the reliable successors to the revolutionary cause of Juche.

instruction on the "Childhood of Kim Il Sung" and the "Childhood of Kim Jong Il." These lessons teach that Kim Il Sung is the divine father of the Korean people. Students are grilled with endless lessons on how Kim Il Sung and his son Kim Jong Il are to be worshipped as absolute deities since they are the protectors and progenitors of the Korean race. History books ascribe all the country's achievements to the duo, including many that are totally unrelated to them. Older children sing songs and hymns to their glory. Younger children are taught to say before meals, "Thank you, Father Kim Jong Il, for offering us this delicious food," while saluting Kim Jong Il's photo.[31]

Juche indoctrination gets heavier as the students get older. By the time students are promoted to high school, Juche indoctrination has intensified to 567 hours each year in four subjects, as shown in Table 9-6.

In addition to Juche religious indoctrination, over 40% of North Korea's language, geography, and nature textbooks are full of material designed to deify the two Kims. Well over half of the content of North Korea's musical education program is devoted to hymns and compositions that worship the Kims. For example, a third-grade nature textbook teaches students, "Respected Father Marshal Kim Il Sung instructed us as follows: Our country is abundant with mountains." Similarly, a sixth-grade language textbook teaches older students, "Let us learn after the virtues of Great Leader Kim Il Sung."

TABLE 9-6. Juche Religious Indoctrination Curricula in North Korean Schools[32]

GRADES	SUBJECT	HOURS
Primary Schools	Childhood of Kim Il Sung	152
	Childhood of Kim Jong Il	152
Senior High Schools	Revolutionary Activities of Kim Il Sung	150
	Revolutionary History of Kim Il Sung	195
	Revolutionary Activities of Kim Jong Il	112
	Revolutionary History of Kim Jong Il	110

History textbooks emphasize that North Korea is the sole legitimate heir to rule over the Korean peninsula. Juche scholars relate how the line of legitimate rule passed from the Tangun founders of Korea around 2333 B.C. to Kokuryo, Balhae (Palhae),[33] Koryo, and ultimately to North Korea. A recurring theme in the North's rendition of Korean history is how these kingdoms unified the Korean peninsula through popular uprisings by farmers against foreigners and "cowardly fellows in the ruling class."

Since the early 1970s, North Korean history books have been totally rewritten and revised in accordance with Kim Il Sung's directives to emphasize Juche ideology and extreme exclusion against foreign powers. For example, in his thesis, "On Enhancing the Role of Social Science in Compliance with the Requirement of Our Revolution at the Present Age," Kim Il Sung wrote, "A study of history must not be aimed at obtaining knowledge about the history of kings and rulers in the feudal era, but at correctly understanding the history of our people's struggles and creativeness." Thus, North Korean history books all agree that Juche has enabled North Korea to be successful in establishing paradise on earth. Since paradise has been achieved, now all that remains is for the people to safeguard their paradise from invasion by foreigners. Through a comprehensive rewrite of their history, North Korea's leadership has cut off its people from their true past and systematically substituted mythology for truth.

One history textbook, *Chosun Tongsa* (*History of Korea*), uses "religion is the opium of the masses" anti-religious jargon to describe the social order of a primitive Bronze Age community:

As classes began to appear and the ruling class seized

power following the collapse of the primitive community, religion, which was the product of ignorance about nature and society, became a tool to attribute all social evils to mysterious and supernatural power, thus to paralyze the class consciousness of the ruled class and to protect the ruling class and its exploiting system. In

Kindergartners under the two Kims' cult indoctrination.

the class society, *religion* was something like *opium designed to paralyze the masses*' consciousness for struggles. In other words, religion was an important means of strengthening the rules of the ruling class.[34]

A mathematics textbook for second graders presents the following problem:

> During the War for the Liberation of our Fatherland [The Korean War], our uncles in the People's Army destroyed a pack of Yankee imperialist bastard jackals and confiscated 224,123 grenades and 265,137 various kinds of explosives. All together, what was the total amount of grenades and explosives obtained?[35]

A language textbook for seventh graders teaches children how to effectively narrate a story:

> The best method for narrating a story successfully is to convey vividly one's experiences, and by doing so one can effectively agitate the listeners to harbor hatred and hostile feelings against the Japanese imperialists and the bastard landlords who had reigned over our society in the past.[36]

The language textbook for eighth graders presents a lesson on proper etiquette:

> Whenever we refer to our enemies, we must use such words as "gangly American bastards," "the noggins of the American bastards," and so on.[37]

School field trips, homework assignments, games, and activi-

ties also revolve around glorifying the Kims. Students must have
Communist Party approval to continue their education after the
tenth grade. During their summer vacations, students must work
for the state. Even after a student graduates from high school, the
Juche brainwashing process continues as North Koreans are told to
use any time off work to visit the numerous Juche monuments,
make pilgrimages to historical and revolutionary sites, and assist
their own children in their Juche indoctrination.

George Orwell's novel *1984* provides further explanation of the
theoretical necessity of brainwashing the nation's youth to ensure
the continuation of the totalitarian system:

> A Party member is required to have not only the right
> opinions, but the right instincts. Many of the beliefs and atti-
> tudes demanded of him are never plainly stated, and could
> not be stated without laying bare the contradictions...He will
> in all circumstances know, without taking thought, what is
> the true belief or the desirable emotion. But in any case an
> elaborate mental training undergone in childhood and group-
> ing itself round the Newspeak words *crimestop, blackwhite,* and
> *doublethink* makes him unwilling and unable to think too
> deeply on any subject whatsoever.
>
> *Crimestop* means the faculty of stopping short, as though
> by instinct, at the threshold of any dangerous thought. It in-
> cludes the power of not grasping analogies, of failing to per-
> ceive logical errors, of misunderstanding the simplest argu-
> ments...and being bored or repelled by any train of thought
> which is capable of leading in a heretical direction.
>
> *Blackwhite*...has two mutually contradictory meanings.
> Applied to an opponent, it means the habit of impudently
> claiming that black is white, in contradiction of the plain facts.
> Applied to a Party member, it means a loyal willingness to say
> that black is white when Party discipline demands this. But it
> means also the ability to *believe* that black is white, and more,
> to *know* that black is white, and to forget that one has ever
> believed the contrary. This demands a continuous alteration
> of the past.
>
> *Doublethink* means the power of holding two contradictory
> beliefs in one's mind simultaneously, and accepting both of
> them. The Party intellectual knows in which direction his mem-
> ories must be altered; he therefore knows that he is playing
> tricks with reality; but by the exercise of *doublethink* he also
> satisfies himself that reality is not violated...*Doublethink* lies at

the very heart…of the Party…to use conscious deception while retaining the firmness of purpose that goes with complete honesty.[38]

The Juche term "class consciousness" is an almost exact match for Orwell's terms crimestop, blackwhite, and doublethink. According to Kim Jong Il, "Conscience [class consciousness] is the mirror of action, and the measure by which to distinguish truth from untruth."[39] For example, compare the following article entitled "Class consciousness, weapon for defending socialism" in light of Orwell's foregoing definitions:

What is an important demand for defending socialism is to firmly arm the popular masses with the working class consciousness. Ignoring the working class consciousness [Crimestop] means destroying the ideological basis of socialism and neglecting the masses' demand for independence and their fundamental interests. The history shows serious lessons that divorce from the viewpoint and position of the working class results in degeneration of socialism. The class consciousness is the ideological and mental source of helping the people keep the confidence in socialism. It also definitely guarantees consistent maintenance of the revolutionary principles in socialist construction.

The revolutionary and socialist principles are, in essence, the working-class principles. Only those steadfast in class consciousness can judge all the matters with the viewpoint and position of the popular masses and always fight to defend the fundamental interests of the revolution [doublethink]. The class consciousness is essential for uncompromising fighting against the imperialists.

Those who have firm class consciousness can struggle uncompromisingly against the imperialists' moves to stifle socialism, deeply aware of their class stand and duty. With the firm class consciousness, the Korean people boast of being consistent in confidence in socialism and strong in the revolutionary principles. They also categorically reject the imperialists' ideological and cultural offensive, economic blockade and military threat and never allow others to hurt the destiny and honor of their fatherland [blackwhite] [*Rodong Sinmun*].

Class consciousness—in the sense of Orwell's crimestop, doublethink, and blackwhite—is also reflected in how North Koreans perceive real-world events using "Juche-speak."

The average North Korean must verbalize the State's definition of terms such as "injustice" on one hand, while living amid real unpunished "injustice" on the other. Finally, notice the *crimestop* in North Korea's elementary principle of education. Teachers must train students "to distinguish between right and wrong" according to the "class consciousness" way. Of course, in North Korea, "right and wrong" must agree with the ever-changing "Juche-speak" definitions of these terms.

Every morning at six o'clock sharp, North Koreans throughout the land are awakened by large loud speakers, placed at one-hundred-yard intervals throughout their towns and villages. At the crack of dawn, these speakers boom anti-God slogans, Juche hymns and propaganda, and call all families to rise and partake in "religious exercises." Citizens are told:

> The nation is under threat of foreign forces bent on destroying paradise on earth...Your only hope remains with the Great Leader...Everyone should keep a constant watch for those who turn from this [Juche] ideology.[40]

These loudspeakers serve as an incessant reminder of "the Party's voice," the necessity of unquestioning allegiance to Kim Jong Il. For example, the people are reminded that Kim Jong Il is their savior, protector, provider, future, and ever-victorious leader of the Juche Communist revolution who has freed them from the fear of being monitored by foreign agencies.

In addition to the steady stream of Juche propaganda, Juche religious-like worship is also enforced throughout North Korea by the Pyongyang Big Brother regime. Juche religious indoctrination continues for the masses at over 40,000 "Kim Il Sung Revolutionary Thought Study Rooms" throughout the cities, villages, and countryside. These "study rooms," which are "pastored" by the local Party officials, serve as surrogate churches for "congregations" which average about 500 people each. People prepare for political study meetings at these study rooms by memorizing the contents of the Party newpaper.

For the privileged core group members who have access to a university-level education, Juche indoctrination continues even further. Pyongyang's Kim Il Sung University maintains six entire departments that specialize in Kim Il Sung and Kim Jong Il. They include the Department of Kim Il Sung's Revolutionary History, the Department of Kim Jong Il's Revolutionary History, the Department of Kim Il Sung's Works, and the Department of Kim Jong Il's Works. A North Korean book on Kim Il Sung University declares the university to be "the highest seat of the Juche-oriented education." The book goes on the describe the mission of the university:

> *The University is raising the quality of education by* further improving the contents of education in conformity with the needs of the revolution and construction and *thoroughly applying the Juche-oriented pedagogics.*[41]

University students' activities include participation in Pyongyang's annual parades by the city's million-plus working people. Their campus is adorned with Kim memorabilia, well-manicured grounds, and, of course, a large prominently located statue of Kim Il Sung.

Let us consider what "thoroughly applying the Juche-oriented pedagogics" means at the university level. For example, this is what *Lectures on National Law*, a textbook used at Kim Il Sung University, states regarding freedom of speech:

> Freedom of speech is widely used in *criticism* and *self-criticism*, thereby giving benefit to the people, and it solidifies the people's democracy and promotes the further development of the people's economy.[42]

The textbook continues:

> Publications, with the workers' active support and participation, play the role of the propagandist in cultivating the socialist idea among the masses, and their principal mission is *to indoctrinate the masses* with revolutionary Marxism-Leninism so that they may be able *to develop their faculty of criticism and self-criticism* and join the task of constructing a socialist country.[43]

Yet, in reality, the Juche religion and the government it sustains cannot tolerate any mechanism of self-criticism whatsoever. True freedom of speech would allow for open criticism of Kim Jong Il, Juche ideology, and the Party without fear of reprisal. So, North Korea redefines such terms to suit their needs.

Kim Jong Il and Party officials often tour North Korea's universities and attend inter-collegiate sporting events. In one such visit, Kim Jong Il attended an October 1997 basketball game between Kim Il Sung University and Kim Chaek University of Technology. Though the propaganda article failed to mention any of the players, or which team won, or even the final score, the names and titles of all of Kim Jong Il's entourage were listed along with the following summary of Kim's post-game pep talk to the teams:

> After seeing the game, Secretary Kim Jong Il congratulated the students on the successful game, saying that the revolutionary and militant students of Korea put their heart and soul into studies of science for the country and people and are good at art and sports activities. He noted with great satisfaction that the two universities have positively contributed to the prosperity of the country by producing many able native cadres and technicians who play a pivotal role in the revolution and construction. It is very important to train the students into versatile persons of ability who will shoulder the future of the country, he said, and gave important tasks for university education [*KCNA*].

Jeremy J. Stone's interaction with Pyongyang's elite was recorded both in his 1991 testimony before a U.S. Senate subcommittee and in the *Journal of the Federation of American Scientists (FAS)*. The following excerpt from Stone's *FAS* article provides an example of the comprehensive impact of Juche education:

> A lecturer, an expert in "Modern Korean Philosophy," waited at his station to help students by answering their questions. Asked if he had any questions about America, he said, "I just hope that you have a correct understanding of our philosophy." He then went on to describe the North Korean political view of South Korea.
>
> "Does everyone here agree that Americans are the problem for reunification?" He responded, "Yes, because it is correct. And the demonstrations in South Korea, every day, show it is."
>
> "Has there ever been a demonstration here on any subject?" "No," he answered, "because we have a people oriented government."
>
> "Has your government ever made a mistake?" He said, "No, never. There were some individuals who had wrong ideas, but we found out in time." Told that Americans would never believe that no mistake had ever been made by the government, he said, "If they come, they will see."
>
> It was the same question I had asked of Chinese in Shanghai during the Cultural Revolution. Asked then whether "Chairman Mao had ever made a mistake," my guide—in the area

then controlled by the Gang of Four—said, "This is an abusive question." In contrast, throughout North Korea, the officials I questioned seemed too brainwashed even to resent the question. They gave a greater impression of believing.[44]

At the end of years of such thorough indoctrination, North Korea's elite are fully indoctrinated to carry on the torch of the revolution as the mainstay of the next generation's Juche faithful.

Juche Myths and Legends

General Kim Jong Il . . . is firmly determined to make Kim Il Sung's nation an ideologically, politically and militarily powerful state forever and build an ideal paradise of humankind and a strong and prosperous country of Juche at an early date.
EXCERPT FROM THE EVER-POPULAR BOOK,
AN EARTHLY PARADISE FOR THE PEOPLE

A key part of North Korea's educational system is to promote an entire concoction of Juche myths and legends until they become accepted truth. Though these legends seem hilariously laughable to an outsider, Pyongyang has done such a remarkably thorough job of promoting them that they have taken on the air of theological truth within the Juche culture.

The system of myths is designed, from the ground up, to validate the false Juche religion. Categories of myths include those about Kim Il Sung, Kim Jong Il, the Kim family, Mt. Paektu, imperialists, revolutionaries, and North Korea as a "paradise on earth." The following discussion provides an overview of Juche mythology.

North Korean mythology gives one the definite sense that Kim Il Sung supposedly had nearly supernatural powers. His notable powers included gifted intelligence along with the capacity to be in several places at the same time. For example, the two Kims would have each had to travel over 340,000 miles (equivalent to making over 113 coast-to-coast trips in the United States) for this to be true.

President Kim Il Sung with the idea of "believing in the people as in heaven" devoted all his life to the welfare of the people. In his reminiscences the president said his revolutionary activities began and continue among the people. After Korea's liberation from the Japanese imperialist colonial rule,

Dear Comrade Kim Jong Il [allegedly] grew up under the care and revolutionary education of the great leader General Kim Il Sung and Comrade Kim Jong Suk, an indomitable Communist revolutionary fighter.

the President made a 550,000-kilometer-long journey, going to the places where the people live and gave on-the-spot guidance to some 18,000 units on more than 8,000 occasions. Secretary Kim Jong Il has made a journey for the welfare of the people as the President did [*KCNA*].

Korea's poor-to-nonexistent road system and Kim Il Sung's fear of flying make the journey part particularly unbelievable. As the next propaganda excerpt shows, the younger Kim seems to be lagging behind his father's superman-like pace of inspections:

> General Secretary Kim Jong Il has led the Korean revolution to a brilliant victory, giving on-site guidance to many units even on red-letter days for 34 years since he started working at the Central Committee of the Workers' Party of Korea. Days of his on-site guidance number 3,693 equivalent to over 10 years, among them 997 red-letter days including his birthdays equivalent to nearly 3 years. On these red-letter days, he gave on-site guidance to more than 2,100 [KPA] units across the country, covering the road of 59,196 kilometers. This clearly proves that he has devoted everything only to the happiness of the people [*KCNA*].

However, the propaganda piece aims to meet the cultural expectation that Korea's Juche leaders were and are Confucian-style servant-leaders. Despite the absurdity of the "proof," such propaganda also shows the high importance these dictators have placed on sustaining their Juche political/religious system through maintaining a solid personal base of power in the Korean People's Army.

North Korea has also invented a variety of absurd legends to idolize Kim Jong Il as shown in Table 9-7.

TABLE 9-7. Popular Legends About Kim Jong Il[45]

LEGEND
– Kim Jong Il's birth was foretold by a swallow.
– At the time of his birth there were flashes of lightning and thunder, and the iceberg in the pond on Mt. Paektu emitted a mysterious sound as it broke.
– A double rainbow appeared over sacred Mt. Paektu when he was born.
– At the age of 4 he smeared a Japanese map with black ink, then a stormy rain poured down on Japan.
– Jong Il supposedly has mastered all knowledge, and his thoughts are studied at great world universities.
– By a touch of Kim Jong Il's hand the sea turned into a fertile land and a deep valley into a paradise.
– Secretary Kim Jong Il had a power of keen observation in his childhood. When he was a child, he found out why chickens raise their bills when they drink water and why there is no black flower.
– Kim Jong Il had extraordinary insight and analytical abilities as a child. He observed that one added to one makes two but it makes greater one in some cases.

Mythographers have yet to claim that Kim Jong Il was suckled by a she-wolf or tutored by centaurs, but they certainly come close. The truth about Kim Jong Il is less remarkable. For example, his only travels outside his homeland have been a short stint of studies in Malta and visits to other Communist countries.

Of course, more and more books about Kim Jong Il emerge from the imaginations of North Korean writers with each passing year. One 1998 book, entitled *Legends about [the] Great Man*, was released on Kim Jong Il's 56th birthday. The book contains 56 legends ranging from the birth of Kim Jong Il to "his immortal feats for the history of the nation" [*KCNA*].

The idolization of Kim Jong Il's family lineage was initiated to both justify the illegitimate process whereby Kim Il Sung seized power and to pave the way for the succession of power from father to son. Table 9-8 provides five examples of the Kim Il Sung's fabricated family background.

TABLE 9-8. Fabrications of Kim Il Sung's Family Background[46]

NAME	RELATION TO KIM IL SUNG	FABRICATION
Kim Ung-u	Great-grandfather	A plain peasant was made into the vanguard commander of the sinking of an American trading vessel, the *Sherman* (the actual leader was Governor of Pyongyang, Pak Kyu-su).
Kim Bo-hyon	Grandfather (paternal)	Ordinary farmers were made into patriots who resisted Japanese aggressors.
Li bo-Ik	Grandmother (paternal)	
Kim Hyong-jik	Father	An oriental medicine pharmacist, who was killed in a raid by Communists, was made into an indefatigable Communist revolutionary fighter and a vanguard of the Communist movement.
Kang Ban-sok	Mother	An ordinary woman was made into a passionate revolutionary fighter and a leader of the Korean women's liberation movement.

One of the most popular terms for Kim Jong Il is "lodestar of Mt. Paektu." It was there that Kim Jong Il, as a toddler, allegedly grew up in the base camp of the anti-Japanese struggle. However, the historical facts that Jong Il was born in Soviet Russia and that Kim Il Sung and Kim Jong Suk were nowhere near Mt. Paektu in 1936 make no difference in North Korea. Their history has been revised and sanitized complete with national parks, battlefields, monuments, tour guides, and souvenirs.

New myths that are taught as facts are constantly being invented for "the three generals of Mt. Paektu" (Kim Il Sung, Kim Jong Suk, and Kim Jong Il). In one of these myths, Kim Il Sung, as a young revolutionary in 1928, is said to have cured an old woman of a disease by simply touching her. His touch is said to have been a cure for any disease. In another new myth, Kim Jong Il in 1988 allegedly resuscitated a veteran anti-Japanese fighter, who had been dying from an incurable disease, by sending Kimjongilia flowers to him. Other new myths chronicle the circa 1938 anti-Japanese battlefield tales that glorify "mother Kim Jong Suk." According to Pyongyang, these revolutionary tales are intended to "greatly encourage the Korean people in the forced march for the final victory" [*KCNA*].

One of the latest fabrications is the "sudden" discovery (after half a century) of more than 200 slogan-bearing trees throughout North Korea. Pyongyang alleges that:

> Those slogans were written by the first generation of the Korean revolution during the anti-Japanese war period, who celebrated the birth of General Kim Jong Il on Feb. 16, Juche 31 (1942) as a great national event and praised him as "bright star above Mt. Paektu" [*KCNA*].

To the casual observer, these slogans seem to be little more than new government-sponsored graffiti that defaces otherwise healthy trees. Yet, since North Korea's tree-slogans praise their current dictator, Pyongyang has declared them to be national treasures.

Much of the other history of North Korea has been rewritten as well. For example, the North Koreans have built a revolutionary museum at Sinchon, south of Pyongyang, to memorialize the alleged mass murder of over 38,000 Korean civilians by American soldiers. Koreans are told that for 52 days from October to December 1950, American Eighth Army soldiers drove civilians off of bridges to perish in icy river waters below. The North Koreans are then told that Americans separated women from children, raped, pillaged, and finally poured gasoline and torched those who were still alive. The North Korean caption for one of the paintings in the Sinchon Museum states:

> On an early December day of 1950, a bestial Yankee Harrison appeared at Wonam-ri, Sinchon County. Looking at mothers and children he said that it was so happy for mothers to be with their children and separated them into two storehouses, giving orders to keep them separated until they died. Then the devils sprinkled gasoline in the storehouses to burn 400 mothers and 102 children mercilessly.[47]

American wartime accounts paint an entirely different picture. Following the successful American amphibious landing at Inchon, Americans defeated the North Korean forces in the south and started driving north of the 38th parallel. In October 1950, as the

North Korea's Sinchon museum blames American soldiers for the Communist slaughter and burning of over 38,000 North Korean civilians at Sinchon during the Korean War.

Americans pushed north toward Pyongyang through the hilly country around Sinchon, resistance stiffened. On various occasions, North Korean guerrillas ambushed and wiped out American patrols. Then their standard mode of operation was to pour gasoline over the bodies and set them on fire. Private First Class Leonard Korgie, from G Company of the 21st Infantry, gives one such eyewitness account from the Sinchon area in October 1950:

> The 1st Cav rode ahead of us in trucks, we marched on foot. A day or so into North Korea we discovered a small but grisly scene. I've seen it in my dreams a thousand times...Some signal unit...had been ambushed by North Korean guerrillas ...*Then the Communists poured gasoline over everything and set it on fire*...We walked among the smoldering bodies.[48]

As the Eighth Army pushed north through Pyongyang in November, North Korean guerrilla activity remained high in the Sinchon area. In fact, after the Chinese intervention in November, Chinese and North Korean guerrilla units actually occupied the area in December 1950. In January 1951, the Eighth Army had to fight its way through Chinese positions at Sinchon while retreating southward. One of the Chinese tactics at the time was to infiltrate groups of refugees and prisoners and then turn on American guards when the opportunity presented itself. In addition to the "scorched earth" policy of the retreating United Nations forces (to deny supplies to the advancing Chinese), that tactic resulted in some regrettable atrocities by allied soldiers. However, many of the accounts presented in the Sinchon Museum appear to be highly exaggerated or distorted. To most American officers and soldiers of the Eighth Army, such atrocities would have been un-thinkable—and certainly impossible for a 52-day period. An alter-nate possibility is that, though some American atrocities did occur, the Communists used the occasion of the American withdrawal as a cover story while they wiped out all the Christians and the rest of Sinchon's populace. Afterward, the history could easily have been revised to support continuing anti-Americanism.

A survey of North Korean propaganda also reveals another prevalent myth. Pyongyang still paints the picture that North Korea is paradise on earth compared to the rest of the world. The popular North Korean book, *An Earthly Paradise for the People*, con-tinues to promote this paradise myth as an inherent part of Juche ideology. The following propaganda excerpt, amid the ongoing famine, surprisingly tones down the "paradise" rhetoric referring to it as being still under construction:

> Our people are a dignified people who are advancing un-der the guidance of General Kim Jong Il, upholding the na-tional flag. No matter how desperately the imperialists may try to stifle the Korean-style socialism, our people are confident-ly advancing with an indomitable revolutionary spirit along the straight road of the revolution chosen by themselves… Our Republic is firmly defending its honor without the slightest vacillation in face of any offensive of the enemy as it is guided by *the general who is firmly determined to* make Kim Il Sung's nation an ideologically, politically and militarily power-ful state forever and *build an ideal paradise* of humankind and a strong and prosperous country of Juche at an early date [*KCNA*].

Never mind that most of North Korea's people are starving and the economy is in shambles. In fact, despite South Korea's economy being 14 times stronger than the North's, South Korea continues to be portrayed as a "brutally poor, miserable place under Uncle Sam's boot heel." Since defection to the South is nearly impossible across the most heavily guarded border in the world, many people in North Korea do not realize the full extent of the less-than-paradise quality of their existence.

The Juche Caste System

Revolution is not made by people's class origins but with their thought.[49]

KIM JONG IL

Citizens all enjoy equal rights in political, economic, cultural and all other spheres of State and public activities.[50]

ARTICLE 51
NORTH KOREAN CONSTITUTION

Since the 1967 implementation of the "Citizens Re-registration Project," everyone in North Korea's "classless" society above age 17 is investigated and categorized in one of three classes. Within these classes, people are further designated to fall within one of about 64 classifications. These classifications serve as the basis for determining what privileges one has during his or her lifetime. How comfortably one lives, what schools are available, what jobs can be obtained, and even how much food one can have to eat, are all based on one's caste designation.

The core group (top 28%) of North Korean society is the elite group from which the privileged members of North Korean society emerge. Core group status is necessary to enjoy the privileges of Pyongyang society. The core group includes Kim Jong Il and his family, along with top government officials (about 200,000 people) and their families who are loyal to Kim Jong Il. Though core group membership does not always exempt one from being jailed, the children of core group families have access to the best schools and positions in the government and the military. Moreover, core group members of the society have priority in obtaining food rationing or food aid, medical treatment, and consumer goods.

In the early 1990s, a Korean described the home of a relative he visited in Pyongyang who was a high-ranking Party official. He noted that the official was leading quite a wealthy lifestyle, despite the famine conditions prevalent among the general populace:

His relative's house was western style with four bedrooms, a living room, a bathroom, two toilet rooms with flush toilets, and there were two watch dogs and a guard dog and a guard post outside the house. The house was furnished with a Yamaha-brand piano, a large-size color TV, a VCR, and audio components which were all the latest Japanese models purchased through Macao. His relative said that they were receiving supplies from the state according to "the degree of loyalty to the Party." Also the dishes at their table were abundant (fish, meat, cakes, etc.). The Party official also boasted of an Omega wristwatch and French suits which his comrade presented him.[51]

Having a core group status, however, does not necessarily mean that one is particularly well-off. For example, three North Korean professors from Pyongyang's prestigious Kim Il Sung University recently visited St. Paul, Minnesota. Their hosts brought them to the Shila Restaurant, one of St. Paul's finest Korean dining establishments. Though the menu was written in Korean, none of the three professors had any idea of what the meat was. One actually licked out his noodle bowl and commented, "This is the first time I have had noodles in about three years." These men showed clear signs of starvation.[52]

A look at North Korea's food distribution system provides additional insight into the restaurant scene described above. North Korea is a socialist country that is supposed to supply the people's daily necessities. However, real life is quite different than the nice-sounding utopian theories of communism and socialism. Distribution of necessities and commodities is based upon class, not upon equality. Senior Party officials are entitled to a daily ration of meat, cooking oil, fruits, vegetables, and cigarettes. Central Party members, high government officials, and high-ranking military officers are entitled to a weekly ration. Other core/elite group members are entitled to a ration every other week. A typical ration includes about six kilograms of meat, eight kilograms of fish, 30 eggs, and 30 cartons of cigarettes. The bulk of the population that is in the "unstable/wavering" class or "hostile/suspect" class receives a ration of rice and/or grain once every two weeks.

The quantity of rations also varies based upon one's social status, occupation, and age. Soldiers receive 600 grams, ordinary workers 450 grams, high school students 400 grams, dependents 300 grams, and the elderly and those under three years of age receive 120 grams. Under such conditions, if one eats three meals per day, the twice monthly ration would be expended in less than a week. Thus, in order to make the food last longer, common people subsist on a diet of porridge. And when the erratic food distribution fails, the already undernourished North Koreans starve.

Given these wretched conditions throughout North Korea,

only core group members are allowed to live in Pyongyang—at least the utopian Pyongyang that foreigners are allowed to see. With few exceptions, only those who look youthful or strong are allowed in the capital city. The old, feeble, and handicapped are weeded out of the Pyongyang populace on a regular basis. This policy is a reflection of the late Kim Il Sung's fetish for youth and may also be part of an Asian anarchist tradition. This is why visitors to North Korea see the same kinds of people when they visit Pyongyang.

Also, private bicycles are prohibited in Pyongyang. Movement by road within the city is always tightly controlled. Buildings are unmarked. Thus, there is no way to determine the purpose of a particular government building, since there are no names, addresses, or symbols to identify it. This atmosphere of extreme anonymity and cloistered privacy extends inside the doors, as well. One eyewitness reported:

> It is all anonymous, it is all private. If you go into one office building room and want to go across the aisle to another passageway or room, you will be blocked by police. You are told as a worker just how you go to work and how you come back, and what hours. There is just no wandering around, no independent travel. Also there are no independent conversations; you do not just go over to somebody's place and chat. Women complain about this a great deal; they can't talk about their children, about their feelings, about anything at all. This is a quotation from a woman: "No one ever visits other homes for talks or the like, because he or she is exhausted after work, and moreover, there is never any time to do so."[53]

The next 45% of North Korea's populace are designated as the "wavering" or "unstable" group. These people are considered to be of questionable loyalty in times of emergency. Members of the "unstable" group are generally specialists, ordinary workers, peasants, desk workers, nurses, and schoolteachers throughout the provinces. "Unstable" people are not allowed to travel to the capital city without special permission. However, an Egyptian journalist and others have reported that there is a slum area in the "model city" of Pyongyang where members of the unstable group live in shanties. These people are the servants who dust the streets, remove the snow, and serve as maids and menial labor. Generally, both the husband and wife must work. The unstable group has very limited access to education, travel, health care, maternity, and other benefits within the DPRK's socialist society.

The unstable group is composed of the masses of North Koreans who have not been fortunate enough to be designated in the core group or unfortunate enough to become part of the "hostile/suspect" group. The people who belong to the unstable group generally do not have any family history of "religionist" activity. When the food supply permits, members of the unstable group have access to the state food distribution system. However, food supplies have been intermittent or non-existent since May 1997. Thus, the unstable group is left, for the most part, to subsist for itself.

"Unstable class" people are always considered to be under the strict surveillance of the Political Security Bureau. One of the ways this surveillance is efficiently accomplished is to keep most of the general populace busy in a never-ending series of meetings. These meetings include project planning meetings, political study meetings, or neighborhood meetings. A vital part of these meetings is to always pressure "unstable people" to show their loyalty to Kim Jong Il, the Party, and Juche ideology.

The bottom group of the caste system is the "suspect" or "hostile" group. "Hostile class" members include former land owners, people of means, westernized intelligentsia, those who cooperated with the Japanese authorities in the past, and descendants of political leaders and relatives who fled to the South. "Hostile" people have no rights. This segment of society is never mentioned in the press and is seldom seen by foreign visitors. They are the drone-like slave laborers of North Korea who generally are assigned dangerous or hard work. People are assigned to the "hostile class" because they or a relative has shown a tendency to oppose, show disloyalty, or otherwise complain about the government. Whole families along with future generations are designated as "hostile" because of the actions of one family member.

The North Korean concept of "family" allows the family to be disgraced for the sins of the father or one family member. This cultural view is radically different from the biblical view: "Fathers shall not be put to death for their children, nor children put to death for their fathers; each is to die for his own sin" (Deuteronomy 24:16). Those individuals and families who are labeled members of the hostile group are under strict political surveillance around the clock. They live in constant fear of real or false accusations against them. For these reasons, the average North Korean citizen is extremely reluctant to carry on any heart-to-heart conversation with someone else, much less a foreigner. In this way, the totalitarian system uses family loyalty—the fear of one person bringing down the entire family—to keep the masses in line. Even the perception of "counterrevolutionary activity" by one could result in the entire family being designated as "subhumans" and sent to a concentration camp.

One of the things that is remarkable—almost unfathomable —to someone outside the North Korean system is how the almost entirely homogeneous Korean people could develop such a caste system. Moreover, the prevalent designation of the roughly 200,000 members of North Korea's concentration camp as "subhumans" further boggles one's mind. Revelations of the existence of both the Juche caste system and the concentration camps represent a shameful embarrassment to Pyongyang. Meanwhile, Pyongyang's regime continues to advertise North Korea as paradise on earth with a perfect classless society.

How could castes have been created under the Juche religious system? Part of the reason is that the North Korean society has largely been sold on the limited Juche view of eternity. This lack of belief in an individual hereafter and a "surveillance-morality" engenders a "live for today" materialistic view of existence. If the extreme opulence of the Su-ryong's lifestyle is any indication, then the Juche worldview, when carried to the extreme, results in hyper-materialism. Loyalty to the Party is valued along with possessions, status, and power. Apart from loyalty, possessions, status, and power, the individual is devalued. In this sense, the only difference between a faithful concentration camp guard and many an inmate may be that one is outside the gate while the other is inside.

International human rights organizations such as Amnesty International and Freedom House maintain that the world's worst human rights violations are being committed in North Korea. The people there live under the strictest controls imaginable. For example, travel certificates are required in advance if one wants to take even a short trip to an adjacent county or province. The Korean Worker's Party maintains tight control over "freedoms" of assembly, speech, and residence. This fear-based system continues to be perpetuated by the unswerving loyalty of the core group whose "faithful revolutionaries" are immensely loyal to their Great Leader Kim Il Sung and Dear Leader Kim Jong Il. With the perpetuation of the Juche religious caste system, individual freedoms and human rights will continue to be whatever Pyongyang desires.

The Juche caste system continues to reign in North Korea—a land that has no laws or regulations designed to protect human rights. Even if such laws did exist, the re-designation of people who are labeled political criminals as "subhuman emigrants" takes them out of the "human" category from the Juche viewpoint. Instead of a society governed by laws, North Korea is run by a system where all instructions come down from the Party. These instructions are considered more important than laws. Those who dare offend the Party will be labeled political criminals, and be sent to the concentration camps.

Concentration Camps

Bastards who escape must be run to the ground and killed one by one. The Honorable Leader's prestige and foreign influence can be hurt more by an escape than by any other thing. So bastards who escape must be killed without mercy.[54]

KIM JONG IL

In the Juche People's Republic there is no such a thing as an internment camp for political criminals.[55]

NORTH KOREAN OFFICIAL

Concentration camps are a byproduct of the Juche religious system, which permits human beings to be arbitrarily classified as non-humans. For the 26-year-period between 1972 and 1998 alone, the Headquarters of the Movement for Improving Human Rights in North Korea estimates that about 400,000 inmates have died in North Korean concentration camps. The total number of concentration camp deaths may be much higher, and continues to rise each day the Juche totalitarian regime remains in power. The high death toll is attributed to the bitterest living environment, forced labor as a means of punishment, frequent arbitrary executions, a large amount of medical experimentation by doctors practicing surgery techniques on otherwise healthy inmates, and serious malnutrition.

Over the five last decades of the 20th century, independent eyewitness accounts confirm both the existence and the gruesome details of North Korea's concentration camps. According to a North Korean document seized by the U.S. during the Korean War (1950–1953), North Korea established its first concentration camps in 1947 to incarcerate various "criminals." By 1958, when North Korea conducted a large-scale political purge, Kim Il Sung's regime began to detain political opponents in the concentration camps. Two decades have passed since Ali Lameda first wrote a book about North Korea's concentration camps entitled *A Personal Account of the Experience of a Prisoner of Conscience in the DPRK* (London: Amnesty International, 1979). This "Lameda Report" covered concentration camp conditions during the 1960s and 1970s. Larry Diamond, co-editor of the *Journal of Democracy*, wrote a 16-page article on concentration camps based on interviews with four North Korean defectors. His "Diamond Report" roughly covers conditions during the 1970s through 1990s. Other former concentration camp inmates and guards have defected and recorded graphic testimony of the ongoing atrocities in these camps. One such defector, former guard An Myong Chol, wrote *Political Prisoners' Camps in North Korea* (Seoul: Center for the Advancement of North Korean Human Rights, 1995). Thus, the best efforts of the North Korean dictators to keep their death camps a secret have failed.

Inside the camps, the conditions are subhuman. Marriages are forbidden, while pregnant women are forced to have abortions as soon as they enter the camps. Guards who are caught raping "subhuman emigrant" inmates are reprimanded, but the inmate victim is killed. If the guard is not caught and a woman becomes pregnant, she is taken out into a field where rocks are piled on her abdomen, and unspeakable tortures are committed before she is finally put to death. Inmates suffer from hard labor for 12 hours a day, and eventually they die from starvation and malnutrition.

North Korea's Ministry of State Security (MSS), or State Security Agency (SSA), wields absolute power within the society without any interference from other government organizations. The Seventh Bureau of the MSS (equivalent to the Gestapo) operates North Korea's death camps where Koreans are imprisoned, designated "subhuman emigrants," tortured, and ultimately killed. Table 9-9 lists directives for camp guards and the MSS regarding treatment of inmates.

The MSS's Third Bureau are human butchers who perform medical experiments on inmates which are every bit as gruesome as those crimes done by the Nazis against the Jews. North Korean

TABLE 9-9. Directives for Camp Guards and the Ministry of State Security (MSS)[56]

NO.	DIRECTIVE
1	The inmates are bloodsuckers who have abused our comrades in the past. They are corpulent, heinous enemies. They are inveterate enemies of the people, and traitors to the state.
2	You must never regard them as human. If you treat them with empathy, you will be treated as an inmate yourself.
3	If you err and kill an inmate, or if you kill an inmate in an accident, we will not hold you responsible. Your authority is unlimited, and you may do as you want.
4	If you capture an inmate with a bad attitude, we will commend you officially. If you capture an escapee, we will open the door to your future.
5	If South Korean Special Warfare Command (SWC) troops parachute into your area, you must form a strong guerrilla front. You must train without any stops to prepare to defend against the SWC.
6	If you allow inmates to make contact with ordinary citizens, you will injure the prestige of the Honorable Leader. You must shoot without exception any inmate who approaches the perimeter fence.
7	Be always alert against the possibility that a spy may sneak into your area. Be ready to detect him.
8	You absolutely must never talk to an inmate, and you must maintain security at all times. When your term of service ends you must continue to maintain security. If you do not, you will become an inmate.

interns are sent to the camps to practice complex surgical procedures on healthy adult and child inmates at so-called "Ideological Indoctrination Areas." For example, every military medical officer is required to conduct at least 50 "experiments" on living people. Thousands of needless amputations, abdominal, heart, spinal, bone, eye, and every sort of imaginable surgical procedures are performed each year on otherwise healthy North Korean concentration camp inmates. North Korean surgeons use the Juche designation of inmates as subhuman to rationalize this ongoing butchery. Once a doctor gains sufficient experience in performing such things as eye surgery, brain surgery, heart surgery, bone surgery, and amputations, he can get a better job at a big city hospital —possibly even in Pyongyang. One such doctor was recently praised in a North Korean magazine for performing his 7,000th brain

**TABLE 9-10. Kim Il Sung's and Kim Jong Il's
Directives on Political Prisoners[57]**

DICTATOR	DIRECTIVES
Kim Il Sung	— We must make class enemies taste clearly the dictatorship of the proletariat.
	— Factional elements are stumbling blocks to our revolution, and the revolution must single them out for eradication.
	— Factionalism produces class enemies who must be annihilated again and again, without fail.
	— Weeds must be eradicated in their season, destroyed to the roots.
	— Exploitative elements and factional elements in the past got fat by sucking the sweat and blood of our people. We must annihilate these elements without regard for their situation today, and push ahead with no further thought of them.
	— I understand class enemies in our Administrative Centers (internment camps) often riot and revolt. We must station Army troops there to see they do not do that again (delivered in 1968).
	— We must commend highly military members of the Camp Guard Force who apprehend escapees, and we must strengthen ideological indoctrination among them so they are hostile toward factional elements.
	— MSS personnel in charge of class enemies must not be induced to feel the slightest humanity or empathy for them. They must execute their control duties always with revolutionary awareness. They must clearly reveal to these class enemies just what constitutes the dictatorship of the proletariat.
Kim Jong Il	— Bastards who escape must be run to the ground and killed one by one. The Honorable Leader's prestige and foreign influence can be hurt more by an escape than by any other thing. So bastards who escape must be killed without mercy.
	— You comrades (MSS and camp guards) must be perfect in your control and your surveillance so that you do not let a single bastard escape, for that would cause the Honorable Leader to worry.
	— The 7th Bureau of the MSS does not exist for production. It exists to deal violently with class struggle. You must strengthen your uncompromising struggle against class enemies and factional elements.

TABLE 9-10. *(continued)*

DICTATOR	DIRECTIVES
Kim Jong Il *(continued)*	– Personnel of the MSS Farm Guidance Bureau (7th Bureau) and the Camp Guard Force must take pride in the fact that they stand on the forward outpost line of our class. They must bring joy to the Honorable Leader by conducting camp control activities without blemish and by preventing any of the emigrants (political prisoners) from escaping.

surgery. The article neglected to mention how many of his patients were death camp inmates. North Korea denies these camps exist.

The concentration camps system grew significantly between 1967 and 1970 as Pyongyang instituted the Juche caste system. This system was implemented through a nationwide ideological surveillance campaign, under the name "Citizens Re-registration Project." In this project, everyone was classified into one of three categories: the core (elite) group, the unstable (wavering) group, or the hostile (suspect) group. Armed with these new classifications, Kim Il Sung issued the notorious "Cabinet Decision No. 149." This decision ordered the summary execution of 6,000 people and detention in concentration camps of another 70,000 people from 15,000 families. About half of these 70,000 people were eventually sent to the "Special Dictatorship Target Areas." These "target areas" were a Juche euphemism for extermination camps.

One of North Korea's more internationally renowned early inmates was French Communist Jacques Sedillot. During the early 1960s, at the request of the North Korean government, Sedillot asked 300 French intellectuals to comment on some of North Korea's propaganda. Their non-receptive responses included questions such as, "How can we believe that Kim Il Sung became leader of a Communist Party at the age of 14 and then actually defeated Japanese troops as leader of a revolutionary army?" In May 1964, Sedillot returned to North Korea to report his findings. Shortly after his return to Pyongyang, Sedillot was arrested, sentenced to a twenty-year prison term, and thrown into a concentration camp. In 1975, due to an international campaign for clemency, Sedillot was released. However, he died in a Pyongyang hospital in January 1976. This tenacious devotee to the international Communist movement had escaped arrest orders by both Spain's Franco and the Soviet Union's Stalin—only to be finished

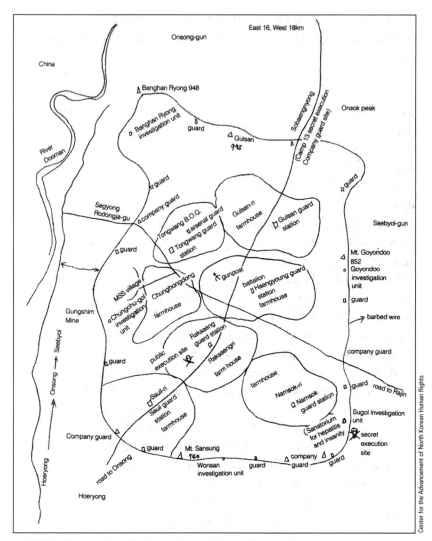

MSS 7th Bureau (Farm Guidance Bureau) Camp 22 drawn by a guard who defected.

off by North Korea's Kim Il Sung.

Following the Sixth Party Congress in 1980, the concentration camps again grew in size. At this Congress, Kim Jong Il was designated the heir apparent and sole successor to Kim Il Sung. This declaration was shortly followed by a major nationwide campaign to deify Kim Jong Il as a Juche god. In the course of carrying out this new propaganda campaign, Kim Il Sung sent about another 15,000 political opponents to the concentration death camps.

Once again in the 1990s the number of inmates in these camps sharply increased. This time, the cause was the tightening of political surveillance over the people. "Political suspects" were arrested at work, at home, and at all hours of the day and night without arrest warrants or advance notice. They were secretly taken away to concentration camps, often with family members. Kim Il Sung instituted this new slaughter because he feared that, if he acted otherwise, his regime might collapse like those in the former Soviet Union and East European countries.

Currently North Korea incarcerates approximately 200,000 prisoners in 12 concentration camps in the areas of Kaechon and Yodok in the South Hamgyong Province, and Hoeryong and Chongjin in the North Hamgyong Province. U.S. Department of State estimates, which report the number of prisoners to be between 105,000 and 150,000, are slightly more conservative. The North Korean authorities officially call these camps "Management Centers" with numbers before the name. In true Adolf Eichmann style, these camps are also referred to by such names as "Places of Exile" and "Districts for New Settlers." "Maximum Security Area" (concentration camp) "emigrants" (inmates) are slave laborers.

The following account of a former concentration camp inmate, defector Sun Ok Lee, gives an example of the special persecution given to Christians at North Korean concentration camps. From 1987 to 1992, Soon was imprisoned at the Kae-Chun Rehabilitation Center in Pyong An Nam-do Province. During her time as a prisoner, she witnessed the execution of numerous Christians. The following is her eyewitness account:

I have seen the execution of Christians at least

How many of this neurosurgeon's 7,000 brain operations were performed on healthy concentration camp inmates?

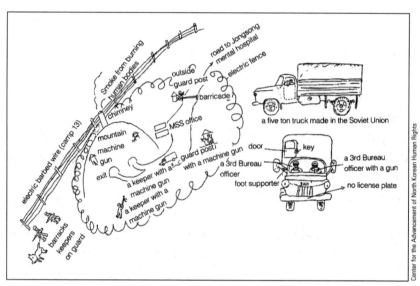

An MSS 3rd Bureau Station in Hwasong, North Hamgyong Province.

once a month. At the rehabilitation center, prisoners were given one day of rest each month. However, instead of allowing rest, the warden always used this time for political and "religious" propaganda of Juche Ideology, which is the worship designed by Kim Il Sung. The first target groups for this rehabilitation were always the Christians in the camp. At our center, there were about 6,000 prisoners, with at least 30 to 40 Christians at any given time. Prison officers brought out these Christians and made them sit face-down on the ground, circled by other prisoners. Then they were asked to deny their belief in heaven and God in heaven. They were told that if they said they did not believe in Jesus or God in heaven, then they would have better treatment in the prison. I did not know about their belief in heaven, or that a God in heaven refers to the Christian faith until I came to South Korea. While I was in prison these years, I did not see a single Christian deny his faith. When these Christians were silent, the officer became furious and started to kick the Christians' stomach, back, face, and any place where it really hurt. Some Christians died.

Many Christians were killed by the death squad, which was made up of young men in their early twenties who were brutal. I could not describe their cruelty well enough. These executioners did not work regularly, but came only for the executions. On the day of the execution, they would usually take a drug to cause them to act like some hungry animal. The executions were conducted in public, and all prisoners were called to observe them. After the bloody executions, all prisoners were made to go around the dead body to say a word of hate to the dead victim and to remind themselves to live with the Communist Party's propaganda. This event created fear among prisoners and much trembling. They could not sleep for many nights.

At the time, I could not understand why these Christians risked their lives when they could have said, "I do not believe," and accept what the officer insisted. I even saw some who sang music as the kicking and hitting intensified. The officers would call the singers "crazy" and take them to the electric treatment room. I saw none come out alive. When they sang these songs, I thought they were really crazy until I escaped to South Korea and heard hymns in church. I never knew what these prisoners were singing until I became a Christian.

Because inmates were forbidden to talk in the rehabilitation center, I never had a chance to talk to a Christian. However, I now remember hearing "Amen."

Christians who came to the Kae-Chun Rehabilitation Center were treated differently, and were often assigned to do the most difficult tasks in the camp. The women had to clean up human excrement. The men worked in front of the furnace used for casting iron where temperatures exceed 1,000° C.

One day I witnessed the killing of Christians with molten iron poured out of a furnace. On that day, eight Christian prisoners were forced to lie on the ground face-down. Officers accused them and punished them unreasonably. The officers became angry and poured hot iron from the furnace on them. I was so shocked watching that I could not believe it. The smell of burning was terrible, yet as they died the Christians were quiet and peaceful...[58]

How is it possible for North Koreans to rationalize these ongoing atrocities against their fellow countrymen and others? As in the case of North Korea's caste system, the basis for North Korea's concentration camps also lies in Juche religious ideology. Juche ideology, like Marxism-Leninism, attracts converts by much idealistic anthropocentric talk—drawing from the Christian concept of the rights and dignity of man. Yet nothing in the Communist philosophy sets forth any such basis for man to have dignity or

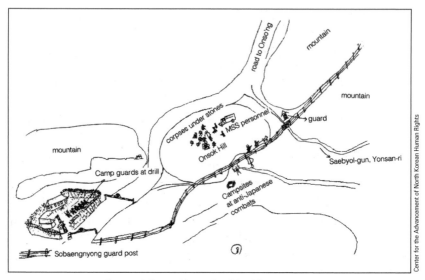

Camp 13 Secret Execution Site "Onsok Peak."

rights. Indeed, every place in history where Communists have come to power they have oppressed people and stripped any meaning from the concept of majority rule through the imposition of totalitarian rule. Thus, under North Korea's Juche system, it is quite easy to arbitrarily designate any number of men, women, and children as subhuman. Juche's designation of concentration camp inmates as non-humans sounds like an Asian rendition of Hitler's mandate to the Nazis that "it is not a crime to exterminate them [the Jews], since they do not belong to humanity at all."[59]

In his May 1991 monograph, North Korea's Dr. Pak Song Duk explains more specifically how, under the Juche religion, individuals may be designated as subhuman.

> To a man, socio-political integrity is more valuable than his physical life. It is his life and soul.
>
> To a man, the private life related to his physical life is indispensable and is also important. But this private life should be subordinated to the socio-political life and one's physical life must serve as a biological means for him to exalt his socio-political integrity.
>
> A man who has been deserted by his community because he has betrayed it and impeded social progress cannot acquire socio-political integrity. *Such a man, though he remains alive, is virtually dead* as a social man. When a man lives only to main-

tain his physical life without socio-political integrity, *he is no better than an animal* that is a slave to physical desire.[60]

Thus, under Juche ideology, when the Party decides that an individual "impedes social progress," he may be deemed not to have any socio-political integrity, consigned to a concentration camp as a subhuman, and treated "no better than an animal." The only reason that most of the "subhuman" inmate "animals" are not killed outright is so the maximum amount of work may be squeezed out of them before they die of starvation or are tortured and executed.[61]

Enforcing Juche in All Areas of Society

The successful application of the Juche idea has changed all domains of society beyong all recognition.

LAND OF MORNING CALM
NORTH KOREAN VIDEOTAPE[62]

Promotion of the Juche culture includes enforcing Juche in all areas of society. Any criticism of socialist ideology in North Korea's one-Party system has been taboo since North Korea's founding. Even wives and husbands never exchange opinions about political matters. Despite what their "Socialist Constitution" says, the people are not allowed the freedom of religion, residence, travel, education, and occupation. During the day, the populace is shackled by Kim Jung Il's so-called "10 Principles for Solidifying the Party's Monolithic Ideological System." By night, the State Security Agency (SSA, the secret police) rules the people with a tight surveillance network.

Though defection is rising, it is extremely difficult within the police state. In October 1996, Kim Jong Il strengthened the border security by organizing a Border Guard Brigade. He also ordered the guards to shoot or arrest those who would attempt to cross the border in search of freedom and food. Guards bring back unsuccessful escapees to North Korean cities with shackles on their feet, and then execute them before the public.

In addition to the almost complete isolation of North Koreans from foreigners, another of the most significant aspects of social enforcement is the relentless emphasis on self-sacrifice and hard work. The population is told that everything can be accomplished through dedication and the proper revolutionary spirit.

"Arduous struggle" terminology is commonplace. This view is evident in the perennial "speed battles" initiated by the leadership to dramatically increase productivity. Another example was the phenomenally bizarre "drink no soup" movement. This idea was apparently designed to improve efficiency by keeping workers on the factory floor rather than going to the lavatory. Still another Juche self-sacrifice idea was to encourage workers to cut back to two meals per day in light of the nationwide food crisis. Other reports out of North Korea depict starving people eating roots. This practice, in part, probably is based on the "arduous struggle" myths of revolutionary guerrillas living in secret bases on Mt. Paektu by subsisting on roots. Thus, from a Juche viewpoint, subsistence on tree roots is a testimony to the zeal of the masses in the ever-victorious arduous Juche revolutionary struggle.

Propaganda

Even if you read foreign literature, your spirit should be your country's.[63]

KIM JONG IL

Thanks to the special state benefits, people live long. The working people have no worries about food, clothing or housing; and enjoy a long life and health thanks to the free medical service.

LAND OF MORNING CALM
NORTH KOREAN VIDEOTAPE[64]

Officially, the North Korean Constitution gives political power to the people. However, real political power belongs to the Korean Workers' Party (KWP). Though the Constitution guarantees such rights as freedom of the press, religion, and speech, North Koreans have extremely little freedom in these areas. For example, all radio and television broadcasts are officially administered under the auspices of the Korean Central Broadcast Committee. However, in reality, these broadcasts are tightly controlled by the KWP. The content of all radio broadcasts is subject to the rigid instructions of the KWP's "Propaganda and Agitation" and "Unification Front" departments. Short-wave radios are banned to prevent North Koreans from hearing information from the outside. All other radios sold in the country are preset to government frequencies.

Radio dials are inspected by State security officials every three months. Should an inspection reveal a broken seal, the owner will be punished as an "ideological offender," since he will be considered to have received foreign radio broadcasts. Only the radios of diplomats are exempted from this extreme censorship. Current news is altered and often withheld from the public. Most North Koreans do not learn of news events until weeks, months, or even years after they have occurred. Loudspeakers that are located in most communal and work areas broadcast a steady stream of propaganda from government radio stations.

Television is under similar State controls. It is illegal to tune into either South Korean or Chinese television stations in the southern and northern provinces near the borders. Interior provinces are not required to have fixed TV channels since the absence of TV satellite dishes means that foreign broadcasts cannot reach these areas. In addition, since television sets in rural areas are quite rare, people have to watch TV in groups.

The main function of these media broadcasts is to conduct a cradle-to-grave process of brainwashing the masses in Juche ideology and indoctination into the "Three Revolution Movement" (ideological, technological, and cultural) as "Juche-oriented revolutionaries." The masses are told that they are "revolutionary weapons" destined to communize the south. News, truth, speed, and even accuracy of information are unimportant by comparison. Accidents and disasters are seldom reported, since such reports would run counter to North Korea's self-proclaimed utopia or could tarnish Kim Jong Il's pristine domestic image. Instead, propaganda focuses on praising Kim Jong Il, the KWP, and Juche ideology. North Korea's totalitarian media control and propaganda are so rigid that few North Koreans outside of a few diplomats and high government officials know much at all about the outside world. What little news the North Korean populace does have tends to be extremely distorted.

People in North Korea receive their information from one or more of the state's propaganda organs. These organs include the *Korean Central News Agency*, the only state news agency; *Rodong Sinmun*, the organ of the KWP; *Choson Inmingun*, the organ of the Korean People's Army (KPA); *Minju Choson*, the organ of the government; *Youth Vanguard*, the organ of the Kim Il Sung Socialist Youth League; *Kulloja*, the monthly magazine of the KWP; and *Kuguk Jonson*, an organ of the National Democratic Front of South Korea (NDFSK).[65]

Another example of the state-controlled media is the *Democratic People's Republic of Korea* (*DPRK*) magazine. *DPRK* is the *Life* magazine of North Korea. Like many European magazines since World War II, *DPRK*'s design and format give every appearance of having been directly patterned after Nazi Germany's *Signal* wartime picture magazine. Like *Signal, DPRK* magazine is more than a social document—it is North Korea's view of itself. A comparison between Nazi Germany's *Signal* magazine and North Korea's *DPRK* magazine is provided in Table 9-11.

To what extent the people of North Korea realize they are being helped is also a big question. Pyongyang insists that rice aid from South Korea and Japan be shipped in unmarked bags. They expressed considerable alarm that a shipment of South Korean noodles arrived in commercially marked boxes. While North Korea has taken the difficult step of admitting its internal problems to the international community, and the North has told the outside world about the flood damage, Pyongyang has not told its own people how bad their situation is—or even that they are seeking help. Any such announcement would run counter to Juche ideology. For example, a 1995 North Korean news report claimed that nationwide floods caused no casualties, and that no one was suffering from shortages of food, clothing, or shelter. Instead, the North Korean announcer proclaimed, "People are ever more cheerful and filled with faith and optimism."[67] A similar propaganda article declared the same Party line:

> Korean socialism centering on the masses of the people
> …has fully met its aspiration and demand. The whole country is seething with enthusiasm to live and work in a revolutionary way…The true looks of Korean socialism is that the leading position and role of the working class are firmly ensured in all aspects of social life, that its spirit and morality, working style and culture prevail in the whole society, and that the [Juche] revolutionary principle of the working class has been strictly adhered to in all aspects of social life…Korean socialism enjoys unquestioned support and trust from all the people [*Rodong Sinmun*].

German reunification presented a propaganda dilemma for North Korea because North Korea had adopted the East German model of management of internal political affairs since Germany was a divided country like Korea. The propaganda solution was to

TABLE 9-11. Comparison of Nazi Germany's *Signal* Magazine and North Korea's *DPRK* Magazine

SIGNAL MAGAZINE[66]	*DPRK* MAGAZINE [*DPRK*]
Signal was meant…to show…the excellent conditions of life in Germany, and the power and might of the German armed forces.	*DPRK* is meant to show the excellent conditions of life in North Korea under Juche, and the power and might of the North Korean armed forces.
[*Signal's*] treatment of action photographs and its collection of color on the war and the homefront in the Third Reich are incomparable.	*DPRK*'s treatment of action photographs is incomparably excellent.
[*Signal*] encouraged Occupied Europe to believe that Anglo-American Liberation would be more cruel and barbarous than life under the Swastika.	*DPRK* encourages North Koreans to believe that any overthrow of Pyongyang's regime would be more cruel and barbarous than life under Juche.
Defeats were hardly ever mentioned [in *Signal*], and then only much after the fact in an optimistic context as temporary setbacks.	Famine, floods and hardship are hardly ever mentioned in *DPRK*, and then only in the optimistic context as a temporary arduous struggle on the path to national reunification under Juche.
[Late in World War II, *Signal*] began to stress the heroism of the soldiers on the front who fought on in spite of all difficulties.	*DPRK* articles stress national reunification and the heroism of anti-imperialist revolutionaries who fight on against all odds in spite of all difficulties.
Domestic devastation by bombing, the anti-Semitic (anti-Jew) holocaust, and the anti-Slavic deportation policies and atrocities in Eastern Europe were never mentioned in *Signal*.	Domestic devastation by flooding, the rising rate of crime, anti-Christian atrocities and North Korea's dozen or so concentration camps are never mentioned in *DPRK*.
As the victories slowed to a halt and reverses were suffered, *Signal* devoted itself to more and more gossip about film stars in the Reich, sporting events, theater and fashion.	In the midst of a floundering economy, floods, droughts and tidal waves, *DPRK* devotes much of its space to gossip about film stars, sporting events, theater and fashion.
According to *Signal*, there were no problems in Nazi Germany.	According to *DPRK*, there are no problems in North Korea under Juche.
Signal, like all good propaganda, is a subtle mixture of truth and fiction.	*DPRK*, like all good propaganda, is a subtle mixture of truth and fiction.

remain silent on East Germany's abandonment of 40 years of socialism for West German–style capitalism. Instead, propaganda shifted its focus to China and Cuba.

Disinformation in North Korea's media leads people to believe that natural disasters occur only in capitalist countries. For example, the main Party bulletin, *Rodong Sinmun*, consists of six pages. The first four pages are devoted to stories worshipping Kim Il Sung and Kim Jong Il. Page five presents fearsome images about "hell on earth" in South Korea. The sixth page presents selected and distorted international news. International news articles portray all the people of the world as studying Juche Thought, a world in awe of North Korea's utopian system, international representatives flocking to Pyongyang to pay homage to the great statue of Kim Il Sung, and capitalism and "imperialists" tottering on the brink of collapse around the world. Most TV evening news broadcasters simply read Party-approved news straight out of *Rodong Sinmun*.

Pyongyang resorts to other extreme measures in its penchant to promote the utopia myth. Foreigners who visit Pyongyang are generally restricted to one of a few variants of a standard "Magic Kingdom" tour, complete with actors playing the roles of churchgoers, hospital staff and patients, and model workers. As part of one of these tours, New York Congressman Stephen J. Solarz and his party were taken to visit the famous hospital that is shown to all VIPs. Solarz reported:

> This hospital is primarily a showcase; many of the patients and doctors are actors and actresses, including the children. You see them not only there, but you see them later on agricultural farms, you see them in industry, you see them marching—you see the same people. We talked to some of the actresses ourselves. Very few people are allowed to use this hospital. Some of its medical equipment is highly technical, from Sweden, West Germany, East Germany, and other countries. But in checking with Swedish sources, I discovered the companies do not send any of their manuals for adjusting the medical equipment. There are no storage areas for a lot of the film and other X-ray tapes. Also, there are no proper electrical outlets. A friend of mine who went to North Korea recently took a picture of one of these machines and then got behind it and showed that it was not even plugged in. It is one of my favorite pictures. The real hospital for the elite

is a secret, private hospital for [Kim Jong Il] and those around him, which has never been publicly exposed.[68]

Pyongyang is presented as the model city, but it most definitely is not. To call it a model city would imply that it should be used throughout Korea as a pattern for other cities. Instead, one informed observer described Pyongyang is less complimentary terms:

> Pyongyang…is basically an arbitrary private city of Kim Il Sung's own creation. It is an expression of his own ego, his own cult views, his fetish against dirt, his fetish for cleanliness. Truck traffic is not allowed during the day, all cars and trucks must be washed before they come through the city gates. All marketing goes on at night. And the residents are checked frequently to see if they are dirty or if they have lice…Until very recently a single road lane in Pyongyang was reserved for [the dictator's] car. There is one subway car that is reserved for him.[69]

Pyongyang's portrayal of North Korea as the ultimate utopian state is one of the greatest hoaxes that continues to be perpetrated through Juche religious propaganda. From the 1960s onward, the North Korean government has used propaganda to teach the people that "North Korea is a paradise on earth." Pyongyang's more recent indoctrination campaigns continue to retain the slogan "North Korea is a paradise on earth" while adding new catch phrases such as "Juche Ideology," "Socialist Paradise," and "Our Human-Centered Socialism." Meanwhile, their paradise-on-earth system has miserably failed to meet the demands of the masses for food and other daily necessities.

North Koreans are told, despite their starvation and poverty, that their Juche socialist utopian system must be protected at all costs. For example, one 1998 propaganda bulletin declared:

> *The anthropocentric socialism built in Korea is the most ideal society of democracy wanted by progressive humankind…*General Secretary Kim Jong Il has worked hard day and night to give full play to the vitality of socialism. By giving on-the-spot guidance to factories, farms, construction sites and units of the people's army without even a day's rest he has brought about a great advance in political, economic, military and all other fields. He is the future of a reunified Korea [*KCNA*].

Another example of the ongoing propagation of the utopia

myth occurred on February 16, 1998. That day, Kim Jong Il's 56th birthday was celebrated by a state-sponsored rally at Pyongyang's Indoor Stadium. Over 10,000 youths and schoolchildren performed in a mass gymnastics show to glorify the dictator-god. Among the exhibition's themes glorifying Kim Jong Il was "Creator of Happiness Who is Building the Paradise of Juche."

North Korea is not unique in its aim to achieve a man-centered utopia. Francis Schaeffer noted:

> Communists speak about "socialism" and "communism," maintaining that socialism is only a temporary stage, with a utopian communism ahead. Over a half century has passed and not only have they not achieved the goal of "communism" anywhere, they have not even come to a free socialism. The "temporary dictatorship of the proletariat" has proven, wherever the Communists have had power, to be in reality a dictatorship by a small elite—and not temporary but permanent. No place with a communistic base has produced freedom of the kind brought forth under the Reformation in northern Europe.[70]

Given that North Korea's well-oiled propaganda machine is a vital element to sustaining the Juche religion, there is no reason to believe North Korea will "change its tune" apart from a radical change in its god-king religious-political system. Instead, North Korea's leader attempts to sustain the status quo with slogans such as "Let us push ahead with the forced march for the final victory!" *Rodong Sinmun* and *Choson Inmingun* (Korean People's Army) 1998 New Year's editorials proclaimed the DPRK's resolve to stay steady on their current course:

> *[North] Korea will firmly maintain the anti-imperialist, independent stand,* invariably pursue the external policy of independence, peace and friendship and make active efforts to bring earlier the victory in the cause of global independence and socialism, *come what may*... [*Rodong Sinmun, Choson Inmingun*].

Pyongyang's leaders know that apart from effective propaganda and maintaining a continuing clamp on communications with the outside world, their claims of success would rapidly be proven false at the onset of any peaceful reunification process with the South. Thus, propaganda and disinformation remain critical to sustaining the Juche religion, while peaceful reunification is not even a viable option.

Fear, Drugs, Terrorism, Counterfeiting, and Sabotage

The heart is deceitful above all things, and desperately wicked: who can know it?

JEREMIAH 17:9 (NKJ)

It should not come as a great surprise that the man-centered Juche religion uses unrighteous means to sustain itself. According to multiple sources, Kim Jong Il has personally directed torture and murder at home and terrorist activities abroad. Pyongyang continues to promote the culture of Juche through propaganda, fear, drug dealing, terrorism, counterfeiting U.S. dollars, and sabotage. Terrorist activities have included the October 9, 1983, bombing deaths of 18 visiting South Korean officials, including Deputy Prime Minister So Sokchun, during a failed attempt to assassinate South Korean President Chun Doo Hwan in Yanggon, Myanmar (formerly Rangoon, Burma). In November 1987, a North Korean agent blew up a Korea civil airliner over the Bay of Bengal, killing all 104 passengers and 11 crew members.[71] A year later, in December 1988, North Korean agent Kim Hyon Hui admitted that she planted the bomb on KAL 858 on orders directly from Kim Jong Il.

North Korean Communists also have an over-fifty-year track record of counterfeiting U.S. currency. In 1946, the first Korean Communist Party–sponsored counterfeiting operation was uncovered and broken up in what is now South Korea. As of November 1998, Seoul's Agency for National Security Planning conservatively estimates that the DPRK produces $15 million of bogus U.S. currency per year.

North Korea also abducts foreigners from time to time. Sometimes these abductions are due to a direct order from Kim Jong Il. North Korea has kidnapped men and women from Hong Kong, Macao, Sweden, France, Italy, the Netherlands, and Japan. These state-sponsored kidnappings are generally ordered for one of three reasons. First, Pyongyang uses foreign abductees to teach their native language and customs to espionage agents and terrorists. Second, Pyongyang's intelligence agencies attempt to obtain valid foreign passports with the real personal data of foreigners. Third, North Korean agents have abducted people to eliminate witnesses to their espionage activities. In one bizarre case, Kim Jong Il ordered his agents to abduct a South Korean movie couple, director Shin Sangok and actress Choi Eunhee, because he wanted their help in making North Korean movies. The pair later escaped via the U.S. embassy in Wien, Austria, after eight years under North Korea's yoke. All told, South Korea's Research Institute on National Unification estimates that, between 1955 and 1996, 3,739 South Korean citizens have been kidnapped by the North, with 442 still remaining in DPRK custody.

North Korea's state-sponsored drug trade and drug smuggling are particularly big business. Despite another poor harvest of food crops in 1997, North Korea had a robust opium crop. It quickly harvested the opium and shipped it to the Russian mob. Opium remains an important export for North Korea so that they can obtain hard foreign currency. There are also other indications that the North Korean government sponsors international drug trafficking on a large scale. For example, the *East Asian Review* reported on February 16, 1998:

> North Korean Ambassador to Mexico, Kim Chang-Shik, was deported by the Mexican government in connection with recent cocaine smuggling involving two North Korean diplomats residing in Mexico...[The] two North Korean diplomats, who smuggled 35 kg of cocaine out of Mexico, were caught by the Russian police on January 17 at the Moscow airport.[72]

On February 18, Kim Dong-Su, a former member of the North Korean mission to the U.N. FAO in Rome, who defected to Seoul twelve days earlier, reported:

> North Korean diplomats, dogged by their Stalinist country's economic woes, often engage in narcotics trafficking and other illegal transactions of goods to earn foreign currency.[73]

Public executions are another example of the continuing Juche reign of terror. Such executions have been confirmed by various international human rights organizations. Even Hwang Jang Yop's remarks mentioned one such execution. Nevertheless, the North Korean authorities continue to deny that these executions occur. So far at least 23 executions have been confirmed through testimonies by defectors from North Korea. Many defectors have personally witnessed and independently confirm how these public executions are conducted. North Korean authorities continue to use executions as a means to ensure that the masses remain under their complete control.

Murderers, rapists, and those who steal grain are executed in public. For example, during 1995 and 1996, over 300 North Koreans were executed by their government for non-Juche black market activity. Also, those who are found guilty of having criticized Kim Il Sung or Kim Jong Il face the same fate. These executions are decided after summary trials. At these "trials," local Public Security Ministry officials (police officers) serve as judge, jury, prosecutor, and attorneys. No lawyers are ever present, and the outcomes of such courts are a foregone conclusion.

Local authorities inform the residents in the area of the verdict through public notices, such as bulletins posted on walls. These bulletins list the contents of the criminal charges, along with the time and place of the executions. The executions are held in open areas before thousands of onlookers. According to defectors, executions in Hamhung were usually held at an open space under a bridge in Shimpo District, in Shinuiju and Chongjin at open spaces by the riverside, in Wonsan on a playground, and in Pyongyang on open spaces near Mt. Obong and Sama-dong.

> Victims are gagged before being shot or hanged in public. In this way, they cannot utter any words, particularly curses against Kim Il Sung or Kim Jong Il. Once their eyes have been covered and their hands tied up, they are ceremoniously executed by four or five public security officials.[74]

The most serious crime in North Korea, however, is that of dishonoring the Great Leader Kim Il Sung, or the Dear Leader Kim Jong Il. Kim Man Chul, a 46-year-old medical doctor who defected aboard a 50-ton boat with his 11-member family, tells the story of the unfortunate fate of his younger brother:

> In the Spring of 1975, my younger brother, Kim Dong Chul, a graduate from Pyongyang Art College, was invited by the Workers' Party to paint a huge portrait of Kim Il Sung. The cause of his misfortune was the fact that he sat his rear end on the "Great Leader's" face. Because the portrait was so huge, it was almost inevitable for my brother to do what he did. However, a Party official who saw this was less than sympathetic and severely criticized him, saying, "To sit on the noble countenance of the Great Leader is an affront to his dignity." From that day on we never heard a word from him again. The secret police simply dragged him away and probably executed him.[75]

North Korea, of course, denies any accusations of human rights abuses or terrorism. For example, on January 6, 1998, the *Korean Central News Agency* announced:

> Worse still, the U.S. is raising the DPRK's abandonment of "terrorism" as a prerequisite to the total lifting of sanctions. *We have nothing to do with terrorism and have long been opposed to any terrorist act.* The U.S. demand for the DPRK's abandonment of "terrorism" means that it would not totally lift the sanctions [KCNA].

Similarly, the DPRK officially rejected the U.S. Department of State's 1998 *Annual Report on Human Rights.* Detailed reports of human rights abuses were attributed to the U.S.'s alleged intention to subvert North Korea's Juche socialist state as part of an overall plan to take over the world.

> The spokesman for the Foreign Ministry of the Democratic People's Republic of Korea (DPRK) commented on the "annual report on human rights" the U.S. State Department made public on Jan. 30...abusing the DPRK groundlessly. The U.S. attempt to force the DPRK to "change the system" and put pressure on it under the pretext of the non-existent "human rights problem" is as foolish and reckless...The spokesman said: It is foolish of the United States, which is unable to mind its own business, to act a "judge of human rights."...The report was motivated by the U.S. never-to-be-attained intention to put the world under its control by interfering in other nations' internal affairs willfully and forcing the "American-style view of value" on them. *The Korean socialism, based on the Juche idea and centered on the masses of the people, is the best social system in the world which fully ensures the masses' rights on the highest level.* The American conception of human rights never works on the DPRK. The U.S. intention to pressurize the DPRK with "human rights problem" is only a daydream. The more loudly the U.S. talks about the DPRK's "human rights problem," the more strongly the Korean people are determined to always defend their genuine socialist system [*KCNA*].

Instead, the North Korea's paper, *Rodong Sinmun*, proclaimed how the utopian North Korea defends human rights whereas imperialist states abuse them:

> Human rights are most ruthlessly violated in imperialist states. It is absurd for them to poke their nose in the internal

affairs of other countries over "human rights issue" and act as a "judge of human rights." Genuine human rights can be guaranteed only in a society whose masters are the popular masses. *The government of the Democratic People's Republic of Korea provides all the members of society with political freedom and right, rights to work, rest, receiving education and medical care and all other rights of social human beings.* That is why the Korean people treasure socialism with the belief that it is a genuine society for the people where a worthwhile and dignified life is guaranteed. Never should it be allowed in international relations that one forces one's own concept of human rights upon other countries or uses it for a sinister political aim [*Rodong Sinmun*].

Minju Choson, the propaganda paper of the government, issued a similar stating:

> Defense of human rights in the capitalist society where all the policies of the state are shaped on the basis of the will and interests of the exploiting class is a camouflage to deceive the working people and cover up the reactionary nature of the bourgeois dictatorship and the anti-social essence of the capitalist system [*Minju Choson*].

The preceding examples show how DPRK propaganda continues to reflect classic key elements of Marxist ideology. Marx taught that every means possible must be used to seek to destroy the "exploiting class." Meanwhile, a mythical class of working people called the "proletariat" would inevitably emerge to establish a utopian society. The problem is that the "proletariat" class never emerges under communism. Instead, wherever communism goes, totalitarian dictators reign and enslave the people. North Korea's Juche system is no exception.

Jeremy J. Stone, as he testified before the U.S. Senate, compared the life under Juche to life in the Oceania of George Orwell's *1984*. During his extensive testimony before the U.S. Senate Subcommittee on East Asian and Pacific Affairs Committee on Foreign Relations, Stone said:

> Among the features in the DPRK in common with Orwell's *1984*, there are "speed-up" campaigns for labor, rewriting of history, completely arbitrary arrests, disappearances, and imprisonment, intense criticism sessions, hate campaigns, many true believers in impossible beliefs and, above all, complete control over contacts with foreigners. Even high officials of

the Government, armored with family relationships with Kim Il Sung and Kim Jong Il, must act with extreme caution in expressing their views internally and, especially, in dealing with foreigners.[76]

Orwell's novel depicted the pervading fear associated with every aspect of life under such a system:

> The thing that he was about to do was to open a diary. This was not illegal (nothing was illegal, since there were no longer any laws), but if detected it was reasonably certain that it would be punished by death, or at least by twenty-five years in a forced labor camp.[77]

Such fear grips North Korea in much the same way. For example, housewives suffer throughout North Korea. Anything they might say to a neighbor could be held against them, their husband, or their children. The impact of this fear is to isolate people from each other within families and within neighborhoods. For example, consider the findings of a visitor who interviewed residents in various apartment buildings:

> Do you know the birth date of any of your neighbors? Do you know where your neighbors have come from? Do you ever sit down and talk with them? Have you ever been in their rooms? The answers are usually no, no, no, no, no. It is a very quick interview.[78]

A former DPRK local official's account provides additional information about why people are so fearful to speak openly:

> According to a DPRK local official now living in the United States, a scientist had his home bugged through his radio set. One day when he came upon some rotten apples among the family's rations, he became angry and said that all the high-ranking cadres take the fresh apples and give the rotten apples to the lower ranks. He then exclaimed: "Kim Il Sung is a son of a bitch." For this comment, the scientist was reportedly executed in 1986. The former local official knows the details of this case because they had been fellow prisoners. A high-ranking DPRK intelligence officer who defected stated that he decided to defect once he found a bugging device in his Mercedes 250.[79]

Under this oppressive regime, any expression of complaints meets with immediate and radical reprisals. The following examples of such reprisals were disclosed by members of the Chongryon (North Korea's General Assembly of Korean Residents in Japan) who visited North Korea in the mid 1980s:

- An incident occurred on April 13, 1983, in which a time bomb was placed in a men's rest room on the 16th floor of the main building of Kim Il Sung University in Pyongyang, together with a leaflet which read, "Down with the Kim Il Sung Dynasty!" This incident was a real shock to the North Korean authorities because it happened only two days before Kim Il Sung's birthday (April 15), and over 140 university students were rounded up and interrogated because of that incident.

- An incendiary incident occurred on October 20, 1983, at an automobile repair shop belonging to the Wonsan Public Security office (police) when a car under repair was set on fire. At that time, the Pyongyang authorities falsely reported that it was an act committed by a South Korean spy. Later it turned out to be a retaliatory act committed by discontented workers belonging to an automobile transportation service center in Wonsan city as an expression of their discontentment against the police officers' overbearing behavior. The offenders were arrested and shot to death without any court trial.

- On February 15, 1984, one day before Kim Jong Il's birthday, some students of Kim Il Sung University who were discontented with the policy of deifying Kim Il Sung and his son, Kim Jong Il, had a framed photograph of Kim Jong Il girdled with black-colored stripes and left it hanging at a waiting hall in Pyongyang Station. At that time seven students of Kim Il Sung University, who came to Pyongyang Station to send off their senior, a University graduate, who was on his way to a new assignment in a rural area, were rounded up by the police; thereafter, all of them and their family members were not heard of.

- On April 10, 1984, there occurred an incident in which someone destroyed the head portion of a Kim Il Sung plaster bust which was placed in the Research Room for Revolutionary History in Haeju Teachers' University. This incident caused the demotion and transfer to other areas of all the faculty staff beginning with the rector. Especially, the ethics professor (in charge of Kim Il Sung thought) underwent ideological screening and was forced to move to another place.[80]

A radical top-down change is required to reverse the Orwellian societal expectations. Without such a change, all loyal North Koreans must continue to live in a constant frenzy of hatred of domestic and foreign enemies, real or imagined. Meanwhile, Kim Jong Il remains firmly in control to lead them in their "arduous struggle" and self-abasement before the totalitarian power and wisdom of the Party and Su-ryong.

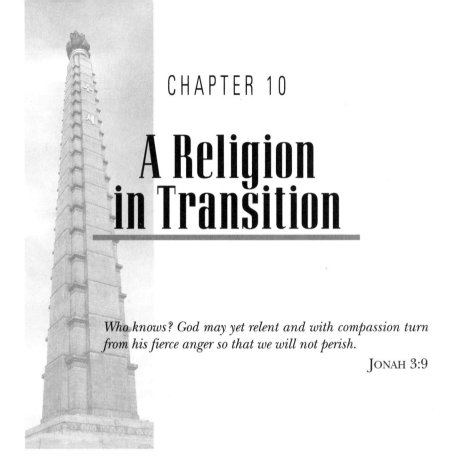

CHAPTER 10

A Religion in Transition

Who knows? God may yet relent and with compassion turn from his fierce anger so that we will not perish.

JONAH 3:9

A s far as world religions go, the Juche religion is quite young. As with the first fifty years of other religions such as Judaism, Christianity, and Islam, Juche is a religion in transition. Like these other religions, Juche now has its own calendar. With the 1990s have come new Juche teachings about "Red Flag ideology," the smooth accession of Kim Jong Il to deity upon the death of Kim Il Sung, and an increasing emphasis on exporting Juche abroad.

The Juche Era Calendar

The use of the Juche era meets the cherished desire of the Korean nation and reflects their ardent worship for President Kim Il Sung, their desire for his immortality and their determination to exalt the history of the leader, the sun, for all ages, holding him in high esteem for all ages.

RODONG SINMUN
SEPTEMBER 12, 1997

A landmark event happened on September 9, 1997. Just in case you missed it, on that date the "Juche Era calendar" was officially instituted. Actually, two months earlier, on July 8, 1997, the Korean propaganda organs already had declared that the Juche Era calendar had begun on the third anniversary of the death of Kim Il Sung. The same declaration also instituted Kim Il Sung's April 15 birthday as the Taeyang-jeol (Solar Day). Evidently the rest of the world did not seem to take notice. So, propaganda publicists did a better job the second time around to advertise the September 9 declaration of the new era. For example, one article proclaimed:

> The whole country was yesterday in deep emotion and joy at this great national event which records the Juche era with 1912 when the respected President Kim Il Sung was born as the sun of humankind, as the first year. The Korean people courteously printed the first Juche era on telegrams, documents and information addressed to Secretary Kim Jong Il, with deep gratitude, unfailing loyalty and devotion to him who ensured the continuation of President Kim Il Sung's history. On Tuesday national news agency and radios started broadcasting with Juche era and capital and local press organs published newspapers on which the Juche era was printed. All transport is operated according to this era. People began to use it in communications and other daily routine. In maternity hospitals across the country babies were given the date of birth with the Juche era [KCNA].

The implementation of the Juche calendar is another important example of the progressive development of the Juche cult religion. Juche's calendar follows the pattern of the Jewish, Christian, and Muslim religions, which each have their own calendar "year zeroes." The Juche Era calendar resets the clock of mankind to synchronize the year zero with the year of Kim Il Sung's birth—1912. That makes the year 1997 to be Juche 86, 1998 to be Juche 87, and so on.

The Juche calendar is a solid indication that Juche is really a religion. Use of Juche chronology, as explained in the September 1, 1997, article, "Juche Era that will shine forever in history of Kim Il Sung's nation," is specifically intended to enshrine the immortality of Kim Il Sung in the collective consciousness of the North Korean people. The following North Korean propaganda excerpts illustrate the basic motivation of Pyongyang to institute the calendar as an act of worship:

> The *use of the Juche era* meets the cherished desire of the Korean nation and *reflects their ardent worship for President Kim Il Sung,* their desire for his immortality and their determination to exalt the history of the leader, the sun, for all ages, holding him in high esteem for all ages. *The Juche era is a symbol of the eternal harmony of the Korean people with the President.* With its institution, our nation and humankind can always live in Kim Il Sung's era, in the history of the sun. *It is an immortal milestone symbolic of the immortality of the era of Juche* created by the President [*Rodong Sinmun*].

Subtle yet significant shifts in terminology can be detected as one studies North Korea propaganda. Accompanying the introduction of the Juche Era, one such almost imperceptible shift occurred. The term "great leader" was used in conjunction with Kim Jong Il:

> The Juche Era is valuable wealth and an everlasting era for the Korean people. It is everlasting because it symbolizes a new era of history, the Juche Era pioneered by President Kim Il Sung under the banner of the Juche idea. It is also...definitely guaranteed by *another great leader, Secretary Kim Jong Il,* who is successfully carrying forward the traditions of Juche. Remaining true and devoted to the ideas and leadership of Secretary *Kim Jong Il is essential for ensuring the eternity of the Juche Era*...Without his leadership, the Juche Era and its eternal viability are unthinkable [*KCNA*].

Until 1997, the term "Great Leader" was reserved exclusively for Kim Il Sung, while "Dear Leader" designated the son. The term "another great leader" shows that, under the Juche religious system, Kim Jong Il is considered to be just as much "god" as his father.

The announcement that supernatural phenomena had occurred heightened the religious sense about the significance of the introduction of the Juche calendar. No, the flooding, droughts, and endemic famine had not miraculously ceased. However, some strange apricot flowers came into bloom next to the Kaesong environmental management building near the demarcation zone.

> Upon hearing the news, a large number of working people in Kaesong rushed to the spot on the morning of September

9, Juche 86 (1997), and were amazed to see the flowers in full bloom. They said that it seemed the flowers commemorated the significant day when the use of the Juche era has begun, praying for the immortality of President Kim Il Sung with deep reverence for him [*KCNA*].

As if the introduction of the Juche calendar and the "mysterious phenomena" throughout North Korea were not enough, Pyongyang also decided to do its very best to institute the calendar throughout the world. Pyongyang launched an unprecedented mass media blitz to announce the year Juche 86 (1997) and the Day of Sun (Kim Il Sung's April 15 birthday). On September 18, 1997, the Congolese Socialist Party led the international community's parade to endorse the new Juche Era. The Russian Communist Party followed suit on September 19, followed by the Romanian-Korean Friendship Association on September 26. In addition, over 60 nations such as Algeria, Bangladesh, Cambodia, Cuba, Egypt, Jordan, Laos, Libya, Mali, Mongolia, Nepal, Pakistan, Peru, and Tanzania commemorated the event. The international fanfare included seminars on works and reminiscences of President Kim Il Sung, celebration meetings, lectures, films, gifts, photo exhibitions, and honorary citizenship in other nations for Kim Jong Il.

However, closer to Pyongyang, the "illegitimate regime of the south" was not as fast to catch the Juche Era vision. Thus, Pyongyang had to initiate a radio and leaflet campaign to comfort the people in the south by telling them that "the institution of the Day of Sun and the Juche Era…is the greatest auspicious event that enables the history of President Kim Il Sung, the great sun of the nation, to be everlasting and the Juche revolutionary cause started by him to be exalted in the world."

On October 8, Juche 86 (1997), the Workers' Party of Korea Central Committee and Central Military Commission issued a lengthy joint declaration that summed up the significance of the new era. This declaration, entitled "Juche Era and Sun's Day, the symbols of the age of independence," stated:

> Under comrade Kim Jong Il's leadership, our Party members and people have cherished the firm faith and will to venerate the great comrade Kim Il Sung as the eternal leader of our Party and people and as the Sun of Juche for all ages, arm themselves…for the completion of the Juche revolution,

and led the Party, the army and the people to rise up under the banner of self-reliance, overcome the economic blockade of imperialists and repeated natural disasters and...win the final victory without fail, overcoming all trials and hardships. *And our country will be reunified at no distant date and the 70 million fellow countrymen will enjoy genuine freedom and prosperity in the homeland of Juche* [*KCNA*].

Red Flag Ideology

Our red flag represents the idea and will of the General to accomplish the Korean revolution.

RODONG SINMUN
SEPTEMBER 30, 1997

In the 1830s and 1840s, a wave of national revolutions swept across Europe influencing many European nations (such as Italy, Germany, and Romania) to adopt tricolored flags. During the Paris riots of January 15, 1831, the red flag made its first modern appearance as the universal symbol of international revolution. This red flag represented a radical simplification over the various tricolored revolutionary flags. In 1849, as Karl Marx systematized Communist ideology, the red flag replaced the black flag of anarchy as the favored flag of the Communist revolution.

Kim Jong Il first used the term "Red Flag ideology" in his November 1, 1994, thesis, "Socialism Is Science" published in *Rodong Sinmun.* His essay explained the term by saying that "this phrase is an expression that my ideology is red." The next year, *Rodong Sinmun* began using the term as an official catch phrase during the commemoration of the 25th anniversary of the founding of the Korean Communist Youth League. For example, an August 28, 1995, article was entitled "Let us hoist high the Red Flag." Another red-flag article that followed was "The Workers' Party is the Party of the Great Leader Comrade Kim Il Sung" (October 2, 1995).

A partial explanation of "Red Flag Ideology" was presented in the January 9, 1996, issue of *Rodong Sinmun,* the propaganda organ of the Korean Workers' Party. In a commentary entitled "The Red Flag Philosophy Is an Expression of the Revolutionary Spirit Based on Juche Ideology," the paper declared that Juche and Red Flag ideology were closely interrelated. Since then, joint editorials of three major newspapers on the first days of 1996 and 1997 called upon the people to abide by the "Red Flag Ideology." Red-flag essays that followed included "On Adherence to Self-Reliance and Nationalism in the Revolution and Construction" (June 19, 1997) and "Let Us Carry Out Completely the Task of Achieving the Reunification of the Fatherland as Instructed by Great Leader Comrade Kim Il Sung" (August 4, 1997).

Like Juche ideology, the "Red Flag Ideology" also calls upon the people to embrace the spirit of self-reliance, the revolutionary struggle and spirit, and to become "bullets" and "human bombs" to protect the Leader. The following 1997 propaganda article demonstrates the "human bombs" connection with "Red Flag Ideology" while notably omitting the term Juche:

> To *defend the red flag is, in essence, a sacred struggle to safeguard the leader.* Secretary Kim Jong Il is the top brain and great standard-bearer of the Korean revolution who is leading the Korean revolution to victory, upholding the red flag.
>
> *Our red flag represents the idea and will of the General to accomplish the Korean revolution* as intended by President Kim Il Sung and his indomitable stamina to defend socialism without wavering under any circumstances. The Korean people are determined to become an impregnable fortress and shield to safeguard the General at the cost of their lives. Their firm determination is to share their destiny with the General forever, upholding him as the supreme leader of the Party and the revolution.
>
> *Holding this red flag, our people are defending the idea of the leader* most purely with resolute revolutionary principles and uncompromising struggle they are most resolutely safeguarding the safety of the leader in the spirit of human bombs and they are highly exalting the absolute *authority of the leader* through their devoted struggle. *If we are to defend the red flag of the revolution, the banner of defending the leader, we should have absolute worship for and unshakable faith in the leader* and follow him with a noble sense of conscience and obligation.
>
> Even if we die while resolutely safeguarding the General, it is glory. It is the unbreakable faith of the Korean people to become an impregnable fortress to safeguard the General at the cost of their lives and deal telling blows to the enemy. No matter how the world may change, they will defend the headquarters of the revolution headed by the General and thus glorify their honor as revolutionaries [*Rodong Sinmun*].

Since then, a new "spirit of the Red Flag" emphasis has emerged in addition to continuing "Red Flag" propaganda. For example, the following 1998 propaganda article presents a sense of the revolutionary meaning of "the spirit of the Red Flag":

> *The spirit of the Red Flag that mirrors the traits of the three generals of Mt. Paektu serves as the banner of the struggle of the true communists. The Red Flag spirit of Mt. Paektu means that one should carry out one's revolutionary task by oneself no matter how difficult it is,* the article says, and goes on: The spirit serves as the driving force with which the Korean people live and fight as the vanguard fighters in defending the leader at the risk of their lives, as the banner of the indomitable spirit under which they rise again even though they fall hundreds of times and as the banner of independence under which they push ahead with the revolution and construction their own way with firm belief in their own efforts. Our society has great potentials as the integral whole of the singlehearted loyalty and filial piety to the leader. It is the noble traits of *the Korean people who inherited the Red Flag spirit of Mt. Paektu to devotedly safeguard the headquarters of the revolution headed by General Kim Jong Il* as the seventh regiment of the Korean People's Army did during the anti-Japanese war. It is the unshakable will of the Korean people to build their country into a powerful one of Juche in the same indomitable spirit that was displayed by the People's Army members in the thick forests of Mt. Paektu. The indomitable spirit of the Korean people is the source of strength for preserving the Juche character and the national character in the teeth of the campaign the imperialists have intensified as never before to isolate and stifle them, as well as the mean acts of renegades of all hues, and *for demonstrating the might of Kim Il Sung's Korea all over the world.* As long as they have the Red Flag spirit of Mt. Paektu, the Korean people will remain as a dignified independent people and Korea as a powerful country independent in politics, self-supporting in the economy and self-reliant in national defense forever [*Rodong Sinmun*].

The recent emphasis on "Red Flag" ideology in North Korea is an indication that Kim Jong Il is attempting to restore the ideological purity of the universal Communist revolution to the Juche religion. The use of "Red Flag" ideology in the context of self-sacrificially returning to basic Communist roots was also reflected in propaganda that accompanied Kim Jong Il's 56th birthday on February 16, 1998.

> Youths and students in Pyongyang met at Kim Il Sung Stadium on Feb. 15 to celebrate the 56th birthday of General Secretary Kim Jong Il. Pak Song Chol,...Vice President of the DPRK,...said that General Secretary Kim Jong Il's birth on Mt. Paektu, the revolutionary sacred mountain, was a great national event which opened a bright future of the Juche revolutionary cause and *prophesied* a brilliant prospect of the homeland. General Kim Jong Il has wisely guided the work of the youth league in every period and every stage of the developing revolution to put the movement of the Korean youths *on a higher stage*, they said. They called upon the youth league organizations, their officials and members to discharge the honorable mission of the youth vanguard of the Workers' Party of Korea, reserve unit and detached force of Supreme Commander Kim Jong Il in the forced march of socialism for the final victory with perseverance, uplifting *the red flag of the revolution* under his leadership [*KCNA*].

Similar radical revolutionary references to the Red Flag have occurred in association with the memory of Kim Il Sung's mother. For example, the 1998 North Korean documentary film, *Gun Reports By the Mother Will Be Everlasting*, depicts Kim Jong Suk taking "a gun of revolution before the sacred Red Flag," to inspire the Korean people to defend Kim Jong Il "at the risk of their lives" [*KCNA*].

Unlike the West, where *red* takes on the connotation of danger, aggression, or warning, the color red in East Asian cultures is viewed in a very positive light. Kim Jong Il has harnessed this cultural symbolism through this new ideology. It is important to remember that, under the Juche system, a new "ideology" is by definition a new divinely inspired religious doctrine. As the following excerpt suggests, Red Flag Ideology is also linked to the new Juche Era concept:

> The Juche era instituted by Secretary Kim Jong Il, representing loyalty of the people and the request of history, is associated with his noble determination to exalt the history of the sun for all ages, holding the president in high esteem as the eternal leader. It *is also associated with the General's idea of the Red Flag* to accomplish the Juche revolutionary cause in any storm and stress no matter how the situation may change [*KCNA*].

Thousands of students wave red flags in unison at a Korean Worker's Party rally.

But how is this new Red Flag concept changing the Juche religious system that has ruled over the North Korean people for decades? Just as Juche took a major philosophical turn away from Marxism-Leninism, Kim Jong Il's recent introduction of "Red Flag Ideology" represents the introduction of a new super-zealot face of Juche for the "Juche Era" of the 21st century. This radical shift may be intended to counter what Kim Jong Il perceives as the threat of growing outside influence on North Korea. With only partial information in hand, Red Flag ideology seems well on its way to keeping the collective consciousness of the "Kim-country" masses focused on Juche purity.

The Problem of Accession

The crisis North Korea is facing is not a "transient crisis"
as North Koreans claim it to be, but a "structured crisis"
derived from its political and social system.[1]

KOH YU HWAN
PROFESSOR OF POLITICAL SCIENCE
DONGKUK UNIVERSITY, SEOUL

Kim Jong Il's 1994 accession to rule North Korea posed more of a Juche theological problem than a political one for Pyongyang. While foreign political theorists wrung their hands worrying about whether Pyongyang's regime would fall apart, the architects of Juche had been hard at work solidifying the ideology, theology, and terminology to be used in Juche-speak. The father-to-son succession of power has been a foregone conclusion since the 1970s. However, the Juche religion where Kim Il Sung was god had to be modified to allow for Kim Jong Il's eventual reign. The introduction of the theory of the Su-ryong in the 1980s was part of this theological preparation for eventual succession.

Upon Kim Il Sung's death on July 8, 1994, Kim Jong Il inherited a shattered economy, widespread famine, and the possibility of a general collapse of the Juche totalitarian system. Kim Jong Il's response was to declare a three-year period of mourning for Kim Il Sung, blame all domestic problems on national disasters and an economic embargo by "imperialists," and suspend any and all substantial reforms.

Pyongyang took immediate action to make it absolutely clear that Kim Jong Il was continuing the major policies of his father. The July 9 nationwide radio broadcast that formally announced the dictator's death also announced that Kim Jong Il would implement a threefold course of action. First, Kim Jong Il would continue to pursue, to its perfection, the great revolutionary task of "Juche," generation after generation, as launched by Kim Il Sung. Second, Kim Jong Il would carry on North Korea's "Socialism Our Way" as initiated by Kim Il Sung. Third, Kim Jong Il would continue to pursue a unification achieved on terms laid down by Kim Il Sung in the context of his "three principles for unification" and "ten-point program on a grand national unity." Eleven days later, Kim Young-Nam's memorial speech reaffirmed that Kim Jong Il's regime would continue to be guided by these policies of the past.

Nevertheless, the death of Kim Il Sung in July 1994 came as a cataclysmic shock to the average North Korean. Their god was dead! With floods of genuine emotion and grief, millions of North Koreans mourned the death of the Great Leader. In the days that followed, Kim Jong Il smoothly assumed leadership under the pretext that "the revolutionary task must be carried out in succession to Kim Il Sung." With the Su-ryong justification for the feudalistic father-to-son succession of power, Pyongyang proceeded to

Flowers surround the body of Kim Il Sung as it lies in state (1994).

accelerate the ongoing deification of Kim Jong Il no less ardently than it had for Kim Il Sung.

One hypothesis surrounding Kim Il Sung's death was that he was quietly assassinated to make room for Kim Jong Il:

> Was the Great Leader himself having second thoughts before he died? A few signs suggest it—and some South Korean journalists and intelligence sources did not hesitate to wonder whether Kim Sr.'s death might have been given a helping hand as a result. While no proof of this exists, what is known is that Kim Il Sung emerged from a semi-retirement of sorts earlier this year and adopted a stronger public role, not long after the nuclear dispute with the U.S. and other countries began sharpening. At the same time, some North Korean officials had asked Chinese physicians for advice on diagnosis of a peculiar brain injury—a wound that insiders said Kim Jong Il had suffered in a car crash last September. The fact that the Dear Leader appeared in public and in seemingly fine condition soon afterward hinted at a possible face-saving attempt to sideline him from duty.[2]

While such "conspiracy theories" make for exciting plots in popular motion pictures and novels, the assassination of Kim Il Sung would have been quite unlikely. In fact, the chronology of the Great

Comrade Kim Jong Il, Supreme Commander of the Korean People's Army, is present at the ceremony for bidding the last farewell to the President.

Leader's regime shows that he had a long record of purging anyone who had even the slightest notion of posing a threat. In any event, Hwang Jang Yop most likely would have both known about and told the world of any such assassination following his defection in 1997. No such announcement has ever been made.

Another theory, proposed by foreign analysts upon Kim Il Sung's death, was that the younger Kim's authority was on shaky ground. For example, two reports shortly following Kim Il Sung's death reveal the rampant speculation that existed outside of North Korea:

> As of last weekend, however, the Dear Leader had still not sewn up his accession. The fact that the announcement of his father's death was delayed a full day and a half suggested to some outsiders that Kim Jong Il was busy *lining up support behind the scenes.* Several hours after the broadcast, a number of top Establishment figures came out with statements of allegiance to him. Even then, he was not styled President—yet. That formality, assuming it comes, will have to wait for some quasi-coronation ceremonies at high councils of the party and state.[3]

To be fair, Kim Jong Il is *not fully in charge*. Pyongyang's policy paralysis is in part a deadlock between the few impotent reformers and an overweening military, who have much to lose from peace. It would be unwise to ignore the warnings of Hwang Jang Yop, the senior North Korean defector, that the comrades he left behind are seriously contemplating the war option. And if their arsenal really includes nuclear weapons, as he claims, as well as chemical and biological toxins, then the potential is there for Kim Jong Il or some mad marshal to go down in history as the greatest killer of Koreans of all time.[4]

Such analysis revealed a general lack of understanding that, under Juche, Kim Jong Il was already officially invested with the power of the Su-ryong. By early 1992, over two years before his father's death, Kim Jong Il was virtually ruling the country. His true accession to power did not occur at Kim Il Sung's death but in his assumption of the following three major power-swaying posts: First Vice Chairman of the newly-instituted National Defense Commission (May 1990), Supreme Commander of the People's Armed Forces (December 1991), and Grant of the title of "Marshall" (April 1992). For example, a 1992 revision to North Korea's Constitution created the NDC and gave it independent and supreme authority over the military. Article 114 of the revised Constitution states:

> The chairman of the National Defense Commission commands and controls all the armed forces...and guides all armed forces and defense construction projects.[5]

Kim Il Sung seemed to share this view also. An April 15, 1992, interview in the *Washington Times* actually quoted North Korean President Kim Il Sung as saying of his son, "Kim Jong Il is the de facto ruler of North Korea."[6]

Meanwhile, South Korean, Japanese, and Chinese scholars considered nuances of language that were lost in the translation to English. For example, while the *KCNA* used the term "Great Leader" for both Kim Jong Il and Kim Il Sung, the Korean version used "ryongdoja" for Kim Jong Il and "Su-ryong" for Kim Il Sung. Thus, East Asian academics asked among themselves, "When will Kim Jong Il become the Su-ryong?"

Thus, unlike the impression created in the international media following Kim Il Sung's death in July 1994, North Korea did not have a questionable process of power succession as is prevalent in many other nations of the developing world. Accession of "the Dear Leader" under the Pyongyang system was already a Juche religious fait accompli and a political foregone conclusion.

After all the speculation, Kim Il Sung's funeral went off smoothly and Kim Jong Il assumed the reigns of power in a seemingly seamless fashion. Juche's god was dead (but lives on in the collective consciousness), long live the new god! Propaganda surrounding Kim Jong Il's succession consistently conveyed this "hail the new god" understanding of Juche accession:

> Though the great leader Comrade Kim Il Sung passed away, the Korean people under the leadership of the dear leader Comrade Kim Jong Il will surely accomplish the revolutionary cause of Juche started by the respected leader [*DPRK*].

> Comrade Kim Il Sung brilliantly solved the question of leadership succession, making sure the revolutionary cause of Juche would be inherited through generations. It was his most admirable greatness for the future of our revolution. Now dear Comrade Kim Jong Il, the illustrious leader of our Party and people, stands at the forefront of our revolution [*DPRK*].

With Kim Jong Il's unswerving endorsement of the Juche totalitarian system, where he now enjoys god-like status, there is little or no likelihood that he would ever willingly turn from the Juche-oriented socialist system.

On October 8, 1997, after completion of the three-year mourning period, Kim Jong Il finally assumed the post of Party General Secretary. Then the mourning was officially extended for an additional year. Finally, on September 5, 1998, North Korea modified its Constitution by abolishing the post of President, eliminating the Central People's Committee, declaring the deceased Kim Il Sung to be Eternal President, and creating the ceremonial post of chairman of the Supreme People's Assembly's Standing Committee. However, the most important aspect of the revised Constitution was that it elevated the post of chairman of the NDC to be head of state. Thus, with the subsequent colorful fanfare and festivities that marked the September 9, 1998, 50th anniversary of the DPRK, Kim Jong Il was officially in control of all of North Korea's political, military, and economic affairs. However, much of this four-year process amounted to merely "smoke and mirrors," since there was no doubt within North Korea that Kim Jong Il was in charge all along.

Even with the seemingly smooth transition of power to Kim Jong Il following the death of Kim Il Sung, there is still the very valid question of, "How will power pass to Kim Jong Il's successor?"—should another such transition ever occur. One look at the history of the accession of Roman god-man emperors provides a wide variety of possible alternatives. The Juche religion can accommodate whichever of these alternatives is chosen simply by proclaiming to the Party and masses that the new leader has inherited the mantle of the Su-ryong. In the final analysis, the actual mechanism of succession is really not that important from the Juche viewpoint anyhow. This is because North Korea's Juche history is continually under revision to create in the masses the collective mind that the Su-ryong desires.

Is Juche an International Religion?

Today the world people call the 21st century the century of Kim Jong Il, the era of Kim Jong Il...The idea of leader Kim Jong Il is the Juche idea...the eternal guiding idea of humankind...His idea is rapidly disseminated on a worldwide scale, sweeps the era and leads the ideological and mental change of humankind and the change of the world.

KOREAN CENTRAL NEWS AGENCY
DECEMBER 1, 1997

On November 16 and December 16, 1997, the North Korean government twice paid the *New York Times* $68,000 to carry a full-page ad praising Kim Jong Il, the leader of North Korea. These ads, entitled "Kim Jong Il Emerges as the Lodestar for Sailing the 21st Century," declared:

The North Korean leader Kim Jong Il is a man of great leadership, remarkable wisdom and noble virtues. He is always with the popular masses sharing the ups and downs of life with them. Indeed, he is equipped with all the qualities a great leader needs. Kim Jong Il, a new leader of the 21st century, will surely break fresh ground in the political, economic, military and diplomatic fields of Korea, succeeding excellently to the cause of the late President Kim Il Sung [*Korean News Service*].

With millions of their citizens starving to death, why would a nation's leadership $136,000 for ads in a newspaper on the oppo-

Kim Jong Il's full-page ad in the New York Times.

site side of the world? The answer to this question emerges as we consider the international aspect of the Juche religion.

Is Juche an international religion? Most of the analysis, so far, has presented Juche as the national religion of a totalitarian feudal demigod. However, Juche religious teachings have an intrinsic international dimension as well.

One of the key indicators of an international dimension of Juche is the view of North Korea's leader that he is leading the way for the international Communist revolution. Both Karl Marx's *Communist Manifesto* and subsequent history show that communism is expansionist. Marx wrote:

> The Communist disdain to conceal their views and aims. They openly declare that their ends can be attained only by the forcible overthrow of all existing conditions. Let the ruling classes tremble in a Communist revolution. The proletarians have nothing to lose but their chains. *They have a world to win. Working men of all countries, unite!* [7]

Today, Communist leaders still have designs on the entire world. Communist Party meetings consistently call for the conquest of the world and destruction of capitalistic power. Ever since Khrushchev declared, "We will bury you," no Communist leader of any stature has ever repudiated that goal.

Kim Jong Il's book *On the Juche Idea of Our Party* (1985), which is a modern day Communist version of Adolf Hitler's *Mein Kampf* (1925), makes the global intent of Juche ideology crystal clear:

> If the might of…the international communist movement is to be rendered indestructible…The present situation demands that whoever desires the security and peace of humanity should unite, irrespective of political views, religious beliefs and social institutions, and rise up in the fight to thwart US imperialist saber rattling and defend world peace.
>
> To achieve the unity of anti-imperialist, independent forces affords the decisive guarantee for halting and foiling imperialist moves…
>
> The socialist forces and the international communist movement, national-liberation movements, democratic movements, the non-aligned movement and all other progressive and peace-loving forces of the world should form an anti-US united front and *strike together at US imperialism* to prevent it from acting recklessly. All the anti-imperialist, independent forces must fight resolutely to check and frustrate the imperialists' frantic

arms buildup and war preparations, get rid of the US imperialists' military bases in other countries, withdraw US troops and nuclear weapons and other means of mass destruction...

Under the banner of anti-imperialism and independence, the Workers' Party of Korea and the Korean people will firmly unite with the socialist countries, the international working class, the non-aligned nations and all progressive people the world over, actively struggle for *the victory of the Korean revolution and the world revolution* and creditably discharge their national and international duties.

The cause of socialism and communism pioneered by Marx will certainly emerge victorious, and *the ideal society of mankind* where the Chajusong of all peoples are fully realized, will surely come.

As in the past, so also in the future, our Party and our people will struggle dynamically to hasten the brilliant future of communism, holding aloft the revolutionary banner of Marxism-Leninism and *the Juche idea.*[8]

The expansion of Juche's influence serves to promote Communist totalitarianism around the globe—particularly in most non-aligned nations which have little or no tradition of a multiparty representative form of democracy. At the core of Communist totalitarianism lies the idea that the masses must surrender all power to the *state*. This *state* is headed up by a dictator for an indeterminate interim period. Communist ideology promises that the interim period, called "the dictatorship of the proletariat," ultimately culminates in a classless utopian society apart from God. North Korea has incorporated these core Communist beliefs into Juche ideology. For example, Pyongyang's *Dictionary of the [North] Korean Language* defines the "dictatorship of the proletariat" as follows:

> Proletarian dictatorship means state guidance of society during the entire period in which the working class thoroughly suppresses all counter-revolutionary elements and crushes imperialism *on a global scale*.[9]

Juche ideology holds that North Korea now stands at the vanguard of world communism revolution. Moreover, as the following 1997 propaganda article shows, Juche is proclaimed as the key to the "developing nations" throwing off the yoke of capitalist nations.

> The end of the Cold War...has worsened contradictions between capitalist countries and developing nations. It is con-

spicuous that the aggressive and predatory nature and policies of the imperialists remain unchanged and their dominationist ambition has grown. The front of their world military strategy has been moved from Europe to Asia…to destroy the bulwark of socialism in this region. It is their final target to bring the Korean Peninsula under their control and, with it as a military strategic point, establish domination over promising Asia and, furthermore, control the world.

The ever undisguised craftiness and knavishness of the imperialists is characteristic of their aggressive foreign policy after the end of the cold war. Vociferating about "security," "mediation" and "cooperation," they intend to create illusions about imperialism, dull the awakening of the people against imperialism and for independence and competitively interfere in internal affairs of regions and countries and infiltrate into them. They are forcing other nations to accept western-style "prescription," claiming that it is "remedy" and "capital idea." Under the cloak of such a dominationist dogma of a new type as the current of global "integration," they are trying to westernize and monopolarize the world.

What is noteworthy in the international life after the Cold War is that new complicated matters have been raised among nations and regions because economic competition has been intensified as never before with primary attention to the economic affair. The most serious lesson given by the post-Cold War happenings to the world people is that *neither independent development of countries and nations nor global independence can be achieved unless they should preserve the Juche character* and the national character and intensify the struggle against imperialism and dominationism [*Rodong Sinmun*].

Thus, Pyongyang views Juche as essential to successfully promote the universal Communist revolution.

North Korea's advocacy of an anti-imperialist coalition of non-aligned, Arab, Latin American, African, and other nations is nothing more than a modern application of the "Unified Front" strategy adopted by the Third Comintern in June 1921. The "Unified Front" is designed to overthrow the main enemy by forming a coalition of all other forces. This strategy is employed when the Communist revolutionary forces are not regarded as strong enough to achieve the goal alone.

This global outlook continues to be reflected in Juche ideology under Kim Jong Il as the 21st century approaches. Propagan-

da presents Kim Jong Il as personifying Juche, proclaiming him
to be the Savior of mankind and the "sun of the 21st Century."

> Today *the world people call the 21st century the century of Kim
> Jong Il,* the era of Kim Jong Il…This is not a prediction and
> prophecy but a scientific judgment and conviction based on
> the realistic recognition of Kim Jong Il's idea and its revolu-
> tionary role.
>
> The idea of leader Kim Jong Il is the Juche idea. He is the
> great master of the Juche idea who comprehensively en-
> riched the Juche idea and systematized it in an integral way and
> has glorified it as the guiding idea in the era of independence,
> *the eternal guiding idea of humankind* with his extraordinary
> intelligence and energetic ideological and theoretical activities.
>
> *Today the world people absolutely follow his idea and theory…*
> Groups and centers for the study of Kimjongilism were formed
> and are active in many countries of the six continents, which
> is given attention as an expression of the unanimous aspiration
> and will of the progressive humankind to win the final victo-
> ry of human liberation according to the idea and will of the
> leader Kim Jong Il. His idea is rapidly disseminated *on a world-
> wide scale,* sweeps the era and leads the ideological and men-
> tal change of humankind and *the change of the world.*
>
> This means that his idea firmly holds the position of the
> guiding idea that illumines and leads the era and that the
> glorious era of Kim Jong Il, a new era, has already started, in
> which the world is transformed and history advances, guided
> by his idea. The *whole humankind* will, no doubt, sing of free-
> dom and live in happiness in an independent new world freed
> from domination and subjugation, aggression and war, in the
> 21st century when the idea of the leader Kim Jong Il, *the sun
> of the 21st century,* whom history and humankind acclaim, will
> be applied comprehensively and will come into bloom [*KCNA*].

North Korean written materials show that, from a Juche worldview, Korea is the center of the world. To be more specific, Mt.
Paektu is Juche's Mount Zion from which Juche emanates to the
world. The ever-widening concentric circles start with Kim Il Sung
(and now Kim Jong Il) at the center. Next comes the Kim family
followed by the guerrillas who fought with him. Moving outward
from the center of this theological solar system comes the Korean Workers' Party elite, the Party, the masses, and finally outward
to the nations of the world beyond. Pyongyang, of course, is the

Foreign dignitaries look on as President Kim Il Sung cuts the red tape to announce the completion of the West Sea Barrage (1986).

holy city of Juche. This core circle controls everything at the top levels of the regime and moves outward to encompass the masses and serve as the glue holding the system together. As the echelon of workers and peasants is reached, grassroots trust gives way to totalitarian control through a power-based incentive system. To some extent, the family is retained as a model for societal organization. Finally, the outer circle distinguishes Koreans from foreigners. This Juche distinction flows out from both the extraordinary ethnic and linguistic unity of Koreans and Korea's history of exclusionism. As the circle keeps expanding, foreigners are brought under the mantle of Kim and his Juche religion. Selected Third World nations that are thought to be ready for the Juche religion are viewed as being in the inner rings, while other unenlightened nations remain on the fringes.

This international aspect of Juche might explain North Korea's August 31 launch of what they claim was a satellite payload over Japan into orbit via a three-stage Taepo Dong-I missile. Initial Western analysis revealed only a two-stage rocket and no indication of a new functional satellite. Japanese Prime Minister Keizo Obuchi also expressed his doubt that the rocket carried a satellite.

However, subsequent analysis by the National Aeronautics and Space Administration (NASA) indicated the North Koreans may have indeed launched a satellite, albeit a non-functioning one.[10]

If it was a satellite, then what sort of satellite did North Korea attempt to launch, and why? According to the North Korean press, the satellite was launched to transmit "the melody of the immortal revolutionary hymns, 'song of General Kim Il Sung' and 'Song of General Kim Jong Il' and the Morse signals 'Juche Korea'" at a frequency of 27 megahertz. The North Korean Foreign Ministry claimed that the launch of the rocket "manifests the iron will and indomitable spirit of our party, army and people who are working hard for the greater prosperity of the country, pulling through difficulties."[11] The North's leaders timed the rocket launch to coincide with the September 1998 celebration of the 50th anniversary of the founding of North Korea by Kim Il Sung. The accompanying mass celebrations in Pyongyang's May Day Stadium were televised to the world. No doubt, the timing of the launch was also set to occur just two hours before U.S. and North Korean diplomats were scheduled to meet in New York City. These meetings were intended to discuss spy satellite photos revealing renewed North Korean construction of nuclear facilities to the northeast of Pyongyang in violation of the 1994 Geneva Agreement. Yet, North Korea's stated intention that the satellite would broadcast Juche-related media to the world is consistent with their belief that Juche truly is an international religion.

Is Juche an international religion that can be exported? The Palestine Liberation Organization's leader Yasser Arafat thought so:

> During his visit to Korea, the Palestinian President Yasser Arafat said as follows: *"The Juche idea belongs to all fighters for freedom* as well as the Korean people."…What he said then proved that all fighters for freedom aspire after independence, sovereignty and the Juche idea [*DPRK*].

North Korean propaganda is consistent in defining the goals of the revolutionary cause of Juche to be both national reunification and "victory in the cause of global independence."

To what degree has the international emphasis to export Juche to other nations been put into practice? Jeremy Stone's remarks, following a 1991 visit to Pyongyang, help to answer this question:

> In the morning, I began to realize how good North Korea must look to the Third World nations with which Pyongyang

often works. The city was huge, and beautiful, buildings and large monuments to the Great Leader. Socialist realist murals abound in a city that is "spic'n' span." The people are adequately, though not in Western terms fashionably, dressed. Resident Westerners say there is no crime, no malnutrition. There is a 99% literacy rate, life expectancy of 65 years and a per capita income of US $800–1200. To the great leaders of Africa, and even to officials from Latin America and India, Kim Il Sung's [and Kim Jong Il's] approach must seem very appealing.[12]

Thus, Pyongyang serves as the poster city of North Korea's allegedly utopian Juche state. Given this realization, it is little wonder that the North Korean government restricts all foreigners, except for special occasions, to the city limits and to specific revolutionary propaganda attractions.

Even so, there are indications that the representatives of various developing nations know exactly what is going on in North Korea. Yet, these foreign representatives are unwilling to criticize North Korea since many of their home nations also have despotic policies. For example, Choi Sung Chul, editor of *Human Rights in North Korea*, quotes an unnamed Peruvian author who wrote a book praising North Korea as a utopian state:

> They [North Korea] have done incredible things in the economy, it is the only Third World country where everyone has good health, good education, and good housing.[13]

When the Peruvian author was asked what he really thought, Choi states that he replied,

> It is the saddest, most miserable country I've ever been in my whole life. As a poet, it strikes bleakness into my heart.[14]

Nevertheless, international relations between North Korea and other non-aligned nations result in a continuing parade of representatives from Cambodia, Cuba, Libya, Yemen, and a host of other nations who pay homage before the statue of Kim Il Sung and praise Kim Jong Il's "benevolent" despotism.

The Juche teachings, in all seriousness, truly hold that the world looks toward Korea for its future. Indeed, all eyes should be on the eternal (though dead) Kim Il Sung and his "immortal" son Kim Jong Il. This Korea-centric international aspect of the North Korean worldview is perhaps one of the most bizarre, yet highly noticeable, legacies of the Juche religion.

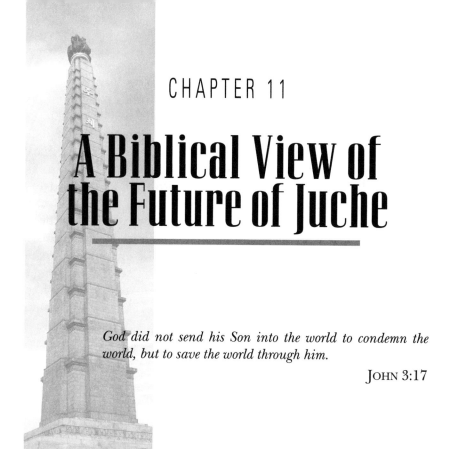

CHAPTER 11

A Biblical View of the Future of Juche

> *God did not send his Son into the world to condemn the world, but to save the world through him.*
>
> JOHN 3:17

A biblical view of North Korea reveals future hope for the country amid an otherwise bleak outlook. Comprehensive passages in the Bible about nations apply to North Korea as well as to other nations of the world. Such passages foretell both judgment and mercy as being in North Korea's future.

North Koreans live in a land where politics and religion have merged through Juche and are in need of both political and spiritual freedom. The Scriptures provide hope, and thus serve as the basis for confident faith that the same God who judged Pharaoh's Egypt will bring the sure promises of His Word to pass in North Korea. For example, the Scriptures repeatedly foretell God's ultimate victory over any and all rulers (including Kim Jong Il) who refuse to acknowledge the reign of the one true God (for example, Psalm 2). Nevertheless, North Korea's government has officially decided against Christianity for the entire nation.

We can see how the evil of communism swept much of the influence of Buddhism, Taoism, ancestor worship, Confucianism, Western imperialism, and even liberal Christian theology out of the

Chinese culture. Without trivializing its horror, throughout the last two millenia of world history, persecution has had the effect of separating the wheat from the chaff—true believers in Jesus Christ from those who are not. Thus, persecution and the preaching of the gospel of a Jesus Christ who is worth dying for have paved the way for the gospel to sweep across China in the greatest wave of evangelism to date in world history. How can a loving God have waited to judge the evil of Juche? God's Word provides the answer. The apostle Peter, who was martyred by the order of the Roman emperor Nero, wrote that the Lord is "patient with you, not wanting anyone to perish, but everyone to come to repentance" (2 Peter 3:9).

This biblical view of the future of Juche takes a final look at whether Juche may properly be considered a religion. Discussion will include how the doctrines of the Juche and Christian religions are diametrically opposed. This biblical view of Juche continues with a comparison of Israel's Mt. Hermon and North Korea's Mt. Paektu. This comparison is followed by a look at the impending downfall of the idolatrous Juche religious system in light of God's inescapable justice, and then presents God's unfathomable mercy toward North Korea in Jesus Christ. Finally, our look at Juche's future culminates in a call to prayer to bring about the downfall of spiritual wickedness in North Korea.

Is Juche Really a Religion?

Juche is the religion of North Korea. They pray to his [Kim Il Sung's] statue for His eternal life and for him to live in their hearts.[1]

GORDON ROBERTSON
CBN "700 CLUB" INTERVIEW

It's important to ask whether Juche is really a religion because, like chameleons, adherents to many false religions claim their philosophy, system of beliefs, or doctrines are a religion only when it suits their needs. Proponents ardently act as if their beliefs are a secular philosophy at times, and yet oppose contrary "religious beliefs" and claim religious exemptions when it is convenient. As we seek an answer to this question, it's helpful to first define the terms *religion* and *secular*.

James Madison defined *religion* in the original Constitution of

the Commonwealth of Virginia to mean "a duty to one's Creator."
The *American Heritage Dictionary* is more specific: "belief in and reverence for a supernatural power recognized as the creator and
governor of the universe."

The *Websters Dictionary* definition of *secular* is:

> *secular:* adj. 1. temporal rather than spiritual: worldly. 2. Not
> religious or sacred. *secularism:* n. The belief that religion and
> religious considerations should be rejected or ignored.[2]

Secular conveys the notion that people can somehow exercise
rule or otherwise conduct affairs in open disregard of God's Word.

Kim Il Sung and now Kim Jong Il have used their own Juche
definitions to carve the figurative pie of life into many fat *secular/
atheist* pieces and a thin *religion* slice. This ideology seeks to use
these definitions to bind, control, confine, eliminate, or otherwise
subvert the values of Christianity. Pyongyang's establishment holds
that Juche is somehow in a special non-religious category, while all
other competing philosophies of life are denounced as *religion.*

The Bible presents faith in God as a righteous response to the
love of God—a duty to our Creator—a relationship with God
through Jesus Christ. Those nations and peoples who rejected
the love and Word of God are referred to as *idolaters* and unbelievers regardless of their belief system. In more recent history,
the term *pagan* has been used to describe unbelievers. The many
biblical injunctions against the worship of false gods and idolatry
remain in solid opposition to the Juche belief system.

There are varying opinions about what does and does not
constitute a religion. The very meaning of *religion* has changed
rapidly within the modern Western world. For example, in 1933,
the U.S. Supreme Court narrowly defined *religion* as "the existence
of a belief in a supreme allegiance to the will of God."[3] Yet, by 1961,
the Court defined *religion* to include both theistic and non-theistic
belief systems:

> Also included under the protection of the religion clauses
> of the First Amendment would be religions which do not teach
> a belief in the existence of God, including Buddhism, Tao-
> ism, Ethical Culture, Secular Humanism, and others.[4]

In that decision, humanism received official recognition as a
religion, and humanists became entitled to free exercise of religion.
The basic anthropocentric tenets of humanism are essentially iden-

tical to those of Juche. Thus, Juche, according to this definition, may be considered to be a religion, too.

Some view Juche not to be a religion because, in their view, any religion requires a Creator who is the Supreme Being. Without a Creator, there is no duty, and thus no religion exists. Others view Juche to be a religion because they prefer a "big tent" view of *religion* that includes any "sincere and meaningful belief which occupies in the life of its possessor a place parallel to that filled by God."[5]

However, disagreement on the proper use of the word *religion* does not avoid the more central issue of institutionalized idolatry. Juche may be safely described as a competing belief system that is firmly set against all who profess faith in Jesus Christ as Lord of lords. Juche's advocates even refer to adherents of competing belief systems as *pagans:*

> Now the North Korea ruling hierarchy has escalated its ideological campaign designed to prevent the entire citizenry from being "contaminated by pagan ideologies." *North Korean ideologists say that all ideologies and culture other than those based upon the Juche idea are "pagan."*[6]

Is Juche really a religion? If one uses consistent terminology and applies the "big tent" definition of *religion* that includes comprehensive belief systems, then Christianity and Juche are both religions. From a biblical view, regardless of whether Juche is a religion, one may categorically state that Juche is a false idolatrous faith that clearly stands in opposition to the kingdom of God, the true church, and the uncensored proclamation of the gospel of Jesus Christ.

Worlds in Collision: Juche vs. Christianity

> *Elijah went before the people and said, "How long will you waver between two opinions? If the Lord is God, follow him; but if Baal is God, follow him." But the people said nothing.*
>
> 1 KINGS 18:21

> *We must stop . . . only seeing these things in bits and pieces. We have to understand that it is one total entity opposed to the other total entity . . . —not just religious reality, but total reality. And our view of final reality—*

> *whether it is material-energy, shaped by impersonal chance, or the living God and Creator—will determine our position on every crucial issue we face today. It will determine our views on the value and dignity of people, the base for the kind of life the individual and society lives, the direction law will take, and whether there will be freedom or some form of authoritarian dominance.*[7]
>
> FRANCIS SCHAEFFER
> *A CHRISTIAN MANIFESTO*

North Korea's Juche-driven society is a world in collision with Christianity because Juche and Christianity are two diametrically opposed, all-encompassing belief systems. Juche principles and faith in their god, Kim Jong Il, clearly dictate the direction of both individual North Koreans and their society. Meanwhile, the faith of Christians in the Word of God, their indwelling by the Holy Spirit, and their unwavering assurance of His final victory over evil guarantee that true Christians will never bow to totalitarianism or forsake their faith in Jesus Christ. These two colliding sets of deeply held views pertain to all areas of life. There can be no compromise.

The Bible declares an unchanging standard of right and wrong. This standard is a reflection of God, who changes not. His laws are fixed, uniform, and universal. Moreover, the Lordship of Jesus Christ covers all of creation. Francis Schaeffer comments:

> True spirituality covers all of reality...It is not only that true spirituality covers all of life, but it covers all parts of the spectrum of life equally. In this sense there is nothing concerning reality that is not spiritual...Christianity is not just a series of truths but *Truth*—Truth about reality...the truth of what is—brings forth not only certain personal results, but also governmental and legal results.[8]

The following discussion explores why Juche and Christianity are two diametrically opposed philosophies, belief systems, or religions (all three are correct definitions for both). The discussion includes how Juche violates the basic principles of biblically acceptable government, and compares Juche ideology with its older philosophical sibling, secular humanism. The chapter concludes by presenting why, from a biblical standpoint, Juche is fundamentally evil.

Juche Violates Biblical Principles of Government

Jesus answered, "It is written: 'Worship the Lord your God and serve him only.'"

LUKE 4:8

One of the fundamental reasons that Juche and Christianity are inherently opposed is that Juche violates the principles of government set forth in the Bible. God's basic purposes of government are to restrain human sin (Romans 13:3,4) and to preserve order (1 Timothy 2:1,2). Because *all* have sinned and fallen short of God's glory (Romans 3:23), rulers are susceptible to temptation, sin, and corruption just as their subjects are. Consequently, excessive power in the hands of rulers has been the classic historical formula for despotism and disaster. Lord Acton once noted, "Power corrupts; absolute power corrupts absolutely."[9] Thus, governments should be designed to prevent too much power from being placed in the hands of any one man (such as the Su-ryong) or group of men (such as the Korean Workers' Party). To do otherwise creates social conditions in which men become proud and corrupt and abuse power.

Historical examples abound of man's vain attempts to build societies upon gods. For example, the ancient Greeks and Romans created a system of gods that, even when considered in total, were not infinite. Instead, these gods were basically no different in thinking than human men and women. Such gods are ultimately dependent on the society that made them. When the society crumbles, the gods tumble. Time and time again, such gods have been proven incapable of providing a sufficient basis to sustain the fabric of a civilization's life, morals, and values.

The Juche god-man system of worship is no exception. Like the Roman system of god-men rulers and idols, Juche does not enable its adherents to relate to the one true God, which is man's number one need. Juche theology (or, if you prefer, ideology) neither deals with the problem of sin, nor guarantees access to eternal life. Thus, the gods of Juche, like the gods of the Romans, are small, petty, temporal, and weak compared to the almighty, everlasting, omniscient God of the Bible.

The Roman Empire also serves as a historical example of the hazard of placing excessive power in the rule of one man. Approximately 2,000 years ago, Rome was threatened and the existence of the empire was in peril. Schaeffer explains:

> Rome, in desperation, turned to Julius Caesar (100–44 B.C.) and made him "dictator for life" in the hope that his authoritarian rule would save the empire. His successor, Octavian (Caesar Augustus) (63 B.C.–A.D. 14), was granted total power, proclaimed the head of the state religion, and was worshipped as Pontifex Maximus. Worship of Caesar, "the spirit of Rome" and "the genius of the emperor" became mandatory throughout the Roman Empire. However, the human emperor-gods were a poor foundation for civilization. Rome fell.[10]

Yet, even as Roman totalitarianism was crumbling, the gospel spread throughout the decaying empire. German philosopher Georg Hegel noted that the spread of freedom from totalitarian rule has coincided with the propagation of the gospel throughout history.

Christians resisted the idolatrous syncretism of worshipping Caesar by standing firm in their conviction to worship Jesus as God and refusing to worship all other gods. This "pagan" refusal to pay Caesar homage by saying, "Caesar is Lord," led to successive waves of Roman persecution and atrocities against the Christians. Another reason for the persecution was that "no totalitarian state can tolerate a group who judge the standards."[11] Since Christians had that standard in the Bible to judge the actions of both individuals and the State, corrupt Roman leaders preferred throwing Christians to the beasts rather than relinquishing their absolute power.

Juche Ideology is Comparable to Secular Humanism

> *Humanism, for all its talk about freedom, can present no philosophical framework to justify freedom. On what basis do we say that the state is limited if God himself has not limited it?*[12]
>
> JOHN EIDSMOE
> *GOD & CAESAR: CHRISTIAN
> FAITH & POLITICAL ACTION*

Juche's North Korean proponents claim that their anthropocentric ideology is unique in all of history and distinct from humanism. However, such claims do not bear up under scrutiny. What exactly is humanism? The *American Heritage Dictionary* defines humanism as:

...a philosophy or attitude that is concerned with human beings, their achievements and interests, rather than with the abstract beings and problems of theology.[13]

Like Juche, humanism elevates man to be the universe's center, supreme value, and sole problem-solver. In contrast, Christianity regards God, not man, as the center, supreme value, and fundamental problem-solver. There is no compromise between these universal opposites.

The man-centered doctrines of both Juche and humanism provide no unchanging principles to state that one thing is right, while the other is wrong. Their anthropocentric universe is impersonal. It is neutral and silent regarding kindness and cruelty, or right and wrong. There are no absolutes. Whether one calls himself a humanist or an advocate of Juche, the result is the same: arbitrary mores replace absolute morals, and political decisions are based on whatever is arbitrary and expedient. Such secularized views reject the fixed base of God's law in favor of a person or a group who arbitrarily decides what is good for a society at any given moment. Such views are directly opposed to Christianity.

The Humanist Manifesto I (1933) and II (1973) proposed the basic tenets of humanism. These documents speak in glowing terms of the supremacy of man and his future. Yet, while they seek to glorify man, they actually debase and degrade him. For example, humanism robs man of the soul and spirit that makes him distinctly superior to animals. In denying the biblical view that man was created in the image of God, humanism holds man to be a mere animal—complex and intelligent, but just an animal nonetheless. This denigration of man as nothing more than an animal establishes a foundation for the disregard for the right to life, denial of privacy, absence of property rights, denial of due process in court, imprisonment without trial, and suppression of free speech. There is no basis for such human rights if, according to the Juche religion, there is no God to guarantee them. Other basic principles held in common between humanism and Juche are contrasted with Christian beliefs in Table 11-1.

Juche's proponents, like the humanists, are determined to eliminate the knowledge of God. Bibles are feared and hated because they give witness to the fact that God has not been silent, but has spoken and intervened in history to provide salvation through Jesus Christ. Adherents of Juche and humanism are so determined in their opposition to God that they are willing to sub-

**TABLE 11-1. Basic Principles of Humanism
Compared to Juche and Christianity[14]**

HUMANISM	JUCHE	CHRISTIANITY
1. God is either non-existent or irrelevant to man.	Same as Humanism	God is eternally self-existent. Jesus died and rose again so man might receive the gift of eternal life.
2. Man is the supreme value in the universe.	Same as Humanism	God is the supreme value in the universe.
3. Evolution is the unifying principle of all life.	Same as Humanism	God is the unifying source and holds everything together.
4. Man is purely a physical or biological creature.	Same as Humanism	Man is a threefold being. Each man has a spirit, a soul, and a body.
5. No absolute morals or values exist.	Same as Humanism	Moral values do exist and are defined in God's Word.
6. Man, through the use of scientific reason, will solve his own problems.	Same as Humanism	Man is utterly unable to solve his own sin problems and must look to the Lord Jesus Christ in faith.

vert the revelation of God even at the high cost of undermining the values that hold society together: truth, respect for property, self-control, generosity, forgiveness, mercy, and unselfish love.

While the Bible does not specifically mention North Korea, Jesus Christ did comment on Juche's man-centered idea. When Jesus revealed to His disciples that He must go to Jerusalem, suffer, be killed, and subsequently resurrected (Matthew 16:21), Peter objected. Jesus identified Satan as the source of Peter's man-centered view:

> Peter took him aside and began to rebuke him. "Never, Lord!" he said. "This shall never happen to you!" Jesus turned and said to Peter, "Get behind me, Satan! You are a stumbling block to me; *you do not have in mind the things of God, but the things of men.*" Then Jesus said to his disciples, "If anyone would come after me, he must deny himself and take up his cross and follow me" (Matthew 16:22–24).

Thus, God's revelation of the necessity of the cross inherently sets Christendom on a collision course with the cross-less, man-centered world of Juche.

Juche is Fundamentally Evil

*Everyone who does evil hates the light, and will not come
into the light for fear that his deeds will be exposed.*

JOHN 3:20

Juche is fundamentally evil because it is uncompromising in its man-centered totalitarianism. Thus, the Juche and Christian worldviews are opposed regarding the very nature of reality and existence. Moreover, the two worldviews will inevitably produce different results in regard to society and law. Juche will uphold the Su-ryong and totalitarianism. Once this good-versus-evil dichotomy is grasped, it is quite simple to recognize that those who advocate "setting aside political differences" for the sake of "unification" are proponents of a philosophically naive and fundamentally flawed proposition. Even so, there are those who seek to engage in rational negotiation and political dialogue while others hope for "reform." Yet, none of these approaches deal with the spiritual reality that the Juche religious system is patently evil. The entire society that is formed around the Juche idea is utterly corrupt. Nothing can change the sinful core of the North Korean system other than repentance and the salvation that is through Jesus Christ alone.

One biblical example of this "worlds in collision" perspective is the view that Kim Il Sung and Kim Jong Il are among the antichrists to which the apostle John referred:

> Dear children, this is the last hour; and as you have heard that the antichrist is coming, even now many antichrists have come (1 John 2:18).

The Greek word for "anti" in this text can have two meanings: "against" or "in place of." Usually this word is translated as "against."[15] Certainly Kim Il Sung and Kim Jong Il oppose and reject God. However, the meaning "in place of" would let us understand that the Kims are two of the surrogate rulers who would usurp the worship that is properly due only to the one Lord and Savior, Jesus Christ.

Kim Il Sung understood better than the Church that these two worldviews are encompassing concepts of reality standing in antithesis to one another. Christianity accommodates unity, diversity, and plurality of leadership. In contrast, Juche uses totalitarianism to enforce "unity." For example, consider the anti-imperialist meaning of the Juche concept of unity:

> Unity is vital to vigorously advancing the peace movement and achieving world peace...All the progressive forces and peace-loving people of the world should unite under the banner of anti-imperialism, anti-war, anti-nuclear and of peace, stand up to imperialists who are escalating aggression and war preparations and deal collective counterblows to the imperialists everywhere their aggressive claws reach [*KCNA*].

This Juche's "unity" is not true unity, but rather religionized Communist uniformity. It is important to understand this overarching principle that transcends any political negotiations or economic agreements. Kim Jong Il seeks to be the only guiding light with the "immortal" Juche idea:

> *The Juche idea* founded by President Kim Il Sung and steadily developed in depth by General Kim Jong Il *is the truth* whose revolutionary significance has already been proved through history and *the only guiding idea of the time with universal justification*. The idea is a compass for the revolutionary movement which indicates the correct road to independence, democratization and national reunification and it is the maxim of the struggle and life that should be cherished by activists all the time [*KCNA*].
>
> No force on earth can keep *humankind from advancing...* Socialism is rapidly sweeping the whole world...In the teeth of obstructions of the imperialists, the peoples in those countries are now advocating socialism and fighting *for carrying its noble idea [Juche] into practice* [*KCNA*].

Throughout the Bible, some rulers and governments are described as good, better, or best. The Bible repeatedly records how nations were judged for being wicked, idolatrous, and immoral in God's eyes. If leaders reject the Bible as the immutable standard for judging human institutions, then we risk elevating "tolerance" in the name of "global peace" as a surrogate standard. Thus, we need to see the authority of the Word of God not only over individuals, but also over all the nations of the earth. Just as U.S. President Ronald Reagan had the boldness to declare the former Soviet Union to be "an evil empire," political and spiritual leaders throughout the world should have the moral fortitude to declare North Korea's Juche totalitarianism to be an evil system.[16]

How do we make such measured judgments of human institutions? We must be able to use biblical standards both to make righteous judgments of human institutions and to proclaim the gospel that saves souls. We need to be able to make qualitative assessments between human institutions on the international level. God is the protector of the good, the better, and the best nation. However, the Bible clearly and consistently shows that God will judge every wicked nation. If we reject unconditional tolerance as the preeminent virtue, we can boldly declare the North Korean government to be evil and rightly declare that the Juche religion of North Korea is idolatry in God's eyes.

Mt. Paektu in the Bible

Everyone did what was right in his own eyes.
JUDGES 21:25 (NKJ)

Let us live our own way!
NORTH KOREA'S KEY PROPAGANDA
SLOGAN FOR 1998 [*KCNA*]

God's Word is filled with examples of the spiritual significance of high places. In contemporary North Korea, Mt. Paektu is one of the key holy places and the most important high place of the Juche faith. Among the many mountains and high places mentioned in the Bible, one—Mount Hermon—appears to bear prophetic significance for understanding what the Word of God has to say about Korea.

Both the Old and the New Testaments refer to Mt. Lebanon. For example, Jesus ascended Mt. Hermon, a 9,232-foot mountain, with Peter, James, and John. It was while Jesus was on top of Mt. Hermon that He was brilliantly transfigured, spoke with Moses and Elijah, and a voice boomed out of heaven identifying Jesus as God's Son (Matthew 17:2; Mark 9:2). However, the biblical account of Mt. Hermon, in the Lebanon mountains, begins in the Old Testament's Book of Judges:

> These are the nations the Lord left to test all those Israelites who had not experienced any of the wars in Canaan *(he did this only to teach warfare to the descendants of the Israelites who had not had previous battle experience):* the five rulers of the Philis-

tines, all the Canaanites, the Sidonians, and the Hivites living in the Lebanon mountains *from Mount Baal Hermon* to Lebo Hamath. They were left to test the Israelites *to see whether they would obey the LORD's commands,* which he had given their forefathers through Moses (Judges 3:1–4).

The Book of Judges records that God left the idolatrous nations around Mt. Hermon because the people of God were untried in warfare and He wanted to test their obedience. Perhaps God has similarly left the idolatrous people around Mt. Paektu to test the obedience of today's people of God, the church, in spiritual warfare. Another parallel with North Korea arises in the last verse of the book of Judges, as it describes the conditions that prevailed in this era: "everyone did as he saw fit" (Judges 21:25). By comparison, North Korea's key propaganda slogan for 1998 was "Let us live our own way!" [*KCNA*].

Later in the Old Testament, Ezekiel 17 speaks parabolically about God taking an uppermost branch off a tree in Lebanon and planting it on the highest mountain (Mt. Hermon). This chapter speaks of God's work of restoration. By the Mt. Hermon/Mt. Paektu typology, we may be encouraged that God will include the rebuilding of His church in North Korea as a part of His plan for the proclamation of the gospel.

In addition, the name of the snowcapped Lebanon mountain range is derived from the Hebrew for "white-headed." Recall that Paektu means "white-headed" or "whitecapped" in Korean. In addition, Mt. Hermon has long been considered to be a sacred mountain in the Middle East (e.g., 2 Peter 1:18). In the Book of Isaiah, the Bible records Satan saying, "I will sit enthroned on the mount of assembly, on the utmost heights of the sacred mountain" (Isaiah 14:13,14). North Koreans refer to Mt. Paektu as the "sacred mountain of Juche."

The Juche belief in Mt. Paektu as the source of the Juche religion is spiritually significant. Throughout the Bible, mountains and high places signify spiritual strongholds.[17] Much prayer is required to dethrone godless religions like Juche. Removal of people's idols through force and policy without dealing with the spiritual root does not create a lasting effect. For example, the Bible records that Josiah's destruction of pagan worship places (2 Kings 23:19–25) pleased the Lord. However, it did not change the hearts of the people, and they returned to idolatry. Thus, prayer along with the proclamation of the gospel in spiritual power and authority is essential to dethrone the Juche spiritual evil symbolized by Mt. Paektu. Jesus said, "If you have faith as small as a mustard seed, you can say to this mountain, 'Move from here to there' and it will move. Nothing will be impossible for you" (Matthew 17:20,21). Thus, Christians need to act in faith to reclaim North Korea's high ground for Jesus Christ.

Mene, Mene, Tekel...God's Soon Coming Justice

"But you his son, O Belshazzar, have not humbled yourself, though you knew all this. Instead, you have set yourself up against the Lord of heaven."
DANIEL 5:22,23

Severe flooding and food shortages have driven many North Koreans not only to the point of eating grass and roots to survive, but also to succumbing to cannibalism. Many Korean and non-Korean Christians alike hold the view that North Korea's recent floods, tidal waves, and food shortages could be God's judgment upon Kim Jong Il's tyranny.

Jonathan Edwards, the early American preacher whose classic sermon "Sinners in the Hands of an Angry God" helped spark the Great Awakening, explained God's role as the ultimate Judge of nations:

> If a nation or people is very corrupt and remains obstinate in the evil way, God generally, if not universally, exercises these threatenings. God is more strict in punishing of a wicked people in this world than a wicked person. God often suffers particular persons that are to prosper in the world and discharges them to judgment in the world to come. But as a people we are punished only in this world. *Therefore God will not suffer a people that grow very corrupt and refuse to be reclaimed, to go unpunished in this world.*[18]

An example of God's swift justice against a wicked ruler and nation is provided in the Book of Daniel. This account records God's judgment upon the Babylonian King Belshazzar in 539 B.C. Feeling quite safe within the seemingly impregnable 60-foot-high walls of Babylon, Belshazzar continued in open rebellion against God.

At a great banquet, a hand miraculously appeared and wrote on the wall, "Mene, Mene, Tekel, Parsin" (Daniel 5:25). The mysterious words meant that God had numbered Belshazzar's kingdom and finished it. The king was weighed in the balance and found wanting, and his kingdom would be divided and given to the Medes and Persians. The Book of Daniel proclaims God's judgment of this evil ruler: "...the Most High God is sovereign over the kingdoms of men and sets over them anyone he wishes. But you [Nebuchadnezzar's] son, O Belshazzar, have not humbled yourself, though you knew all this. Instead, you have set yourself up against the Lord of heaven" (Daniel 5:21–23). That very night, Belshazzar's life was taken. According to the ancient Greek historian Xenophon, the Medo-Persian army, led by Cyrus, redirected the Euphrates River and then conquered Babylon by marching in along the dry river bed. The Medo-Persians threw down the gates, and the city's defenses were rendered worthless. Proud Babylon was sacked.

Belshazzar's Babylon had been weighed in God's balances and found wanting. One might well conclude that Kim Jong Il's Juche state of North Korea has also been "weighed in the balance and found wanting." Thus, whether or not Kim Jong Il actually sees miraculous handwriting on a wall, his continuing rebellion against God assures North Korea of God's soon coming justice.

God's Provision of Mercy in Jesus Christ

Lord, I have heard of your fame; I stand in awe of your deeds, O Lord. Renew them in our day, in our time make them known; in wrath remember mercy.

HABAKKUK 3:2

A biblical analysis, which makes a clear case for the inevitable judgment of God upon North Korea and its Juche idolatry, is incomplete without also presenting His perfect provision of mercy in Jesus Christ. God's justice and mercy met at the cross where Jesus of Nazareth was crucified for the sins of man. Thus, the good news of the gospel is that Jesus Christ did not come to kill and destroy, but to seek and save the lost and to give us spiritual life (John 3:17; 10:10).

Our attitude and prayer for North Korea should be like that of the prophet Habakkuk, who pleaded in intercession with the Lord. Habakkuk prayed that the Lord would have mercy on Israel despite His judgment upon them for their open rebellion. Even Jesus' disciples required a divine heart transplant through the power of the Holy Spirit to change their attitude toward those who reject God's Word. Jesus still commands his present-day disciples to pray for their enemies:

> "I tell you: Love your enemies and pray for those who persecute you, that you may be sons of your Father in heaven. He causes his sun to rise on the evil and the good, and sends rain on the righteous and the unrighteous" (Matthew 5:44,45).

Thus, the business of today's Church is not to specialize in judgment or major in "giant-ology" (the fear of spiritual enemies), but rather to declare God's provision of mercy in Jesus Christ. Yet how does God's mercy coincide with His soon coming justice?

Contrary to the belief of some, the God's justice and mercy run hand-in-hand throughout the Bible from Genesis to Revelation. Book such as Daniel in the Old Testament and Matthew 24 and Revelation in the New Testament agree on God's ultimate judgment of evil. Similarly, the book of Jonah provides an Old Testament picture of God's amazing provision of mercy to a god-hating rebellious nation.

What the Bible tells us about the prophet Jonah helps us understand God's heart toward the people of North Korea. One should remember that the Old Testament, outside the book of Jonah, documents that Jonah was an actual prophet of Israel from the region of Galilee who lived in the seventh century B.C. (2 Kings 14:25). Jesus also taught that Jonah was a real historical figure (Matthew 12:39–41). If Jonah had lived today, his television set would have been filled with news broadcasts vividly displaying Assyrian atrocities against Jonah's countrymen and many other nations. The Assyrians were the first truly military society. Their ruthless slaughter was legendary, and, as with modern North Korea, no effort or expense was spared to increase the army's efficiency.

In addition to Assyrian cruelty, Jonah had another reason to want God to judge Nineveh. Israel's king paid tribute to the Assyrians under Adad-nirari III, meaning that Jonah and his countrymen in Galilee had to pay heavy taxes to meet the required tribute. Not surprisingly, Jonah resented the Assyrians; he wanted God to destroy them. Given this background, it seems very reasonable that when God told Jonah to go to Nineveh and preach, Jonah ran in the other direction until God finally got his attention through the use of a great fish. "Then the word of the Lord came to Jonah a second time" and Jonah, the ultimate reluctant missionary, finally obeyed and went to Nineveh.

God's message, that Jonah preached to Nineveh, was short and harsh: "Forty more days and Nineveh will be overturned." When Nineveh repented, Jonah was angry with God for responding with mercy.[19] However, the real message of the account is God's attempt to change Jonah's heart. After all his preaching, Jonah still did not have God's heart toward the lost because he had failed to repent of his own unforgiveness.

> The LORD said, "You have been concerned about this vine, though you did not tend it or make it grow. It sprang up overnight and died overnight. But Nineveh has more than a hundred and twenty thousand people who cannot tell their right hand from their left, and many cattle as well. Should I not be concerned about that great city?" (Jonah 4:10,11)

Like Jonah's initial view of Assyria, people throughout the world need to have a clear view of North Korea's totalitarian system. People should see Juche for what it actually is—not an alternative "ideology," but a false religion that keeps an entire people in both spiritual and physical bondage. However, the Lord's words to Jonah show that God expects something more from Christians. Christians—including all intercessors and would-be missionaries to North Korea—need to have the heart of Jesus to seek and save those who are lost. Jesus' parable about forgiveness in Matthew 18:21–35 gives a powerful illustration of the necessity for Christians to truly forgive others since God has forgiven them an immeasurably large debt of sin. As in the case of Jonah, the Church needs Jesus' heart of restoration toward North Korea:

> "You have heard that it was said, 'Love your neighbor and hate your enemy.' But I tell you: *Love your enemies* and pray for those who persecute you" (Matthew 5:43).

How can the Church respond? Certainly, the first response should be prayer. As a result of such prayers, the many ministries that have been reaching out in the love and mercy of Jesus Christ toward North Korea generally have selected one of three creative access strategies: *"front-door"* ministry, *"back-door"* ministry, and *humanitarian food aid* ministry. "Front-door" ministries, such as the Center for American–North Korean Understanding, William Carey International University, and the Christian Broadcasting Network seek to build a bridge of understanding between the people of the

United States and the people of North Korea. All the methods used by these organizations are legally authorized by the U.S. Department of State, where required, and are conducted with the foreknowledge and approval of the North Korean government. Some of the successes achieved by the front-door ministries include the opening of a permanent CNN news bureau with correspondent Mike Chinoy in Pyongyang, and the donation of laser medical technology and associated training of North Korean doctors by U.S. doctors. Another success was establishing an agreement to assign a Christian adjunct faculty professor from William Carey International University (Pasadena, California) as a guest history professor at Kim Il Sung University in Pyongyang. Center for American–North Korean Understanding groups have attended Free Economic and Trade Zone meetings in the Rajin-Sonbong area, made frequent visits the Pyongyang area, and hosted North Korean delegations to the United States when U.S. Department of State approval was forthcoming. Those Christian organizations who espouse the front-door approach tend to steer away from controversial issues in favor of "friendship evangelism."

The second of the three categories of ministries are "back-door" type ministries. These ministries use creative methods to both directly strengthen the North Korean underground church and get the gospel into North Korea. Just two of the many back-door ministries are The Voice of the Martyrs and Cornerstone Ministries International. These groups smuggle Bibles into North Korea by the ton, float Scripture balloons across the border, train underground church leaders, and even provide food and monetary assistance directly to underground Christians. The North Korean government, which persecutes the underground church, does not approve of these organizations, their goals, or their methods.

The third group of Christian ministries are humanitarian aid organizations. These ministries provide famine relief shipments to mitigate the ongoing starvation and suffering in North Korea. Christian humanitarian aid organizations include most major U.S. and Canadian Christian denominations, networked Korean-American churches, and numerous para-church ministries such as Food for the Hungry International. Some of the networked churches work through non-Christian humanitarian relief organizations such as the United Nations' World Food Program. However, Christian famine relief organizations tend to take a "no strings attached" attitude, whereas food aid from various governments and some non-Christian humanitarian aid organizations is more likely to be interrupted by North Korea's ongoing controversial international incidents that are the trademark of its brinkmanship diplomacy. Together, these three ministry strategies combine to show the love of Jesus Christ to both Christian and non-Christian North Koreans.

The Church should continue in all three of these creative access strategies, as God empowers Christians to reach out to North Korea. Regardless of which strategy is preferred, believers should not lose sight of God's vision for North Korea. Those who read their Bibles carefully will see North Koreans among the multitude of people in the apostle John's vision of heaven:

> And they sang a new song: "You are worthy to take the scroll and to open its seals, because you were slain, and with your blood you purchased men for God *from every tribe and language and people and nation*" (Revelation 5:9).

Yet, we must remember that it is only the transmission of the gospel that is the difference between whether the followers of Juche (or anyone else, for that matter) perish or are saved. The apostle Paul declared:

> "Everyone who calls on the name of the Lord will be saved." How, then, can they call on the one they have not believed in? And how can they believe in the one of whom they have not heard? And how can they hear without someone preaching to them? And how can they preach unless they are sent? As it is written, "How beautiful are the feet of those who bring good news!" (Romans 10:13–15)

Today, the cross of Jesus Christ, who alone offers us spiritual life, must be lifted up in the midst of North Korea's spiritual desert of death as a beacon of hope and love. Jesus said, "But I, when I am lifted up from the earth, will draw all men to myself" (John 12:32).

A Call to Spiritual Warfare Against Juche

> *Lift up your heads, O you gates;*
> *be lifted up, you ancient doors,*
> *that the King of glory may come in.*
> *Who is this King of glory?*

The Lord strong and mighty,
the Lord mighty in battle.

PSALM 24:7,8

The light of the gospel is shining continually. However, the god of this world has blinded the minds of men (2 Corinthians 4:3,4). This spiritual blindness results in the gospel being hidden to those who are in unbelief. Jesus Christ has called the church to prayer against Satan. Our prayers can lift the veils from blinding the minds of unbelievers in North Korea to the gospel so they may be truly free to believe.

The Great Commission is one of spiritual conquest, not the accommodation of evil. According to the Bible, Jesus' goal for the saints is not to merely *know* that Juche is fundamentally evil, nor even to achieve *an understanding* with Pyongyang's totalitarian government. Rather, Jesus' command to the church is to extend the kingdom of God in North Korea through the power of the proclamation of the gospel. North Korea's merger of politics with religion under Juche in no way makes North Korea exempt from Jesus' "Plan A" Great Commission mandate for the church. No "Plan B" for North Korea exists. We must never forget that the bottom line of the New Testament ultimatum to North Korea is no less pointed than Jonah's words to Nineveh: "Forty more days and Nineveh will be overturned" (Jonah 3:4). The New Testament rendition of the divine ultimatum is equally blunt: "believe or perish" (Luke 13:5; Mark 16:16).

Likewise, let us not pretend that Jesus is not interested in the government of nations. Psalm 22 and Matthew 28:18–20 clearly establish the supreme authority of Jesus Christ over all earthly governments. No ruler or nation is free to redefine what is good and evil apart from God's Word.

Furthermore, all true Christians are ambassadors for the King of kings (2 Corinthians 5:20; Ephesians 6:20). Imagine, for a moment, if your country sent an ambassador to another nation that bribed, subverted, or bought the silence of your country's ambassador. Certainly, you would rightly conclude that your ambassador had committed a treasonous act worthy of the most severe punishment. The "official" Korean Christian Federation churches are led by such false ambassadors whose primary allegiance is to Juche's gods, not to Jesus Christ. However, the church at large, in primary allegiance to Jesus Christ, must guard against any temptation—in the name of cross-cultural understanding, world peace, national reunification, or tolerance—to compromise the divine ultimatum of the gospel for the people of North Korea. Just as Satan used Peter in an attempt to compromise Jesus' resolve to achieve His victory at the Cross (see Mark 8:33), saints should be discerning about any influences that urge the church to compromise her mission to proclaim the gospel.

Reliance on well-intentioned and well-financed missionaries alone is insufficient to provide a lasting impact apart from prayer and dependence upon God's power. For example, in 1947, U.S. General Douglas MacArthur challenged America's churches that they could convert Japan to Christianity if they sent 1,000 missionaries.[20] The American churches sent over 2,500 missionaries along with 10 million Bibles in the Japanese language. American leaders unwittingly misrepresented the gospel by telling Emperor Hirohito and his people that they needed Christianity to support a democratic government, not because they needed salvation in Jesus Christ.[21] The Japanese retained democracy. However, since the evil was not defeated through prayer, the Japanese, for the most part, rejected Christianity. Apart from prayer, the military and economic might of the United States proved insufficient to tear down the evils of Shintoism.

The Bible assures the church that it is well-equipped through fasting, prayer, the Word of God, and the power of the Holy Spirit to tear down the evils of Juche.

> For though we live in the world, we do not wage war as the world does. The weapons we fight with are not the weapons of the world. On the contrary, they have divine power *to demolish strongholds.* We demolish arguments and every pretension that sets itself up against the knowledge of God, and we take captive every thought to make it obedient to Christ (2 Corinthians 10:3–5).

Yet, it is entirely appropriate to ask the question, "Is the church praying correctly for North Korea?"

At any given hour of the day and night, believers in South Korea are praying for a supernatural breakthrough in North Korea so that the "people of God" may worship openly. Pray for North Korea! Saints—pray for North Korea. Pray against the evils of Juche through the resurrection power of Jesus Christ who is "far above all rule and authority, power and dominion, and every title that can be given, not only in the present age but also in the one to come" (Ephesians 1:21). Pray for the Christian minority in North Korea's underground church to be given courage and be sustained in their faith. Pray for a spirit of repentance and reconciliation within the Korean churches and among missionaries to heal the deep wounds that split Korea's church a generation ago. Pray for the government officials to relax their attitudes toward Christians and Christian outreach. Pray for the Lord of the harvest to raise up, equip, and empower Christian witnesses to North Korea. Pray that this country, a place once thought to be the birthplace of revival in Asia, will again have a strong and growing church, blessing the people of the land. As one Korean-American missionary friend told me upon seeing the physical starvation of his people:

> There is more at stake in Korea than starvation, as tragic as that is. People die, yes—but without the gospel, many Koreans face eternal death.

My personal conviction is that the gospel shall be proclaimed as a witness throughout the whole world—including North Korea.

Do not be afraid, little flock, for your Father has been pleased to give you the kingdom (Luke 12:32).

Psalm 2

Why do the nations conspire and the peoples plot in vain? The kings of the earth take their stand and the rulers gather together against the LORD and against his Anointed One. "Let us break their chains," they say, "and throw off their fetters." The One enthroned in heaven laughs; the Lord scoffs at them. Then he rebukes them in his anger and terrifies them in his wrath, saying, "I have installed my King on Zion, my holy hill." I will proclaim the decree of the LORD: He said to me, "You are my Son; today I have become your Father. Ask of me, and I will make the nations your inheritance, the ends of the earth your possession. You will rule them with an iron scepter; you will dash them to pieces like pottery." Therefore, you kings, be wise; be warned, you rulers of the earth. Serve the LORD with fear and rejoice with trembling. Kiss the Son, lest he be angry and you be destroyed in your way, for his wrath can flare up in a moment. Blessed are all who take refuge in him.

Recommended Reading

Allen, Horace N. *Things Korean. A collection of Sketches and Anecdotes.* New York: Fleming H. Revell Co., 1908.

An Myong Chol. *Political Prisoners' Camps in North Korea.* Seoul: Center for the Advancement of North Korean Human Rights, 1995.

Billington, James H. *Fire in the Minds of Men: Origins of the Revolutionary Faith.* New York: Basic Books, Inc., 1980.

Choi Sung Chul, ed. *Human Rights in North Korea.* Seoul: Center for the Advancement of North Korean Human Rights, 1995.

Eidsmoe, John. *God & Caesar: Christian Faith & Political Action.* Westchester, Illinois: Crossway Books, 1984.

Hur, Sonja Vegdahl and Ben Seunghwa Hur. *Culture Shock! Korea: A Guide to Customs & Etiquette.* Singapore: Times Editions Pte Ltd, 1988.

Kang In Duk. "North Korea's Policy on Religion." *East Asian Review*, vol. 7 no. 3 (Autumn, 1995): 91–100. Seoul: The Institute for East Asian Studies, 1995.

Kang Wi Jo. *Christ and Caesar in Modern Korea: a History of Christianity and Politics.* Albany, NY: State University of New York Press, 1997.

Kim Il Sung. *Reminiscences With the Century*, Volumes 1–4. Pyongyang: Foreign Languages Publishing House, 1992. *Kim Il Sung University.* Pyongyang: Foreign Languages Publishing House, 1982.

Kim Jong Il. *Let Us Exalt the Brilliance of Comrade Kim Il Sung's Idea on the Youth Movement and the Achievements Made Under His Leadership.* Pyongyang: Foreign Language Publishing House, 1996.

_____. *On the Juche Idea of Our Party.* Pyongyang: Foreign Language Publishing House, 1985.

More Love to Thee (videotape). Bartlesville, Oklahoma: Voice of the Martyrs, Inc., 1994.

Otis, George, Jr. *The Twilight Labyrinth: Why Does Spiritual Darkness Linger Where It Does?* New York: Chosen Books, 1997.

Orwell, George. *1984.* New York: Harcourt Brace Janovich, Inc., 1950.

Rhodes, Harry A. *History of Korea Mission Presbyterian Church U.S.A. 1884–1934.* Seoul: Choson Mission Prebyterian Church U.S.A., 1934.

Savada, Andrea Matles. *North Korea: A Country Study.* Washington, D.C.: Library of Congress Federal Research Division, 1993.

Schaeffer, Francis A. *A Christian Manifesto.* Westchester, Illinois: Crossway Books, 1984.

_____. *How Should We Then Live?: The Rise and Decline of Western Thought and Culture.* Westchester, Illinois: Crossway Books, 1983.

Stone, Jeremy J. *Testimony to U.S. Senate Subcommittee on East Asian and Pacific Affairs Committee on Foreign Relations.* 25 November 1991. Transcript. http://www.fas.org/nkorea/nktest.html.

The Human Rights Situation in North Korea: The Reality of Self-styled Paradise. Seoul: The Institute for South–North Korea Studies, 1992.

Underwood, H.G., *The Call of Korea.* New York: Fleming H. Revell, Co., 1908

U.S. Navy Reports Investigating the Loss of the Schooner General Sherman, 19th Century. Microfilm rolls 251, 252. Washington, D.C.: U.S. National Archives Navy Maritime Group, 1866, 1867.

White, Tom. *North Korea: The Battle Continues.* Bartlesville, Oklahoma: The Voice of the Martyrs, Inc., 1996.

End Notes

Chapter 1. Introduction

1 James Walsh, "North Korea—A World Without Kim: The last Stalinist's sudden demise leaves his realm more enigmatic than ever," *Time*, 18 July 1994.

2 Ibid.

3 This number is not a typographical error. North Korean propaganda routinely ascribes superhuman powers and feats to Kim Il Sung and Kim Jong Il.

4 Nature's display of trees blooming out of season and the sun bursting through the fog are interpreted as heavenly omens. What this and other similar propaganda attempts to show is that heaven welcomes both Kim Jong Il's personal presence and his political decisions. In the Juche religion, such phenomena are the equivalent of the pagan practice of reading animal entrails. Of course, Juche omens are always in favor of Kim Jong Il!

5 "In a 'Slow Motion' North Korea Famine, Church Aid Makes Slow Progress," *Lutheran World Relief News* (New York), 3 June 1997.

Chapter 2. Central Juche Teachings

1 "Statements of Leader Kim Jong Il," *The People's Korea* (Tokyo: DPRK web magazine), 14 May 1998.

2 "Juche Ideology," *Koreascope* (Seoul: web magazine).

3 "Quotations of Leader Kim Jong Il," *The People's Korea* (Tokyo: DPRK web magazine), 13 May 1998.

4 In his book *On the Juche Idea of Our Party*, Kim Jong Il describes the three basic Juche social attributes of man to be *Chajusong, creativity,* and *consciousness.*

    Chajusong is the Juche concept of the collective social life attribute that a man is not born with, but is given to him by society. "It can be said that man's Chajusong is the requirement and reflection of social life, social practice." The attribute of Chajusong replaces the biblical concept that every human life is intrinsically valuable because man is uniquely created in God's image (Genesis 9:6), with the concept that man is unique because society gives him the social attribute or value of Chajusong.

    Creativity is the Juche social attribute of a "man who transforms the world and shapes his own destiny purposefully."

    Consciousness is the Juche social attribute of a "man who determines all his activities designed to understand and reshape the world and himself." [Kim Jong Il, *On the Juche Idea of Our Party* (Pyongyang: Foreign Languages Publishing House, 1985), 4, 5.]

5 Li Yang Su (Vice Editor-in-Chief, Korean Central News Agency), interview

with author, Virginia Beach, Virginia, 8 October 1997; and Kim Jong Il, *On the Juche Idea of Our Party*, 20, 21.

6 Lee Wha Rang, "What is Jucheism?" *Korea WebWeekly* (Seoul: Korea Nationalists Association), 12 September 1997.

7 Klaus Steinberger, "Hyong," *Traditional Taekwon Do and Other Martial Arts* (Munich, 1999) (web magazine).

8 Francis A. Schaeffer, *A Christian Manifesto* (Westchester, Illinois: Crossway Books, 1984), 24.

9 Kim Gahb Chol, "The Principle of Separating Economics from Politics and Prospects for Improvement in South-North Relations," *East Asian Review,* vol. 10 no. 2 (Seoul: The Institute for East Asian Studies), 31.

10 Lee, "What is Jucheism?"

11 Kang In Duk, "Party Secretary Hwang's Defection: North Korea Now on the Brink of Collapse or Change," *The Korea Overseas Information Service* (web magazine, 1997).

12 Lee, "What is Jucheism?"

13 *Dogmatism* is defined by Kim Jong Il in his book *On the Juche Idea of Our Party*, 18, as: Those who "endeavor to imitate mechanically established theories and [the] experience of others, without taking into consideration the historical conditions and specific realities in our country where a colonial and semi-feudal society was in existence…dogmatism was a serious obstacle in the way of revolution."

14 Lee, "What is Jucheism?"

15 "Political Ideology: The Role of Chuch'e," *Country Missing* (Washington, D.C.: U.S. Library of Congress, 1993).

16 Japan's Professor Murooka Tetsuo, of Tokyo's National Institute for Defense Studies, notes that, in 1949, Kim Il Sung was first given the title of *Su-ryong* (meaning "leader"), long before the term ever took on its later "Great Leader" meaning.

17 Kang, "Party Secretary Hwang's Defection."

18 Murooka Tetsuo (Professor, National Institute for Defense Studies, Tokyo, Japan), interview with author, Virginia Beach, Virginia, 26 February 1999.

19 Jeremy J. Stone, "North Korea: Hermit Kingdom Faces Hard Choices," November 1991 (Washington, D.C.: Federation of American Scientists website).

20 "Quotations of Leader Kim Jong Il."

21 "The Workers' Party of North Korea," *Koreascope* (Seoul: web magazine).

22 Ibid.

23 Stone, "North Korea: Hermit Kingdom Faces Hard Choices."

24 George Orwell, *1984* (New York: Harcourt Brace Janovich, Inc., 1950), 174.

25 Kim Jong Il, *Let Us Exalt the Brilliance of Comrade Kim Il Sung's Idea on the Youth Movement and the Achievements Made Under His Leadership* (Pyongyang: Foreign Language Publishing House, 1996), 9.

26 "Neither Major Policy Changes nor Fresh Developments in Sight," *Korea Her-*

ald (Seoul), 5 June 1998.

27 "Quotations of Leader Kim Jong Il."

28 *The Human Rights Situation in North Korea: The Reality of Self-styled Paradise* (Seoul: The Institute for South-North Korea Studies, 1992), 18.

29 J. Edgar Hoover, *Masters of Deceit* (New York: Holt, 1958), 301.

30 Lee, "What is Jucheism?"

31 Steve McCabe, "Jucheism???," *Korea WebWeekly* (Seoul: Korea Nationalists Association), 15 September 1997.

32 Pak Song Duk, "Christianity and Juche Idea" (Pyongyang: Juche Idea Division of the Social Science Institute, 1991), 9. Remarkably, aside from the title, there is absolutely no discussion or mention of Christianity in this monograph!

33 "Quotations of Leader Kim Jong Il."

34 Kim, *Let Us Exalt*, 17.

35 "Neither Major Policy Changes nor Fresh Developments in Sight."

36 Kim Jong Il, *On the Juche Idea of Our Party* (Pyongyang: Foreign Languages Publishing House, 1985), 18.

37 Stone, "North Korea: Hermit Kingdom Faces Hard Choices."

38 James Walsh, "North Korea—A World Without Kim: The last Stalinist's sudden demise leaves his realm more enigmatic than ever," *Time*, 18 July 1994.

39 Aidan Foster-Carter, "Korea's Leadership Crisis: Neither North nor South are facing up to their destiny," *Asiaweek*, 30 May 1997.

40 James Nash, "North Korea," personal papers (Ann Arbor, Michigan: University of Michigan, 1995).

41 Francis A. Schaeffer, *How Should We Then Live?: The Rise and Decline of Western Thought and Culture* (Westchester, Illinois: Crossway Books, 1983), 251.

42 McCabe, "Jucheism???"

43 Li Yang Su, interview with author, 12 October 1997.

44 *The Korean Christians Federation* (Pyongyang: The Central Committee of the Korean Christians Federation, 1994), 1.

45 Kang In Duk, "North Korea's Policy on Religion," *East Asian Review*, vol. 8 no. 3 (Seoul: The Institute for East Asian Studies, 1996), 95.

46 Jimmy Carter, *Living Faith* (New York: Random House, Inc., 1996), 139.

47 Tom White, *North Korea: The Battle Continues* (Bartlesville, Oklahoma: The Voice of the Martyrs, Inc., 1996), 4.

48 "Corporatism and the Chuch'e Idea," *Country Missing* (Washington, D.C.: U.S. Library of Congress, 1993).

49 Stone, "North Korea: Hermit Kingdom Faces Hard Choices."

50 Barbara Slavin, "N. Korea Opens Doors to U.S. Christians," *USA Today*, 26 February 1997: 11A.

51 Billy Graham, *Just As I Am* (New York: HarperCollins, 1997), 497.

52 Slavin, "N. Korea Opens Doors to U.S. Christians," 11A.

53 Graham, *Just As I Am*, 631.

54 Kim Il Sung, *Reminiscences With the Century*, vol. 1 (Pyongyang: Foreign Languages Publishing House, 1992), 34, 35.

55 "Quotations of Leader Kim Jong Il."

56 "Kim Jong-il appears at N. Korea anniversary parade," *Reuters*, 10 October 1995.

57 "Personality Cult of Kim Jong-il," *Koreascope* (Seoul: web magazine).

58 Walsh, "North Korea—A World Without Kim."

59 Ibid.

60 "Albright Says Economy Key to N. Korean Peace," *Reuter Information Service*, 22 February 1997.

61 Some sources indicate that Kim Jong Suk was born in 1919. However, this writer opted to use the year of her birth (1917) from North Korean sources.

Chapter 3. The Spiritual Dimension of Juche

1 "Statements of Leader Kim Jong Il," *The People's Korea* (Tokyo: DPRK web magazine), 14 May 1998.

2 Billy Graham, *Just As I Am* (New York: HarperCollins, 1997), 616.

3 Richard Wurmbrand, *Was Karl Marx a Satanist?* (Glendale, CA: Diane Books, 1976), passim.

4 Peter E. Prosser, *Knowing How to Operate in Signs and Wonders* (Virginia Beach, Virginia: Regent University, 1996), 88.

5 Ibid.

6 Sarah Barry, "World Mission History" (Seoul: University Bible Fellowship, 1999) (web magazine).

7 Dan Wooding, "North Korea Wants to Re-enter the World But on its Own Terms," *Christian Herald*, 6 September 1994, 3.

8 Francis A. Schaeffer, *A Christian Manifesto* (Westchester, Illinois: Crossway Books, 1984), 130.

9 John Eidsmoe, *God & Caesar: Christian Faith & Political Action* (Westchester, Illinois: Crossway Books, 1984), 10.

10 Luther Hess Waring, *The Political Theories of Martin Luther* (Port Washington, New York: Kennikat Press, 1910 (reprinted 1968), 2.

11 "The Pleasure Team," *Koreascope* (Seoul: web magazine).

12 Choi Sung Chul, ed., *Human Rights in North Korea* (Seoul: Center for the Advancement of North Korean Human Rights, 1995), 234, 235.

13 Ibid.

14 Nicolai Timenes, Jr., *Defense Against Kamikaze Attacks in World War II and Its Relevance to Anti-Ship Missile Defense, Volume 1: An Analytical History of Kamikaze Attacks Against Ships of the United States Navy During World War II* (Arlington: Center for Naval Analyses, November 1970), v.

15 For one of classical analyses of Senjinkun in English, refer to John W. Dower, *War Without Mercy* (New York: Pantheon Books, 1986).

16 Dennis and Peggy Warner, with Commander Sadao Seno, JMSDF (Ret.), *The Sacred Warriors, Japan's Suicide Legions* (New York: Van Nostrand Reinhold Company, 1982), 5, 6.

17 For recent Bushido studies, see Eiko Ikegami, *The Taming of the Samurai: Honorific Individualism and the Making of Modern Japan* (www.hup.harvard.edu/ S97Books/S97.Catalog/taming.samurai.html), and Kyotsu Hori, "The economic and political effects of the Mongol Wars," in J. W. Hall and J. P. Mass, eds., *Medieval Japan: Essays in institutional history* (New Haven: Yale University Press, 1974).

18 Warner, *The Sacred Warriors*, 76.

19 "Statements of leader Kim Jong Il."

20 This recanting lasted until 1992, when Emperor Hirohito died and his son assumed power. His son reinstituted the Daijosai ceremony, thereby returning Japan to the sun goddess. The nationally televised ceremony cost the Japanese government nearly US$ 53 million.

21 For further reading on the Japanese view of Daijosai, see the following websites: Nanzan Institute for Religion & Culture (www.ic.nanzan-u.ac.jp/ SHUBUNKEN/jjrs/jjrs.html), Institute for Japanese Culture and Classics, Kokugakuin University (www.kokugakuin.ac.jp/ijcc/index.html), and the International Shinto Foundation (shinto.org/menu-e.html).

22 Shinto shrines vary both in size and in whom they enshrine. A shrine in a village might be very small. One shrine may have Amaterasu, the Sun Goddess, while another might enshrine Admiral Togo and so forth. Additionally, the Emperor's portrait (goshin'ei) with his empress was kept in a small house in every public school in both Japan and its outer territories for bowing and later for worshiping by students.

23 Some have dismissed this legend as fiction. Others have noted the significance of this belief in which a god had, of his own accord, left heaven to become a man. Still others have interpreted this legend to mean that even deities think that present life in Korea is better than the wonders of the hereafter. This last view, which is reflected in the Korean proverb, "an earthly field of dung to the wonders of the afterworld," is also reflected in contemporary Juche "live for today," and "protect our paradise" beliefs.

24 For example, DPRK propaganda, national educational curricula and even a 1997 speech by the DPRK's vice president all refer to dictator Kim Jong Il's birth on Mt. Paektu, Korea's sacred ancestral mountain. However, Kim Jong Il was actually born in the ex-Soviet Union.

25 Sang Hun Choe, "N. Korea Said To Be Training Bombers," *Associated Press* (Seoul), 19 September 1998.

26 "Quotations of Leader Kim Jong Il," *The People's Korea* (Tokyo: DPRK web magazine), 13 May 1998.

27 "The Contradiction of North Korea Nation is Deepening," *Petrel*, 19 October 1997.

28 "Quotations of Leader Kim Jong Il."

29 Li Yang Su (Vice Editor-in-Chief, Korean Central News Agency), interview with author, Virginia Beach, Virginia, 29 October 1997.

30 Pak Song Duk, "Christianity and Juche Idea" (Pyongyang: Juche Idea Division of the Social Science Institute, 1991), 9.

31 Ibid.

32 Will and Ariel Durant, *The Lessons of History* (New York: Simon and Shuster, 1968), 50, 51.

33 Michael Schuman, "Defector Highlights Korean Culture Gap: Capitalism Might Not Cure All if Impoverished North Falls," *The Wall Street Journal,* 2 October 1997, A19.

34 "Women," *Citizens' Alliance to Help Political Prisoners in North Korea* (Seoul: web magazine, 1998).

35 Jeremy J. Stone, "North Korea: Hermit Kingdom Faces Hard Choices," November 1991 (Washington, D.C.: Federation of American Scientists website).

36 Chun Hong Taek, "The Characteristics and Function of the Second Economy in North Korea" (Seoul: Korean Development Institute), April 1997.

37 Dan Wooding, "Big Changes Inside 'The Land That Time Forgot,'" *Christian Herald,* 19 November 1994, 4.

38 "The Role of Religion," *Country Missing* (Washington, D.C.: U.S. Library of Congress, 1993).

39 Ibid.

40 Chung Doo Hee, "The Heritage of the Chosun Dynasty Appearing in the North Korean Description of History," *East Asian Review,* vol. 10 no. 1 (Seoul: The Institute for East Asian Studies, 1998), 31.

41 Thomas Hosuck Kang, "Why the North Koreans Behave As They Do" (Washington, D.C.: Confucian Publications, 1997).

42 Kim Jong Il, *Let Us Exalt the Brilliance of Comrade Kim Il Sung's Idea on the Youth Movement and the Achievements Made Under His Leadership* (Pyongyang: Foreign Language Publishing House, 1996), 12. Furuta Hiroshi (Professor, University of Tsukuba, Japan) presented an alternative view based on his analysis of North Korean documents. Professor Furuta believes that numerous examples of usage and ideas, including the concept of "filial piety," are borrowed from those of the Japanese empire rather than from traditional Korea. Furuta notes that the ghostwriters of Juche ideology, including Hwang Jang Yop, were educated by the Japanese and/or studied in Japan before becoming Communists as adults. For example, Professor Furuta notes that Hwang Jang Yop used an idiomatic phrase from old Japanese poem written in ancient Chinese upon his arrival at the Kimpo Airport after his 1997 defection.

43 "Tradition and Modernity in North Korea," *Country Missing* (Washington, D.C.: U.S. Library of Congress, 1993).

44 Kim Son Hwi, "Q & A: Christianity in DPRK," *The People's Korea* (Tokyo: DPRK web magazine), 20 July 1997.

45 *The Korean Christian Federation* (Pyongyang: The Central Committee of the

Korean Christian Federation, 1994), 1, 2.

46 J. S. Conway, *The Nazi Persecution of the Churches* (New York: Basic Books, 1968), 48.

47 On a more humorous note, the Korean Christian Federation was not quite as thorough in its September 2, 1997, bulletin regarding Mrs. Ruth Bell Graham, wife of international evangelist Billy Graham. The *KCNA* announced, "Ruth Bell Graham, *widow of Rev. Billy Graham*, U.S. religious leader, and her party arrived here today." On that date, Dr. Graham was still quite alive and pressing on in his preaching ministry.

48 Stone, "North Korea: Hermit Kingdom Faces Hard Choices."

49 Tom White, *North Korea: The Battle Continues* (Bartlesville, Oklahoma: Voice of the Martyrs, Inc., 1996), 8.

Chapter 4. Juche's Spiritual Archenemy: The Church

1 Lee Wha Rang, "What is Jucheism?" *Korea WebWeekly* (Seoul: Korea Nationalists Association), 12 September 1997.

2 Kim Il Sung, *A Selection of Kim Il Sung's Works, vol. 1* (Pyongyang: Korean Workers' Party Printing House, 1967), 173.

3 "Quotations of Leader Kim Jong Il," *The People's Korea* (Tokyo: DPRK web magazine), 13 May 1998.

4 Kang Wi Jo, *Christ and Caesar in Modern Korea: a history of Christianity and politics* (Albany, NY: State University of New York Press, 1997).

5 McLane Tilton, Captain, USMC, personal papers (Archives and Library, Historical Branch, Headquarters, Marine Corps) (May 20, 1871) as quoted in Carolyn A. Tyson, *Marine Amphibious Landing in Korea, 1871* (Washington, D.C.: Naval Historical Foundation, 1966), 8.

6 E. M. Cable, *United States Korean Relations, 1866–1871,* English Publication no. 4 (Seoul: YMCA Press, 1939), 62.

7 Varying accounts and much confusing exists surrounding the *General Sherman* incident. For example, though the *General Sherman* was a commercial vessel, some Korean accounts describe the *General Sherman* as a warship because the crew had firearms. One writer even mixed up the 1866 *General Sherman* massacre account with the 1871 U.S. naval expedition which landed a force on Kangwha island near Seoul to come up with an entirely new "revisionist" historical account [Cooper Leggett, "Letters to the Editor: Act of Colonization?" *Korea Herald* 2 February 1998]. This fictional account alleges that the *General Sherman* was never burned and the crew never was killed. To further confuse historians, in 1866, there were five U.S. commercial vessels were named *General Sherman,* none of which were the ship that was burned in Korea in 1866! [Washington, D.C.: U.S. National Archives Navy Maritime Group]. Actual accounts and interviews of Korean participants from the 1866 and 1867 U.S. Navy reports investigating the loss of the schooner *General Sherman* 19th century are located on microfilm rolls 251 and 252 in the U.S. National Archives.

8 Harry A. Rhodes, *History of the Korean Mission Presbyterian Church U.S.A.*

1884–1934 (Seoul: Chosen Mission Presbyterian Church U.S.A., 1934), 171, 172, as quoted in Kang, *Christ and Caesar in Modern Korea*, 12.

9 One version of this story relates that the two friends were executed at the border. The charge? Bringing in a foreign religion!

10 Tilton, personal papers as quoted Tyson, *Marine Amphibious Landing in Korea*, 8.

11 Ibid., 6.

12 William Newton Blair, *Gold in Korea* (Topeka, KS: H. M. Ives and Sons, Inc., 1957), 103–105.

13 Tom White, *North Korea: The Battle Continues* (Bartlesville, Oklahoma: The Voice of the Martyrs, Inc., 1996), 1.

14 Ibid., 2.

15 *The Human Rights Situation in North Korea: The Reality of Self-styled Paradise* (Seoul: The Institute for South-North Korea Studies, 1992), 68.

16 Tom White, "The Road Home," *The Voice of the Martyrs*, June 1998 (Bartlesville, Oklahoma), 5.

17 Isaac Lee, "Come Forth!," *Cornerstone Ministries Monographs*, October 5, 1992 (Seattle, Washington: Cornerstone Ministries, International), 1, 2.

18 Kang In Duk, "North Korea's Policy on Religion," *East Asian Review*, vol. 8 no. 3 (Seoul: The Institute for East Asian Studies, 1996), 95.

19 Ibid., 94.

20 White, *The Battle Continues*, 1.

21 Isaac Lee, *Cornerstone Ministries Monographs*, 19 April 1993 (Seattle, Washington: Cornerstone Ministries, International), 1, 2.

22 Cornerstone Ministries International, phone interview by author, 27 June 1997.

23 Dr. Cho, a 74-year-old former Presbyterian minister, was born in North Korea and met Kim Il Sung on three occasions. In 1990, Dr. Cho lectured on Christianity at Pyongyang's Kim Il Sung University, while visiting relatives. He donated about 3,000 books on religion to North Korea.

24 White, *The Battle Continues*, 1, 2.

25 *More Love to Thee* (videotape) (Bartlesville, Oklahoma: The Voice of the Martyrs, Inc., 1994).

26 Isaac Lee, *Cornerstone Ministries Monographs*, 22 June 1993 (Seattle, Washington: Cornerstone Ministries, International), 1, 2.

27 "North Korea Eyewitness Report: Execution of the 'Heaven People,'" *The Voice of the Martyrs*, March 1998 (Bartlesville, Oklahoma: The Voice of the Martyrs, Inc.), 6, 7.

28 Isaac Lee, *Cornerstone Ministries Monographs*, 7 December 1992, 2, 3.

29 Isaac Lee, *Cornerstone Ministries Monographs*, 19 April 1993, 1, 2.

30 Thomas J. Belke, "Starving Souls, Starving Bellies in North Korea," *Not By Might*, vol. 3 no. 3 (Jasper, Arkansas: Parthenon Gospel Church, 1997), 3.

31 Choi Sung Chul, ed., *Human Rights in North Korea* (Seoul: Center for the Advancement of North Korean Human Rights, 1995), 233.

32 *Reuters,* 6 February 1998.

33 James Pringle, "North Korea a Starving Society Descending into Medieval Barbarism," *London Times,* 5 February 1999.

34 Belke, "Starving Souls, Starving Bellies," 3.

35 Thomas J. Belke, "Isolated North Korea Is in Throes of Serious Spiritual Famine: Observers call Christians to pray for a spiritual breakthrough in their communist country—which they say is 'under a curse,'" *Charisma,* November 1997 (Lake Mary, Florida: Strang Communications), 27.

36 Belke, "Starving Souls, Starving Bellies," 4.

Chapter 5. Origins of Juche

1 Lee Wha Rang, "What is Jucheism?" *Korea WebWeekly* (Seoul: Korea Nationalists Association), 12 September 1997.

2 James H. Billington, *Fire in the Minds of Men: Origins of the Revolutionary Faith* (New York: Basic Books, Inc., 1980); and Francis A. Schaeffer, *How Should We Then Live?: The Rise and Decline of Western Thought and Culture* (Westchester, Illinois: Crossway Books, 1983). Dr. Billington, a leading expert on Marxist-Leninism, is the Librarian of Congress.

3 Walter Martin, *The Kingdom of the Cults* (Minnesota: Bethany Publishing, 1982), 338, 339.

4 Lee Wha Rang, "What is Jucheism?"

5 Ibid.

6 Timothy J. O'Brien, "Foreign Investment in North Korea" (Dallas, Texas: Southwestern Legal Foundation Symposium), 20 June 1995.

7 Although the large-scale second Chinese offensive ("Second Campaign") occurred at the end of November, the actual date of the Chinese intervention was October 14, 1950. [Edwin P. Hoyt, *The Day the Chinese Attacked: Korea, 1950: The Story of the Failure of America's China Policy* (New York: McGraw-Hill Publishing Company, 1990)].

8 "The Origin of the North Korean Regime," *Koreascope* (Seoul: web magazine).

9 Steve McCabe, "Jucheism???," *Korea WebWeekly* (Seoul: Korea Nationalists Association), 15 September 1997.

10 Kang In Duk, "Party Secretary Hwang's Defection: North Korea Now on the Brink of Collapse or Change," *The Korea Overseas Information Service* (web magazine, 1997).

11 Lee Wha Rang, "What is Jucheism?"

12 "Political Ideology: The Role of Chuch'e," *Country Missing* (Washington, D.C.: U.S. Library of Congress, 1993).

13 Timothy J. O'Brien, "Foreign Investment in North Korea" (Dallas, Texas: Southwestern Legal Foundation Symposium), 20 June 1995.

14 "Juche Ideology," *Koreascope* (Seoul: web magazine).

15 "Political Ideology."

16 Ibid.

17 Ibid.

18 Ibid.

19 Ibid.

20 North Korea's signing of the Non-Proliferation Treaty in 1985 should have resulted in them allowing international inspections of their nuclear facilities within the 18 months that followed. However, to date, North Korea has never allowed foreign International Atomic Energy Association (IAEA) experts to inspect their nuclear facilities.

21 Jeremy J. Stone, "North Korea: Hermit Kingdom Faces Hard Choices," November 1991 (Washington, D.C.: Federation of American Scientists website).

22 Chun Hong Taek, "The Characteristics and Function of the Second Economy in North Korea" (Seoul: Korean Development Institute), April 1997.

23 Ibid.

24 Ibid.

Chapter 6. Juche Holy Sites

1 Charles Fenyvesi, "The Communist Cult of the Dead," *U.S. News & World Report*, 21 July 1997, 18.

2 "North Korea Eyewitness Report: Execution of the 'Heaven People,'" *The Voice of the Martyrs*, March 1998 (Bartlesville, Oklahoma: The Voice of the Martyrs, Inc.), 7.

3 State holidays and Juche holy days are basically synonymous since Juche is the state religion.

4 Dan Wooding, "North Korea Wants to Re-enter the World But on its Own Terms," *Christian Herald* 6 September 1994, 3.

5 Ibid., 3.

6 Tom White, *North Korea: The Battle Continues* (Bartlesville, Oklahoma: The Voice of the Martyrs, Inc., 1996), 7.

7 "Statements of Leader Kim Jong Il," *The People's Korea* (Tokyo: DPRK web magazine), 14 May 1998.

8 Klaus Steinberger, "Hyong," *Traditional Taekwon Do and Other Martial Arts* (Munich, 1999) (web magazine).

9 *Secret Camp on Mt. Paektu* (Pyongyang: Korea Pictorial, 1990), 1.

10 Ibid.

11 Ibid., 13.

Chapter 7. The Juche Worldview

1 "Statements of Leader Kim Jong Il," *The People's Korea* (Tokyo: DPRK web magazine), 14 May 1998.

2 Joy Yunhee Choi, interview by author, Virginia Beach, Virginia, 11 February 1997.

3 "World tempted to help in hope of making change," *Associated Press* (Seoul: The News and Observer Publishing Co.), 15 September 1995.

4 Kim Tae Seo, "Changes in the North Korean Power Structure, and the Kim Jong Il Regime on a Track," *East Asian Review*, vol. 10 no. 4 (Seoul, Korea: The Institute for East Asian Studies, 1998), 18, 19.

5 During 18-27 May 1980, radical students, with the aid of North Korean agents, seized a well-stocked government armory in Kwangju, South Korea. Over 50,000 other students then took to the streets to protest against martial law. On May 27, ROK troops recaptured the city in a bloody two-hour battle against armed students. Approximately 2,000 people were killed and 1,740 demonstrators arrested. Later, on September 17, 1980, South Korea's current President Kim Dae Jung was sentenced to death for his involvement. However, the U.S. persuaded President Chun Doo Hwan to suspend the sentence and, instead, exile Kim to America. Ironically, in 1976, Chun was convicted and sentenced to death for treason and for ordering troops to massacre civilian demonstrators. Then, in December 1997, President Kim Dae Jung pardoned the ex-President Chun—the very man who had once pardoned him from death.

6 The Hanchongyon Incident is described in Chapter 8.

7 The National Security Law (NSL), enacted by the ROK in November 1947, broadly outlined terrorist acts. In December 1958, the National Assembly expanded the NSL to include imprisonment for anyone who "benefited by disturbing the people's minds by openly pointing out or spreading false facts."

8 "North Stresses Economy In New Year Editorial," *Choson Ilbo* (Seoul) 2 January 1998.

9 Chung Doo Hee, "The Heritage of the Chosun Dynasty Appearing in the North Korean Description of History," *East Asian Review*, vol. 10 no. 1 (Seoul: The Institute for East Asian Studies, 1998), 38.

10 Korean Embassy website (Washington, D.C.: Republic of Korea embassy, 1999).

11 Chung, "The Heritage of the Chosun Dynasty," 36.

12 Dong Yong Seung, "Changes in the Surrounding Situation, and Measures to Vitalize Economic Cooperation Between the South and the North," *East Asian Review*, vol. 10 no. 4 (Seoul, Korea: The Institute for East Asian Studies, 1998), 75, 76.

13 The first North Korean infiltration tunnel under the DMZ was discovered in 1974. By October 1978, two more such tunnels were discovered. On March 1990, during the 445th session of the Military Armistice Commission's investigation of the fourth tunnel, the North Koreans openly admitted to tunneling underneath the DMZ.

14 "Hwang Details Depths of North Korea's Plight," *Korea Herald* (Seoul), 11 July 1997.

15 James Nash, "North Korea," personal papers (Ann Arbor, Michigan: University of Michigan, 1995).

16 Choi Sung Chul, ed., *Human Rights in North Korea* (Seoul: Center for the Advancement of North Korean Human Rights, 1995), 235.

17 Kim Il Sung, *Reminiscences With the Century,* vol. 1 (Pyongyang: Foreign Languages Publishing House, 1992), 33–35.

18 Ibid., 35.

19 *The Revolutionary Martyrs Cemetery* (Pyongyang: Korea Pictorial Pyongyang, 1989), 1.

20 Ibid., 11, 12.

21 The complete version of this account notes that the North Koreans took a non-Christian Japanese delegation to the "Christian" Jangchung Cathedral and Pongsu Church. Such actions, along with the mention of the Korean Religionists Council objectives, demonstrate that, from the Juche religious vantage point, all *religionists*—Christian or otherwise—can be controlled and used to promote Juche.

22 "N. Korea Slams South's Invite of Japanese Emperor," *Reuters* (Tokyo), 11 October 1998.

23 Cameron W. Barr, "N. Korea's Feast and Famine," *Christian Science Monitor,* 18 February 1999.

24 Ibid.

25 Bill Clinton, "Why I'm Going to Beijing," *Newsweek,* 29 June 1998, 28.

26 Koh Yu Hwan, "The Continuation of the North Korean Socialist System in the Post Kim Il Sung Era," *East Asian Review,* vol. 9 no. 1 (Seoul: The Institute for East Asian Studies, 1998), 72.

27 On January 23, 1968, the U.S. Navy electronic intelligence ship *USS Pueblo* was attacked and seized by North Korean gunboats. North Korea claimed the vessel had violated their territorial waters. Though a U.S. Seventh Fleet task force took station off the coast of North Korea, no reprisals were taken. Almost a year later, on December 22, 1968, the North Korea released the 82 crewmembers following a complicated agreement. The agreement required the U.S. to sign a statement admitting that the vessel had been engaging in espionage with the understanding that the U.S. would subsequently denounce the document. [Ernest R. Dupuy and Trevor N. Dupuy, *The Encyclopedia of Military History from 3500 B.C. to the Present* (New York: Harper & Row Publishers, 1970), 1311.]

28 On April 15, 1969, a North Korean fighter plane shot down a U.S. EC-121 reconnaissance aircraft 90 miles off the North Korean coast in international airspace, killing 31 airmen.

29 Reinhard Drifte and Hyock Sup Lee, "The Internationalization of the Korean Security Issue: A Way Forward," *The Korean Journal of Defense Analysis,* vol. 7 no. 2 (Seoul: Korea Institute for Defense Analyses, 1995).

30 *Dictionary of Politics* (Pyongyang: [North] Korean Social Science Press, 1973), 913.

31 Lee Seok Soo, "Dynamics of the Relationship Between North Korea and the U.S.: Policy, Capability, and Policy Performance," *East Asian Review*, vol. 10 no. 4 (Seoul, Korea: The Institute for East Asian Studies, 1998), 110.

32 Fred C. Iklé, "U.S. Folly May Start Another Korean War," *The Wall Street Journal*, 12 October 1998, A18.

33 "World tempted to help in hope of making change."

34 *CBN News*, 11 November 1997.

35 Colin L. Powell, *My American Journey* (New York: Random House, 1995), 605.

36 Ibid.

37 Lee Seok Soo, "Dynamics of the Relationship Between North Korea and the U.S.," 100.

38 "N. Korea Ready To See Nuclear Pact With US Broken," *Reuters* (Tokyo).

39 Yoo Jae Ik, "Arms Control and Korea's Security," *East Asian Review*, vol. 10 no. 4 (Seoul, Korea: The Institute for East Asian Studies, 1998), 56.

40 Choi Sung Chul, ed., *Human Rights in North Korea*, 106.

41 Drifte and Lee, "The Internationalization of the Korean Security Issue."

42 Antoaneta Bezlova, "N. Korean famine is good business for town in China: By bartering across border, 'local people can both make money... (and) ensure there is no mass migration across the frontier'," *USA Today*, 12 June 1997, 9A.

43 Taeho Kim, "The Changing Nature of China's Influence over North Korea in the Post-Cold War Era," *East Asian Review*, vol. 10 no. 4 (Seoul, Korea: The Institute for East Asian Studies, 1998), 50–52.

44 Choi Sung Chul, ed., *Human Rights in North Korea*, 240, 241.

45 Bezlova, "N. Korean famine is good business," 9A.

46 Chung Doo Hee, "The Heritage of the Chosun Dynasty Appearing in the North Korean Description of History," *East Asian Review*, vol. 10 no. 1 (Seoul: The Institute for East Asian Studies, 1998), 53.

Chapter 8. Hwang Jang Yop: The Architect of Juche

1 Koh Yu Hwan, "The Continuation of the North Korean Socialist System in the Post Kim Il Sung Era," *East Asian Review*, vol. 9 no. 1 (Seoul: The Institute for East Asian Studies, 1998), 66.

2 Ibid., 69, 70.

3 For example, on January 21, 1999, the *Washington Post* reported that Kim Kyong Pil, an economics official in the DPRK mission in Berlin, Germany, defected to the U.S. with his wife.

4 Hahn Ho Suk, "The Real Hwang Jang Yop: Was He a North Korea's George Washington or a Senile Old Man?" *Korea Webweekly* (Seoul: Korean Nationalists Association).

5 Ibid.

6 Jeremy J. Stone, "North Korea: Hermit Kingdom Faces Hard Choices," November 1991 (Washington, D.C.: Federation of American Scientists website).

7 Ibid.

8 Seoul's Institute for East Asian Studies has published a detailed list of approximately 60 high-level government officials known to have been purged in the
last few decades. Analysts believe that this list is only the "tip of the iceberg."

9 Stone, "North Korea: Hermit Kingdom Faces Hard Choices."

10 Ibid.

11 Hahn, "The Real Hwang Jang Yop."

12 Ibid.

13 Koh, "The Continuation of the North Korean Socialist System," 74.

14 Hahn, "The Real Hwang Jang Yop."

15 Ibid.

16 Mr. A., who reportedly opened a small trading business in China in 1993,
used the business as a front to assist North Korean escapees in China to
defect to South Korea.

17 Hahn, "The Real Hwang Jang Yop."

18 Ibid.

19 Ibid.

20 Kang In Duk, "Party Secretary Hwang's Defection: North Korea Now on the
Brink of Collapse or Change," *The Korea Overseas Information Service* (web magazine, 1997).

21 Ibid.

22 "Hwang Details Depths of North Korea's Plight," *Korea Herald* (Seoul), 11
July 1997.

23 Ibid.

24 "No Signs of Kim Jong Il Formally Taking Over," *Korea Herald* (Seoul), 11
June 1997.

25 "Hwang Jang Yop's speech," *Choson Ilbo* (Seoul), 10 July 1997.

26 "No Signs."

27 Ibid.

28 Kang, "Party Secretary Hwang's Defection."

29 Ibid.

Chapter 9. Promoting the Culture of Juche

1 George Orwell, *1984* (New York: Harcourt Brace Janovich, Inc., 1950), 17.

2 "Women," *Citizens' Alliance to Help Political Prisoners in North Korea* (Seoul: web
magazine, 1998).

3 Michael Baker, "Empathy Wins Trust of Wary N. Koreans," *The Christian Science Monitor*, 6 October 1997.

4 "Quotations of Leader Kim Jong Il," *The People's Korea* (Tokyo: DPRK web magazine), 13 May 1998.

5 Ibid.

6 "Statements of Leader Kim Jong Il," *The People's Korea* (Tokyo: DPRK web magazine), 14 May 1998.

7 Jeremy J. Stone, "North Korea: Hermit Kingdom Faces Hard Choices," November 1991 (Washington, D.C.: Federation of American Scientists website).

8 Choi Sung Chul, ed., *Human Rights in North Korea* (Seoul: Center for the Advancement of North Korean Human Rights, 1995), 104.

9 Koh Yu Hwan, "The Continuation of the North Korean Socialist System in the Post Kim Il Sung Era," *East Asian Review*, vol. 9 no. 1 (Seoul: The Institute for East Asian Studies, 1998), 69.

10 "N. Korea's own food reserves run dry, forcing it to rely on aid," *Virginia Pilot*, 13 April 1998, 2.

11 Jing Dong Yuan, "Building Peace on the Korean Peninsula: Major Power Interests and Arms Control Process," *East Asian Review*, vol. 9 no. 1 (Seoul: The Institute for East Asian Studies, 1998), 65.

12 "NK Food Shortage Estimated At 1 Million Tons In 1998," *Choson Ilbo* (Seoul), 30 December 1997.

13 "Neither Major Policy Changes nor Fresh Developments in Sight," *Korea Herald* (Seoul), 5 June 1998.

14 Kim Tong Il, "Prospects of North Korean Agriculture," *The People's Korea* (Tokyo: DPRK web magazine, 1997).

15 Chung Doo Hee, "The Heritage of the Chosun Dynasty Appearing in the North Korean Description of History," *East Asian Review*, vol. 10 no. 1 (Seoul: The Institute for East Asian Studies, 1998), 43.

16 Jing, "Building Peace on the Korean Peninsula," 65.

17 Hong Soon Jick, "Pyongyang's Economic Opening and Security Policies Under the Kim Jong Il Regime," *East Asian Review*, vol. 10 no. 2 (Seoul: The Institute for East Asian Studies, 1998), 105.

18 "Quotations of Leader Kim Jong Il."

19 Choi Sung Chul, ed., *Human Rights in North Korea*, 123, 124.

20 The West Sea Barrage is a system of locks for ships and long low dams between the sea and fresh water to allow for irrigation. The barrage prevents the salt water from flowing into the estuary at high tide to preserve the fresh water from salt so it can be used for irrigation.

21 Choi Sung Chul, ed., *Human Rights in North Korea*, 123, 124.

22 "Quotations of Leader Kim Jong Il."

23 Taeho Kim, "The Changing Nature of China's Influence over North Korea in the Post-Cold War Era," *East Asian Review*, vol. 10 no. 4 (Seoul, Korea: The Institute for East Asian Studies, 1998), 43.

24 "Drive for Economic," *Korea Central News Agency* (DPRK), 15 January 1998.

25 "North Korea Says No to Reform," *The Associated Press* (Seoul), 18 September 1998.

26 Ibid.

27 "Quotations of Leader Kim Jong Il."

28 *The Human Rights Situation in North Korea: The Reality of Self-styled Paradise* (Seoul: The Institute for South-North Korea Studies, 1992), 20.

29 Kim Jong Il, *Let Us Exalt the Brilliance of Comrade Kim Il Sung's Idea on the Youth Movement and the Achievements Made Under His Leadership* (Pyongyang: Foreign Language Publishing House, 1996), 6.

30 Ibid.

31 *The Human Rights Situation in North Korea,* 20.

32 "Personality Cult of Kim Jong-il," *Koreascope* (Seoul: web magazine).

33 The Balhae (Palhae) kingdom was located in what is now roughly southern Manchuria and North Korea.

34 Chung, "The Heritage of the Chosun Dynasty," 31.

35 *The Human Rights Situation in North Korea,* 21, 22.

36 Ibid., 21.

37 Ibid.

38 Orwell, *1984,* 174–177.

39 "Quotations of Leader Kim Jong Il."

40 Tom White, "The Road Home," *The Voice of the Martyrs,* June 1998 (Bartlesville, Oklahoma: The Voice of the Martyrs), 6.

41 *Kim Il Sung University* (Pyongyang: Foreign Languages Publishing House, 1982), 2, 3, 8.

42 Choi Sung Chul, ed., *Human Rights in North Korea,* 302.

43 Ibid.

44 Stone, "North Korea: Hermit Kingdom Faces Hard Choices."

45 James Walsh, "North Korea—A World Without Kim: The last Stalinist's sudden demise leaves his realm more enigmatic than ever," *Time,* 18 July 1994.

46 "Idolization of the Kim Family Lineage," *Koreascope* (Seoul: web magazine).

47 *The Sinchon Museum* (Pyongyang: Foreign Languages Publishing House, 1982), 17.

48 Donald Knox, *The Korean War: An Oral History* (New York: Harcourt Brace Janovich, 1985), 392.

49 "Quotations of Leader Kim Jong Il."

50 *The Human Rights Situation in North Korea,* 27.

51 Ibid., 28, 29.

52 Choi Sung Chul, ed., *Human Rights in North Korea,* 233.

53 Ibid., 233, 234.

54 An Myong Chol, *Political Prisoners' Camps in North Korea* (Seoul: Center for the Advancement of North Korean Human Rights, 1995), 22.

55 Ibid., 63.

56 An, *Political Prisoners' Camps,* 38.

57 Ibid., 22.

58 "North Korea Eyewitness Report: Execution of the 'Heaven People,'" *The Voice of the Martyrs*, March 1998 (Bartlesville, Oklahoma: The Voice of the Martyrs, Inc.), 6.

59 Pak Song Duk, "Christianity and Juche Idea" (Pyongyang: Juche Idea Division of the Social Science Institute, 1991), 9.

60 An, *Political Prisoners' Camps*, 59.

61 *Land of Morning Calm*, videotape (Pyongyang: Mokran Video, 1995).

62 "Quotations of Leader Kim Jong Il."

63 *Land of Morning Calm.*

64 The National Democratic Front in South Korea (NDFSK or NDFS) is a bogus organization that was created by Pyongyang as a rallying point for pro-North activists in the South.

65 S. L. Mayer, ed., *Signal: Hitler's Wartime Picture Magazine* (London: Bison Publishing Company, 1976), ii, 1, 3–6.

66 "World tempted to help in hope of making change," *Associated Press* (Seoul: The News and Observer Publishing Co.), 15 September 1995.

67 Choi Sung Chul, ed., *Human Rights in North Korea*, 232, 233.

68 Ibid., 234.

69 Francis A. Schaeffer, *How Should We Then Live?: The Rise and Decline of Western Thought and Culture* (Westchester, Illinois: Crossway Books, 1983), 127.

70 "Bible Stories and Kim Jong Il's Ruling Style," *Koreascope* (Seoul: web magazine).

71 "Major Events Around the Korean Peninsula (December 1, 1997–February 28, 1998), *East Asian Review*, vol. 10 no. 1 (Seoul: The Institute for East Asian Studies, 1998), 127.

72 Ibid.

73 "Public Executions," *Koreascope* (Seoul: web magazine).

74 *The Human Rights Situation in North Korea*, 132.

75 "Jeremy Stone's North Korea Testimony," November 1991 (Washington, D.C.: Federation of American Scientists website).

76 Orwell, *1984*, 174.

77 Choi Sung Chul, ed., *Human Rights in North Korea*, 234.

78 *The Human Rights Situation in North Korea*, 35.

79 Ibid., 64–66.

80 Erwin W. Lutzer, *Hitler's Cross* (Chicago: Moody Press, 1995), 79.

Chapter 10. A Religion in Transition

1 Jing Dong Yuan, "Building Peace on the Korean Peninsula: Major Power Interests and Arms Control Process," *East Asian Review*, vol. 9 no. 1 (Seoul: The Institute for East Asian Studies, 1998), 60.

2 James Walsh, "North Korea—A World Without Kim: The last Stalinist's sudden demise leaves his realm more enigmatic than ever," *Time*, 18 July 1994.

3   Ibid.

4   Aidan Foster-Carter, "Korea's Leadership Crisis: Neither North nor South are facing up to their destiny," *Asiaweek*, 30 May 1997.

5   Chang Moon Sug, "Expansion of Japan's Security and Military Roles and Its Influence on Northeast Asia," *East Asian Review*, vol. 9 no. 2 (Seoul: The Institute for East Asian Studies, 1998), 88, 89.

6   "Chronology of Korea" (Washington, D.C.: Korean Embassy website, 1999).

7   Karl Marx, *The Communist Manifesto* (1848, reprinted Chicago: Regnery, 1954), 81, 82.

8   Kim Jong Il, *On the Juche Idea of Our Party* (Pyongyang: Foreign Languages Publishing House, 1985), 136-139.

9   Choi Sung Chul, ed., *Human Rights in North Korea* (Seoul: Center for the Advancement of North Korean Human Rights, 1995), 322.

10 "N. Korean Satellite Described As a Dud," *Washington Times*, 11 September 1998.

11 "North Korea: It Wasn't a Missile," Seoul: *The Associated Press*, 4 September 1998.

12 Jeremy J. Stone, "North Korea: Hermit Kingdom Faces Hard Choices," November 1991 (Washington, D.C.: Federation of American Scientists website).

13 Choi Sung Chul, ed., *Human Rights in North Korea*, 228.

14 Ibid.

Chapter 11. A Biblical View of the Future of Juche

1   Gordon Robertson television interview by Pat Robertson, "Visit to North Korea," *The 700 Club* (Christian Broadcasting Network Television), 3 October 1997.

2   *Webster's II New Riverside Dictionary* (New York: Berkley Books, 1984), 625.

3   Francis A. Schaeffer, *A Christian Manifesto* (Westchester, Illinois: Crossway Books, 1984), 54.

4   *Torcaso v. Watkins*, 367 U.S. 488, 495, n. 11.

5   Schaeffer, *A Christian Manifesto*, 54.

6   Choi Sung Chul, ed., *Human Rights in North Korea* (Seoul: Center for the Advancement of North Korean Human Rights, 1995), 285.

7   Schaeffer, *A Christian Manifesto*, 51.

8   Ibid., 19, 20.

9   John Eidsmoe, *God & Caesar: Christian Faith & Political Action* (Westchester, Illinois: Crossway Books, 1984), 17.

10 Francis A. Schaeffer, *How Should We Then Live?: The Rise and Decline of Western Thought and Culture* (Westchester, Illinois: Crossway Books, 1983), 20, 21.

11 Ibid.

12 Eidsmoe, *God & Caesar*, 85.

13 Ibid., 131, 132.

14 Ibid.

15 James Strong, *Strong's Exhaustive Concordance* (Grand Rapids, Michigan: Baker Book House, 1980), "Greek Dictionary of the New Testament," 13 (no. 473).

16 Former U.S. President Jimmy Carter, while using the Bible as a standard in his personal life, refrains from publicly using the Bible to declare North Korea to be an evil nation. Instead, he views using the biblical standard for judging governments in terms of good or evil as a "major impediment" to global peace (Carter, *Living Faith,* 139). In contrast, the Bible does not present "aversion to war and suffering" as the ultimate ideal with the view that we must be willing to deal with totalitarian dictatorships.

17 The Bible is filled with examples of the spiritual significance of high places. A sample of the spiritual abomination that these idolatrous pagan high place practices represent may be found in 1 Kings 11:3–11; 12:31,32; 13:2,32,33; 14:23; 15:14; 22:43; and 2 Kings 12:3; 14:4; 16:4; 17:9–11,29,32; 18:4,22; 21:3; 23:13,15,19,20; 23:13–25.

18 John Dawson, *Healing America's Wounds: Discovering Our Destiny* (Ventura, California: Regal Books, 1994), 46.

19 The Bible records that eventually harsh judgment did fall upon Assyria (e.g., Nahum 3:7, Zephaniah 2:13) and Nineveh was destroyed. However, Nineveh's final judgment did not occur until about 200 years after Jonah in 612 B.C. when it was destroyed by the Babylonians, Scythians, and Medes [T. Alton Bryant, ed., *The New Compact Bible Dictionary* (Grand Rapids, Michigan: Zondervan, 1967), 403).]

20 "Christianity Seen as Chief Hope of Japan by Gen. MacArthur," *The Washington Post,* 11 January 1947, 13.

21 Lawrence S. Wittner, "MacArthur and the Missionaries: God and Man in Occupied Japan," *Pacific Historical Review,* February 1971, 82, 83, 89.

Resources

Other Resources Available from The Voice of the Martyrs

The Answer to the Atheist's Handbook
Pastor Richard Wurmbrand
Atheists assert that there is no God. How can they be sure? This answers the many questions and arguments they present, leaving the atheist with a question: "How do you know?" (Paperback, 171 pp.)

The Oracles of God
Pastor Richard Wurmbrand
Pastor Wurmbrand emerged from 14 years of prison in Communist Romania not with a melancholy, defeated testimony, but with one that was victorious and overcoming, awakening the world to the plight of Christians in restricted nations. During his imprisonment, he spent much time talking to the Lord and meditating on His Word. *Oracles of God* explores God's wisdom about life, enabling you to become His mouthpiece. (Paperback, 171 pp.)

Between Two Tigers
Compiled by Tom White
From forbidden baptisms and secret meetings to imprisonment, Christians in Vietnam pay a great price for their faith in Christ. Caught between Communist police and tribal religions, their many victories are evidence of God's faithfulness. *Between Two Tigers* is a collection of testimonies from today's persecuted Christians in Vietnam. (Paperback, 192 pp.)

Videos by The Voice of the Martyrs

North Korea: More Love to Thee
How do Christians survive in one of the most tightly controlled nations in the world? A powerful presentation depicting public executions and the sufferings of Christians in North Korea. (40 minutes)

Leaping China's Great Wall
For decades, faithful Christians in China have defied their Communist government to meet secretly to worship God and proclaim the gospel. This video is a rare opportunity to meet Chinese Christians in their homes, share their sufferings, and rejoice in their victories. Leap over China's Great Wall and fellowship with these courageous believers. (30 minutes)

Faith Under Fire
Faith Under Fire brings to life interviews with Christians who face persecution head-on. You will meet Zahid, once a persecutor of Christians until God gave him a "road to Damascus" experience and allowed his faith to grow under persecution in his Muslim homeland. You will visit a Chinese pastor's home and witness the "strike-hard" policy that Christians now face. And you will gain insight from the plight of Linh Dao, a Vietnamese teenager dealing with the arrest and imprisonment of her father for his work in the underground church. *Faith Under Fire* will challenge you to ask the question, "Is my faith ready to hold up under fire?" Don't miss this chance to be inspired by stories from the other part of the Body of Christ. (30 minutes)

The Voice of the Martyrs has available many other books, videos, brochures, and other products to help you learn more about the persecuted church. In the U.S., to request a resource catalog, order materials, or receive our free monthly newsletter, call (800) 747-0085 or write to:

> The Voice of the Martyrs
> P.O. Box 443
> Bartlesville, OK 74005-0443

If you are in Canada, Australia, England, or New Zealand, contact:

> The Voice of the Martyrs
> P.O. Box 117
> Port Credit
> Mississauga, Ontario L5G 4L5
> Canada

> Release International
> P.O. Box 19
> Bromley BR2 9TZ
> England

> The Voice of the Martyrs
> P.O. Box 598
> Penrith NSW 2751
> Australia

> The Voice of the Martyrs
> P.O. Box 69-158
> Glendene, Auckland 1230
> New Zealand